NORTHWEST EXPLORATIONS

Northwest Explorations

By
GORDON SPECK

Edited by
L. K. Phillips

BINFORDS & MORT, *Publishers*
Portland · Oregon · 97242

AUTHOR'S PREFACE

IN WRITING the story of the explorations of the Pacific Northwest, I had two goals: to give a fresh interpretation to the early history of the region and, at the same time, call attention to contemporary events in other parts of the New World.

It is my hope that those who enjoy the human side of historic persons will find in these pages a new insight into several of them. I have tried to portray their struggles for power and glory, their amorous intrigues, their fights for pelts and great wealth. All the attributes of high adventure raced through the lives of those Northwest explorers—hardship, sacrifice, accomplishment; feasting, drinking; plunder, rape, and murder. Now and again I have endeavored to recapture something of the current scene.

Though every effort has been made to avoid error, perfection is too much to expect. My explanations, criticisms, and estimates have always been based on historic information, but they remain my own interpretations and are therefore fallible.

GORDON SPECK

ACKNOWLEDGMENTS

THIS VOLUME could not have been written without the help of two distinct groups, the students who attended my history classes and a much smaller group of scholars and specialists.

The students stimulated my researches that I might deserve their respect and challenge their attention. Many of the interpretations and incidents included are ones they found most interesting.

For their patient assistance, I am indebted to the staffs of libraries, museums, and galleries in Seattle, Portland, San Marino, St. Louis, Montreal, Three Rivers, Toronto, Quebec, and London. I wish to pay tribute to C. S. Kingston, Eastern Washington College of Education, who many years ago first interested me in Northwest history; to Dr. C. J. Brosnan, University of Idaho, who taught me that historic figures were also very human beings and should be treated as such; to Miss Mary Lytle, who aided in obtaining valuable material from the Library of Congress; to Miss Beulah Russell, who translated much data from Old French, Spanish, and Portuguese, which is not included in standard versions of histories of the Northwest; to Jon Speck for preparing the maps; to Harold Huseby for valuable suggestions regarding arrangement; to Mrs. Elizabeth Barnett and Miss Edith Price, who laboriously transposed my longhand into type; and finally to my wife, Lillian, who never lost confidence that this volume would eventually be finished and published.

G. S.

CONTENTS

PART ONE—BY SEA   PAGE

1   *The Fifteenth Century World* 3

2   *Pacific Explorations Before Columbus* 6

3   *The Voyage of Hwui Shan* 8

4   *Renaissance Explorations* 14

5   *Balboa Discovers the Pacific Ocean* 15

6   *Cortez Establishes Spanish Power* 26

7   *Romance and Myth of the Pacific* 28

8   *Cabrillo and Ferrelo Explore a New Coastline* 31

9   *Sir Francis Drake, Buccaneer Deluxe* 34

10   *Gali Observes the Coastline South* 44

11   *Vizcaino Surveys North to Old Oregon* 45

12   *Russia Enters the Pacific* 53

13   *Vitus Bering, the Outlander* 55

14   *Russians in the North Pacific* 74

15   *Spain Returns* 79

16   *Juan Perez Reaches 55° North* 81

17   *Heceta and Quadra Head a Great Spanish*
        Expedition 86

18   *James Cook, Trader-Geographer-Explorer* 92

19   *Hanna Sails into the North Pacific* 109

20   *La Perouse Starts Around the World* 110

21   *James Strange Goes to Nootka* 112

22   *John Meares, English Trader* 113

23   *Lesser English Traders* 123

24   *Spain's Last Try for Power* 126

25   *Vancouver Maps the Northwest Coast* 128

26   *Gray Discovers the Columbia River* 151

27   *The End of Northwest Explorations by Sea* 163

CONTENTS—*Continued*

PART TWO—BY LAND   PAGE

1   The Search for the Western Sea 167

2   Radisson and Groseilliers at Hudson Bay 168

3   The de la Verendryes, an Exploring Family 180

4   Jonathan Carver's Famous Book of Travels 191

5   Hearne Lays the Ghost of Anian 199

6   Alexander Mackenzie Discovers a Great River........213

7   Lewis and Clark Reach the Pacific 235

8   Fur Trade and Exploration 262

9   Manuel Lisa, the Indians' Friend 264

10   Astor and the Pacific Fur Company 275

11   The "Tonquin" Goes to the Columbia 279

12   Hunt and the Overland Astorians 300

13   The North West Company of Canada 316

14   Trade and Trading Methods 322

15   Nor'Westers as Explorers 329

16   David Thompson Discovers Athabasca Pass............334

17   Rocky Mountain Men 342

18   Jedediah Smith Defies the Spaniards 353

19   The Rocky Mountain Fur Company 359

20   Dr. John McLoughlin, American Citizen 365

Bibliography 373

Index 379

PART ONE —
BY SEA

Cathay

INDIA superior

Quinsay

Terra fla

Archipelagus 7448
insularum

Zipangri

Chamaho

Panuco Inf. Tonucard

Lucatana

Temistitan

Inf. pdonum

Nou

Caugra

Inf. infortu
nate

Ienfan

Mare pacificum

MAP OF THE NEW WORLD

From Munster's Cosmographei, Basil, 1550. This map shows Japan (Zipangri), China (Cathay),
and India to be near North America. The Oregon Coast was unknown, but a river is indicated
in the location of the supposed River of the West.

SIR FRANCIS DRAKE

Master mariner and the world's greatest pirate, Sir Francis Drake terrorized the entire Spanish Main during the Elizabethan age. (From the portrait by Jodocus Hondius, Flemish engraver)

Juan Rodriguez Cabrillo (left) in October, 1542, arrived at Port Conception, the farthest north landing yet made on the Pacific coast of North America. Sebastian Vizcaino (right) in the seventeenth century, faithfully inscribed in his log a complete account of his Pacific coast experiences as far north as Old Oregon. (Huntington Library)

Two famous Russians: Vitus Bering, the Dane (left), in the eighteenth century led two memorable Russian expeditions, proving that the New World is more than an arm of the old World. Alexander Baranof (right) was the first and most notorious of the governors of the Russian American company.

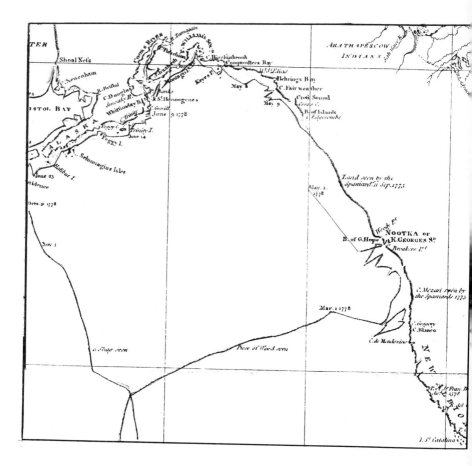

PART OF CAPTAIN COOK'S NORTHWEST CHART, 1778

The route of Cook's ships, *Resolution* and *Discovery*, on the Captain's third Pacific venture. In March, 1778, he sailed from the Sandwich Islands for the Northwest coast, reaching, March 7, 44°, which is now part of Oregon.

Of 47° he wrote, "It is in this very latitude where we now were that geographers have placed the pretended strait of Juan de Fuca. But I saw nothing like it; nor is there the least probability that ever any such thing existed." Ironically, he sighted and named Cape Flattery, which guards the opening to de Fuca. He then coasted slowly north, stopping at Friendly cove (Nootka). He little realized that he had left the mainland. (From Cook's *Atlas*)

CAPTAIN JAMES COOK

Spanish fears were embodied in the Englishman, James Cook, captain in His Majesty's service. World trader, geographer, explorer, he made three voyages into the Pacific, the last and greatest being the one to the Northwest coast in 1776. (From the portrait by Sir Nathaniel Dance of the Royal Academy. Most statues and busts of Cook have been copied from this original picture in the Painted Hall at Greenwich. An ocean view in the background, the new map which his voyages made possible, and the book he was writing, are all suggested in the picture.)

Nathaniel Portlock (left), of the Royal British Navy, in 1785 was licensed to monopolize the direct trade between the Northwest coast and China. That same year, Louis XVI sent the great navigator, La Perouse (right) on a round-the-world trip to seek the Strait of Anian and survey the fur trade. (Huntington Library)

Charles William Barclay (left) receives credit for the discovery of the Strait of Juan de Fuca in 1787. At Nootka Sound the following year, English trader John Meares (right) built the *Northwest America*, the first ship known to be built in this part of the world. (From the portrait by Sir William Beechey in Meares's *Voyages*)

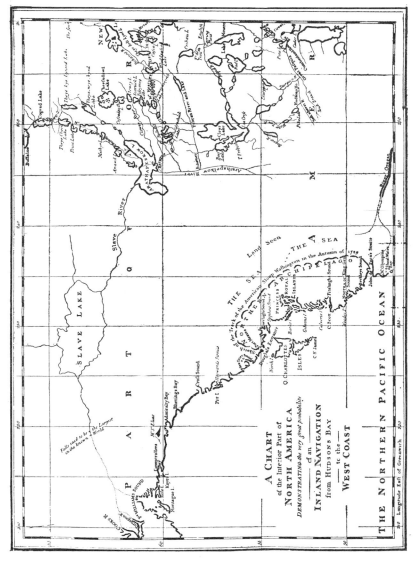

PART OF LIEUTENANT JOHN MEARES'S FAMOUS MAP

This is the supposed track of the sloop, *Lady Washington*, in 1789, from Meares's *Voyages*, published in London the following year.

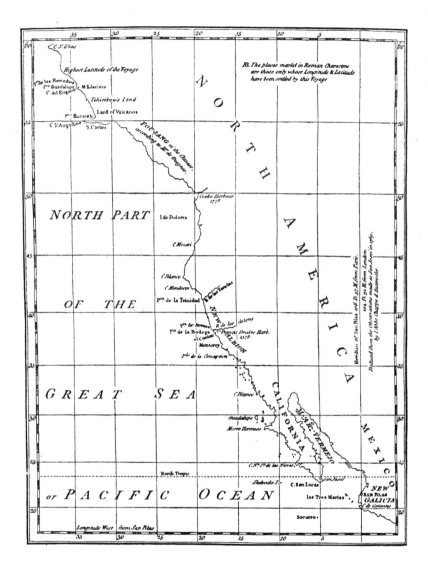

MAP OF QUADRA'S VOYAGE OF 1775

Credit for the outfitting and prosecution of this perhaps greatest of all Spanish voyages, from Mexico north, goes to Antonio Bucareli, Viceroy of New Spain, 1771-1779. Explanation at the top of the map reads: "The places marked in Roman Characters are those only whose Longitude & Latitude have been settled by this Voyage." (From *Miscellanies*, published in London, 1781, by Daines Barrington, noted jurist and author)

51390

CAPTAIN GEORGE VANCOUVER

In the meager number of truly great explorers, Captain George Vancouver ranks with the finest. He sent his men scurrying into every inlet of the Northwest coast to draw the most detailed maps ever laid down by an Anglo-Saxon on a voyage of discovery. (From the portrait in the National Gallery, London, by Lemuel Abbott, noted English portrait painter, 1760-1803. The map outlined on the globe shows Vancouver's Northwest explorations. Presumably the books are those he was writing for publication by the government, *Vancouver's Voyages*, London, 1798)

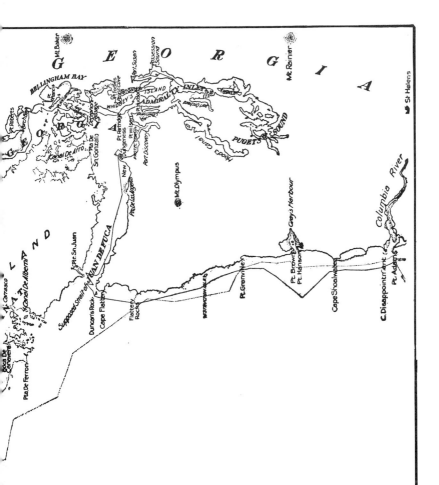

VANCOUVER'S CHART OF PUGET SOUND

This chart was made during Vancouver's historic visit to the Pacific Northwest in 1792, the fateful year of Robert Gray's discovery of the Columbia river. (Reproduced from the map in the original *Atlas*, London, 1798)

A VIEW OF THE HABITATIONS IN NOOTKA SOUND

In the late eighteenth century, Nootka was a busy little port. It had become the center of all activity on the Pacific Northwest coast south of the Russian posts. To its harbors came ships from Spain, England, the Orient, the Sandwich Islands, and from Mexico. (Reproduced from the plate in the original *Atlas of Cook's Voyages*, London, 1798)

VILLAGE OF THE FRIENDLY INDIANS AT THE ENTRANCE OF BUTE'S CANAL

Of these friendly villagers on the mainland of British Columbia, Vancouver noted that they bartered "a plentiful supply of fresh herrings and other fish . . . in a fair and honest way for nails." (By W. Alexander of Vancouver's Expedition, from an on-the-spot sketch by T. Heddington)

CHESLAKEE'S VILLAGE IN JOHNSTONE'S STRAITS

On a tour of this village with the Indian chief, Vancouver found it "pleasantly situated on a sloping hill, above the banks of a fine fresh water rivulet. . . . It was exposed to a southern aspect, whilst higher hills beyond, covered with lofty pines, sheltered it completely from the northern winds." (By W. Alexander from an on-the-spot sketch by J. Sykes)

SLOOP *DISCOVERY* ON THE ROCKS IN QUEEN CHARLOTTE'S SOUND

Discovery was the famous ship that Captain Vancouver sailed when he passed but missed the muddy mouth of the turbulent Columbia. (By W. Alexander from an on-the-spot sketch by Zachary Mudge)

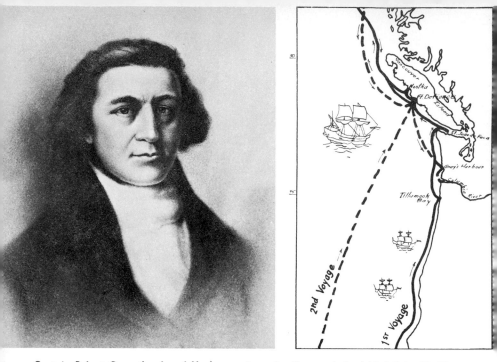

Captain Robert Gray, the shrewd Yankee mariner who discovered the fabled Columbia River. More than any other single person, he helped win the Oregon Country for the United States.

Gray's route during his second voyage, when he discovered the Great River, on that historic morning of May 11, 1792.

THE *COLUMBIA* AND THE *WASHINGTON*

When Captain Robert Gray exchanged ships with Captain John Kendrick, he was unwittingly foretelling the naming of the Columbia river.

Full rigged and 212 tons burden, Gray's famous ship, the *Columbia Rediviva*, gave the river its name.

MEARES AT ENTRANCE OF FUCA STRAIT, JUNE 29, 1788

On the right is Tatoosh Island. Meares claimed to be the discoverer of the strait but it had already been seen by Barclay. (From Meares's Voyages)

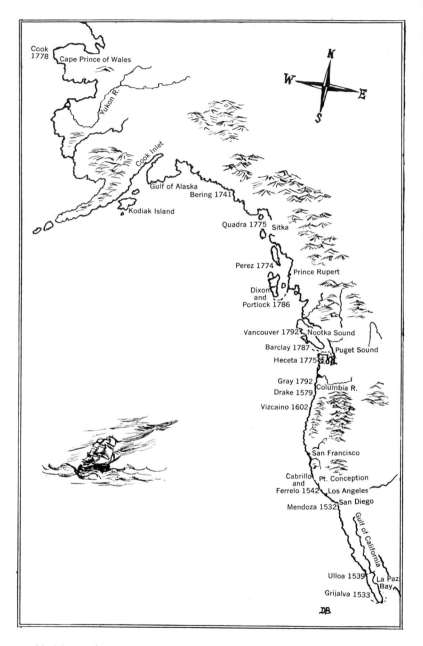

Maritime explorations on the Pacific coast of North America, 1532-1792.

1

THE FIFTEENTH CENTURY WORLD

FIVE HUNDRED YEARS AGO, the known world was very small, somewhat smaller than Europe today. The Sahara bounded it on the south, Gibraltar and the British Isles on the west, the lands of the Teutons on the north, and the fabled Orient on the east. To the average man, all else was "chaos and black night."

It is true that adventurers and explorers had traveled up the north coast of Europe, had discovered Iceland, and visited the southern tip of Greenland. Evidently around A. D. 1000, Norsemen even touched the American coast in the region now called New England, and since before the birth of Christ ships have regularly called at northern Africa. Europeans knew of India and the Malay peninsula, and for centuries carried on indirect trade with China at the great fairs of Samarkand, Bokhara, and Khiva.

But the commoner of the fifteenth century was unaware of these far horizons of the traders and explorers. During the nearly thousand years separating the fall of Rome from the Renaissance, so harsh was the struggle for existence that men's minds were deadened to progress. Serfs planted, nobles wooed, and the clergy expounded, but all to no apparent purpose. Hunger, disease, and war continued to be the usual lot of the masses; velvets and pageantry that of the nobles. The work of changing this ancient pattern became the profound task of the Renaissance. Out of it came some of the most turbulent and brilliant epochs in human history, as well as a galaxy of fabulous names: Elizabeth, Drake and Raleigh, Balboa, Cortez, and Vizcaino; and, two centuries later, James Cook, Robert Gray, Lewis and Clark, and John McLoughlin, to mention only a few.

Fully to understand why the common seamen of those early Spanish, English, and Portuguese navies willingly faced death to hunt their fortunes overseas, we have to remember the ignorance, poverty, and social corruption of that day. Besides, adventure and the lure of the unknown were as persuasive then as now. Men like Columbus and Lindbergh will always seek new worlds.

Many motives led the nobility to discovery and exploration but all were largely based on economics, nationalism, and religion. Just as the ordinary seaman felt the pressure of poverty, so did noblemen and business leaders feel the impact of lower incomes and profit rates. Constant wars and the inroads of barbarians had critically upset the commercial world. Northern Europe had no sooner adjusted itself to the invading Norse tribes than southern and eastern Europe were cut off from the Orient by the insurgent Mongols and Turks. International trade became hard pressed to make a profit acceptable to the owners. New routes to old markets and sources of supply were imperative, and these had to be seaways because the enemy controlled the overland tracks.

Although the spirit of national unity bloomed slowly in Europe, by the late fifteenth and early sixteenth centuries it was playing an active part in pushing back old boundaries. Spain was united under Ferdinand and Isabella; England became conscious of nationalism under the Tudor, Henry VII; and the Portuguese, French, and Dutch were on the threshold of national development. Leaders like Prince Henry of Portugal and, later, Elizabeth of England wanted to advance their nations as well as themselves.

The third great force leading to exploration was religion. The Christian gladly risked his life to find a new route to escape the sword of the "infidel Turk" and acquire the silk, spices, and incense of the "heathen Chinamen." "To divert . . . treasure from the infidel and secure it for a Christian nation was an enterprise fitted to kindle a prince's enthusiasm." [1]

At the beginning of the Renaissance, missionaries and traders were entering China and Japan, but the religious interests of Europe were neither centered in missionary work in the Orient nor in hatred of the Moslems. John Huss, who challenged the infallibility of the Church and was condemned to death by the Council of Constance in 1415, was but a forerunner of a long line of religious zealots, eventually represented in America by the Pilgrims, Anne Hutchinson, Roger Williams, Jason Lee, and Marcus Whitman. So widespread was religious concern, so insistent its pressure on both noble and commoner, that it account-

1.—John Fiske. *The Discovery of America*, volume 1, page 317.

ed for many of the greatest explorations and settlements. Trader Joliet took the missionary Marquette with him; LaSalle had the priest Hennepin.

Small as the fifteenth century world was, and cursed with ignorance, intolerance, and war, it was yet blessed with farsighted businessmen who were willing to risk life and fortune to retain old markets or acquire new ones. It had a growing sense of nationalism which placed the good of the nation above the desires of the individual and it possessed a religious consciousness that was ready to face either the stake or the wilderness for its faith. And it had an insatiable appetite for geographic knowledge that was not satisfied until the last lingering corners of the New World were being mapped and conquered four centuries after Columbus.

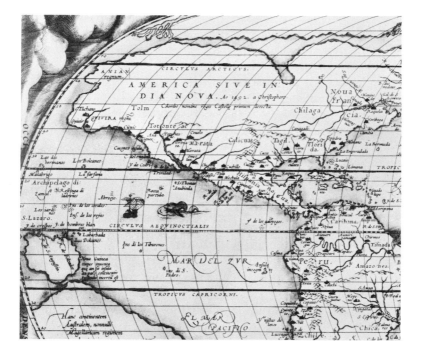

Part of the Ortelius map of 1570. Note that Anian is shown as a country facing the North Pacific, and the legendary Quivira is located in modern California. Ortelius was the Latin name used by Abraham Oertel, 1527-1598, Flemish geographer whose atlas, *Theatrum Orbis Terrarum,* long remained the basis for geographic works. (Library of Congress)

PACIFIC EXPLORATIONS BEFORE COLUMBUS

THE FULL STORY of the Pacific Northwest coast starts long before the fifteenth century. That coast was as surely visited by Orientals earlier than Christopher Columbus as was the Atlantic coast by Norsemen during those same pre-Columbian eras. To find just how much before, we have to examine the first knowledge of the New World. For centuries at least, irregular communication existed between the Orient and America prior to the Spanish period. The Orientals themselves have traditions of ancient activities in the New World; and many travelers and students have noted the similarity of social customs, religious rites, arts, and languages of the ancient Orientals and the early Americans. Alex von Humboldt[1] points out the almost identical signs of the zodiac used by the Tartar-Mantchoos and the Mexicans. The tiger, hare, serpent, monkey, dog, and bird are found in each in that order.

The Reverend W. Lobscheid[2] shows that the principal buildings of both the Chinese and Central Americans are erected above ground on elevated sites and that the roofing materials in each case are convexed and concaved tiles; also that "the anchors of their boats are the same as we find them in Japan and the north of China . . . with four hooks without a barb." He suggests, too, that the worship of the serpent in Mexico is not far removed from the honor paid the more dignified dragon in China:

"They resembled the Chinese and (Buddhist) Japanese in their ideas of the transmigration of the soul; in the monastic forms and discipline; in their penances, ablutions, alms-givings, and public festivals; in the worship of their household gods; in the devotions of the priests to the study of the vows and rites of the cloister; in the incense and chants of their worship; in their use

---

1—"Views of the Cordilleras and Monuments of the Indigenous Nations of America," quoted in Edward P. Vining's *An Inglorious Columbus; or, Evidence that Hwui Shan and a Party of Buddhist Monks from Afghanistan Discovered America in the Fifth Century, A. D.,* page 148.

2.—"Grammar of the Chinese Language," quoted in Vining, page 155.

of charms and amulets; in some of their forms of burning their dead, and the preservation of the ashes in urns, and in the assumption of the right to educate the youth." [1]

The word *llama* or *tlama* in the Mexican indicates "medicine men," and the *lama* of the Tibetans and Tartars is their physician as well as their religious leader. The figure of a cross-legged Buddha is common to both peoples. According to Karl F. Neuman,[2] the customs of courtship and marriage among the Aztecs resemble those of present-day Kamchatka.

Some early American inscriptions have many of the features of a written language and may have been read in columns from the top to the bottom, Oriental fashion. Coins, utensils, and objects of adornment, dug up at numerous points along the Pacific coast of North America, are clearly Asiatic in origin and of ancient vintage. How these artifacts arrived in the western hemisphere is partially answered in the tale of Hwui Shan, who returned to China in A.D. 499, reporting a voyage to Fu-Sang by five Buddhist monks twenty-one years earlier.

1.—Vining, page 157.
2.—"Eastern Asia and Western America, according to Chinese Authorities of the Fifth, Sixth, and Seventh Centuries," quoted in Vining, page 99.

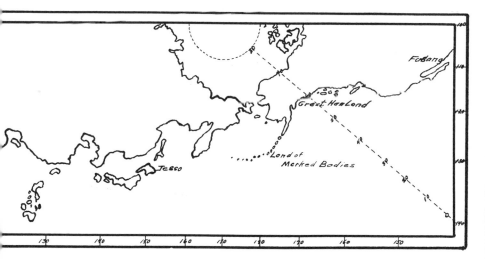

Place names for the famous voyage of Hwui Shan, fifth century Oriental traveler
to the western world.

THE VOYAGE OF HWUI SHAN

OF ALL THE TALES told about Orientals or by Orientals, two stand out in the imagination of the western world: the wanderings of Marco Polo and the voyage of Hwui Shan. And they are both wrapped in the haze of fourteen centuries.

According to official documents of the Sung dynasty, Hwui Shan lived and worked during the fifth century of the Christian Era. In A. D. 458, he left the mainland of China, proceeding to Japan by way of the Yellow sea. From there he traveled along the Kurile islands to Kamchatka, then to the Aleutians and Alaska, where he stopped to observe the customs of the natives. Going southward he eventually landed in Mexico, where he stayed to learn the culture of its people. From Mexico, Hwui Shan insisted that he passed to the Country of Women. In 499, he reported his findings to the official historian of China. This scholar considered the journey of enough importance to be included in the state records.

America has never quite reconciled itself to being visited by an Oriental ten centuries before Columbus, and Westerners generally have taken a dim view of Hwui Shan. Yet scholars have gone to great length to analyze the evidence supporting his claims. The possibility of such a journey is obvious to those familiar with the coast line and ocean currents of the North Pacific. The journey from China to Mexico is primarily a progress from west to east, not north to south as it is falsely projected on the Mercator maps. From land point to land point the distance is never more than two hundred miles, easily covered by the most primitive craft. Besides, a strong warm ocean current follows this exact route from the coast of China to that of Mexico and is so powerful that a boat once caught in it is easily carried to American waters. In fact, so strong is the Japan current that a disabled boat could not avoid arriving in those waters even if it wanted to.

8

There is the modern case of the *Ryo Yei Maru,* eighty-five-foot, one-hundred-ton fishing schooner from Misaki, Japan. On December 5, 1926, it left its home port on a fishing cruise. Almost a year later and with only two bodies of the original crew of twelve aboard, it was sighted off Cape Flattery by the freighter *Margaret Dollar* and towed to Port Townsend, Washington.[1] Clearly the journey from Japan to the Pacific coast of North America could easily have been accomplished by Hwui Shan in a well-equipped vessel.

What actual evidence did this traveler leave to convince us of the truth of his claims? Hwui Shan had a knack for describing with minute detail those things peculiar to a country or a people. He selected the essential though obvious differences, and was more interested in recording these than in making casual references to an inferior culture. A glance at the map will indicate the regions Hwui Shan visited and the names he gave them. Northeast of Japan proper is the Island of "Jesso;" the Aleutians are the "Country of Marked Bodies;" Alaska is the "Great Han Country;" and that vast region called California by the Spanish was "Fu-Sang" to Hwui Shan. He made little note of Jesso, already familiar in China, but in the "Country of Marked Bodies," he commented on the three lines painted on the faces of the men to show their rank in the community;[2] and, what was stranger, he mentioned the absence of walled cities.[3]

Pleased by the friendliness and hospitality of the Aleutians, he said, "The People of the land are of a merry nature, and they rejoice when they have an abundance, even of articles that are of little value. Traveling visitors do not prepare food for their journeys, and they have the shelter of . . . the inhabitants' dwellings." [4]

Although Hwui Shan undoubtedly stopped in Alaska, more in-

1.—The log of the vessel revealed that a few days after leaving port, engine trouble developed. Before this could be remedied, a typhoon caught the hapless craft, and the long drift across the Pacific began. The quarantine officer at Port Townsend said there was little doubt that cannibalism had been resorted to when the members of the crew faced starvation. See Gordon R. Newell's *S. O. S. North Pacific.*
2.—The great Scots explorer, Alexander Mackenzie, reported that the same markings were still used when he traversed that region thirteen centuries later.
3.—Vining, pages 319-321.
4.—Same.

teresting here are his descriptions of the land to the south, Fu-Sang, which was the same general region called *Baja California* by the Spanish:

"Fu-Sang is situated twice ten thousand li[5] or more to the east of the Great Han country. That land is also situated at the east of the Middle Kingdom.[6] That region has many Fu-Sang trees, and it is from these trees that the country derives its name. . . Their first sprouts are like those of the bamboo. The people of the country eat them and the fruit, which is (formed) like a pear but of a reddish colour. They spin thread from their bark, from which they make cloth. . . . They also manufacture a finer fabric from it. In constructing their houses they use planks, such as are generally used when building adobe walls.

"According to their rules they have a southern and a northern place of confinement. An offender who has transgressed but slightly enters the southern place of confinement, but if he has sinned heavily he enters the northern place. . . . If there is pardon for him, then he is sent away to the southern place . . . but if he cannot be pardoned, then he is sent away to the northern one. Those men and women dwelling in the northern place of confinement, when they mate and bear children; the boys are made slaves at the age of eight years, and the girls at the age of nine years. The criminal is not allowed to go out, up to (*or* at) [7] the time of his death.

"When a nobleman has committed a crime, the people of the country hold a great assemblage and sit in judgment on the culprit, in an excavated tumulus.[8] They feast and drink before him, and bid him farewell when parting from him, as if taking leave of a dying man. Then they surround him with ashes there. For a single crime (*or* a crime of the first magnitude) , only one person (the culprit) was hidden (*or* sent) away. For two crimes (*or* a crime of the second magnitude) , the children and grandchildren were included in the punishment. For three crimes (*or* a crime of the third magnitude) , seven generations were included in the punishment.

"They have cattle-horns, of which the long ones are used to

5.—Chinese miles.
6.—China.
7.—In this passage, parentheses indicate possible translations.
8.—Burial mound.

contain some of their possessions, the best of them reaching twice ten times as much as the capacity of a common horn. They have horse-carts, cattle-carts, and deer-carts. The people of the country raise deer as cattle are raised in the Middle Kingdom. From milk they make Koumiss.[9] They have the red pears kept unspoiled throughout the year, and they also have tomatoes. The ground is destitute of iron, but they have copper. Gold and silver are not valued. In their markets there are no taxes or fixed prices.

"When they marry, it is the custom for the son-in-law to go and erect a house outside the door of the dwelling of the young woman. Morning and evening he sprinkles and sweeps (the ground) for a year, and, if the young woman is not pleased with him, she then sends him away; but, if they are mutually pleased, then the marriage is completed, the marriage ceremonies being for the most part like those of the Middle Kingdom." [10]

Such descriptions leave little doubt that, in the fifth century, Hwui Shan actually visited the New World, even though some of the passages in his story are not entirely clear. For example, it has long been thought that horses as known today were brought here by the Spaniards; and perhaps the application of *peaceful* to the pre-Aztec inhabitants of Mexico causes speculation about Hwui Shan's definition of the term. On the other hand, the Aztecs may have defeated and absorbed these earlier tribes just because they were peaceful. The horse may have been native and died out. What Hwui Shan thought was a horse may have been another animal seen at some distance, or he may simply have made a mistake.

Such errors, if they are errors, do not condemn the rest of the evidence. To disregard the whole story for certain exaggerations and inaccuracies would call for like treatment of the records of the Spanish explorers. Even Jamestown and John Smith would have doubtful authority, as well as the explorations and work of the French up the St. Lawrence and about the Great lakes. Each would become but a shadow of the imagination. Hwui Shan's story abounds in proofs of accuracy and he faithfully cites too many American customs to be dismissed as a mere romancer.

Not that he was above exaggeration or bold misstatements. For

9.—Liquor.
10.—Vining, pages 265-293.

centuries the Orient had a legend regarding the existence of a mythical Kingdom of Women, where strange, half-human beings reigned and weird customs ruled still more weird females, whose hairy, breastless bodies became pregnant without the aid of males; whose young were capable of prodigious feats at tender years. It was believed to be a land dominated by ruthlessness, mystery, and gruesome femininity. Hwui Shan describes what he "saw:"

"Its people's manner of appearance is straight erect and their colour is a very pure white. Their bodies are hairy, and they have long locks, the ends of which reach to the ground.

"At the second or third month, bickering, they enter the water.[11] They then become pregnant. They bear their young at the sixth or seventh month. The female-people are destitute of breasts in front of their chests, but behind, at the nape of the neck (*or*, back of the head) they have hair-roots (short hair, *or* a bunch of hair, *or* a hairy organ), and in the midst of the white hair, it is pleasing to the taste (*or* there is juice). They nurse their young for one hundred days, and they can then walk. When three or four years old they become fully grown. This is true! When they see a human being, they are afraid, and flee to one side. They venerate their mates.

"They eat the salt-plant. Its leaves resemble the Sie-Hao,[12] but its odour is more fragrant and its taste is saltish." [13]

This account is probably merely another version of the old tale so often heard in both the Orient and the Occident during the early middle centuries of the Christian era.

Out of some sixty descriptions of American culture which Hwui Shan gives, only a fraction have been challenged, such as his statement regarding horses and his comments on distances traveled. The question of distance usually hinges upon the length of the *li*, generally considered one-third of the English mile. If such were the case, his accounts are not inaccurate. Generally, both European and American scholars accept this Oriental visit of fifteen hundred years ago, concerning themselves only with its importance. At first glance it has little. The Orientals did not come regularly and the voyage did not deeply affect China.

11.—The character for *water* also means *migration*.
12.—A species of Chinese absinthe or wormwood.
13.—Vining, pages 303-309.

But Hwui Shan could have greatly influenced the natives of the Pacific coast. If we credit him and the other Buddhist monks, then they may have introduced into the western hemisphere a higher civilization than that developed by native tribes. The calm, peaceful philosophy of the East was far superior to the bloody culture of the Aztecs. How many millions enjoyed that milder rule before the coming of the Aztecs we can never know.

This though is sure—to have lived under a culture softened by the teachings of Buddha was better than to have lived under the rigors of paganism. And undoubtedly the man who would have been responsible for spreading this happier way of life was the monk, Hwui Shan.

Two great Spaniards: Vasco Nunez de Balboa (left), with his discovery of the Pacific ocean, sparked a long series of international events. In the sixteenth century, Hernando Cortez (right) conquered Mexico and established Spanish power in the Pacific. (Huntington Library)

4

RENAISSANCE EXPLORATIONS

IMPORTANT AS THE PRE-COLUMBIAN VOYAGES were to America, the expeditions of the Portuguese and Spaniards during the Renaissance outranked them. The great voyages in the interval between these periods were not directly concerned with the story of Pacific Northwest explorations, so they will be mentioned only briefly.

Long before the Renaissance reached its peak, Prince Henry of Portugal had founded his navigation school. Fernandez had gone to Cape Verde, and Gomez to the Cape Verde islands. Dias had rounded Good Hope in 1497 and de Gama had arrived at Calicut the following year. While the Portuguese were accomplishing these things, Isabella and Ferdinand financed Columbus to the Azores; the British Cabots reached the coast of Newfoundland; and Ojeda and Amerigo Vespucci landed in Guiana. At the beginning of the sixteenth century, Cortereal arrived off Labrador and Ponce de Leon hunted a fountain in Florida.

It was still assumed that the coasts so far discovered were merely unknown parts of the Asiatic seaboard. By 1513 the islands and coasts of the Caribbean were fairly well explored, but it had taken a half century to get a rudimentary idea of the New World. Though this tardy geographical knowledge slowed settlement, attempts were made to investigate the interior regions about the Caribbean and to plant colonies as headquarters for more extensive exploration.

The discovery of the Pacific was the direct result of such circumstances. The Spaniard Ojeda, with whom the unscrupulous Amerigo Vespucci made his first voyage, had established the town of San Sebastian on the mainland of Central America. When this colony was badly in need of supplies, a relief ship was sent out. On it was that poor, ugly, red-haired Spaniard, Balboa, who for the first time was attracting some attention.

14

5

VASCO NUNEZ DE BALBOA
DISCOVERS THE PACIFIC OCEAN

VASCO NUNEZ DE BALBOA was born into a society top-heavy with lace, castled moats, and long swords. It was then about 1475 and Spanish life was a maze of political trickery, religious intrigue, and downright debauchery; great wealth and great poverty were often side by side. Yet it was also an age of bravery, of honesty, and a time which bred men. Weaklings perished because no laws enforced social justice for them. They were ruthlessly swept aside by men and women in whose blood coursed the fighting spirit of generations of soldiers of fortune.

Balboa's family was noble in a provincial kind of way, and doubtless young Vasco played, fought, and got into trouble much as young boys have done ever since fathers learned the benefits of corporal punishment. Soon after the first reported voyage of discovery, he came to the New World to seek his fortune. Though he did not add greatly to the family wealth, he did carve his name high on the roster of Spanish conquistadors who for three centuries ruled the American tropics.

Close on Columbus's report of discovery, the Atlantic boiled with caravels loaded with nobles, gentlemen, friars, soldiers of fortune, debtors, criminals, freebooters, and pirates, many of whom Columbus swore did not deserve water from the hand of either God or man.[1] All were headed for the "Indies" to make a fortune in a day and then return to Spain to live in an aura of lace, perfume, and beautiful women. These dreams had some basis in fact, for the "Indies" were storehouses of vast wealth, to be tapped by daring and imaginative men. Before venturing upon a journey to the Spanish Main, though, the traveler did well to arrange his earthly affairs, for he knew that he had only a rare chance of returning alive, and even rarer of returning wealthy.

1.—Arthur Strawn. *Sails and Swords,* page 3.

No ship's captain ever dreamed of sailing with a small crew. Beri-beri, scurvy, storms, shipwreck, savages, and common starvation often cut a crew down to one-tenth of its original strength. Magellan left Spain with three hundred men and returned with eighteen. Balboa ended his quest with disaster for himself but immortality for his name.

Something was known of Central America before Balboa crossed it. Ojeda had attempted to colonize on the mainland, using as a base of supplies the rude town of San Sebastian,[2] which he had established in the West Indies. Balboa himself had traveled about enough to know that the Indians on the eastern shore of the Gulf of Uraba used poison arrows and were none too friendly.[3] Though the general outline of the Atlantic coast of Central America was fairly well known soon after the discovery of the New World, ignorance of native food supplies and poor transportation brought Ojeda's colony to the verge of starvation within a year.

Two ships, manned by a motley crew of men of fortune and fitted out in San Domingo with food, horses, and general colonial supplies, were dispatched to relieve San Sebastian. In charge of this expedition was a lawyer, Encisco, ill fitted to govern. He had ability but not the leadership that whips a jungle into an organized community, making men obey because they want to.

Actual details of this relief voyage to San Sebastian will probably always be lost among the lofty imaginings of those exciting days. History here mostly strays into "his story."

Some time after Encisco had sailed well out of sight of land, there was a commotion on the overcrowded decks of the little vessel. The head of a barrel marked "pork" burst and out stepped the jaunty Balboa with his huge, ferocious hound, Leoncico, the "Little Lion." [4] Another story reports that Balboa was wrapped in sail cloth and remained hidden until he thought it safe to emerge. A few historians feel that both tales merely romanticize a commonplace ruffian. Whether from a keg with a hound or from a sail without a hound, what matters is that Vasco Nunez de Balboa did emerge. From that moment until his severed head rolled in

2.—Fiske, volume 2, page 370.
3.—Same, page 371.
4.—Strawn, page 22.

the Acla sands five or six years later, he never ceased being the most loved and most despised, most trusted and most feared exponent of Spain in Central America.

On making his appearance he was immediately placed under restraint. Stowaways are seldom popular and they certainly were not in those troubled times. Balboa knew that he was taking his life in his hands in thus hiding aboard a ship manned by such cutthroats as gathered under Encisco. But his debts in San Domingo were great. He had borrowed and defaulted, begged and failed to repay, until his slave-worked plantation at Salvatierre had been seized by his creditors; and there was danger of his arrest for debt. After ten years at Santo Domingo he was a hopeless bankrupt. He decided to stow away and have at least a fighting chance for fame and fortune. Besides, he was in his prime at thirty-five.

Tall and well proportioned, he was also fearless and restless. Not waiting to be challenged as to his right aboard, he took the initiative, knowing that a strong arm, a good sword, and a clear head were welcome to any ship's master. On those strengths he based his defense. Readily admitting to Encisco that his presence was irregular, he cautioned the other that as a friend he, Balboa, was more valuable than as an enemy. He even boasted of being the best swordsman there. Furthermore he was. Of all those aboard he said he knew most about the mainland; only he knew its Indians and its fevers. His eloquence won the crew. Here was a soldier of fortune, a gentleman, yet one who understood the desires and fears of commoners, one who gambled with them and against them, doing both with equal grace.

Balboa was never after that without friends; in the six remaining years of his turbulent career he never again gambled entirely alone. He was always supported by men who had heard this gay, vaunting defense of his worth and who later had seen him prove it.

At first, though, Encisco was furious, ordering that Balboa be put in chains and cast ashore on the first island; virtually a sentence of death. Only Balboa's oratory saved him. He enlisted as a member of the crew and little more is heard of him until the mainland was reached. He ingratiated himself with the best of the crew, kept his wits about him, and found out that Encisco was unpopular with his men.

By the time the ship landed, Balboa had laid the groundwork for his own leadership by deftly playing Encisco's followers against their enemies until his own clique had control. However, he was too wise to claim open leadership until a situation developed which made his seizure of power seem necessary to the security of the expedition.

Ojeda's camp was a failure and Encisco began almost at once to build new cities. When Balboa convinced the leaders that because the Indians on the eastern shore of the Gulf of Uraba were unfriendly it would be better to build their new city on the western shore, Encisco had the good sense to heed the advice. This was the first wedge in Balboa's program to achieve control. Thereafter Balboa saw to it that he was more and more often looked to for leadership and counsel. Playing one group of leaders against another, he gradually became the central figure of the tiny colony. This was in December of 1510.

After helping establish a new colony Balboa turned his attention to gold, at the same time wisely providing for the permanent support of the camp by planting crops. He established friendly relations with a nearby Indian encampment:

"I have taken care that the Indians of this land are not ill-treated, permitting no man to injure them, and giving them many things from Castile, whereby they may be drawn into friendship with us. This honorable treatment of the Indians has been the cause of my learning great secrets from them, through the knowledge of which large quantities of gold may be obtained and your Highness will thus be well-served." [5]

The next step was to acquire the treasure which the natives had accumulated in camp. Even as the Spanish valued it, this varied from the slight value of small trinkets to considerable sums, yet all of the wealth was not in gold. At one time Balboa took several hundred pearls from a single camp. Though these did not compare in value with Oriental pearls, still they were desirable prizes.

Meanwhile Balboa heard tales of even greater riches westward. He must also have heard rumors of a large body of water in that quarter because he decided to go into the interior, hoping to find both treasure and a new coastline.

5.—Strawn, page 91.

He had been on the mainland nearly two years when, in 1512, he began—and continued for many months—a series of long letters to Ferdinand, King of Spain. In one he tells of the ease with which units of gold could be obtained in the New World:

"The Indians describe them as being the size of oranges or of a fist, and others like flat slabs." [6]

Gold was so plentiful that the natives "do not care to keep it in baskets; . . . all the rivers in these mountains contain gold; and . . . they have very large lumps in great abundance. Their method of collecting the gold is by going into the water and gathering it in their baskets. They also scrape it up in the beds of streams, when these are dry." [7]

However, the main reason for his long letters was a defense of his sudden rise to power. Because of the way he had achieved this, he was naturally reported to the court as a usurper. In another letter Balboa described the hardships of a commander:

"And if the person who is entrusted with the government of this land remains in his house and leaves work to others, no one else he can send in his place can manage the people so well, or fail to make mistakes which may cause the destruction of himself and of all who are with him." [8]

In the same letter he tells how he has led his men stripped naked through stinking tropical swamps, all, of course, for the glory of the King. Such boasting was usual then and the King expected it. The simple truth often sounded too unattractive to curry royal favor, and fifteenth century political office seekers exaggerated and misrepresented for exactly the same reason as modern ones. So Balboa filled his letters to the court with truths, half-truths, and pure imaginings, all with the one purpose of strengthening his case before the King.

In his short, sharp struggle for control of the colony, he made many friends, especially among the Indians, but many enemies among his own company. Ex-commanders Ojeda and Nicuesa were openly hostile. In fact, by 1512 Balboa had become so embroiled in suits and counter suits that he was in danger of being

---

6.—Strawn, page 102.
7.—Same, page 103.
8.—Same, page 92.

taken to Spain for trial. Facing this supreme test disclosed his real nature.

He understood quite well that his trial, if one took place, would be merely a contest between lies on one hand and boasting on the other, and that success would rest entirely on whether his command in Darien could bring more gold into the coffers of Ferdinand than that of his enemies. Balboa was charged with graft in public office, yet he knew that the court neither expected nor desired a clean administration of its colonial ventures; it wanted gold and the promise of gold. It desired fame and the assurance of grandeur. Balboa might easily have gone to Spain and lied his way out of his predicament. He could have bought witnesses who would have testified to his honesty.

There was something in Balboa which made him shun the easy way. True, he shipped away in the night to escape his creditors, but he stowed aboard a ship bound for hardship and disaster, not one bound for civilization and ease. Other commanders fought the Indians, stole their gold, raped the native daughters, and left enemies. Balboa fought the Indians, bargained for their gold, and married a chief's daughter as a sign of perpetual friendship. Furthermore, he took this marriage seriously. He and his native wife lived in a peculiarly happy union for the few remaining years of his life.

When he was at last ordered to Spain for trial, he again chose the difficult way. The existence of Mexico was unknown; Peru was a rumor. His forthcoming trial gave Vasco Nunez his greatest and last complete gamble with the gods. He determined to bring to his trial a genuine claim to greatness that would offset the charges against him.

During his months in the jungle, Balboa had developed an enormous enthusiasm for dogs; and when, on September 1, 1513, he gathered his company of two hundred men for this last hazard, he had on hand a small pack of bloodhounds. Doubtless some of them were a result of "The Little Lion's" amorous affairs. Balboa had trained his dogs to hunt Indians, and "The Little Lion" had been so well disciplined that his master vowed he could tell the difference between a friendly and an unfriendly Indian. In any case, after a successful attack on an Indian village, the dog received a soldier's full share of the loot.

Balboa faced a tremendous task. When preliminary surveys for an isthmian canal were being made in 1853, a British naval officer, C. J. Provost, of H. M. S. *Virago,* attempted to cross the isthmus but was forced to withdraw because of the nature of the country. The buildings of the canal at Panama baffled the best brains of one country and took the combined engineering skill of another even partially to conquer the fevers and jungles of that region. Yet the Spanish conquerors triumphed over it with only frail human muscles.

Three weeks after leaving Santa Maria on the Atlantic, the party attacked an Indian village, killed six hundred natives, captured a large supply of food, and appropriated a considerable amount of gold and pearls. The next day, September 24, 1513, Balboa and sixty-seven of his men began ascending the rise which separates the Atlantic from the Pacific. The rest of the expedition stayed in the recently captured camp. Five days later Balboa reached the Gulf of San Miguel, thus realizing his dream of making an enduring contribution to mankind.

Many point out that he was unaware of having discovered the Pacific. Nevertheless he did know that he was gazing on a different body of water from the one he had just left, for he called his discovery the South sea.

The Spaniards remained about a month on the shores of San Miguel, gathered more pearls and gold from the natives, who told them of a land to the south where gold and pearls were as common as sand; where great rooms were piled high with treasures; and whose entrance could be reached only after a water journey of many days. The tale undoubtedly referred to Peru. Balboa at once started planning a second expedition to the South.

First he had to report his success to Santa Maria. He started back on November 3, 1513. The return was fairly easy because, as usual, he had made friends with the inhabitants not only at San Miguel but also along the route. On January 5, he arrived at the Indian settlements controlled by the native chief, Ponca; and on the seventeenth at his father-in-law Careta's village. This was excellent time. He rested two days in Careta's camp before pushing on to Santa Maria, which he reached before the end of the month.

Meanwhile disaster approached Nunez, swiftly and relentlessly.

Having grown exasperated with the conflicting claims and counter claims of the leaders on Terre Firme, the mainland, the Spanish throne determined to send yet another governor to rule. Pedrarias Davila was chosen. He arrived on June 30. Pedrarias was as subtle as Encisco was crude, as ruthless as Balboa was considerate. He sensed the vast opportunities in the New World for personal grandeur and wealth—if one were not over-scrupulous.

Pedrarias was a moral pervert. Lacking nobility himself, he could not recognize integrity of thought or action in others. Even the careful Fiske calls him a two-legged tiger.[9] The Spanish historian Oviedo is said to have amused himself trying to estimate the number of murdered souls Pedrarias would be called upon to atone for on Judgment Day and to have arrived at two million as a fair figure. Fiske says [10] that twenty thousand murders traceable directly to the inhuman Pedrarias is not an excessive number. Open enmity with Pedrarias was the same as signing a death warrant. He did not defeat his enemies; he butchered them.

Because of discovering the Pacific, Balboa hoped to be confirmed as governor of the isthmus, but even as he tramped home from San Miguel, Pedrarias was on his way to the New World. This new governor was past seventy years of age and time had not sweetened him. With him he brought as co-conspirators fifteen hundred soldiers of fortune and necessary equipment. On reaching Darien he set about readjusting the public offices to fit his own plans. Naturally he came in conflict with Balboa.

With Pedrarias was Encisco, the same lawyer with whom Balboa had had his adventures as a stowaway, and, later, as usurper. As chief constable under Pedrarias, Encisco now planned to get revenge on Balboa, his first act after landing being to arrest the other on various charges. Trial and acquittal followed immediately but Balboa's position was delicate. He had enthusiastic followers but no legal status with Pedrarias as governor.

Again Balboa chose the hard way out of a difficulty. Since no one loved the governor, save possibly the equally despised Bishop Fonseca, Balboa could have led an open revolt. He chose conciliation. For two years he and Pedrarias avoided an open break. Balboa used his influence at court to protest Pedrarias's inhuman

9.—Fiske, volume 2, page 377.
10.—Same.

treatment of the natives. When news of this reached the governor, neither man any longer pretended friendship, yet both wanted to avoid open warfare. The Bishop of Darien, Juan de Quevedo, offered a compromise scheme, suggesting that Pedrarias permit Balboa to go in search of Peru, in return for which favor and to bind the bargain Balboa would be betrothed to the daughter of Pedrarias. In this way Pedrarias would rid himself of a trouble-maker and Balboa would be free from the restrictions and impositions of an unjust governor. The detail of Balboa's earlier marriage to the chief's daughter did not bother either the governor or the bishop since they considered the Indian marriage merely a matter of convenience with no moral or legal status.

Balboa disagreed. He had married Careta's daughter not only because of political strategy but also because of genuine respect. This had developed into real devotion. He finally agreed to the betrothal scheme as the most logical solution. Furthermore, the girl was in Spain and had no intention of coming to America; and Balboa was in America with no thought of returning to Spain. Pedrarias was more anxious to be rid of Balboa than to hasten the actual marriage of his daughter. Balboa was more eager to be on his way to Peru than to haggle over a betrothal he had no intention of consummating in marriage. So the bargain was struck and Balboa was committed to the Peruvian venture.

He set up his base of operations at Acla, a newly-founded town north of Darien. Since the journey to Peru had to be made by water and he could neither build nor acquire a ship, Nunez set about the unbelievable task of taking four ships apart at Acla and transporting them by hand labor across the isthmus.

There were no trails and navigable rivers; the jungle was as dense as if man had never penetrated it. The passage from Acla to the Pacific is one of the darkest pages in the life of Vasco Nunez de Balboa.

Tireless himself, he drove his Indian carriers until they literally fell dead at their work, to be replaced by others who in their turn succumbed. But to call him a mere slave driver is to misunderstand him, though even his friends admitted that in this ghastly venture he worked to death at least five hundred Indian slaves. His enemies charge him with the death of two thousand. It is true that he left the wretched bodies of slaves along the route to the Pacific and fame, yet he himself did not stand idly by and curse them. Wherever the heat was greatest, the way roughest and most impassable, there was Balboa, struggling, sweating, slaving with his slaves. His Indians died on the trail, but not at the end of the lash. The master did not die perhaps because he was sustained by a vision of achievement which he could not explain to his slaves. The first ships ever to plow the Pacific under the hand of a Spaniard were those ships from Acla.

When ready for the voyage, save for pitch and iron, Balboa heard rumors that Pedrarias was to be succeeded by a new governor. If he sent now for pitch and iron, he risked having the treacherous governor countermand the Peruvian expedition. On the other hand, the new governor might frown upon another's attempt to gain fame and fortune. Balboa finally decided to send to Pedrarias for the materials, instructing his messengers to spy out the situation and to wait for the new governor, if that seemed wiser.

Just as these events were taking place on the Pacific, Pedrarias heard that Balboa did not intend to marry his betrothed, but was secretly planning to escape to Peru, seize the wealth, and set up an independent principality. Garavito, as craven a renegade as ever disgraced Spain in the New World, carried this rumor to Pedrarias. In love with Balboa's Indian wife, Garavito tried to seduce her but was rebuffed by the loyal girl. It is not clear whether Balboa caught Garavito at his attempted seduction or whether his wife informed him afterward. Anyhow he sharply reprimanded Garavito and warned him thereafter to attend to his own affairs. Ignoring Balboa's leniency, the other merely hated his benefactor and plotted his death. The rumor he carried to Pedrarias of Balboa's supposed treachery was part of this plotting.

Pedrarias was delighted at any tale which offered him an excuse to get rid of his rival, but he was careful. He sent a friendly letter to his pledged son-in-law asking him to return at once as consultant in some important business. Balboa was met at the outskirts of Acla by a company of soldiers under command of Francisco Pizarro, who had served under Balboa and was considered a friend. Pizarro arrested Balboa, leading him before Pedrarias, who immediately found him guilty of treason. Before day's end, Vasco Nunez de Balboa's headless body was ready for burial in the sands of Acla. Even his enemies criticized his speedy execution.

"Contemporary witnesses . . . were unanimous in their expressions of esteem for Balboa and of condemnation for the manner of his taking off." [11] He was a "wise and true-hearted man . . . humane, honest and sagacious." [12]

Had he been permitted to finish his work, the hatred of the Incas, resulting from Pizarro's barbaric policy, might have been averted, for Balboa never defeated his purposes by embittering his slaves.

It is impractical to separate a man from the age in which he lived, unfair to judge him outside it. At times, with a St. Francis compassion, he climbed above the general sordidness of the colonial period; occasionally he sank to the depths of Cortez and Pedrarias. Whether he was noble or scoundrel, four centuries have kept alive his name and his work, and chances are that he will never be forgotten. In some ways he was the most important Spaniard of his time. His colonial policies successfully adjusted relations between natives and Spaniards and his discovery of the Pacific sparked that long series of international events still in the future.

11.—Fiske, volume 2, page 384.
12.—Same, pages 378-379.

6

HERNANDO CORTEZ ESTABLISHES SPANISH POWER

AFTER 1513 the Pacific became a world focal point. Systematic expeditions were formed for map-making and settlement, but most of the voyages had as their chief purposes the discovery of a passage across the continent—the imaginary Strait of Anian—, the finding of new gold or pearl fields, or occasionally the introduction of Christianity among the aborigines. These expeditions generally stemmed from the Spanish government set up in Mexico.

Through Velazquez, governor of Cuba, the Crown in 1519 sent Hernando Cortez to Mexico to explore and conquer that region for the mother country. Later the governor regretted his commission to Cortez, who defied new orders by sailing to the mainland where he captured the Indian woman, Marina, for use as a guide and interpreter. Cortez then resigned his command into the hands of his men but was promptly elected captain-general, thus becoming free from the governor's dictates. To keep his men from returning home, he burned two of his three ships. Meanwhile Panfilo de Narvaez had arrived to relieve him of his command. Cortez met and defeated him, then pillaged the city of Mexico.

Within two years he began consolidating his victories, personally pushing across Mexico to the Pacific at three different points. In 1522 he founded San Blas as a base for further explorations but his plan was cut short by his summons to Spain to answer for misconduct. Having successfully refuted the charges, he again married and returned to Mexico to start the last phase of his spectacular career.

Only his later activities bear particularly on the discovery of the Pacific Northwest. Hernando Cortez decided to retire personally from active exploration and, instead, equip and send out such expeditions as would be necessary to find the waterway

26

which everyone believed must connect the Atlantic and Pacific oceans. In 1532 he sent Diego Hurtado de Mendoza north to look for the Strait of Anian. Mendoza got as far as San Diego and probably touched at a second place on the coast but his ships were wrecked and he lost his own life. The following year Cortez outfitted Becerra and Grijalva to continue the search for the strait but this expedition also failed, though some pearls were found in the Bay of La Paz in lower California.

After three years Cortez himself returned to the lists. He got as far as La Paz, where he founded the colony of Santa Cruz, only to see it fall as the others had; distances were still too great to keep contact with supplies. In 1539 he organized his last expedition, choosing his cousin Ulloa as commander of three vessels. Scurvy broke out and only one ship returned the next year to Mexico. The other two were eventually lost but not before Ulloa had explored the Gulf of California, rounded its southern extremity, and reached 28° north on the California coast.

His fortune now exhausted, Cortez went back to Spain to plead for money from Charles I, but the king did not favor aid to an aging man who could perform no future services for the Crown. Disappointed, the old conqueror returned to the New World where he died, December 2, 1547.

Hernando Cortez was as brave as Balboa, but not so wise. His vision of the future of Spain in America was as splendid, but not so humane. His men loved him, though, and many of his biographers insist he was not cruel when measured by the standards of his century. Whatever the estimate of his character, his career was decisive in establishing Spanish power in the Pacific. During his life and largely through his activities, Old Mexico became definitely Spanish.[1]

1.—Spanish activity was not confined to the west coast. While Cortez was in Mexico, Alvarez had discovered a "river of great size" in the Gulf of Mexico, probably the mouth of the Mississippi river or Mobile bay. In 1521 Cordillo had likewise further examined the coast of Florida. That same year Magellan's men had gone around the world; ten years later Pizarro conquered Peru.

In 1528 the Spaniard, Ayllon, attempted a settlement of six hundred colonists at a place he called San Miguel. This spot was identified eighty-five years afterwards with the English Jamestown.

7

ROMANCE AND MYTH OF THE PACIFIC

MANY MYTHS and legends have become an inevitable part of the story of the Pacific. For centuries a popular notion held that somehow there was a way from the Orient to Europe. After Marco Polo returned to Europe in 1295 to report that such a passageway did exist, the search was on. The spices, gold, and silks of the East became the lodestars of men's imaginations; and for more than five centuries a constant pageant of ships searched for that passageway.

Columbus himself was but the most famous of all those who spent their lives seeking the mythical, mysterious route, which came gradually to be called the Strait of Anian. Supposedly there was an Asiatic province of "Ania." Because the New World was considered a part of Asia and because "Ania" was located "somewhere in the interior" may account for the name. Or, Anis Cortereal on his reputed Atlantic trip in 1501 could have called it after himself. Whatever its source, the name originally appeared in print in Richard Hakluyt's *Divers Voyages*.

From the time the first Spaniards came to Central America, Panama was the popular place to look for the strait. One of the purposes of Cortez's invasion of Mexico was to discover it. When South America had been delineated as a continent and Magellan had fruitlessly searched for the passage, at last driving his *Trinidad* through the Straits of Magellan, general opinion placed Anian north of Panama. Clearly it was not south of there. And because the Americas were considered projections from Asia, it was visualized as a rather short passage.

As Spaniards, Portuguese, Englishmen, and Frenchmen pushed farther north, the strait was always just around the next headland, just beyond the fog. Hardy mariners were always on the verge of sailing into it. The search had progressed as enthusiastically on the Atlantic coast as on the Pacific, but when there was no more eastern coast to explore, the bulk of attention turned to the western. Of the many attempts to find the strait, some are far more famous than others.

In 1554 Menendez de Aviles vowed he met a man who had sailed from ocean to ocean in a French boat. Some Spaniards were sure that Drake had found the strait and returned to England by way of it instead of around Africa as he said. Indeed, Drake had hoped to do just that.

Maldonado, the Portuguese, went before the Council of the Indies in 1609,[1] claiming the prize they offered for the discovery of Anian. He said he had entered the strait off Labrador in 1588 and sailed into the Polar sea, then into the Pacific at 60° north. The plains of Canada, the Rockies, and—just at 60° north—Mounts Logan and St. Elias apparently did not interfere with his seamanship. Even the Council of the Indies doubted his story and withheld the prize.

Most popular of all these mythical trips, if it was mythical, was Juan de Fuca's in 1592. According to his account he had been in charge of a Spanish expedition and had sailed far northward along the Pacific coast. There he had found a waterway just beyond 47° north. He said he went eastward through the strait. Evidently he had no difficulties with the Cascades, Rockies, Bad Lands, or high sagebrush deserts of the West. De Fuca reported all this to Michael Lok in Venice in 1596. A quarter of a century later it became part of that famous book of fact and fiction, *Purchas, His Pilgrims*. Though de Fuca did not sail through North America and there is no proof that he made any voyage in the New World, it is certainly true that a great strait lies not far beyond 47° north latitude. It is fitting that his name was given to that strait.

Even such level-headed men as John Smith of Virginia were firm believers in the Strait of Anian. When Pocahontas reputedly rescued him from the stake on the Chickahominy river in 1607, he was looking for a way to the Pacific.

Sometime during 1708 [2] a fantastic tale appeared in the London *Monthly Miscellany*. Admiral Bartholomew de Fonte, probably as mythical as his voyage in 1640, entered a river on the Pacific at 53° progressing by means of an elaborate network of

---

1.—The Hudson river was discovered in the same year. Two years earlier the English had finally founded a permanent colony at Jamestown.
2.—All the original thirteen colonies except Georgia were now settled.

lakes and rivers to the interior, where he met a Boston ship from "Maltechusets." [3] Meeting such a ship of course proved the existence of the strait. That he neither captured the ship nor brought back any physical proof of his voyage did not keep Europeans and Americans from accepting the story at face value.

Year after year the tall tales went on. In 1617 [4] the entire Southwest was declared to be an island. California had been "circumnavigated" in 1620; and two years later Diego de Penalosa, ex-governor of New Mexico, claimed to have sent an expedition northeast of Santa Fe. He said the party had encountered a very wealthy region along an inland sea.

The Charter on the Hudson's Bay company in 1670 advised its traders to keep a sharp lookout for the strait. In the year of American independence from England, Captain Cook was on the Pacific searching for a Northwest passage. This was after almost three centuries of exploration and colonization.

Men continued to seek the old heroic wealths, fabled fountains, and golden cities as eagerly as ever. Passing decades pushed the passage farther and farther northward but not until Roald Amundsen guided his *Gjoa* from the Atlantic to the Pacific, in 1906, did the long search end.

3.—Hubert Howe Bancroft. *History of the Northwest Coast,* volume 1, pages 115-118.

4.—Jamestown had been founded a decade and Santa Fe even longer.

The *Gjoa*, in which Norwegian polar explorer, Roald Amundsen, navigated the Northwest Passage, completing his journey in the summer of 1906. The vessel is now in Golden Gate Park, San Francisco.

8

JUAN RODRIGUEZ CABRILLO and BARTOLOME FERRELO EXPLORE A NEW COASTLINE

DA VACA'S STORY of the Seven Cities of Cibola spurred the Spanish imagination more than any event since Cortez's dumping of the Aztec riches into the lap of Castille. Each succeeding Mexican viceroy carried on the work of exploration. While Coronado hunted in the interior for the cities of Cibola, plans were going ahead to dispatch two ships from Navidad to search along the coastline northward for the Strait of Anian. Juan Rodriguez Cabrillo, a Portuguese, was in command and Bartolome Ferrelo, chief pilot, was in charge of the second ship.

Their vessels were poorly built and badly equipped. The smaller, with no deck, was wide open to the pounding of the sea. During the early Spanish period on the Pacific, sailors-of-fortune often faced the unknown in ships which the toughest of modern mariners would not use even in coast trade in the summer season.

Cabrillo's ships were manned with conscripts and natives; volunteers were rare. Ship after ship had gone out seeking pearl beds and spice islands, only to disappear forever. Many companies had started overland hunting gold and gems, only to have their bones disintegrate in tropic wastes.

Cortez had no trouble collecting a company because his record was successful and, though a harsh leader, he was personally popular. Less favorably known, Cabrillo and Ferrelo had to rely on conscripting crewmen. They left Navidad on June 27, 1542, coasting leisurely up the western shore of lower California to San Quentin. From the signs and general behavior of Indians he met along the way, Cabrillo believed they were trying to explain that they had recently seen other white men to the east. Probably the natives had met either some of Coronado's party or Alarcon as he was pushing up the Colorado.

Three months later, Cabrillo reported entering San Miguel bay but he probably went into San Diego harbor. Cabrillo's main concern was discovering the Strait of Anian; harbors along the route were merely useful in case of storm. Despite his indifference, it is likely that his was the first European party to land on what is now the State of California. He rested there six days and made a cursory study of the Indians, deciding that they were peaceful and timid. His knowledge of human nature was not so accurate as his seamanship, for soon the natives fired on and wounded three of his men.

By now the two commanders had received their first inkling of how violent the California coast can be even in October. They spent four days running from San Diego to San Salvador Vitoria, their name for Catalina island. The distance was about a hundred miles. They visited San Pedro and Santa Monica, on the tenth of October coming to Ventura.

Here the natives met them in canoes. When they told of white men they had seen and heard about to the eastward, Cabrillo thought they might merely have had word from the Indians he had already encountered. They also mentioned a great river nearby. The Spaniards were not sure that "river" meant the same to the Indians as it did to them, and they could gain no clear notion of how close the supposed river was. Nor could they be certain that the natives had really seen it. Still, any large river was interesting to the explorers of the sixteenth century because the sought-after strait might easily appear as a great river in the minds of others. Possibly these Indians at Ventura referred to the Colorado river or one of those rivers emptying into San Francisco bay.

Cabrillo and Ferrelo next moved north, landing at Point Conception on October 18.[1] This was the farthest north landing yet made on the Pacific coast of North America. Here a storm drove the ships south to the San Miguel islands. For a full month the California seas roared and frothed and the two ships were separated for four days. Cabrillo, who had broken an arm, ordered the ships to carry on after his accident; but the elements took over, driving them again northward, and close to San Francisco bay, though they were unaware of it.

Reversing itself, the storm blew the ships relentlessly south to

1.—Charles E. Chapman. *History of California, the Spanish Period,* page 78.

the San Miguels. They finally hove to at the islands. For three months they tried to recover but more trouble followed. On January 3, 1543, Cabrillo died and Ferrelo became chief in command. Cabrillo's last orders were to carry on the search for Anian.

About the middle of February, Ferrelo resumed the cruise, getting as far as 42° 30′, about the mouth of the Rogue river in Oregon. He did not land and there is no proof that he even actually saw the coastline at that point. On the first of March such a storm broke that even Ferrelo, veteran of sea rampages, gave up hope, called all hands, and took the final vows for death. But once more they were saved by a sudden wind change. The men, though, were still in serious trouble: food was short and the deckless ship was on the verge of foundering every time a wave broke over it.

Drifting south, the ships became separated on March 4, not meeting again until they arrived at Cerros island three weeks later. With supplies gone and crews exhausted, both ships proceeded to Navidad in the middle of April.

Though the expedition did not find the Strait of Anian, it added eight hundred miles to the known coast of the Pacific. Slowly the outline of North America was taking shape on the sixteenth century maps. Little by little the best minds of the age were beginning to suspect that if the New World were a peninsula of Asia, it jutted from an entirely different part and was much larger than hitherto imagined.

Two centuries were to pass before the peninsula idea was entirely abandoned.

9

SIR FRANCIS DRAKE, BUCCANEER DELUXE

BECAUSE OF THE DUKE OF ALVA'S TREATMENT of the Low Countries, the English were coming to hate the Spanish, and religious differences added fuel to that hatred. Freebooters, receiving letters of marque from leading citizens of the English coast towns, preyed on Spanish commerce wherever they found it. As conditions in the Low Countries became more offensive, Queen Elizabeth herself took a stand upholding her freebooters, even knighting Francis Drake for the piracy he committed against the Spanish in the New World.

Drake was born about 1541 of a mother whose name is unknown and of a father who was a minor minister of the gospel. Nevertheless, the boy Francis became locally well known before he reached his majority. Because of financial trouble and religious persecution, the family had moved into Kent and taken lodging in a derelict hull moored along the Medway.

While still very young, the boy went to sea, mastering the art of navigation while building a glamorous reputation for himself. Physically and mentally he was well equipped to seize and hold a place in Elizabethan life. No character of the sixteenth century had a more romantic, stirring setting than Drake. No individual was more keenly alive, more genuinely a part of the fire of the times. He understood the intrigues and passions, the desires and fears of those strenuous years before the Armada, and he capitalized every opportunity to use his knowledge for the glory of both Francis Drake and England.

He had "a dancing vitality in the eyes which might break out at any moment into merriment, or equally into a tantrum of hot temper," [1] And he always had to be doing something. He hated idleness like the devil, one of his contemporary biographers says. His tongue was sharp yet his jests were ready—when his impatience had vented itself. Everyone around him needed to be

---

1.—E. F. Benson. *Sir Francis Drake,* page 15.

smart; he found stupidity intolerable. On shore there was no hanging around pot-house or brothel, nor had he any use for loose women or bawdy talk, though when it came to oaths, he himself was accomplished. Drake was a strict sea captain, quick to punish, but he was just, and fast to recognize merit and industry. He had a pat on the back for a willing boy whenever the young one did not deserve a clout on the head.

He exercised charm and those who served under him loved him in spite of his iron discipline. They readily trusted a man who had such complete self-confidence and who so often triumphed over the most desperate situations. Nor was Francis Drake a man to rest on his oars; no sooner had he achieved one task than he looked for, and always found, another.

There was a different side to the man though. He was overbearing and imperious, recklessly impatient of restraint, incapable of cooperation. If he never forgot a loyal friend, he never forgave an injury or ceased praying God to help him avenge it. His thirst for honor was insatiable; he bragged, bawled, and delighted in flattery.[2] Yet grievous as these faults were, most persons readily forgot them in his greater virtues.

Such was the man who left an abandoned hull on the Medway and fought, intrigued, and laughed his way to the Spanish Main, spreading destruction and fear; collecting silver, wines, and pearls.

When he was about twenty-one, Drake shipped to the West Indies as second in command under Captain John Lovell. Little is known of the details of this expedition beyond the fact that the Spanish raided the ship at Rio de la Hacha and Drake lost his entire fortune. He never forgave the Spanish. He robbed, pillaged, and burned throughout the best years of his life; and every piracy was to avenge his own loss at Rio de la Hacha. That he robbed the Spaniards of much more than they took from him did not stop his plundering whenever he got the chance.

Back from the Indies, he joined a slaving ship booked for the Portuguese coast, West Africa, to pick up a cargo of blacks for sale in the West Indies. This traffic in human flesh apparently affected Drake no more than it did any other buccaneer of that century.

Aided by Hawkins—the same Hawkins whose name is second

2.—Benson, pages 15-17.

only to Drake's in the annals of English piracy—he attacked the little town of Rio de la Hacha, seized, sacked, and sailed away to San Juan de Ulua, by Vera Cruz. There he found some Spanish treasure ships, but a "great ship" hove in sight and he withheld his attack on the Spaniards' promise that the English might depart in peace, a promise they soon broke. Financially the trip was a failure but this only increased his determination to wipe out the memory of San Juan de Ulua as well as that of Rio de la Hacha.

In 1569 Francis Drake quietly left England and as quietly entered the waters of the West Indies. He purposed seeking out the Spanish bases of supplies, the chief towns, the treasure routes, in fact thoroughly acquainting himself with the region so that he could attack the enemy intelligently and efficiently. After reconnoitering he went to England, where he obtained the *Swan* and then returned to the Indies. Again in Spanish waters he selected a secret harbor within easy reach of that important terminal for the Peruvian silver trains, Nombre de Dios. Not only was this town the terminal for the overland mule trains from Panama and Peru but it was within striking distance of the Chagres river, down which the gold was sometimes floated from Vente Cruz to Nombre de Dios. He scouted briefly about this town, then sailed for England to prepare for his great offensive against the Spanish.

His third trip to the West Indies, in 1572, was ominous. He had two ships, the *Swan* and the *Pasha,* with a complement of seventy-three men in both crews. Drake himself had selected each member, and only one was over thirty.

After the usual routine preparation the expedition left Plymouth, May 24, 1572, arriving at its secret harbor on July 12. On going ashore, Drake found a note, left by a sailor who had remained behind from the previous voyage, informing him that the Spaniards had discovered the secret harbor. Drake decided to use it anyhow. He argued that it might not have been the Spanish who discovered the harbor; that even if it were, they would think that since the secret was out he would not use the retreat. He said the easiest way to solve the problem was to mislead the enemy by using the very port they felt sure would not be used. So there Drake built his fort, his base of operations for raiding the Spanish Main.

Resourceful and clever daredevil that he was, Drake was no superman. In his first attack on Nombre de Dios he captured the town but missed getting the booty. He himself was wounded and his men had to content themselves with seizing a large supply of wine. Next he attempted to waylay the mule trains but a twig snapped, a young soldier lost his head and fired a musket too soon, and a million-dollar prize slipped away.

Drake was too astute a buccaneer to strike again in the same place so he changed his sphere of activity to Cartegena where he captured two frigates and some smaller vessels. In all of these episodes his success depended almost entirely upon surprise. He sent his men ashore in the night, quietly captured some strategic outpost, and compelled a frightened Spanish soldier to tell what he knew of the defenses and riches of the town. Then swiftly he attacked, plundered, and deserted the place, all within a few minutes.

During the rest of the night and a good share of the next day he would sail as far as possible to reach some isolated camp for the next evening's assault. So rapid were Drake's raids, so brilliant his plans, that town after town and galleon after galleon fell prey to him, not because they were defenseless but because they were bewildered and afraid. The entire Spanish Main was terrorized. Actually the Spaniards were ready to be robbed by anyone capable of frightening them and Drake was easily equal to that. Undoubtedly he often invaded small towns and took unimportant ships merely to impress on his enemies that no one of them was safe from his wrath. Deliberately he molded for himself a legend of frightfulness. As a showman Drake was unequalled in the Elizabethan age.

The next few months were filled with success. Raided silver trains, captured galleons, plundered towns—these made up the days and nights of the men from Devonshire, all of whose escapades were overlaid with good fellowship, laughter, wine, and song. The crew got back to Plymouth on a Sunday morning in August of 1573, ready to go anywhere or do anything on the high seas that the fertile imagination of their commander could conjure. And their commander was already laying plans, probably aided by Elizabeth herself, for a still more daring expedition to the Spanish realm of the New World.

Before his last and greatest adventure Drake had been in Ireland but his affairs there were completely overshadowed by his New World exploits. With renewed zest he returned to his first love, taking vengeance on the Spanish. The original objective of "piracy pure and simple though of high adventure" [3] later included plans to annoy the enemy in the Pacific as well as search for the Strait of Anian. If they could find such a passage through North America, they meant to return to England that way. Otherwise they were going to attempt the most daring of all maritime feats, sailing on around the world.

Drake's five ships were lavishly outfitted with the best materials and the most modern equipment available. In the crew were 164 men.

After one or two false starts, he left Plymouth in November of 1577,[4] making stops at Morocco and at the Cape Verde islands. Shortly afterwards he sighted and captured a Portuguese ship. Though England was not at war with Portugal, Drake could make no such fine distinctions in the matter of enemies, particularly since the Portuguese had on board a pilot familiar with the coast of Brazil. Because Drake was sailing for Brazil and could use a good pilot, this luckless seaman found himself headed for the New World rather than for his homeland.

Land was sighted north of the Plata on April 5, 1578. As the ships headed south, Drake had difficulty keeping the various units of his fleet in touch with each other. At the port of St. Julian they were attacked by natives; and, though the English were capable of defending themselves, these attacks along with the hazards of the sea undermined their morale.

More trouble was brewing. When the expedition left England, a certain Doughty, one of the commanders and a personal friend

---

3.—Benson, page 103.

4.—Drake was making his North Pacific cruise during the lapse in Spanish activity between Cabrillo in 1543 and Gali's observations in 1584. In these same years there was plenty of action on the Atlantic. Gilbert was at Newfoundland and Raleigh was struggling with his failing colonies, only five years after Drake was searching for the galleons on the North Pacific.
   During the same year that the ill-fated Roanoke colony was attempted, 1587, Thomas Cavendish, another Englishman, sailed into the Pacific, almost repeating the Drake episode.

of Drake's, for some reason decided to mutiny against Drake. The affair leaked out and, at St. Julian, Drake ordered a company ashore to try Doughty for high treason. No event in Drake's career more indelibly stamps him as a man of ability than this trial of his friend. The treason court convened under strictest rules, Drake himself acting as chief judge as he was expected to. Witnesses were heard and the verdict of guilty was reached with the same efficiency that might have been expected had the culprit been a common seaman instead of Drake's most trusted captain.

Drake knew that to free Doughty was to invite mutiny among the other commanders. Besides, his sense of justice outweighed his regard for his friend. Doughty received a fair trial, his guilt was proved, and his head was cut off, all in the customary manner. Some say that Drake spent the afternoon closeted in his cabin with Doughty, that they lunched, opened a bottle of wine, and had a long chat, after which they left the cabin arm in arm, walking down the sand to the block, where Doughty bade his friend an affectionate farewell.

Afterwards Drake remained at St. Julian for more than six weeks making repairs, resting his men, and planning for the future. On August 17, 1578, he hoisted sail and set the course directly for the Straits of Magellan. Passage through these is always difficult but to early mariners it was a nightmare of plunging seas, interminable gales, and easy shipwreck. When Drake finally reached the "South Sea," three weeks later, of the original five ships only one remained. It was the *Pelican,* later called the *Golden Hind.* Then a great storm seized this last ship, driving her far south toward the Antarctic Circle. This final disaster convinced Drake that no large continent of inhabitable land existed south of Tierra del Fuego.

Turning north again, he landed on and named the Elizabethides. On October 30, 1578, he set sail for the coast of Chili, and, on December 5, reached Valparaiso, that part of the world for which the entire expedition had been planned. Drake wasted no time before beginning the attack on Spanish ships in the Pacific. His first windfall was the *Grand Captain of the South* with eight thousand pounds sterling and more than seventeen hundred jars of wine aboard. Indeed, the *Grand Captain* must have been a welcome sight after the weary months of rounding the Horn.

After disposing of this prize, Drake pushed steadily northward along the coast of South America, pirating as he went. Nothing was too small to interest him; nothing too large to prevent his attacking, if he foresaw even a remote chance of success. He was disappointed in the amount of booty from the *Callao de Lima* but was soon comforted by news of *Our Lady of the Conception,* loaded with gold. He took off in hot pursuit. The chase grew more exciting as it neared the finish, and the English closed in on the galleon. The treasure ship yielded thirteen chests of coined silver, twenty-six tons of silver bars, eighty pounds of gold, and several boxes of jewels and pearls. Such a haul satisfied even Drake and he decided to start for home.

Three factors determined the return route. Drake had been able to ravage the Pacific coast only because he struck without warning and seldom twice in the same place. To go back by the way he had come would be foolhardy; Spanish men-of-war and armed merchant ships would be ready for him. To return around South America would throw him into the storms off Cape Horn at the very worst time of year. The decisive factor was news that the annual galleon from the Philippines, with its splendid prize in Oriental goods, was about due off Mexico or California coasts. Here was an opportunity no first-class buccaneer could overlook, so Drake decided to return to England by sailing far northward, where, if he found no straits, he would cross the Pacific to the Indies, then go around Africa and home. He would combine piracy with science, making a serious attempt to find both the Strait of Anian and the Manila galleon. This voyage into the North Pacific gave England strong claim to the western slope of North America.

Drake pillaged as usual on his way up the northern coast. On April 4, 1579, he captured a frigate in charge of Captain Don Francisco Zarate. Drake's treatment of his enemies was always unusual, often unique, sometimes bizarre. He might set a captured crew ashore, unharmed, many miles from a settlement merely for the sake of inconveniencing them by compelling them to walk to port. Or he might, as in the case of Zarate, take one or more aboard the *Golden Hind* and offer a lavish display of wealth. Zarate reported that Drake treated him most sumptuously, showing him flasks of perfume which he boasted Elizabeth had given him and letting him eat in the captain's cabin where meals were served with much ceremony. However, Drake's love of ceremony was just a relaxation from his sterner attributes and the Spaniard frankly called Drake the greatest living seaman.

The *Golden Hind* put into Guatulco on the coast of Oajaca on April 15, 1579. This was the last Spanish port Drake touched in the New World. From Guatulco north, he was in waters most likely to be traversed by the Manila galleon. Despite constant watch for it, he was to be cheated of his last prize. Perhaps the galleon heard of the *Hind* and eluded her or maybe chance kept them apart. In any event, on June 5, Drake reached 42° north off the coast of what is now Oregon, without sighting any Spanish ships.

Considerable doubt exists regarding the exact latitude north touched by the English. Drake claimed he sailed as far as 48°. Evidence he left suggests that he landed at Chetka cove, 42° -3' north. It was this phase of Drake's activities which England used two and a half centuries later as the basis for her claims to the Pacific Northwest.

Throughout the run from Mexico to Chetka cove—if such it were—the men complained of the cold. The ropes froze stiff and, even though it was June, ice and snow covered the mountains. This report has caused much discussion, some serious, some ironic. Natives of the Pacific coast of California make light of it. Of course it is possible that the contrast between the tropics and 40° north was so great that Drake's crew thought they suffered more than they actually did. But to accept such an explanation one must assume that Drake's men were either lying outright about the ice and snow or were too stupid to know ice when they saw it. Besides, the crew was composed of men who had sailed in every climate, under all possible weather conditions, from the tropic calms to the gales off Cape Horn. Hardened as they were by years before the mast, it is hard to believe that a sudden change of weather could completely upset their judgment.

Some authorities say that the Pacific coast experienced an unusual summer and that conditions actually were as reported; still others avow that Drake got much farther north than 42°, perhaps ten or fifteen degrees beyond 42°. This would certainly put them in a more rigorous climate.

On leaving the cove,[5] Drake ordered the *Hind* to sea, and they dropped back to about 38° where they hove to and the ship's party went ashore. There they laid claim to the land for Elizabeth. Drake, the explorer, was less efficient than Drake, the pirate, and at 38° as at 42° his record is so inaccurate that it is not certain just where he touched. It was thought to be San Francisco bay until the discovery that the "Bay of San Francisco" was an old term for what is now called Drake's bay, which is generally accepted as the harbor that they reached. Bodega bay is sometimes taken for the site, but it does not fit Drake's own reference to a "convenient and fit harborough." The description does fit Drake's bay with its white banks and cliffs.

The Indians whom Drake met at this port thought the English were gods. Their "bloudie sacrifice" was distressing to the Englishmen but during the course of the ceremonies the peace pipe was smoked and Drake took the entire proceeding as indicative that the natives were swearing their allegiance to Elizabeth. Probably nothing was remoter from the thoughts of the Indians.

Drake rested five weeks; then, with the ship's stores replenished, he headed the *Golden Hind* for the Farallones.[6] From there he went to the Philippines and then around Good Hope to Elizabeth and home. Plans were later outlined for establishing English colonies on the Pacific coast. Ships were dispatched for this purpose but nothing came of it.

Drake's last years do not deeply concern the Pacific Northwest. He lived them as he had his young manhood and his prime, wreaking vengeance upon the Spaniards. In 1585 he led a new plundering cruise to the West Indies, ten years later making his last voyage. He died a year after this, January 28, 1596, in West

---

5.—John Drake, a cousin of Francis aboard the *Hind*, told Spanish officials at Rio de la Plata that Captain Francis gave the land that is situated in 48 degrees the name of New England, that they remained there a month and a half, taking in water and wood and repairing their ship.

It is more probable that Drake left the cove almost immediately because he stayed several weeks in California, sailing from there on July 23.

6.—During his run from Guatulco north, Drake had picked up a Chinese pilot "who knew the navigation of the Pacific." See Benson, page 164.

Indian waters off Porto Bello. Tropical sickness had taken heavy toll. And, when Drake passed away, two of the ships were piled high and set afire as his body was lowered at sea. It was a proper last salute to England's master mariner and the world's greatest pirate.

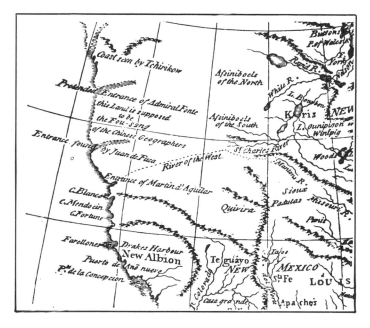

MAP OF WESTERN AMERICA, 1778

From *History of America* by William Russell. Note the River of the West, with its source near the Missouri.

FRANCISCO DE GALI OBSERVES THE COASTLINE SOUTH

BY 1564 the Spaniards had conquered the Philippines and established regular trade with Manila. Despite a flourishing commerce, Spanish merchantmen constantly avoided the California shore. Westward, they were carried directly to the Orient by prevailing winds and currents. On leaving the Orient, they sailed northward until the Japan current caught and bore them east into American waters and on down to Mexico. In all this roundabout journey they carefully shunned the coast itself, adding no new knowledge to that supplied by Cabrillo and Ferrelo in 1542 and 1543.

In the later sixteenth century this trade with the Orient had grown so profitable that it overshadowed the dread of contacting the stormy American coast. If the Manila trade were to prosper, the long voyage east required a halfway haven of some sort. This station not only had to be available to galleons in distress but also fortified against activities such as Drake's.

For these reasons, Francisco de Gali, in command of one of the Manila ships, was ordered to approach the coast on his return from the East in 1584 and search out a likely harbor. De Gali sailed from Macao east by northeast until within two hundred leagues of the American coast, about latitude 37° north. He observed the coastline southward to Mexico, mentioning Cape Mendocino; perhaps he or someone in Mexico named the cape in honor of Viceroy Mendoza. One more geographic discovery joined the expanding knowledge of the Pacific coast.[1]

1.—Meantime the Spanish crown did not allow the Atlantic to go unnoticed. While the Philippines were being conquered, Angel de Villafrane was making an ineffectual attempt to colonize at Port Royal sound on the South Carolina coast.

The English were also busy on the Atlantic. Sir Humphrey Gilbert took possession of Newfoundland in 1583; the following year Raleigh began his unsuccessful attempts to establish an English colony at Roanoke. After sinking a private fortune and still unsuccessful, he could announce, "I shall yet live to see it an English nation."

SEBASTIAN VIZCAINO SURVEYS NORTH TO OLD OREGON

OLD WORLD AFFAIRS inevitably colored the New World. Almost a century had passed since the discovery of America and Spanish power was fading. England, fast becoming the second power in Europe, was Spain's natural rival in the New World.

By the late sixteenth century Spaniards began to realize that large fortunes could not be had without work. The conquest of the Philippines made this more tolerable though, for even the nobility found it pleasant to involve themselves in financing and manning a Manila galleon, which might easily return a thousand units of wealth per hundred units of labor. If the Spaniards never quite stopped hoping for an easy fortune, at least they no longer expected to find another Inca kingdom beyond every range of hills. Gradually they settled down to the less exciting but stabler business of trading with the Orient.

The Manila trade was no summer's holiday. Grotius and his exposition of international law were a half century away and piracy was a fine art. The science of navigation had progressed very little beyond the compass and the astrolabe. The tropics were still a horror of becalmed days and sweltering nights; the deep still held man-eating and ship-swallowing monsters which superstitious sailors had feared since men first went to sea. More real than all the rest was the ever-present threat of violent death. Fears of starvation, scurvy, and cannibalism were the constant companions of those who sought riches in the Manila trade.

Sebastian Vizcaino, a native of Huelva, engaged in this strenuous business. In New Spain he was a chief pilot in his majesty's service, where he had a colorful career. Several years earlier, in November of 1587, when the North Pacific was raided by Cavendish, Vizcaino was one of the losers on the galleon *Santa Ana*

45

with its 122,000 pesos of gold.[1] On another trip to Manila, three years later, Vizcaino was more fortunate; he invested 200 ducats and made a profit of 2,500 ducats.[2] Then he decided to do some pearl fishing. He applied for a license but legal difficulties held him back till the Count of Monterey arrived in New Spain, giving him authority to seize and exploit any lands he wished in California. Afterwards repenting of this liberal charter, the viceroy tried to countermand it but Vizcaino had already sailed away. This was in March of 1596.

Many real leaders were blocked by weak administrators who failed to catch the vision of the New World's potentialities and who tried to keep their authority by revoking the actions of their subordinates. Fortunately for America, its future was in the hands of its soldiers of fortune, adventurers, and pioneers.

Before the close of the sixteenth century Spain decided to secure her claims to lands on the Pacific by carefully exploring the entire coast and establishing the fortified harbors already mentioned. Gaspar de Zunig ay Acereda, who succeeded to the viceroyalty, commanded Vizcaino to lead the expedition. Besides his sailors, Vizcaino took with him soldiers, pearl fishers, four Franciscan monks, the wives of some of the soldiers, and even horses. The friars sincerely hoped to spread the gospel. Though their success was trifling, they opened the way for others more fortunate.

The expedition sailed from Acapulco, its first important stop being La Paz. Winter had now set in but Vizcaino determined to push northward, using La Paz as a base of operations. When he sailed north on October 3, he left the largest of his three ships there. From the start the venture seemed doomed. A storm forced him to put into shore; and, later, as a small boat was taking a party of the Spaniards to the ships, the Indians fired on them, hitting one of them on the nose. The arrow itself was harmless enough but it started a disastrous chain of events.

In the excitement created by the arrow, the small boat capsized. The heavily clothed and armed soldiers were helpless. Nineteen drowned and only five managed to swim to safety.[3] Vizcaino then put back to La Paz, where he found his colony in trouble. The

---

1.—Herbert Ingram Priestly. *Mexican Nation—a History*, page 90.
2.—Charles E. Chapman. *History of California, the Spanish Period*, page 124.
3.—Same, page 127.

land was barren; distances were great; the weather was too stormy for pearl fishing. On top of all this, food was short and the men constantly quarreled over the Indian women. Late in October he ordered the main body of the expedition to return to New Spain.

Vizcaino himself and forty picked men attempted once more to carry out the original purpose of the undertaking, but it was too late in the year. Neither the ships nor the men could endure the coast storms. Giant waves smashed the rudder chains and Vizcaino limped back to New Spain, having done little of permanent value.

No sooner had the survivors rested and regained their health than their spirits rose accordingly and they planned a new expedition. The Council of the Indies, that ever-present and all-powerful governing body of New Spain, had decreed that Vizcaino be replaced. Monterey, at first lukewarm regarding Vizcaino's ability, now advised the council to reappoint him to the post of commander. After some delay, Vizcaino in 1599 was placed in charge of this new venture, which was concerned only with explorations. Colonization was to be left to others.

Because the Spanish areas on the Pacific were being invaded by enemies searching for Manila ships, Vizcaino delayed his departure until 1602. When final orders arrived, they contained some strict rules. He was to look for no bays, noting only those he happened to see. He was to disregard the Gulf of California and proceed north only as far as Cape Blanco. He was to make no settlements and his men were to have no relations with the Indians.

To offset these narrow orders, his equipment was the best. There were three ships: the *San Diego* for the commander, the *Santo Tomas* under Gomez, and the *Tres Reyes* under Aguilar. Attached to these were the regular crews, with reasonable provisions for necessary replacements. A map maker and three Carmelite friars completed the personnel.

On May 5, 1602, all was ready, sails were hoisted, and Vizcaino was launched on the explorations which made him famous in Pacific annals.

Those familiar with this ocean know its temperamental moods. Almost from the start, Vizcaino had trouble with contrary head winds. Shorelines which from a distance looked inviting proved treacherous wastes when approached. Often they could not get fresh water for long periods. Of a pool the crew used for replenishing the water supply, he remarked, "It was not very fresh and was green, but the bottles we carried were filled with it." [4]

Though the Spaniards had sailed from Acapulco early in May, they did not reach San Diego until the beginning of November. Sixty years earlier Cabrillo had entered the same bay, calling it San Miguel. Vizcaino does not refer to Cabrillo's entrance, either being ignorant of it or thinking it unworthy of notice. After a ten-day rest, Vizcaino sailed again, November 24, sighting and naming Catalina island. He found the Indians there both friendly and generous. Not only did the chiefs invite the Spaniards to visit the villages, but they offered each of the sailors at least ten women for personal companionship. It is a tribute to the leadership of Vizcaino and the discipline of his men that they continued northward without taking advantage of the natives. An amazing thing about these early adventurers is not the fact that they sometimes had indiscriminate sex relations with the natives, but rather how often they turned down such offers.

A good wind held from Catalina island until the ships rounded Point Conception, reaching what we know as Monterey bay on December 15. The men were delighted, thinking the harbor an excellent way station for the Manila ships and the Indian population desirable from both economic and missionary viewpoints. Actually this bay is a mediocre harbor but to the tired seamen it likely seemed much better than it was.

With winter, disease and starvation became inevitable. Supplies grew scarce and many men took sick. Vizcaino decided to send Gomez with the worst cases back to Acapulco to obtain fresh supplies and make a preliminary report on their progress. Gomez left California with thirty-four men; he arrived in Acapulco with only nine. Such were the odds in the sixteen hundreds. More than a century and a half was to elapse before Captain Cook of the British navy made the first real headway in controlling scurvy, one of the commonest causes of expedition failures.

After Gomez's return, Vizcaino ordered the *San Diego* and the *Tres Reyes* to proceed northward, since they had not yet reached

4.—Chapman, page 132.

42°, the point cited in their orders as the northern extremity of their voyage. On the way, Vizcaino saw Drake's bay though a contrary head wind prevented his landing. When early in January they rounded Cape Mendocino, he felt that he had fulfilled his orders, that he had searched north as far as was reasonable considering the weather and the men's health.

He resolved to return to New Spain but another North Pacific wind rose, driving the Spaniards still farther into unknown regions. Vizcaino reported that at one time only two sailors of his entire crew were able to climb to the main top sail. The rest were either below in their bunks or too feeble to risk themselves aloft. The wind reached such velocity that the able men could hardly keep on their feet; and the sick were mercilessly thrown from their beds, to crawl back the best they could, nursing their bruises and cursing their luck—or praying to their saints, according to their personal convictions.

In nine days the wind quieted and Vizcaino ordered his ship about. With the wind behind them they could have made the return trip easily had it not been for illness; they were too weak to stop to rest. Even had they found a convenient harbor, they could not have raised the anchor once they had dropped it. Much of this weakness resulted from their inability to eat, their mouths being sore from a prolonged diet of ship's stores. Vizcaino headed for the mainland hoping to get fresh food. He reached Mazatlan on February 18, 1603, with only five men capable of going ashore for help. These happened on a pack-train with a supply of food which they managed to acquire. With it the crew's health was restored, and a month later the *San Diego* ran into Acapulco, having completed what was perhaps the most trying expedition so far undertaken along the Pacific coast.

Meanwhile Aguilar and the *Tres Reyes* had trouble. The storm which blew Vizcaino beyond 42° north separated Aguilar from his commander, driving him at least to 41°, where one of the friars said he had sighted a great river. Aguilar then turned about, coasting south to Navidad.

The work of both Vizcaino and Aguilar was important. Cabrillo and Ferrelo had covered the same coastline as Vizcaino but had not kept documentary records of their findings; Vizcaino faithfully inscribed in his log a complete account of his experiences on the Pacific coast as far north as Old Oregon. The result was that, with the exception of San Francisco bay, the Spaniards were familiar with the entire west coast of America from Panama to 42° north; and they thoroughly sprinkled it with place names honoring their church holidays, their viceroys, and their kings.

Aguilar left no such record, yet his name is only slightly less famous than his commander's because after his last voyage a hunt began for "Aguilar's river." Certainly no "great river" exists anywhere close to 41° or 42° north latitude. Several small streams empty into the Pacific in the approximate latitudes mentioned by Aguilar, the Rogue river in Oregon being the best known now. This is not a great river but under certain light conditions and at flood time its volume appears greater than it is. The legend of "Aguilar's river" spread rapidly, many a mariner keeping a sharp lookout for it while cruising up and down the coast en route to the Orient. Several expeditions sailed north, with this river as one of their objectives. This might have been the fabled Strait of Anian which remained a will-o'-the-wisp until Samuel Hearne finally laid it to rest in 1771.

Vizcaino's reward on reaching home after a year in the North was command of the next Manila galleon, but before he could sail, an unfriendly viceroy took the command away. Several years later, in 1611, Vizcaino again engaged in a huge project. Rumor held that somewhere in the Pacific were two valuable islands, "Rica de Oro" and "Rica de Plata," which would be better way stations for the Manila galleon than anything Vizcaino had discovered along the mainland coast. Reputedly these islands contained an inexhaustible supply of precious metals. The project of a rest station on the mainland was abandoned, Vizcaino instead being ordered to search for these islands. He was also to take back to Japan several merchants who had attempted to negotiate a trade agreement in Mexico. In his turn, Vizcaino was to secure certain trading rights with the Japanese.

But Sebastian Vizcaino was no diplomat. Because he refused to practice certain required etiquette of the Nipponese court, an unfortunate quarrel arose. He then left to search for the islands. Not finding them, he was forced back to Japan for supplies and reconditioning. As a result of his earlier unwise conduct he was poorly received, though he did finally obtain another ship. He sailed for Mexico in 1613. So unpleasant had the Spanish-Japanese relations become that both missionaries and foreign businessmen were thereafter excluded from Japan, that nation entering its long period of seclusion which was not broken until the time of Admiral Perry.

Search for "Rica de Oro" and "Rica de Plata" was Vizcaino's final, significant official act. His death in 1615 checked several other statesmanlike schemes having to do with the California coast and his expeditions ended almost a century of Spanish activity on the west coast of America. For the next 150 years nothing much happened in the story of the Pacific Northwest.[5]

This decline in Spain's interest in the Pacific was partly due to the gradual weakening of Spanish power in the Old World. In 1588 her famous Armada came to grief and the Armada represented Spain's supreme attempt to maintain her position as mistress of the seas. Its failure meant less Spanish concern abroad.

5.—This same century and a half witnessed high drama on the Atlantic seaboard. The year following Vizcaino's return to Mexico, Champlain made the settlement called St. Crois. The London company founded Jamestown in 1607; and, by 1609, Hudson had done his work.

Ten years later the New World saw the establishment of representative government in Virginia. This was accompanied by the introduction of negro slavery into the colony in the same year. The Pilgrims left England for the New World in 1620; three years later Manhattan was settled. Maryland and Rhode Island were founded between 1632 and 1636. Harvard college was founded in 1636. The New England Confederation, the first serious attempt at unified action by the colonists, was organized in 1643 for protection against the Indians and the Dutch.

Two years later King George's war was fought, also the Pequot. Great Britain published her Navigation Ordinances controlling colonial commerce between 1651 and 1672, and the Dutch were driven from Long Island during these same years. The Huguenots had come; the Carolinas were settled; and in 1670 the famous Hudson's Bay company, which was to play such an important part in developing the Pacific Northwest, was organized in London under the elaborate title of "The Government and Company of Adventurers of England trading into Hudson Bay."

The Jerseys were settled; King Philip's war was fought; Bacon's rebellion had stirred Virginia; and the British Crown was quarreling over colonial charters.

William Penn gave a home to the Quakers in 1681, but soon came the disgrace of the Massachusetts witchcraft trials, spurred on by the fanatical Cotton Mather. Old World wars cast their shadows on the new continent, and just at the end of the century King William's war dragged out its course.

In 1713 the Peace of Utrecht gave Acadia, Newfoundland, and the Hudson bay region to England. James Oglethorpe brought poor debtors and other outcasts to Georgia in 1733, founding this southern colony as a home for them and as a bulwark against the Spaniards in Florida.

Spain no longer wished the Strait of Anian found, for England dominated the seas as well as the lands on the Atlantic.

If the Northwest Passage were found, it would give England easy access to the wealth of the Orient and make her round-the-world commercial trips very profitable. She could sell and buy goods on the Atlantic coast of the New World, continue through the strait to the Orient, sell and buy again, then return home, having made handsome sums on each transaction. But if no strait of Anian were discovered, she would be blocked from access to the East except by the long way around South America; that way lay almost entirely through Spanish waters.

Spain was both selfish and logical in her attitude that, since she could not control the Strait of Anian if it were found, she no longer wished it to be discovered.

Sitka as it looked when Baranof ruled there. (Engraving by I. Clark from a drawing by Captain Lisianski, London, 1814. Courtesy National Park Service)

12

RUSSIA ENTERS THE PACIFIC

FEARFUL SUCCESSIONS have marked the imperial throne of Russia. There were seven centuries of barbarism, war, and plunder from Rurik in 862 to Ivan the Terrible in 1547; and another century of rape, incest, brute force, and national expansion elapsed from Ivan the Terrible to Peter the Great.

Peter came to the throne with a mighty will and a clear vision of the possibilities of his country, but few rulers have exercised less control over their own vices or demanded greater sacrifices from their subjects. Peter's character was steeped in excesses. Indeed, he was "the most tempestuous hero and beastlike man that ever ascended the throne of the Russias." [1]

He slaughtered his subjects when they revolted; he tortured captured highwaymen; he probably murdered his own son by frightening him to death; and it is said that he cut off the heads of prisoners while drinking a toast to each. He was hard, ruthless, and half savage, but he was "the Great" for all of that. He understood the needs and desires of his people and labored with his own hands on the docks of the East India company at Amsterdam to learn the crafts of the Occident so that he could impart them into Russia. He gathered the best artists, scientists, and mechanics of Europe around him and strove mightily to lift himself and his people above the quagmire of medievalism.

In the days before his death, Peter lay screaming with pain aggravated by self-indulgence, yet his thoughts were as much of Russia as of himself for he spurred his mind to plan as great a scientific expedition as the civilized world had yet seen. The boundaries of his empire were to be searched out. Russia was to know how vast she was.

Kamchatka is more than five thousand miles from St. Petersburg and nearer six thousand if one counts the turnings and twistings of practical routes. In the days of Peter every mile be-

1.—A. C. Laut. *Vikings of the Pacific,* page 4.

yond the Urals led through a mysterious region of bleak, frozen tundras, impassable mountain torrents, forests infested with timber wolves, and hard-eyed barbarian Kurds, Tartars, and Siberians. It was into this forbidding area that Peter projected his final imperial orders; this unknown hinterland was to be charted as a monument to Russia's barbaric prince.

Five weeks before the end of his reign, Peter gave specific orders to Count Apraxin, his admiral, to organize this exploration. The actual task was entrusted to the outlander, Vitus Ivanovich Bering. Bering was instructed to build two boats at Kamchatka and to sail northward until he determined the exact location of the American coast. He was to collect detailed information and prepare a chart of the coastline. The expedition was then to return to Kamchatka.

13

VITUS BERING, THE OUTLANDER

VITUS BERING was born in Horsens, Denmark, in 1681. Although his parents associated for many years with the leading persons of their city, they never achieved personal prominence.[1] Their home had the elements of respectability but boasted few luxuries. Vitus went to sea at an early age aboard the ships of the East India company and in 1703 traveled as far as the East Indies. Later, he entered the navy which Peter was building along Anglo-Danish lines. The first years of his Russian service were spent on the Baltic andBlack seas. He was held in high repute and Admiral Cruys, one of Peter's most trusted officers, was his intimate friend. It was because of his friendly association with Cruys, backed of course by his experience on the Baltic and Black seas, that Peter later chose Bering to explore the Russian hinterland eastward and northward of Kamchatka.

Bering was in the midst of an active career in 1720 when he suddenly retired from the navy to an estate in Finland. He may have abandoned his naval career because of powerful enemies in the admiralty or merely because of dissatisfaction with a ruling regarding the promotion of foreign officers beyond certain grades. Peter recalled him from retirement to lead the most famous of Russian expeditions.

What sort of man was this Dane? Was he a leader of men or did fate shuffle him into a position of great responsibility? His early training fitted him for the practical seamanship required for the new responsibility. As a sailor he had been to the borders of the Pacific, and he had access to the best geographical knowledge of his time. But early training and knowledge are not neccessarily attendant on leadership.

A leader must possess intuition when all advisers oppose him. Vitus Bering did not have this intuition. His personal bravery

---

1.—One of the Bering women on the maternal side had succeeded in marrying two mayors in the course of her life; perhaps no mean achievement in any age.

was second to none. His patience, perseverance, and sense of justice were superior to those possessed by most men, but the task assigned to him demanded a will which brooked no interference. Bering was too considerate to use force and his crew repaid him with disrespect, intrigue, and insubordination. Probably "In many respects Bering was unqualified to lead such an expedition into a barbarous country." [2]

Bering was no longer young. He was well into middle life before his real work was even suggested to him and the eighteenth century was not one in which men conserved their strength. One was old at forty-five and a patriarch in another ten years. In addition, Bering's task was such that its prosecution was not a question of his ability or will but rather of possibility. History deals gently with his shortcomings because he accomplished much in spite of them.

Bering's First Pacific Expedition

The Russians were familiar with the tales of the Strait of Anian which had kept the Spanish and English agog for two centuries but they took no stock in such nonsense. Bering's instructions to search out the boundaries of Asia included scant reference to this mythical waterway. To be sure, he was to keep his eyes open, but he was not to search for it, as Peter the Great was especially interested in knowing if Russia and America joined north of Kamchatka as practically all the maps of the day indicated. Another geographical problem was the body of land off Kamchatka reported by Popoff, the Cossack, in 1711, but such semibarbarian leaders could seldom read or write and any geographical information they acquired became unreliable long before it reached St. Petersburg. To eliminate fanciful geographical tales and to solve the riddle of America's relationship with Asia were the essence of Bering's orders.

The delays and inefficiencies of Bering's expedition were due to Russia's new and almost annoying faith in her scientific men. These savants meant well but were not explorers and they often gave advice impossible to follow. This plus natural delays incident to outfitting the expedition caused months to drag by before Bering left St. Petersburg.

2.—Peter Lauridsen. *Vitus Bering, the Discoverer of Bering Strait,* pages 75-76.

In the meantime Peter passed on to whatever reward his barbaric greatness deserved and Catherine ascended the throne. She wisely recognized the importance of Peter's interest in the Pacific and reappointed Bering to his command. Even with this added support, February of 1725 arrived before the expedition got under way. Bering had as seconds in command Martin Spangberg, a hot-headed but efficient lieutenant, and Alexis Tchirikoff, a Russian of more than ordinary ability. Tchirikoff left St. Petersburg January 28, 1725, four days before Peter died.

Bering assembled great quantities of supplies and equipment because of the distances to be covered and the nature of the territory. He had almost a thousand horses, two thousand leather sacks for flour, twenty or thirty boats for river use, and hundreds of auxiliary items. The gathering of this mass of baggage and equipment probably was Bering's first major mistake. Explorers generally have done their best work when least encumbered with baggage. Lewis and Clark covered a distance comparable to that traveled by Bering but carried less equipment and fewer supplies; Alexander Mackenzie penetrated as deep into the frozen North as Bering and did it virtually alone. Time after time Bering's trek across northern Asia was delayed almost to disaster because of his enormous luggage. Boats had to be built, streams bridged, winter quarters and supply depots constructed, barracks thrown up, and countless other tasks done, most of which were necessary because of his supplies. To have traveled with none would have been suicidal, but to carry too many was almost as bad.

The long trek from St. Petersburg to Kamchatka was unbelievably dreary. Tchirikoff went on ahead and Bering followed on the first of February. It was March before they reached Tobolsk, and May before the assembled party left that city. From May until September was spent reaching Ilimsk where the expedition passed the winter of 1725-1726. Bering sent Lieutenant Chaplin on to Yakutsk to inquire about further supplies while he himself went southward to Irkutsk for aid and information from the governor of the province. Spangberg was instructed to build fifteen barges forty-five feet in length as well as an additional twelve boats to be used in getting to Yakutsk.

Tchirikoff started for Yakutsk in May, Bering got under way some time later, and by the middle of June the entire expedition had arrived. The forces then were divided, Spangberg setting out on July 7 by the river route to Okhotsk. The overland parties took several routes. On August 16, Bering himself started for Okhotsk, which he reached late in October.

The men immediately built huts for protection during the coming winter. Spangberg became winter-bound en route and was reduced to eating dog harness and shoe leather. Bering sent a rescue party but even with this aid Spangberg did not get to Okhotsk until January, 1727. The rear guard under Tchirikoff fared almost as badly as Spangberg's party, not reaching salt water until midsummer. Even when the various divisions finally arrived at Okhotsk, they were hundreds of miles from the western edge of Kamchatka and, because of the devious route to be followed, almost as many more miles from the Pacific coast.

Work began at once on the *Fortuna,* the first of the two boats which Bering had been commanded to build. When it was finished the Russians embarked across the Sea of Okhotsk. They arrived at Kamchatka without incident but still had the difficult crossing of the peninsula before them. From Bolsheretsk to the fort at the mouth of the Kamchatka river was 585 miles across a mountain range higher than the Rockies. No wonder the men became discouraged and Bering himself had his faith sorely tried.

Although it took three years for them to get from St. Petersburg to Kamchatka, the real expedition had not yet started. The necessary delay caused by building another boat could not be blamed on Bering; it was both impractical and against Peter's orders to search out the extent of Asia by overland routes.

Eventually the *Gabriel* was launched on the Pacific coast of Kamchatka, July 9, 1728, and the actual work of the expedition began. The explorers headed north into the Pacific. Supplies were short, the crew subsisting on oil and dried fish. In spite of inadequate food, dense fogs with which Bering seemed strangely unfamiliar, and almost open hostility among some of the men, Bering sailed northward. He kept close to the shore, making his observations as carefully and completely as his equipment permitted. Cape Chukotski was doubled on August 9 and two days later St. Lawrence island was sighted and named. On the thirteenth, the *Gabriel* was in what is now known as Bering strait.[3] Had it been a clear day, the men could have glimpsed the American coast. Bering's critics blame him for being so near the Alaska shore without discovering it, but such criticism seems unfair. His course north and south was logical if he were to learn whether Asia and America joined north of Kamchatka. He had no reason to believe that North America jutted so close to Asia.

The course held northward until the sixteenth when latitude 67° 18′ was reached. After a parley with his officers, Bering decided to return to Kamchatka, feeling that Peter's wishes had been fulfilled. The coast was no longer visible to the north and there was no indication of a land connection to the east. Bering himself favored going back to their base, fearing that the unfriendly natives would prove too dangerous for the crew of the *Gabriel*. On August 17, the ship was again in the narrowest part of the strait, where Diomede island was discovered and named; and, at 5 p. m., September 2, 1728, it arrived at the harbor on the lower Kamchatka river.

Bering has been accused of cowardice for not wintering north of latitude 67° as he then could have finished his work the next summer, discovered Alaska, and charted it without the long round trip to St. Petersburg which eventually took nearly ten years to complete. This criticism is only partly valid for his supplies were nearly exhausted. Any living off the country should have been done on the way from St. Petersburg to Kamchatka rather than north of the 67th parallel. Nevertheless, Bering should have known that the North Pacific does not freeze over in the middle of August. Perhaps he should have accomplished more while there.

He refitted the following year and tried to sail directly east toward America, but a storm drove him back. This venture failing, he turned homeward and was in St. Petersburg with his reports in March of 1730.[4] Disappointment awaited him in St. Petersburg. The scientists and geographers of Europe had predetermined opinions regarding the status of the Northern coasts of Asia and America. Facts reported by Bering were received

3.—Captain Cook is usually credited with popularizing the term, "Bering strait."
4.—The return over the same six thousand miles which took him three years before was now accomplished in one year. This fact indicates how much his supply trains slowed the outward journey.

coolly by many geographers and openly ridiculed by some. Nevertheless he received the loyal support of a number of scientific leaders.[5]

There are records of a few other adventurers in the region about this time. Not long after Bering's return to St. Petersburg, a vessel under the command of either Michael Gvosdeff or Ivan Federoff reached the Alaska coast and sailed along its shores for two days. Whether the voyage was planned deliberately or the ship was blown into Alaska waters by a storm is not known. The event took place in 1731 or 1732, which means that the Russians were probably the European discoverers of America from the west. Of course, for several generations the Spanish had possessed some knowledge of this coast, but their explorations did not yet extend north of California.

The Chukchi, most warlike of all Siberian natives, apparently were aware of the existence of Bering strait and the North American mainland. Although the Russians had captured and partially subdued the Chukchi, these natives had supplied no fresh geographic information.

In the year 1732,[6] a Russian named Krupischef was driven by a storm across the narrow part of Bering strait.

Bering's Second Pacific Expedition

Bering himself never doubted the success of his first expedition. A Copenhagen periodical published an article in 1730 which indicated that Bering fully realized the importance of an ocean route from Russia to Japan.[7, 8] He recommended to the admiralty that further explorations be undertaken at once. In this he was not entirely unselfish for he believed that it would be to his personal advantage, as well as for the glory of Russia, that he explore and chart the entire western coast of America to establish trade relations.

Since both Bering and Tchirikoff were aware of the Gvosdeff

5.—Strangely enough Bering's conclusions were accepted in the rest of Europe more enthusiastically than in Russia.

6.—James Oglethorpe established his colony for debtors and malcontents in the wilds of Georgia that same year.

7.—Lauridsen, pages 35-36.

8.—This ocean route was not traversed until 1878, when the *Nordenskjold* finally sailed along the northern coast of Eurasia. See Clinton A. Snowden's *History of Washington*, volume 1, page 127.

voyage, the second Pacific expedition would not be adventure into the unknown, but that does not make it less important.

Anna was now on the Russian throne. In spite of the doubts cast on the scheme by some members of the admiralty and academy, her advisers were enthusiastic about the additional exploration of the Pacific, proposed by Bering. Anna issued general orders for a thorough exploration of the coast of America, according to Bering's suggestions.

To understand the delays attending the organization of the second expedition, it is necessary to remember that in 1730 the Russian academy, admiralty, and senate were powerful groups. Each of these assumed a special right to regulate and advise Bering on any further work he might undertake in the northern and eastern parts of the Empire.

Bering had visions beyond mere exploration. He advised the establishment of iron works in Siberia,[9] a better system of administration, and a more honest collection of taxes. He recommended that certain educational facilities be innovated and that new herds be introduced to bolster the inadequate food supply. Bering had an intelligent idea of what Siberia needed, but he did not dream of attempting reforms personally.

Anna had no sooner given her permission for a second expedition than the academy, admiralty, and senate all started planning for the venture. Each group took the attitude, "Who better to entrust with all things than the man who understands the problem?" First one group then another added to and modified Bering's proposals until the unfortunate Dane was submerged by an avalanche of advice.

It was three years from the time Bering returned to St. Petersburg from Kamchatka before his new expedition set out for the Pacific. The Russian government was anxious to make it as spectacular as possible to throw a luster around their leader Anna. The loss of a few hundred lives, the useless expenditure of thousands of dollars, and the probability of unattained goals were overlooked. Peter gave Bering his first orders in a scant paragraph, but the academy, senate, and admiralty spent three years completing the details of his second.

Bering's final instructions would fill a volume. They can be

9.—Two hundred years later, Josef Stalin carried out Bering's advice.

classified into six groups: he was to make astronomical observations both on land and sea; thoroughly prosecute the geographical exploration and study the natural history of the regions traversed; examine the races encountered, not only from historic but also from ethnological viewpoints; discover America from the Pacific; chart the Arctic and East Siberian coasts and build lighthouses. As a minor venture he was to discover Japan from the North Pacific and Christianize the natives of Siberia.

The orders for each of these amazing labors were expanded into myriad details. He was directed to mail a report of his progress to St. Petersburg every few days notwithstanding the absence of any trace of a postal system east of the Urals. In fact, one of Bering's lesser duties was to establish an adequate postal system as he went along.

The personnel of each department of the expedition consisted of scores of scientists, assistant scholars, laymen, and common laborers. When the first detachments of the second Pacific expedition began to leave St. Petersburg in February of 1733, they represented the most astounding aggregation of equipment and men ever to leave on such an enterprise. Besides the scientists and pseudo scientists, there were twelve doctors, seven priests, two dozen officers—who considered the whole thing a mild sort of banishment—carpenters, bakers, Cossacks, sailors, soldiers, wives and children, scouts, two landscape painters, five surveyors, four thousand horses, nine wagonloads of scientific paraphernalia including thirteen- and fifteen-foot telescopes, a library of several hundred volumes, and seventy reams of paper on which to jot down findings. In all, there were five hundred persons and tons of equipment.

As if this bewildering mass of men and things were not confusion enough, more than half of Bering's officers were foreigners. His own hands were tied by the stipulation that no major act could be ordered until a junta of officers and scholars had discussed the matter. The one man who should have had supreme power was denied it, yet he was held responsible for the success or failure of the entire undertaking.

Bering could not have been ignorant of the complications which would arise from such a state of affairs. Just as he had been unable, or unwilling, to choose between baggage and speed on his first expedition, so now he could not force himself to choose between excess baggage and multiplied interests on the one hand and speed and unity of purpose on the other. A wiser commander would have resolutely opposed the interferences of the scientific and political groups and made it clear that either the expedition was to be under his supreme command and its objectives limited to those one man could reasonably attain, or that there would be no expedition as far as his leadership was concerned. Such a stand might have taken from Bering the opportunity to explore on the Pacific, but much more likely it would have resulted in submission to his wishes as he was the ablest person for such an expedition. Bering attempted to meet the problem by co-operation and mild remonstrances but his half-hearted objections were swept aside and further instructions issued in their place. Thus handicapped he started again on the long journey across Siberia, which was to terminate for him in a frozen grave.

The first contingent under Spangberg, Bering's old lieutenant, left St. Petersburg in February, 1733, and Bering himself got under way the following month. Besides the capable, energetic, and practical Spangberg, Bering was fortified by having Tchirikoff command one of the divisions. Tchirikoff was valuable to any expedition, not only because he was well informed and courageous but because his nobility of character and sense of chivalry did much to soothe natures made raw by the hardships of the North.

The first winter was spent at Tobolsk just across the Urals; the following summer in pushing as far as Yakutsk, on the Lena, where ships were built for exploring the Arctic coast. The main force set out again in June, 1735, for the journey to the Pacific. Bering himself remained at Yakutsk a number of months.

This second expedition repeated the first in many unpleasant ways. The general route led from Yakutsk to the Aldan, up the Aldan to the Maya, to the Yudoma, over the Stanovoi mountains, down the Urak to its mouth, then by sea a mere three miles to Okhotsk. Such a route, easy enough to delineate on a map, was not easy to traverse with supplies estimated to last six years. Little or nothing had been done to prepare for Bering's heterogeneous company even though scouts went ahead to warn the Siberian officials to have equipment and accommodations ready. The officials refused to do anything. There was no legal way to compel them and Bering would not use force.

More than a thousand Siberian exiles, dreary outcasts of semifeudal Russia, dragged barges mile after mile against the currents of Asia's rivers. At the end of the day they dropped, too exhausted to do more than mutter curses at their masters. Food ran short in spite of the enormous supplies, and horses which should have been beasts of burden were eaten and their work done by half-starved exiles. The days were often oppressively hot, the nights freezing. Three times on the way from civilization to the Pacific, boats and barges had to be built. In the higher altitudes men and animals often struggled up partly frozen rivers, alternately stumbling along the shores and wading in the icy water. When they finally arrived on the Pacific, three years after the main forces had left the Lena, they found their progress again blocked by unfriendly officials.

Major-general Pissarjeff, harbor master at Okhotsk, was a typical example. This renegade had been a favorite of Peter's. He was well educated and accepted in the best circles of Russian official society, but he was an evil man. As he had been convicted of more than one offense against society and his country, Peter had him branded, knouted, and exiled to Siberia. With this dubious background Pissarjeff became an evil genius at Okhotsk. When Bering's forces arrived, Pissarjeff was about sixty years old, but as restless, ruthless, and dissolute as ever. This might have been expected for "All Russian officials were corruptible, and the honest men among those who stood nearest to Peter himself could literally be counted on one's fingers." [10]

Spangberg, a fiery and arrogant dictator by nature, soon quarreled with Pissarjeff but Bering refused Spangberg's request to take five men and put the old ruffian out of the way. For almost six years Pissarjeff did everything possible to wreck the expedition, but in the end he overplayed his hand and was forced by Spangberg to flee from Okhotsk to Yakutsk.

The expedition left St. Petersburg early in 1733, but seven years later its main objective, the discovery and charting of the American coast, had not yet begun. These seven years were not

10.—Lauridsen, page 85.

wasted, though, for ships had been sent to chart the Arctic coast of Asia and Spangberg had drawn his maps of Japan. Nevertheless the venture was not really successful. More than $200,000 had been spent, and Bering was severely criticized for not doing something more spectacular. He was accused of being inefficient, of having no system, of grafting for his personal benefit, in fact of being a general failure as a commander. Even his wife was arrested and her baggage searched for goods supposedly not her own. Tchirikoff was encouraged to investigate the expedition's affairs in Siberia. Bering was inefficient in many respects, readily admitting that his personal strength was no longer sufficient to cope with his problems. But to accuse his expedition of being a failure and to indict him for graft was a great injustice, for he had accomplished much and showed no evidence of graft.

Despite his troubles, Bering at last built the *St. Peter* and *St. Paul* at Petropavlovsk, Avacha bay, Kamchatka. They were two-masters, eighty feet long, twenty-two feet in beam, and a little more than one hundred tons burden. They carried fourteen two- and three-pounder guns as protective equipment.

Sails were hoisted on June 4, 1741,[11] for the second Pacific expedition. All of the preceding May had been consumed in getting the Russian officers to agree on a route, which turned out to be the wrong one. Some years before, Juan de Gama claimed to have sighted a land mass at latitude 45° and this nonexistent Gamaland became the first objective of the expedition. Valuable time was wasted hunting for a land which was as unreal as Hwui Shan's Land of Women. Only one hundred casks of water were on board the *St. Peter,* a small amount for its crew of seventy-seven. Tchirikoff on the *St. Paul* was no better equipped. Most of the crews of both vessels were criminals conscripted for the trip, and the minor officers were a brawling, quarrelsome lot very little better than the ruffians they tried to rule.

After a fruitless search for Gamaland, a junta finally decided to sail northward. Supplies for only five months remained in the holds, although Bering had originally intended to stay two years on the American coast if and when it were discovered. This laud-

---

11.—About this time the natives on the Atlantic coast were causing the settlers so much trouble that in 1743 the New England Confederacy was formed to combat them.

able plan was canceled of course because of lack of provisions.

Bering and Tchirikoff reached latitude 46° on June 12, 1741, where a gale separated the vessels which never met again. The historian Lauridsen [12] says that Tchirikoff made no attempt to keep with Bering, but Snowden[13] blames the storm for the separation. Whatever the cause, it is necessary to trace the further work of the two ships separately.

After the storm, Bering sailed as far north as latitude 49°, then went back to 46° to look for Tchirikoff. He accomplished nothing during June. His health had been poor for some time and by the first of July he was down with scurvy. The middle of July found his crew on half rations of water and still he had achieved nothing significant. He called a council which decided to sail northward. The fogs so common in the North Pacific cleared away and the crew of the *St. Peter* sighted land on July 16. The coast was visible for four days as the ship slowly sailed toward it.

Opinion differs concerning the exact date Bering sighted the American coast. The commander himself says July 16, some journals make the landfall on the eighteenth, while others advance the date to the twentieth.[14] The exact place was the coast where Mt. St. Elias rears its summit eighteen thousand feet above the sea and the discolored water indicates that a river enters the ocean. Bering announced that this was the American coast, while admitting to himself and his intimates that he was lost and that the enthusiasm of his men over the discovery was premature.

Kayak island is generally accepted as the point of this first anchorage of the *St. Peter*. Men went ashore for water and fuel. They found recently inhabited huts containing several household tools and utensils similar to those used by the natives on Kamchatka. The inhabitants themselves were not about, but after sailing sixty miles farther, the party encountered natives on the Shumagin islands. Bering himself did not leave the ship for he was ill and irritable and wanted to get under way again as quickly as possible.

Among the most prominent of the many scientists attached to the expedition was the German naturalist, George William Steller.

12.—Lauridsen, page 139.
13.—Snowden, volume 1, page 128.
14.—Hubert Howe Bancroft. *History of Alaska,* page 79.

Like many gentlemen of his profession, he was enthusiastic, and he often overrated the importance of his studies as they applied to the work of the expedition. When the *St. Peter* anchored at Kayak, Steller went ashore with the crew and fell to work collecting specimens. Steller liked Bering, as did most of the men, but at Kayak he and the Dane had seriously disagreed over policies.

Bering's original journal has long since been lost, and the only record regarding his first landfall is the one left by Steller, whose journal discloses that Bering refused to allow the crew ashore for fear of the natives. He permitted Steller only ten hours inland to collect specimens and make observations. The naturalist remarked bitterly that ten years were spent preparing for a ten-hour expedition. There is much justice in this complaint. Had Bering been as impatient of delay in Siberia as he was at Kayak, the *St. Peter* could have spent two years on the American coast as originally planned and still would have had supplies to reach home in relative comfort.

But Bering faced a grave situation. The crew was sick and baffled by the constant fogs; the food had dwindled to a three months' supply; they were lost on a strange, and for all they knew, unfriendly shore; and their charts were worthless, for the coast ran southward instead of northward as their maps indicated. These facts, together with the bickerings of the officers, persuaded Bering to sail at once.

Anchor was weighed, and the *St. Peter* coasted along the shore in a general northwest direction. On August 1, soundings at Ukamok showed three feet of water under the keel. From Kayak to Ukamok, Bering took as complete observations as his facilities allowed; and while the *St. Peter* pushed on toward Asia he kept constant vigil. At a council called on August 10, it was decided to sail for home because one-half of the crew had scurvy and there were but two months' supplies and twenty-five casks of water left.

Land was close on August 30, and, as the crew was very weak, Bering ordered a landing. Most of the sick had to be carried ashore. Shumagin, one of the crew, died during the process, and in his honor the name Shumagin islands was given to the group. Discipline had become so lax that when some of the crew were sent for fresh water, they refused to heed Steller's advice, filling the casks with brackish water, though fresh water was available a short distance inland. Naturally, the bad water made the crew even sicker. Such episodes indicate how deeply the hates of the uneducated crew had grown toward the bookish, but often very practical, Steller.

Storms were almost constant, the natives sometimes caused trouble, and when the ship tried to make headway many of the men had to be carried because they were too weak to move to their posts. Steller remarked, "The general distress and mortality increased so fast that not only the sick died, but those who pretended to be healthy, when relieved from their posts, fainted and fell down dead; of which the scantiness of the water, and the want of biscuits and brandy, cold, wet, nakedness, vermin and terror were not the least causes." Bering had been in bed for weeks and Waxel, the second in command, took over the actual work of navigation. Steller quarreled with everyone, the men grumbled and fought, Bering complained, the rigging froze stiff and broke, gear rotted away, and fogs, snow, and sleet made progress almost impossible. During some days they sailed only twenty miles; during others, none. In spite of everything, Bering did his best to keep the work of the expedition progressing and the maps he made are far above the average of that time.

Land was sighted on November 5. Bering opposed Waxel's order for a landing because the time was short. If Kamchatka were ever to be reached, it must be soon. Only six casks of water remained, the season was far advanced, and a few more men ill with scurvy would mean a helpless crew. It seemed wiser to Bering to gamble on the nearness of Avacha bay than to waste time landing on one more unknown island. But he was overruled and on the nights of November 5 and 6 Waxel and Steller supervised the unloading of some of the men and supplies. The *St. Peter* was driven into a small harbor, safe for the present.

At no time during the eight years since the forces had left St. Petersburg was good judgment more imperative, but at no time were less courage and common sense displayed. At first the men refused even to work together, paying no attention to the orders of their officers. Later, however, this situation partially righted itself when by mutual agreement the crew divided into three sections, one to hunt, one to furnish the wood—often carried six or eight miles—, and a third to be responsible for the cooking. The officers had wrangled for days previous to November 5 over whether to hunt for winter quarters northward, to go to one of the landfalls encountered during the summer, or to push on to their base at Avacha bay on Kamchatka. Fate took a hand in the guise of the landfall of November 5 and for a week the men hastily unloaded their supplies. Bering believed they were lost but Waxel was certain they were just off the mouth of Avacha bay. Pursuing his own way as usual, Steller began preparing for winter. As was so often the case, both Steller and Bering were right. Had they harmonized their differences, they might have avoided the misery of the past summer, for their combined opinions would have carried some weight with the men. Bering was only too well justified in believing they were not at Kamchatka and should attempt to reach it. Steller, too, was right.

Since Bering had been overruled and the party had landed on what is now called Bering island, the logical thing was not to waste time plunging hither and thither as Waxel was doing but to prepare for the long Arctic nights ahead. After reconnoitering for two days they discovered that Bering was right; they were on another uncharted island. Building materials were nonexistent, yet the sick crew must be housed. Men with scurvy could not be cured by rest alone. Plants to counteract the disease had to be obtained.

On Bering island, Steller reached a nobility of soul and devotion to service which should eliminate any irritation felt over his shortcomings. He was indefatigable, he searched for good water as he had done at the Shumagin islands, he gathered what few plants the island afforded, he nursed the men, superintended sheltering both the sick and the partially able-bodied, and by his complete self-denial and unselfishness placed his name next to Bering's and Tchirikoff's on the memorable roll which made up the staff of the second Pacific expedition.

Since the island provided no suitable building materials, crude pits were dug in the sand. The sick were placed in these shallow half-graves and covered with all manner of things. Wildlife was everywhere and food, though somewhat restricted in variety, was plentiful.[15]

15.—Later Steller found time to explain to the men the importance of the

The men carried Bering ashore on the tenth of November, carefully protected from the deadly fresh air which had proved fatal to nine of the confined crew during the process of landing.

A great storm arose on November 28 which snapped the cables of the *St. Peter* and drove her out to sea only to reverse itself and drive her headlong back to land and wreck her beyond repair. Hope was at a low ebb. It was December; five underground huts housed the crew and served as hospitals; men were dying every day; and the blue Arctic fox, unafraid, swarmed over the camp, eating the dead and attacking the dying; holes in the walls of the sand caverns were chinked with frozen bodies of clubbed foxes; the giant sea cow[16] was hunted and eaten; men struggled for miles to obtain wood that a tiny fire might keep bodies and souls together one more night.

Bering himself sank rapidly, dying on the morning of December 8, 1741. He died as he had lived, mildly and without violence. Sand from the sides of his dugout had kept trickling over him, and at last he gave up trying to keep it clear. He said it warmed him, and he used what strength remained to urge the others on to hope and action. He no longer grumbled or quarreled. Steller nursed him as if he were one of his own family. Both men, sensing the end, laid aside their differences, ending their relationship amiably as it had begun.[17]

pelts available on the island. As a result, furs valued at more than $100,000 were taken to Russia by the remnant of the crew that survived.

16.—The sea cow, now extinct in the North Pacific, was an enormous animal. Early voyagers reported it to be twenty to thirty feet long and to weigh up to three tons. Its home was the Commander islands, of which Bering island is a part.

17.—The two best accounts of Bering's death are in F. A. Golder's *Russian Expansion on the Pacific,* pages 211 and 212:

(a) "One may say that he was half buried while still alive. Sand from the walls of the pit in which he lay continually rolled down upon his feet and covered them; and he finally no longer allowed it to be cleared away. He felt a warmth from it, he said, which was also transmitted to the upper parts of his body. And so he was soon buried in sand up to his waist; indeed, when he finally died, they had to dig him out of it in order to give him a fitting interment." (excerpt from Muller's *Sammlung Russicher Geschichte,* volume 3, page 238)

(b) "He almost died from hunger, thirst, cold, emaciation, and sorrow; and the dropsical swelling in his feet, which he had had for a long time as a result of having contracted tertian ague, was aggravated by the cold and driven into his abdomen and chest; and finally, gangrene having attacked the lower part of his body, caused his death about two hours before daybreak on December 8.

"As painful as his passing necessarily seemed to his friends, just so

It is indeed regrettable that Bering's advice was not followed, for his life might have been spared, and certainly the misery of the winter on the Commander islands would have been avoided. His death left Waxel in authority but the other's weak hold on the men led to recurring threats of mutiny.

With the passing of winter, the crew broke up the old ship and built a new one forty feet long. By the middle of August the *St. Peter,* as the new boat was named, was ready to try for Avacha bay. The departure from Bering island on August 16, 1742, was tinged with regret, for the men, though hardened, were human and they had buried on the island more than twenty-five of the crew of seventy-seven. Eight days after hoisting sail the new *St. Peter* was within sight of Kamchatka and on August 27 it reached Avacha bay.

Several months later, Waxel, accompanied by Steller, set out for St. Petersburg. The naturalist had contracted tuberculosis in the North and died of exposure on the homeward journey.

Tchirikoff's Adventure on the St. Paul

In the meantime, what had happened to the *St. Paul* after the fateful storm of June 12, 1741, had separated it from the *St. Peter?* When the storm abated, the *St. Paul* was allowed to drift in hope of sighting the *St. Peter.* Later, a course was set southeast to latitude 48° but on June 13 a council decided it was useless to search longer and the *St. Paul* under the command of Tchirikoff continued as an independent expedition.

Tchirikoff was off the Alexander archipelago July 13, 1741, and two days later was four miles off Cape Addington. Technically, Tchirikoff, not Bering, deserves credit for the discovery of America from the west for he arrived at Cape Addington thirty-six hours before Bering reached Kayak. History has given

---

marvelous was his resignation and preparedness for death, which came upon him while he was still in full possession of his reason and speech. He himself was convinced that we had been cast upon an unknown shore; yet he did not wish to discourage the others by making such an assertion, but rather cheered them on in every way possible to hope and action.

"We buried the body of the departed one that day with Protestant rites near our quarters, where he lies among his adjutants, a commissary, and two grenadiers; and at our departure we marked the grave with a wooden cross, which was to serve at the same time as a token of our possession of the land." (excerpt from Steller's *Pallas' Neue Nordische Beytrage,* volume 6, pages 8-9) .

the Dane the credit, however, for his was the mind and spirit behind the expedition and only chance brought Tchirikoff to the coast of America before him.

The *St. Paul* experienced her share of fog and bad weather, but by July 17 she had drifted to Sitka sound. Here it was decided to fill the water casks and do some exploring. A boat with a crew of ten men under the command of Abraham Dementieff was outfitted and lowered. It contained supplies for several days and carried a small brass cannon for protection. Tchirikoff worked out a simple system of signals to keep in touch with the landing party. For some time this crude communication was successful, but when the party went inland the signals became fewer, finally ceasing altogether. Tchirikoff waited a reasonable time, then dispatched a second boat under Sidor Savelief to investigate the whereabouts of the first and to order the entire detachment back to the ship. Again the signals failed. No word has ever been heard of either crew. Some authors believe they were massacred by the natives,[18] while others suggest they were drowned in the treacherous currents of Sitka sound.[19]

Tchirikoff would gladly have sent still a third detachment could he have afforded the risk. Already he had lost a fifth of his crew, both small boats were gone, and a storm was coming. Furthermore, if the fifteen or more men already ashore were unable to defend themselves it was improbable that five or six more would alter their situation. In the light of such conditions, Tchirikoff hoisted sail and ran out to sea. Whatever the fate of the two boatloads of men, they were the first Russians to land on North America within historic times if we except the indefinitely reported adventure of Gvosdeff.

After the storm, Tchirikoff returned to Sitka hoping to pick up the small boat crews. The supply of fresh water was very low and he abandoned the search, heading northwest. The *St. Paul* sailed close to shore in spite of the dangerous fog, rain and storms. For days at a time it just drifted. When the fog did rise, somewhere off Kodiak island, they got a glimpse of Alaska. The stormy weather was followed by a calm, and it was September 8 before the *St. Paul* reached Adakh island. Indians came off in

18.—Laut, page 49.
19.—Golder, page 187, *note*.

canoes but nothing important resulted from this contact with the natives.

The men were on half-rations, and of course scurvy was rampant. Tchirikoff himself was ill and from September 26 there was at least one death every day.

After leaving Adakh island, the *St. Paul* again was allowed to drift. On October 2 the crew recognized signs of the Asiatic mainland, and land was sighted October 8. It was essential to reach Kamchatka because Yelagin, the pilot, was the only man aboard able to handle the helm. In fact, when the ship reached Avacha bay, the crew sent up distress signals for aid in entering the harbor.

The second expedition was at last completed. The cost in life and treasure had been enormous, but the voyage was a success. Few expeditions in the history of the New World accomplished more. While the work of Spangberg and the other lieutenants has not been stressed here, it should be remembered that they charted the Asiatic coast from the Ob eastward, discovered Japan from the north and proved it to be an island empire, again demonstrated that the Strait of Anian was mythical, and mapped that long stretch of coast from Sitka to the Bering sea so well that navigators need never again be lost in those waters, as Bering himself admitted at Kayak.

Surely such successes more than repaid Russia for the loss in life and money. The scientific world did not grumble at the amount or accuracy of the information obtained. The Russian imperial government realized the value of the work, even though it refused to accept all the conclusions of the explorers. The officers and men who returned to their homes were rewarded by promotions and pensions.

Vitus Bering had many weaknesses but his contemporaries credited him with bigness of soul, a tireless spirit, and dogged determination. These qualities alone place him very high on the roster of leaders. "He was, in school language, a 'plodder'; he did the work before him faithfully and to the best of his ability. From this point of view Bering may be called great."[20]

20.—Golder, pages 213-214.

14

RUSSIANS IN THE NORTH PACIFIC

IN SPITE OF THE VALUE OF THE PELTS TAKEN to Asia by the crew of the *St. Peter*, the Russians gave little official notice to the potential wealth in the North Pacific described by Steller. No further attempt to explore the Alaska mainland was made until 1766.[1]

Some members of the crew which had wintered on Bering island sold their pelts, receiving such high prices for them that they organized independent forays among the islands east of Kamchatka in search of more. These expeditions, if such they could be called, were haphazard affairs. The boats used were seldom more than crude barges held together with leather thongs. They carried no navigator's equipment, often not even a compass, and the men themselves seldom were fitted to be masters of any ship out of sight of land. As time went on, many men not originally connected with Bering's voyages engaged in a wild scramble for the pelts of the blue fox and sea otter. At least a third of all who left Kamchatka never returned, but the profits of those who did were large and caused others to take the risk.

These independent ventures were so numerous in the two decades following Bering's second Pacific expedition that they aroused the interest of Catherine II. In 1766 she ordered Lieutenant Synd to make a thorough investigation of the fur trade. He sailed from Okhotsk around Kamchatka and north to latitude 66°. The next year a second trip took him even farther; it is possible that he landed on the American coast. His work indicated official Russian interest but was otherwise unimportant.

Captains Krenitzin and Levaschef were dispatched in 1768 to survey the islands between Asia and America. Each was in charge of a small vessel. They sailed from Kamchatka and wintered on the Fox islands, returning in October of 1769 with valuable

1.—The Treaty of Paris which ended the French and Indian war in 1763 left the entire North American continent northwest of the Great lakes open for exploitation by fur traders. The English soon invaded the region, but if the Russians had been more progressive they might have established the stronger foothold.

cargoes of furs but with half of the crew dead from scurvy. The geographic survey, the real purpose of the voyages, had not been carried out. The pelts, however, excited interest. Two years later, in 1771, the first voyage was made from the Pacific coast of the Russian domains to another Pacific port frequented by Europeans.

Details of the piracies of Count Mauritius Benyowsky have no place in a history of the Pacific Northwest, but a summary of his escapades is essential to the history of the fur trading era. Benyowsky, a Pole by birth, became entangled with the Russian police. He was apprehended, convicted, and exiled to Kamchatka. On the way to Kamchatka he planned to escape when the party reached the Pacific. His scheme involved the seizure of a ship for a piratical cruise. He enlisted the aid of other exiles; and, when they reached Bolsheretsk on the inner side of Kamchatka, these allies, aided by an intrigue with the governor's daughter, enabled Benyowsky to carry out his plan. The *St. Peter* and *St. Paul* were seized, provisioned, and sailed to Bering island where other escaped exiles joined the group. Benyowsky's course took him from Bering island to the islands off Alaska, then to either the Ladrones or Luzon, and finally to Macao where he disposed of his furs. These pelts were the first from the North Pacific to reach China by water. From this piracy grew the lucrative fur trade which played such an important part in the history of the Pacific Northwest.[2]

One of the first fur companies to operate in Alaska waters was organized in 1781 [3] by Gregory Schelikof, Ivan Gollikof, and others. Schelikof left Okhotsk with three vessels in August, 1783. He was more energetic than Krenitzin or Levaschef and for three years explored the Alaskan coast as far east as Prince William sound. He established several small colonies, the principal one on Kodiak island.

None of these brigands used caution to perpetuate their supply of furs. They robbed the natives, burned their huts and storehouses, and made enemies of the people who should have been their friends.

2.—After many hardships Benyowsky turned up in Baltimore, Maryland, about 1786, and interested the local merchants in a scheme to capture Madagascar. He was killed on the island while attempting to fulfill his plans.
3.—The Articles of Confederation were ratified in March of the same year.

Because these reckless activities took place in territory claimed by Spain, she soon dispatched a protest to Russia. Paul I, who ascended the throne after the death of Catherine the Great in 1796, answered the Spanish complaint two years later by issuing a ukase consolidating the independent Russian traders into the Russian American company. This organization was to have a monopoly for twenty years of all coastal commerce north of latitude 55°. In addition to the fur business, the company was to be responsible for further explorations as well as the propagation of the Greek faith among the natives.

The Russian American company was organized like any modern business house which maintains branches. The directory of the company was in St. Petersburg. A general manager with headquarters established in 1805 at New Archangel[4] represented the company in North America. The Alaska area was subdivided into several districts, each supervised by a subgovernor. Each district had several storehouses, or factories, and was ruled by an overseer in charge of the immediate territory. Employes enlisted for a term of years and were under semimilitary discipline.

The same organization functioned in government matters, each subordinate officer having less power than the official directly above him. There was no appeal from the governor's rulings except to the directory in St. Petersburg, impossible in most cases.

Alexander Baranof was the first and most notorious of the governors of the Russian American company. He had spent many years in the northland and had been with Schelikof on his first expedition. Baranof was stationed at Kodiak when Vancouver arrived there in 1794. The man was a throw-back to a coarser, more feudal age. Never completely happy unless completely drunk, he was still no besotted offscouring of Russian society. His huge, bald head never became so befuddled with the fumes of revelries that he did not know what he was doing. He had the strength which Bering lacked, but was without the refinements of character which made Bering a mild and charming gentleman. Baranof struggled all his life against great odds, never asking or giving quarter. When his caravans were pillaged and he became a bankrupt in Siberia before his fur trading days, he grimly accepted the challenge, gambling his future on the fur

4.—The present Sitka.

business. When his boats were wrecked and his men struggled to shore exhausted and disheartened, his tongue lashed them into activity, then gathered the wreckage and supplies together for a new start. When annoyed by a troublesome fellow who robbed him and incited the natives against him, Baranof ordered the culprit to report for trial. This bluff succeeded so well that the rascal actually gave himself up and was promptly shipped to Siberia.

Baranof was an autocrat who followed legal forms and instructions only if they suited his purpose. He is sometimes pictured as a mental giant who fought against great odds to achieve the impossible, succeeding at last in laying in the lap of the Czars an empire half the size of European Russia. Sometimes he is described as a crude, ill-tempered martinet who won his place in Russian America by intrigue, inhuman violence, debauchery, and robbery. Probably neither picture is completely true. The first excludes the shadows and emphasizes the highlights, while the second overplays the shadows.

Baranof was indeed an uncouth, severe disciplinarian who achieved his successes by violence and deceit, but he was also humanely energetic and resourceful. Whatever he did was for the ultimate good of his people and when his long rule at Sitka was over, thirty years after he first embarked from Kamchatka, a company auditor found not one penny misappropriated and not one evidence of graft or corruption. For thirty years he caroused, cursed, reveled, and labored among his natives and furs, but always he maintained a scrupulous honesty insofar as his personal wealth was concerned. He never hesitated to do anything legal or illegal which would resound to the credit of Russia and his company. With all the power in his hands, thousands of miles from any restraint by Russian directory, Baranof issued just and compassionate regulations for the fur men.[5] These regulations were not always enforced.

Baranof often refused to obey orders which he thought were contrary to the best interest of the company.[6] This policy of

5.—Robert Greenhow. *The History of Oregon and California*, page 271.

6.—Such an instance occurred in 1805-1806 when Von Resanoff was sent to Alaska to reform and regulate the company's affairs. Von Resanoff had failed to arrange an advantageous treaty with Japan and when he arrived at Sitka he was anxious to regain his prestige and assuage his injured vanity.

devotion to the fur traders and the company resulted in prosperity for the organization and near poverty for himself. After thirty years of service, Baranof was arbitrarily removed from office and forced to beg a passage home. He was cast off without reward or consideration when he was no longer useful to the company he had served with such devotion.

Had Russia been more vigorous and bestirred herself, her dominions could have been expanded with relative ease as far south as California. The Spaniards were too listless and impotent to put up more than slight resistance. In fact, for a century and a half Spain had made no pretense of resisting encroachment along her Pacific coastline. From the time of Bering's explorations to 1775, Russia had a free hand in the North but did little about it. With the revival of Spanish interest and the coming of the English and American traders, her opportunities as a colonizing force in America were no longer important, even in the North.

He ordered all trade between Americans and Russians to stop. Count Romanzoff, minister of foreign affairs, suggested to John Quincy Adams, the American representative in Russia, that the two countries sign a treaty forbidding Alaska trade between Russia and America.

The proposal was wrecked when Russia claimed territory south of the Columbia river. Baranof had been carrying on considerable trade with Boston and relied on the Yankee ships for supplies. The situation in Alaska was ironical. At the very time Resanoff issued his orders his settlement was practically without food. In the end, he thought too much of his own comfort to enforce his orders. Just as Sitka faced starvation, an American vessel, the *Juno* from Rhode Island, was welcomed into the harbor.

15

SPAIN RETURNS

FOR FIFTEEN DECADES following Vizcaino's return in 1603, there is no record of any Spanish ships on the Northwest coast.[1] Seldom has the history of any section of the globe been stranger. From Balboa to Vizcaino, Spain feverishly expanded northward from Mexico. Then, abruptly, her activity stopped, to be resumed four generations later with all its early vigor and purpose.

During that long lull Spanish power in Mexico was almost nonexistent. The viceroys and friars accomplished nothing of permanent value and the galleons carried little of the old wealth to and fro. Yet outwardly Old Mexico was about the same. The Spanish flag still flew over Mexico City; viceroys came and went; friars huddled in their missions, thinking more of personal comfort than of heathen souls; and the Occident and the Orient continued trading. But the old fire was gone. The military defeat, the Inquisition, and the economic greed which engaged the homeland echoed strongly in America.

Mines which had yielded quantities of silver to Cortez's followers were now idle, not always because the ore had run out but because the Indian slaves had died. There were not enough negroes to carry on the work and the Spaniards indolently refused to help. When Carlos III came to the throne in 1759, he ushered in a new period of exploration. All the old motives for exploration still existed—the desire for expansion, for the discovery of the Strait of Anian, hope of finding a Northwest port—but the prime factor in this reawakened interest was Russian activity in the New World.

1.—These same years were crowded with events on the Atlantic. The original English and French colonies had been planted; the Indians had been partially driven across the Appalachians; the fierce struggle for personal and religious liberty had waxed and waned; the inter-colonial wars had forced the French from the St. Lawrence and the Ohio valleys; and just at the close of the period the English colonies were about to appeal to arms to achieve political and economic freedom as they had before appealed to reason and moral force to achieve personal and religious freedoms.

Neither Bering nor Baranof expected to stir the idle Spanish power two thousand miles southward, and as the fur trade grew more inviting, the Russians pushed farther and farther south. Eventually Spain got news of this encroachment. As early as February of 1773, and possibly five years before that, Spanish officials knew about the activities of the independent Russians who had followed Bering into the North Pacific. Carlos was advised to check the Russian advance. In Mexico, Jose de Galvez, the visitador-general from 1765 to 1771, and Viceroy Croix had begun the occupation of California. In 1769 the San Diego mission was founded and soon Spanish power spread up to San Francisco.

The king planned to continue this expansion into Alta California, with orders issuing from Mexico City. Croix turned the entire "occupation program" over to Galvez, who was much more energetic than the customary visitador-general. He scheduled four expeditions, two by sea and two by land. Of these four, only one concerns the history of the Northwest coast, the maritime expedition under Juan Perez.

16

JUAN PEREZ REACHES 55° NORTH

WITH HIS LONG CAREER as seaman-trader, Juan Perez was among the most notable figures to appear so far in the history of upper California. Having been in command of the Manila galleon and on official errands along the California coast, he understood the terrors of the Pacific and the importance of a good harbor on the Northwest coast for galleons trading between the Orient and Mexico.

Not much is known about him personally, though he must have suffered the same hardships as other explorers. He was eminently practical, moderately efficient, well trained in the ways of the sea, and a fair leader of men. Neither a far-sighted organizer like Balboa nor a dreamy romancer like Coronado, Perez was a man to be followed and obeyed. Quietly, with no fanfare, he dedicated his life to exploring the Northwest coast of America. If his exploits were never spectacular, they were never complete failures. Undoubtedly these attributes influenced Galvez and the officials in Madrid when they chose him to lead one of the four northern expeditions.

Perez received final orders on December 24, 1773. He was to take the *Santiago* with a year's supplies and embark from San Blas for the missions at San Diego and Monterey. After discharging the cargo at these ports he was to run to sea until he reached 60° north latitude. And the voyage was to be conducted in strict secrecy. If possible, the *Santiago* was to avoid "speaking" a foreign ship. If one were encountered and questions asked, Perez was given form answers: if he met a foreign ship below Monterey, he was merely carrying supplies to that place; above Monterey, he had been blown out of his course.

At 60° north Perez was to turn his ship south and make a careful search for harbors advantageous to the Manila trade. Orders were to land often, take possession, erect a cross, and plant a bottle containing a record of the act of possession. There were to be no settlements but Perez was to gather all possible information regarding suitable sites for colonies. On his way south from 60°, should he come across a Russian or other European settlement, he was to double back and take possession of the region above such settlement. Interference with inhabitants in areas above San Francisco was forbidden, but information about them was insisted upon.

On January 24, 1774, the *Santiago*, with a crew of eighty-eight including officers, hoisted canvas and headed north from San Blas. Several church officials were aboard. These gentlemen, along with supplies for the missions, were delivered in due time to both San Diego and Monterey. Although a ship "from home" was always occasion for celebration, at San Diego, Perez received a more joyful welcome than usual, the colony at that time being on the verge of starvation. On May 9 he reached Monterey, his last port before going north. Here he paid considerable attention to the needs of the expedition.

More than a month he and the crew rested at Monterey, refitting and supplying the ship from the limited facilities of that small port. The *Santiago* set sail again on June 11 but was only off Point Pinos on the fifteenth. Two days later they were out of sight of land but still making no headway. In fact, by the twenty-fourth, they had lost so much latitude that they were down to the Santa Barbara islands. A wind change sent them north once more as far as Monterey on the twenty-ninth. These three wasted weeks took immense toll of both supplies and health. Psychologically the expedition was in danger of defeat before leaving home waters.

Continuing favorable winds helped, though, and by July 4 they had reached 42° north.[1] There they replenished their water supply. Their goal was 60°. In latitude 51° 15′ Perez ordered a sharp lookout for a likely port, but on July 18, at 55°, they had not yet found a landing place. Perez ordered the *Santiago* brought around and followed the coast south to Cape North, 54° 15′. As in most cases of early exploration, opinion differs

---

1.—While Perez was fighting his way north, the call was issued for convening the First Continental Congress to deliberate in secret the fate of American liberties.

as to the exact place where the ship hove to, but probably it was somewhere on the Queen Charlotte islands.

Perez' personal shortcomings robbed him of the honor of discovery that these islands were not attached to the mainland. Where no imagination was demanded, he was a good commander, an efficient seaman and fairly successful trader, but he was unfitted for the role of great explorer. His very practicality prevented his taking necessary risks. Besides, he lacked the intellectual curiosity which is the prime asset of those who would penetrate the unknown.

Although he sailed along the coast to 54° 15′, he was evidently not interested in investigations which would have let him into the seaway between the Queen Charlotte islands and the mainland. He said that the strange currents of what is now called Dixon entrance prevented this. The excuse sounds weak. Juan Perez had spent too many years at sea not to know that such currents meant something more than a strange tide rip. Had he possessed either the tenacity or curiosity of a great explorer he would have stayed to solve that case. Northward he saw Prince of Wales island and Cape Muzon but he explored neither.

In short, Perez did not seriously attempt the really important things for which his orders provided. The few natives with whom he came in contact could seldom be enticed aboard for questioning, and the Spaniards carried little iron or other goods for trading, even had the Indians been interested. The natives did sell them a few sea-otter skins, the value of which was unknown to the Spaniards, who were more concerned with the fact that the Indians had iron-tipped arrows and knives.

Unable to get needed supplies, cursed with scurvy, and having failed to discover a likely port, Perez at last ordered the ship to sail for home. This command clearly shows Perez' shortcomings. At 55° and for many miles both north and south, the coast of America has a number of mediocre harbors, yet Perez found none. Fresh water is only less abundant than salt water, yet the crew of the *Santiago* received short water rations. The region certainly had adequate greens for the scurvy-stricken but Perez saw none. Steller, the naturalist, easily collected such greens along the same coast.

Perez's weakest excuse for turning back was bad weather. This had not barred Magellan or Drake or Bering from their goals, yet a few midsummer storms stopped Perez. These facts do not indict Perez of cowardice—he had faced too many storms in the Manila trade to be accused of that—but they do indict him as an explorer.

Having turned south, he sighted snow-capped peaks from 54° 48′ to 53° 8′, on July 23 and 24. The route lay close along the shores of the Queen Charlotte islands as far south as 52° but heavy fog prevented careful examination. By August 5 the weather cleared and two days later Perez anchored at 49° 30′, a point he called San Lorenzo, which is generally believed to be Nootka sound.

Indians came to trade a few furs. Perez tried to land but was held back by a heavy wind. He felt compelled to cut the cables and run to sea. A southerly course carried the ship by Mt. Olympus on August 15. Afterwards the pilot, Martinez, asserted he had sighted the Olympics on the Washington coast. If he did, it is odd that no mention was made of this in the journals and logs of the trip. However, Martinez may have seen Mt. Olympus and not realized its importance. Many high peaks are observable between 55° and 48°, and one more, at the time, may have made no particular impression on anyone. On the way south from Nootka the *Santiago* crossed the mouth of Juan de Fuca strait but the Spaniards were unaware of this.

While on the Northwest coast, Perez meant to look for Aguilar's river but was stopped by storms. Several days he was out of sight of land, then about August 21 he again saw it. On the twenty-sixth he passed the Farallones and the next day hove to at Monterey.[2] There the crew rested until October 9, when they left for San Blas. On November 3 they arrived in Mexico where Perez reported to Bucareli, the new viceroy.

2.—This was nine days before the Continental Congress met at Philadelphia. Though on the opposite side of the continent, there was some similarity between the task of Perez and that facing the Congress. The Congress met to repulse the encroachments of a European power on American rights; Perez made his tedious journey to stave off another European power, Russia.

Both were concerned with a struggle over liberty of action and territory.

It was as inevitable that others besides Spaniards should share in the wealth of the Pacific as it was that the English could not hope to keep exclusive colonial control on the Atlantic.

The voyage was a disappointment. Perez had accomplished none of the things his orders called for, though he had added some information about the Northwest coast of America. Having reached 55° north, he laid the background for the eventual American claim—under the terms of the Spanish cession—to "fifty-four forty or fight" and "he had given to his nation whatever of credit and territorial claims may be founded on the mere act of first discovery."[3] Also, for the first time in Spanish-American history, a major expedition escaped without enormous loss of life from disease. Scurvy had of course broken out and interfered with the efficiency of the crew but only one man died from it.

On analyzing Perez's work, Bucareli—possibly the ablest of the viceroys of New Spain—charitably concluded that, under the circumstances, Perez achieved as much as could be expected. Nevertheless, Bucareli was not satisfied. He immediately started planning a new and more elaborate survey of the Northwest coast.

3.—Bancroft. *History of the Northwest Coast,* volume 1, page 157.

17

BRUNO HECETA AND BODEGA Y QUADRA HEAD A GREAT SPANISH EXPEDITION

BRUNO HECETA AND JUAN FRANCISCO DE LA BODEGA Y QUADRA, lieutenants in his Majesty's service, became joint leaders in this new expedition. Credit for the outfitting and prosecution of this perhaps greatest of all Spanish voyages from Mexico north goes to Viceroy Antonio Bucareli. With keen understanding of what the conquest of Alta California would mean to Spanish power in America, he left nothing undone to achieve that end.

Heceta chose the *Santiago* as his flagship and Juan Perez as his pilot. The consort ship, tiny thirty-six foot *Sonora,* sometimes called the *Felicidad,* was under the command of Juan de Ayala. Heceta's instructions followed closely those previously given to Perez, except that Heceta was to go north to 65°.

Several other vessels besides the *Sonora* accompanied the expedition but these were not expected to sail north with the *Santiago,* and would have no bearing on this story were it not that the commander of one of them, the *San Carlos,* became insane shortly after the voyage began. This called for a change of commanders. Ayala was transferred to the *San Carlos* and Bodega y Quadra to the *Sonora.*

The expedition left San Blas on March 16, 1775,[1] carrying a year's supplies for 106 men. Because of her small size, the *Sonora* was towed. This seemed the best way to keep commands together and make fastest headway. The California coast in March often produces surprisingly vicious storms, and this was the case that year. High winds and bad weather so retarded Heceta and Bodega that by May 21 they were only up to Monterey. Provisioned as they were for a year, they did not stop. Anyway Monterey would more likely have asked for aid than given it.

1.—The arms and military supplies which occasioned the battle of Lexington and Concord a month later were already being gathered at Concord, and the minute-men farmers were even then going about their daily tasks with an air of expectancy.

None of the northern ports offered more than rudimentary facilities for refitting.

The two ships proceeded steadily into the North Pacific, keeping well out to sea until June 7, when they were again close in at 42°. They then sailed slowly south along the coast to Trinidad where they turned on June 19, steering out to sea once more to take advantage of prevailing winds, which Perez assured Heceta would come from a southerly quarter. These winds would allow the ships to sail easily along the coast, simplifying the work of exploration. By the end of June both ships were some three hundred miles off shore.

The winds came but Perez was wrong as to their direction— they came, not from the south, but from the northwest. Despite this setback, Heceta and Bodega y Quadra glimpsed land on July 11 at 48° 26' and began a vain search southward for an inlet. Two days later they were at 47° 23' north, the Point Grenville of modern maps. They discovered Destruction island, calling it Isle de Dolores.

They satisfactorily settled one disputed point; they found that de Fuca's strait was not between latitudes 47° and 48° north. Unfortunately for Heceta, he was a few miles too far south to get into the strait which does exist in those latitudes, so credit for its exploration was reserved for another expedition. Heceta does have the honor though of being commander of the first European expedition to set foot on what is now the State of Washington, for part of his crew landed on that coast, July 14, 1775.[2]

The Indians, friendly and eager to trade, understood the general routine of barter with white men. Though Heceta's crew was the first to land on the Washington coast, for centuries the natives had gone even to Alaska during the fishing season. Such trips naturally brought them into contact with the Russian traders of the Far North.

Quadra and the little *Sonora* were up the coast a few miles from Heceta and the *Santiago*. There were many Indians about but the *Sonora* men were not suspicious, as indeed they had no occasion to be. Because the ship's water supply was short, Quadra

---

2.—Eleven days before this, Washington had assumed command of the Continental army.

decided to send a boat ashore to superintend replenishing it. Placing Pedro Santa Ana in charge of six men, he dispatched them on an errand culminating in the death of all seven. Probably the Spaniards came upon some of the Indian smokehouses and tried to rob the natives of their food, getting themselves killed for their efforts. Anyhow the savages came off in their canoes, surrounded the schooner, and appeared quite hostile. Taking fright, the Spaniards opened fire, killing six natives.

All this took place on the fourteenth of July, 1775. On the same day a council was held regarding the future of the expedition. Even these Spaniards hesitated going farther into the unknown North in such a small craft as the *Sonora,* a frail carrier indeed on which to pin the hopes of Quadra's crew for a safe return. At sea she was at the mercy of every wind and tide she encountered; yet her commander insisted that the work of the expedition was not yet complete and that they must push on. Heceta wanted to return home, not because he was afraid but because he felt his responsibilities had been discharged.

Heceta and the council at last agreeing to Quadra's plea, they hoisted sail that evening, July 14, and drove again westward. Perez advised turning south but Quadra overrode his objections.

On July 30 the vessels became separated. How this happened is not known. The weather was bad but there were no storms such as would have made separation inevitable. Some historians believe that the two captains, feeling they could accomplish more alone, secretly agreed to part.

Following the advice of a later council, Heceta turned about and sailed toward land but in a northerly direction. On August 10 he sighted land in the vicinity of Nootka. Perez, who should have been less disturbed, constantly urged a return to Monterey or some southern port. He seemed to have deadly fear of the threat of scurvy and the stormy regions north of 42°.

Though Heceta's records are not clear on the point, he possibly sighted Clayoquot or Barclay sounds. He reported keeping close in to shore and generally enjoying fine weather, yet he missed the entrance to Juan de Fuca's strait. There are several explanations for this. One of the simplest is the likelihood of a local, low-hanging fog or haze which obscured the entrance. In those lati-tudes of the Pacific, though the sun may shine brilliantly all day, a comparatively near landmark or headland may be completely hidden by fog or haze. Generous critics praise Heceta for investigating the coast as carefully as he did. After all, many great explorers before him had missed de Fuca and were not called to task.

When on August 15, a crowd of natives surrounded the ship, the crew recognized some who were involved in the massacre a month before. The Spaniards tried to lure a few of them aboard to seize and hold as hostages, but the natives were too shrewd for such a trap.

Two days later the *Santiago* was off 46° 15', the latitude of the mouth of the Columbia river. Heceta named the site Bahia de la Ascuncion. Few instances in maritime annals have more pathos than Heceta off the Columbia in August of 1775. He had spent his life on the sea, had fought with it and conquered it countless times, all as an unconscious part of training for his great task —the exploration of the Northwest coast. He was to be defeated by a combination of circumstances entirely beyond his power to alter or control.

The Columbia, like most great rivers, pours great quantities of silt into the sea; this sediment plus the natural differences in coloring between fresh and salt water discolor the ocean for miles beyond the bar. Heceta noted the discoloration, felt the strong current sweep the *Santiago* out of her course, and knew that he was actually at the mouth of a great river; yet he was helpless to investigate. Scurvy had struck his crew with fearful force, leaving his men unable to man a boat. He said, "If we let go the anchor we should not have enough men to get it up." In spite of this he did try twice to ease the *Santiago* over the bar and into the calmer waters inside, yet each time he failed.

Further effort would have been useless. Bruno Heceta knew he had found a great river but he also knew he would be denied proof. One course was open—to hurry back to Mexico before the emaciated crew grew too weak to steer the ship. He gave orders to sail, leaving the secret of the Columbia to another to solve.

He passed Mendocino on the twenty-sixth and was at Monterey three days later.[3] Heceta had received orders to stop at San Francisco bay on his return, but he missed it. Perhaps this was just

3.—A final effort was made the same month to adjust affairs in the English

as well, for of his crew of forty-five, thirty-five were landed at Monterey, too ill to continue the voyage, and of the ten remaining, one died before reaching home.

The *Sonora* and the *Santiago* had lost sight of each other on July 30. The next day Heceta sailed far out to sea in search of Quadra. Probably he was merely trying to gain time for exploration in face of the opposition of his crew and Perez. By going out to sea, he could have reasoned that the landward drift would place him farther north than he would otherwise be able to reach. That there was virtually no chance of running into Quadra, Heceta well knew. This is one of the major pieces of evidence for the surmise that the two commanders were quite willing to continue the voyage apart.

As for the *Sonora,* she kept to the west until August 5, when she was 45° 55′ north and some 170 leagues off shore. At that point a change of tactics became necessary. Food was always scarce and Quadra's water supply was low. During a meeting of officers and crew the situation was presented in such a light that all agreed, because of the approaching crisis, to continue north.

The modern reader is often intrigued by the spirit of these sailors and their loyalty to Quadra as a leader. Originally forced aboard ship at point of arms, now short of food and water, attacked by scurvy and fear, they still agreed to penetrate deeper into the unknown.

An August 15 the *Sonora* was off Sitka, where Quadra named Mount Jacinto, now Edgecumbe. They cruised north to 58°, formally taking possession at two points and carefully examining the coast beyond the previous Perez voyage. Not until September 8 did Quadra turn south, when most of his men were seriously ill. Often only the officers could work, and even they were in critical condition. The commander himself was down with the fever yet ordered a sharp lookout. From 53° 54′ to 47° north, he could see the coast; from 44° 30′ to 42° 49′ he searched for Aguilar's river, but only discovered Bodega bay.

A month later the *Sonora* reached Monterey where the sick were taken ashore and arrangements made to send the *Sonora* and *Santiago* down to San Blas. They arrived November 20.

Two days out from Monterey the unromantic but able Juan Perez died. Like many before and after him he gave his life to the exploration of the Pacific. Though slightly recognized, few Spaniards worked harder for the glory of the realm. Much of the credit for the success of the Heceta and Quadra expedition belongs to Juan Perez and his quiet advice.

By now Spain had almost completed her task. The Pacific coast of North America had been observed from Mexico to Alaska; and, though Puget sound had not been explored, no reflection fell on the ability of the men from San Blas and Acapulco. "On the Perez, Heceta, and Bodega voyages alone, Spain had spent more than 50,000 pesos," [4] a considerable sum for those days.

Results of the voyage were not published at once. Bodega was permitted little leisure however and was soon recruited by Bucareli to sail to Peru with Areche, visitador to Peru. He had hardly returned from the South before he was dispatched to explore still farther along the Alaska coast.

He left San Blas in February of 1779 and arrived safely enough. Missing the Russians at Kodiak island, he returned in 1780, thinking the North had no foreign encroachment. Even then the Russian American company was exploiting the fur sources from the Aleutians east and south; and the English under Cook and Meares, Vancouver and Dixon, and a host of others, were on their way into the Spanish realm. Ignorant of all this, about 1780 Spain canceled all voyages such as Perez, Heceta, and Quadra had undertaken. Despite Quadra's being at Monterey when Vancouver was entertained there by Jose Dario Arguello in 1792 and the fact that Quadra was still in command of a fleet of ships, the Spanish set up no effective interference.

Aside from this apathy, Spain's record from 1513 to 1779 is notable. Fifteen expeditions had been sent from Mexico into the North, [5] giving Spain the clearest title to the Pacific coast south of Alaska.[6]

4.—Chapman, page 280.
5.—Snowden, volume 1, page 74.
6.—The Spanish Crown had not been too busy on the Pacific to take part in affairs on the Atlantic. Carlos III did not forget that England was Spain's greatest enemy and he secretly lent the Continental Congress $200,000 to aid in carrying on the war against England. In 1779 Carlos declared war on this old enemy, not, though, as the ally of the colonies.

18

JAMES COOK,
TRADER-GEOGRAPHER-EXPLORER

SPANISH FEARS were embodied in James Cook, captain in His Majesty's service. At the very time when Perez, Heceta, and Quadra were trying to prove that there was not the slightest danger of foreign encroachment on the Pacific, the Englishman, Cook, was plowing the Pacific on his way into that region.

Neither glamor nor great dignity attended the birth of James Cook in the village of Marton, Durham county, October 27, 1728. His father was a "servant in husbandry" and both parents were honest, sober workers of the solid laboring class of England. James was one of nine children.

The elder Cook in due time put the boy in school under the tutelage of one Dame Walker. Shortly afterwards the father was promoted to the superintendency of a farm near Great Ayton, North Riding, owned by Thomas Skottow. Skottow generously placed young James in the day school there where he acquired groundwork in writing and arithmetic. The lad was not yet thirteen when his father apprenticed him to a haberdasher at Straiths, a small fishing town nearby. But James Cook was not destined to be a merchant of hosiery and cravats; even then he was full of the "fever of the sea." Following a disagreement with his master he was discharged. This immensely pleased young James and doubtless caused no great loss to the haberdashery shop.

John and Henry Walker, Quakers of Whitby and owners and operators of several vessels engaged in the coal trade, needed another apprentice. Here was James' chance. For seven years his apprenticeship papers held him to the coal trade, but he seemed to like this for when his time was up he stayed on first as common seaman, and then as mate. During these years he lived a normal, industrious, and creditable life; but in 1755 when war between England and France flared up again, he did a startling and unaccountable thing. To escape impressment into the royal navy, he ran away and hid. Why he preferred the coal trade to royal "ships of the line" is puzzling. He suffered no attack of nerves or fear; he was a brave man both physically and mentally. Few commanders of modern times have been calmer, more poised, than he; and these qualities were already manifest when he suddenly scuttled away and hid.

His basic forthrightness soon returned, though, and he came out of seclusion, almost before his contemporaries were aware that he had disappeared. He immediately enlisted in the English navy, deciding to make the royal service his career.

Shortly after this episode he came to know Sir Hugh Palliser and the two remained lifelong friends. To Sir Hugh, Cook owed much of his success in the navy. He never forgot this debt.

The decade of 1755 to 1765 was busy for the new recruit, who spent a good portion of those years in the New World working at routine tasks connected with the campaigns against the French in Canada. He charted the channel of the St. Lawrence between the Island of Orleans and Quebec. This was, of course, secret and had to be done at night. Cook was forced to keep a constant vigil for both Indians and French, and the Indians were more dangerous. On one occasion he saved his life only by scrambling awkwardly from the front end of his boat just as the savages scrambled into the rear. Still, such details were only the usual hazards of his job, and after helping in the capture of Quebec he continued his charting, giving England a new plan of the lower St. Lawrence.

Few men care to live by war alone and James Cook was not of these. He found time to woo and wed Miss Elizabeth Batts, in England in 1762, even though his work prevented his being much more than a casual visitor at his own fireside. His biographers testify that in his homelife as in all other relationships he was honest, kind, and just. But the sea was his first and greatest love.

After the Treaty of Paris in 1763, Cook was again sent to Canada to continue his surveying. Still later he was ordered to Newfoundland under the direct supervision of Sir Hugh Palliser. This in turn led to his promotion to marine surveyor of Newfoundland and Labrador from 1764 to 1767. So far the life of this talented Englishman had been prosaic, a bit dull in fact, except for some trifling adventures connected with the capture of Quebec. But these years were indirectly to play a large part in the success of his explorations, for during them he acquired the invaluable habits of sobriety, careful living, keen judgment, and accurate thinking.

Between the epoch-making escapades of Drake and the year 1765, England had taken very little interest in either the western half of North America or the Pacific ocean. She had been too busy in Europe with her wars for power and in India with her struggles for an Oriental empire. After the French had evacuated Canada and Clive had wrested India from Dupleix, when British imagination was casting about for more worlds to conquer, she for the first time really saw the North Pacific coast with its limitless possibilities. And the most powerful factor which has ever motivated any nation lay behind the English venture in the Pacific—commercial interests.

A full century earlier the great Hudson's Bay company had been formed in England as a result of the activities of those unstable Frenchmen, Radisson and Groseilliers. In the succeeding hundred years this company grew from a small, unimportant commercial partnership to a mighty business empire, rivaling in power such classic trade combines as the Medici house and the East India company. Hudson's Bay company constantly expanded westward and England naturally wanted to find some route by which she could easily cross the vast regions under its sway. In 1745 Parliament offered 20,000 pounds for the discovery of the Strait of Anian, but the Great French war put a stop to any such project. In 1776 the prize offer was renewed and Cook was induced to try for it.

He made three trips into the Pacific, adding many illustrious pages to the record of the British navy. Because the first two voyages had nothing to do with the story of the Northwest coast, only an outline of each will be given.

Through the influence of powerful friends in the admiralty, Cook was commissioned to undertake a combined scientific and trading voyage into the South Pacific. An astronomical observation on the course of Venus offered a good excuse to invade Spanish waters — since England and Spain were temporarily at peace — and Cook left England in 1768, proceeding to Tahiti which he used as a base. He explored extensively about New Zealand and Australia and introduced a limited but well-chosen variety of domestic plants and animals to the natives there. That the natives promptly killed and ate most of the breeding stock did not discourage Cook, for when he was commissioned in 1772 to make a second voyage into the South he took along more animals, doing his best to place them at a safe distance from the dwellings of the natives.

The second voyage, in search of a subcontinent in the Antarctic, failed to reveal the land mass but did add a great deal to the scientific data on the ice barrier in sub-Arctic waters. Besides, the Englishman established pleasant and profitable relationships with many of the natives on the South Sea islands; and, what is more important humanly speaking, he discovered a method for controlling and almost eliminating the scurvy. On his first voyage he had the spare sails brought out and aired and the entire ship thoroughly smoked as a preventive measure against illness; but on the second trip he chanced on a better method.

As part of his regular ship's supplies Cook had taken along a considerable quantity of wort. From this he made a watery beverage for his men. He noted the tonic effect of the drink and when signs of scurvy appeared among them he gave them a small portion of this mixture. So successful was the treatment that on the second voyage, which lasted almost three years, not one man died of scurvy. Wort should not receive all the credit though, since the natives often supplied the ship's cook with fresh fruits and vegetables which were doubtless more valuable than the other.

All manner of honors were heaped upon Cook when he returned from the second trip. He was made a post-captain and appointed a captain of Greenwich hospital, this second position giving him a comfortable income and social prestige. He was elected a Fellow of the Royal Society, which even struck off a medal in tribute to his success.[1]

Such was the background of training and tradition of Captain James Cook when he was invited to dinner by the Earl of Sand-

---

[1].—These medals were cast in at least two forms, twenty-guinea ones gold and ten-guinea ones silver. The King, Queen, and Prince of Wales; and the King of France, and Empress of Russia all received these complimentary medals. That peer of American colonial cosmopolitans, Benjamin Franklin, was also honored with one.

wich and Sir Hugh Palliser one evening shortly after his return from the South Seas. As the conversation turned to scientific exploration, both Sir Hugh and the Earl regretted that no one was available for an extensive trip into the North Pacific such as Cook had just finished in the South. They dwelt sympathetically on the hardships the captain had already endured for the sake of science and his country, adding that an appreciation of human endurance forbade their asking him to undertake a third voyage because he had already done enough and deserved a long rest at the expense of a grateful people and government.

The ruse worked. Before the evening was over Cook had volunteered to lead the North Pacific expedition, and the three friends were deep in a discussion of details.

A close scrutiny of the man who was to embark on this now famous voyage reveals some interesting traits. What were the personal qualities which achieved for this erstwhile farmer lad a place with Francis Drake and Robert Scott? At the start of this great expedition he was forty-eight years old, an excellent sailor and commander. He was a keen observer of men and events, and though of scant formal education, he would have been considered well read in any society in any age. Probably Cook's main strength, and weakness, was over-tenacity. Perseverance often shifted to plain stubbornness which sometimes got him into dangerous situations and eventually cost him his life.

Strong human sympathy and understanding seasoned his firm discipline. Cook hated harshness as a method of control but when necessary could and did inflict severe punishment. "It is well known that Cook called the naturalists 'damned disturbers of the peace' and that he more than once threatened to put them off on some island." [2] There is no evidence that he carried out the threat.

He was inquisitive but stolid, and rarely showed any symptom of romance. This lack of color in his intellectual life often throws the varied episodes of his career into tiresome patterns. He studied all phases of his work but that study was routine. He did not enter the Pacific in search of high adventure, fame, fortune, and the love of mere doing, but rather because duty demanded that he,

2.—Lauridsen, pages 137-138.

an officer in the King's service, undertake the tasks assigned him.

There was nothing of Francis Drake, or Hawkins, or even Walter Raleigh in James Cook. He was quite incapable of dreaming their dreams or partaking of their kind of adventure. If he killed a man he did it because the man interfered with a preconceived plan of action, not because he hated the fellow. If his ship dropped anchor in a tiny hill-crowned habor, it was because its waters were scientifically best suited for his ultimate purpose, not because a beloved enemy might venture by, or because the waters were sweet and cool on shore and a man might relax there and become, for the moment, less than an explorer. If he took an enemy's village or captured a chieftain, it was not for the fun of the loot or the joy of the conquest, but because the village was an essential step toward another and more important goal.

Yet few explorers have approached their voyages with greater determination to succeed and few have succeeded more consistently than Cook. Though usually unassuming and mild mannered, when he did lose his temper, he lashed out with astonishing spirit. His men respected his judgment, which was nearly always right; they trusted him, and felt secure under his command, but it is doubtful if the common deckhand on any of his ships could ever be said to have loved him in the way the Devonshire boys loved Drake or McLoughlin's voyageurs loved him.

This then was the man that the Earl of Sandwich and Sir Hugh Palliser had selected for the great voyage. Preparation was begun at once and the two ships, *Discovery* and *Resolution,* were outfitted for this third Pacific expedition. The *Discovery* was listed as three hundred tons with a crew of eighty while the *Resolution* was half again larger with a crew of more than a hundred. Cook took command of the *Resolution* and Charles Clerke of the smaller vessel.

Having already spent many months in the South Seas on his two previous voyages, the sponsors advised Cook to proceed into the Pacific as much along his old route as possible and to observe the results of his former attempts to improve the lot of the natives, as well as do a bit of trading on the side. He was to sail by way of Good Hope, New Zealand, and Otaheite to New Albion, a name generously applied to all that region between the known Spanish realms [3] and the half-known Russian aggressions to the north.

On arrival at New Albion, the two ships were to be refitted and then go north along the coast to 65°. Cook had orders not to molest the Spaniards nor any other settlers on the way, but he was secretly instructed to seize all lands for England not yet claimed by others.[4] The British were either excessively ignorant of the Spanish and Russian claims in the Pacific or they were relying on the trickery of "ignorance of the facts" to wedge a claim into the already explored coast, for of course the Spaniards and Russians had both antedated Cook's venture. It is true that Drake in his turn had preceded the Spaniards, but at the time Cook volunteered his third trip to the Pacific, Drake's work had received little if any recognition. At least such may be inferred from the secrecy attached to the land-claiming phase of Cook's instructions.

Following proper celebration,[5] the *Resolution* and *Discovery* sailed from Plymouth on July 12, 1776.[6] From first to last Cook had the enthusiastic support of Palliser and the English people.

The importance attached to Cook's trip and the nonchalance with which he was dispatched into waters controlled by Spain— a possible, and as it turned out, unofficial, ally of the revolting

---

3.—Viceroy Bucareli of New Spain received definite orders to hinder Cook as much as possible in his Pacific work, though the two countries were nominally at peace. See Chapman, page 327.

4.—Chapman, page 264.

5.—Attached to the expedition was John Ledyard, American adventurer extraordinary. The story of his life is a tale of high ideals, grand plans, human misery, and stirring adventure with highlights and shadows enough to thrill the most fantastic. Born in New England and trained for missionary work, Ledyard gave up that life for one of adventure.

He lived with the Iroquois Indians; enlisted in but was immediately discharged from the British army; went with Cook on his last voyage; deserted from a man-of-war off Long Island in 1782; returned to Europe and attempted to organize an exploring expedition to the Northwest coast of America. Failing in this, he eventually set out afoot across Northern Asia with the Pacific as his goal.

After incredible hardships he reached Lake Baikal, where he was arrested and ordered from the country. He then started to explore the interior of Africa but died at Cairo from an overdose of vitriol. Thomas Jefferson received much of the impetus which culminated in the Lewis and Clark expedition from Ledyard with whom he had talked about the Northwest while both were in Europe.

6.—The American colonies had already been in open revolt for more than a year; the Declaration of Independence had been published eight days previously. While England could not yet have known of that event, she was well aware of the revolt.

colonies—sheds some light on how casually England took the revolt in the New World. In fact, a number of influential colonists hoped to conduct the war on a high and sportsmanlike plane to avoid interruptions in the routine life of the people. Benjamin Franklin, minister extraordinary to France, issued the following instructions to Yankee captains:

> To all Captains and Commanders of armed Ships acting by Commission from the Congress in the United States of America, now in war with Great Britain.
> Gentlemen,
> A ship having been fitted out from England before the commencement of this war, to make discoveries of new countries, in unknown seas, under the conduct of that most celebrated navigator and discoverer, Captain Cook, an undertaking truly laudable in itself, as the increase of geographical knowledge facilitates the communication between distant nations, in the exchange of useful products and manufactures, and the extension of arts, whereby the common enjoyments of human life are multiplied and augmented, and science of other kinds increased, to the benefit of mankind in general.—
> This is therefore most earnestly to recommend to every one of you, that in case the said ship, which is now expected to be soon in the European seas on her return, should happen to fall into your hands, you would not consider her as an enemy, nor suffer any plunder to be made of the effects contained in her, nor obstruct her immediate return to England, by detaining her, or sending her into any other part of Europe, or to America; but that you would treat the said Captain Cook and his people with all civility and kindness, affording them, as common friends to mankind, all the assistance in your power, which they may happen to stand in need of. In so doing, you will not only gratify the generosity of your own dispositions, but there is no doubt of your obtaining the approbation of the Congress, and your other American owners.
> I have the honor to be, Gentlemen,
> Your most obedient, humble servant,
> B. FRANKLIN
> Minister Plenipotentiary
> At Passy, near Paris,
> this 10th day of March, 1779.
> from the Congress of the
> United States, at the Court
> of France.

The gentlemen in Congress could not bring themselves to be so humane in the treatment of an enemy. They not only refused to ratify Franklin's magnanimous proposal but specifically ordered the seizure of Cook and his ships if they were encountered anywhere on the high seas.

The *Resolution* and *Discovery* were not the pride of England's navy, nor was Cook England's most renowned commander, but had the home war office understood the seriousness of the American revolt, it is at least possible that they might have suggested postponement of the third Pacific venture. Instead, Cook had orders to find a strait leading from the Pacific into Hudson or Baffin bay. Still more blood and treasure were poured out to discover the undiscoverable. Yet in a way it is a mark of distinction that these explorers struggled for three centuries toward a goal they believed in.

Cook's first major port of call was Table bay, Cape of Good Hope, on October 18, 1776. As on earlier trips he took along for the Pacific natives some carefully selected breed stock—two cows, a bull, several calves, and sixteen sheep. Wary of the natives' appetites, Cook brought the animals ashore at night for grazing. The sheep he placed in a pen for safe keeping, but dogs got into the pen, scattering some of them.

At the time, the colony was under the nominal control of the Dutch, and Cook appealed to the officials for redress, but got no help. Next he established relations with some scoundrels in port who, for proper considerations, returned part of the sheep. This incident merely points up the nature of James Cook. The Dutch might claim and have complete authority over Table bay, yet the sheep were his and he would go to any length to get them back. If this could be done through usual channels, very well, but if reference to blackguards of the port were necessary, that too was all right. To this tenacious Britisher the essential thing was repossession of his property. Cook's greatest single weakness was his tendency to overestimate the value of property. Given a choice between the loss of a ship's boat and risking the life of a member of his crew, he unhesitatingly risked the life for the material thing.

Not that he was inhuman or entirely lacking in a sense of human values, he just symbolized the materialism of the Industrial Revolution which was rounding into shape. Yet he often was excessive, going to great lengths to regain trinkets. Many times in the course of his thousands of miles in the Pacific he endangered his own life and the lives of his crew by forcing the return of a hatchet, a knife, a yard of this, or a pound of that. It should be added though that he took every precaution to avoid injury to his men while regaining his property.

Despite the episode at Table bay Cook purchased several

more animals for the Pacific natives. Among his stock when he at last made ready to sail were two bulls, two stallions, two rams, two heifers, two mares, several ewes and goats, a number of rabbits, and some poultry. How British sailors must have hated the job of tending such a collection on the high seas! Nevertheless Cook's contribution to the domestic animal life of the South Pacific was notable and both the crew and commander must share the credit. The animals were to be distributed mostly in New Zealand but left elsewhere along the way, when conditions seemed suitable.

After rounding the Cape of Good Hope on November 10, Cook turned toward the South Pacific islands, where he spent a year among the islanders, renewing acquaintances with native chiefs, opening new channels for British enterprise, and distributing his livestock. This latest cargo he placed well out of reach of the natives. Occasionally he took the animals far inland, hiding them in a grassy, moist valley, hoping they might multiply before the hunters found them.

Sometimes he exacted the most binding promises from the chiefs regarding the care of an animal before releasing it into their care. This sense of responsibility in Cook reached a higher level in his humane treatment of the natives, particularly native women. So seriously did he consider the problem of relationships that he issued the following orders regulating trade with the natives:

1. To endeavour, by every fair means, to cultivate a friendship with the natives; and to treat them with all imaginable humanity.

2. A proper person or persons, will be appointed to trade with the natives for all manner of provisions, fruit and other productions of the earth; and no officer or seaman, or other person belonging to the ship, excepting such as are so appointed, shall trade, or offer to trade, for any sort of provisions, fruit, or other productions of the earth, unless they have leave so to do.

3. Every person employed on shore on any duty whatsoever, is strictly to attend to the same; and if by any neglect he loseth any of his arms, or working tools, or suffers them to be stolen, the full value thereof will be charged against his pay, according to the custom of the navy in such cases, and he shall receive such further punishment as the nature of the offense may deserve.

4. The same penalty will be inflicted on every person who is found to embezzle, trade, or offer to trade, with any part of the ship's stores, of what nature soever.

5. No sort of iron, or anything that is made of iron, or any sort of cloth, or other useful or necessary articles, are to be given in exchange for anything but provision.

J. Cook.

Regarding the treatment of native women he said:

"This conduct (seduction) of Europeans among savages, to their women, is highly blameable; as it creates a jealousy in their men, that may be attended with consequences fatal to success of the common enterprise, and to the whole body of adventurers, without advancing the private purpose of the individual or enabling him to gain the object of his wishes. I believe it has generally been found, amongst uncivilized people, that where the women are easy of access, the men are the first to offer them to strangers; and that, where this is not the case, neither the allurements of presents, nor the opportunity of privacy, will be likely to have the desired effect.

"This observation, I am sure, will hold good throughout all the ports of the South Sea, where I have been. Why then should men act so absurd a part, as to risk their own safety and that of all their companions, in pursuit of a gratification which they have no probability of obtaining." [7]

At another time Cook refused to allow his men to go ashore because venereal diseases had broken out among them and he did not wish to expose the islanders.

Satisfied that he had done all he could in the South Pacific, Cook turned north early in the spring of 1778.[8] Running a general northern direction he discovered and hastily investigated the Sandwich islands, named in honor of his friend and patron, the Earl of Sandwich. His work at the islands and along the Northwest coast received scant attention either in England or America. The contemporary Andrew Kippis, in his *Captain Cook's Voyages Around the World,* gave four hundred pages to the voyages and expeditions but a mere fifty of them concerned the third

7.—Andrew Kippis. *The Authentic and Complete Narrative of Captain Cook's Voyages Around the World,* pages 289-290.
8.—This was the winter George Washington spent at Valley Forge.

Pacific expedition, and these were quite general and rudimentary. Because the book had wide circulation in both England and the United States, it must have represented the popular conception of the captain's work.

From the Sandwich islands Cook sailed for the Northwest coast, reaching, on March 7, 1778, 41°, which is now part of Oregon. Bad weather then drove him south, where the crews named Cape Perpetua and Foulweather. Again they turned north and at 47° started searching for de Fuca's strait but soon gave this up, deciding no such strait existed.

Cook wrote, "It is in this very latitude where we now were that geographers have placed the pretended strait of Juan de Fuca. But we saw nothing like it; nor is there the least probability that ever any such thing existed." [9] Hubert Howe Bancroft argues that Cook's attitude was fortunate, for had he taken another he might have bolstered the de Fuca tale, lending strength and dignity to an untruth. But had he not been so easily discouraged, he might very conceivably have discovered the present de Fuca and explored Puget sound. Ironically, he did sight and name Cape Flattery, which guards the opening to de Fuca. He then coasted slowly along to Vancouver island where he remained at Friendly cove (Nootka) for almost a month, trading with the Indians and observing their ways.

Cook was particularly interested in the fact that the natives had beads, iron, and spoons—articles which proved they had had contact, at least indirectly, with Europeans. Yet he was loath to admit it. Kippis reasoned that the iron and beads must have come to the Pacific from the Atlantic side of the continent, and "whencesoever these articles might be derived, it was evident that they had never had any immediate intercourse with the Russians; since if that had been the case, our voyages would scarcely have found them clothed in such valuable skins as those of the sea otter." [10]

In the immediate vicinity of Friendly cove, Cook sighted bear, fox, deer, and wolves; he recorded the April thermometer readings which ranged from a low of 42° F. to a high of 60°; he investigated the fishing grounds and shrewdly remarked that

9.—Bancroft, page 170.
10.—Kippis, pages 353-354.

there was evidence that the Northwest coast often had runs of fish which might be valuable; he studied the tools and weapons of the Vancouver island Indians closely enough to note their similarity to those used by the Eskimos and Greenlanders; he saw the natives carrying dried heads and hands about, concluding that such gruesome trophies were evidence of cannibalism.[11]

Sad experience taught him that the natives were honest traders but expert thieves and that they neither feared nor were curious about the white men or their ships. It is doubly strange, considering his years of dealing with primitive people and his having spent a month trading and fraternizing with these, that he still failed to learn of a waterway into the interior.

Next to being a great explorer, James Cook was a great trader and he and his crew learned the value of a pound of iron or a pretty ribbon. Cook himself won promises from the chiefs that they would trap and save pelts for him, biding his return; but the common sailors seized the present opportunity, collecting a large quantity of furs. These they used to replace their summer blankets, later selling the furs in China for ten thousand dollars.

From Friendly cove, Cook sailed north, sighting Edgcumbe, Fairweather, and St. Elias mountains. At 60° he went ashore on Kaye's island, now Kayak, where he left a bottle and two silver twopenny pieces as evidence of his landing. Farther west he discovered the present Cook's inlet and Dutch harbor. At Prince William sound he met the Alaskan Eskimos, from whom, as already noted, he got the idea that there must have been previous overland contacts with Europeans. Actually both Cook and Clerke were wrong because these contacts had been maritime, not overland.

Of the two commanders, Clerke was occasionally keener witted. When the *Discovery* reached Shumagin islands, Clerke came into possession of a Russian note carrying two dates, 1776 and 1778. He passed it along to his commander supposing that Cook would attempt to have it translated, but Cook disregarded it. At Unalaska, Clerke received a second Russian note, delivering it also to Cook, who again let it go unheeded.

This negligence highlights one of the chronic weaknesses of the

---

11.—Alexander Begg. *History of British Columbia,* page 20.

English seaman — his reluctance to admit that other nations are likely to do anything of importance. Cook was so unimpressed with the possible value of the Russian notes that he did not even keep a copy of them. Clerke at least had thought them worthy of Cook's attention. Probably the notes were not important historically, but still Cook blundered. Ignorant of their content, he assumed a haughty, detached attitude; and though he admitted the notes indicated he had been wrong and the Russians had been ahead of him, beyond that his sense of superiority would not permit him to go. He could not conceive of the Russians' doing anything important.

Both Clerke and Cook were at fault on another score. Those were strenuous and dangerous years along the Alaska coast. With shipwreck and disaster common, the notes might have been pleas for help. Ordinary decency demanded that they at least be translated.

When Cook later came upon Ismyloff, a Russian trader, he was probably chagrined to discover how deeply the Russians had penetrated the Alaska fur trade; yet even then he really learned very little about all the Russian activity in the North Pacific.

After rounding into Bering sea, Cook continued north and on August 9, 1778, was off Cape Prince of Wales. He crossed over to the Asiatic side of the strait and then back to the American coast, after which he sailed north until the ice floe of the Arctic compelled the *Resolution* and *Discovery* to turn about at 70° 44′.

From the presence of so much ice and a careful examination of the coast north of 60° the commanders concluded that any passageway into Hudson or Baffin bays must be beyond 72°. They recrossed to the Asiatic side in September, coasting south along the shore of what is now Northern Russia, finally sailing for the Sandwich islands to spend the winter.

Neither of the leaders was quite satisfied with results so far, deciding on another trip north the following season. It was necessary then that their wintering place provide not only rest for the crews and some degree of safety and pleasure, but also repairs and provisions for the ships. The Sandwich islands filled these requirements. Although the run from Alaska to the islands is many hundreds of miles longer than from Alaska to Friendly cove—which also could have served as a wintering place—Cook considered the climate of the islands sufficiently superior to make the extra distance worth while. For many years his views were shared by virtually all explorers and traders entering northern waters.

The very strength of purpose which had carried Cook over major obstacles cost him his life. When his ships first returned to the islands, the natives had given them a hearty welcome. The crews went ashore and arranged equipment for the winter, even building a few huts. Relations with the natives continued pleasant for some time, though the English had to keep a constant watch on every movable object, no matter how trifling. The simple-minded islanders, not understanding private property, stole whatever they could. Cook and Clerke generally managed to get back the largest items by seizing an important native and holding him hostage.

As thievery increased, the natives grew careful not to be caught aboard ship at the time a sizable theft became known. This, of course, made Cook's plan less effective. Thefts and reprisals culminated on the night of February 13, 1779, when the natives stole the cutter belonging to the *Discovery*. It was missed next morning and Cook led a command of marines ashore to coax one of the chiefs aboard as a hostage. The chief and his two sons seemed willing enough to go but the boys' mother objected. During the ensuing hubbub stones were thrown and shots fired. While trying to cover the retreat of his men, Cook was knocked semi-conscious with a club and almost drowned before he could scramble to his feet and continue fighting.

In the end he lost his footing and the infuriated natives stabbed and clubbed him and tore his body to pieces. His remains were left to the indignities of the islanders, and not until several days later were part of his bones regained and buried at sea with appropriate military honors.[12]

Cook himself would likely have admitted that the cutter was not worth a human life, yet his peculiar sense of duty demanded that he risk his own life and that of members of his crew to retrieve a relatively unimportant piece of property. Nevertheless, Cook's defenders point out that the cutter was a major piece of

---

12.—This summary of events resulting in Cook's death originated with a Mr. Samwell, whose journal of the Cook voyage is extensively quoted by Andrew Kippis in his book.

irreplaceable equipment; also that the commander was involved with the "principle of the thing"; and if native thefts were unpunished, there would be no end to them. All of which is true but does not completely analyze Cook's methods of dealing with the primitive peoples he encountered in both the South and North Pacific.

The orders he had issued on relations with the natives were inadequate to deal with the thieving; they failed to provide for eliminating it. On his earlier voyages in the South Pacific, Cook had been annoyed by this stealing, yet had devised no scheme for stopping it. Rather he spent his misguided energy perfecting a plan whereby stolen goods could be recovered. This tactical blunder eventually cost several lives, both English and native. Most other English or Yankee traders to the Pacific soon learned that the only way to be even reasonably safe from the nimble fingers of the natives was by refusing to allow them aboard ship at all, or only in very limited numbers. Even under these conditions some disasters happened; occasionally whole ships passed from human knowledge.

Still, James Cook ranks high among modern navigators and explorers. He opened a vast new field of profit to traders and added much to the geographic and scientific lore of his time.

After his death Clerke took over command of the expedition, moving to the *Resolution*. Lieutenant Gore was given command of the *Discovery*. As Cook's death occurred in February, time was short before the date set to start north for a second summer off the Alaska coast, and Clerke was determined to carry out the original plans.

On this trip they continued as far as the ice fields, then turned south along the Russian coast. Clerke concluded, as had Cook the previous year, that if any passage existed from the Atlantic into the Pacific in the northern hemisphere, it was north of the southern limits of the ice floes.

The English followed the Kamchatka shore to Petropavlovsk where Clerke died. Gore took charge of returning the two ships to England. Arriving there he found the mother country in open warfare with her American colonies. Even the scientific results of the third Pacific expedition were not published for four years,[13]

13.—Snowden, volume 1, page 99.

and all attempts at further exploration were abandoned.

War is never a permanent barrier where fortunes are to be made, so now the sailors who had been with Cook and Clerke boasted how great wealth could be won in the fur trade. Had they not sold their old bed furs for ten thousand dollars? Had they not seen how eager the natives were to trade valuable furs for cheap iron? Had they not been able to buy the choicest products of the South Seas and the softest pelts of the North for a yard of ribbon or a rusty nail? The era of the maritime fur traders was about to open. That this mighty yet sordid struggle for fur was to end in the extinction of a species, would likely not have bothered Cook's common sailors, had they known. For this savage struggle against both nature and the Indians, Cook's expeditions laid the groundwork.

Organization of the fur trade along the Northwest coast was difficult because the East India and South Sea companies had charters calling for monopolies of trade in the Indies; and, in the eighteenth century, this coast was but a faraway segment of the hazy Indies. But the monopolies did not long check the coming of the fur men. Special treaty rights between the Portuguese and the Chinese threw open the port of Macao to western trade and the independent British traders soon hit upon the subterfuge of flying a Portuguese flag in order to enter the closed areas reserved for the companies with the monopolies.

19

JAMES HANNA
SAILS INTO THE NORTH PACIFIC

NOT UNTIL SIX YEARS AFTER the mutilated bones of James Cook were consigned to the waters off the Sandwich islands did another Englishman enter the North Pacific. This man was James Hanna, the year 1785.

Because company monopolies technically closed the Pacific to all independent traders, Hanna must have practiced some trickery to escape the penalties of trading in those seas. He left Macao in April of 1785, perhaps flying the Portuguese flag, though, according to Bancroft,[1] he may have been licensed under the British East India company. His boat was only sixty tons, and manned by a small crew of twenty.

From Macao to Nootka the voyage was uneventful, the Englishmen arriving in August and receiving a cool welcome from the natives. Though the Pacific coast Indians had not yet become hostile to all white men, they were increasingly suspicious. With much labor and some luck, Hanna managed to trade the Indians out of 560 sea otter skins, worth around twenty thousand dollars, hardly enough to make the voyage a success but sufficient to invite plans for a larger one.

Hanna did some exploring during the summer months, naming Sea Otter harbor and St. Patrick bay (St. Joseph) before turning his brig for Macao in September. He arrived at the Portuguese port during December and immediately made preparations for a second and more pretentious voyage. Hanna outfitted a new boat, the *Sea Otter*, twice the size of his first one. By August of 1786 he was back at Nootka.

He was disappointed. He got only fifty pelts; the natives either could not or would not sell them. He tried trading along the coast, working through the rest of August and all of September. On October 1, having purchased only fifty more skins, he started for Macao. There his later wanderings are lost in a maze of Oriental commerce.

1.—Bancroft, volume 1, page 173.

COMTE DE LA PEROUSE
STARTS AROUND THE WORLD

MEN AND SHIPS crowded fast along the Northwest coast in the years following Hanna's voyages. Through the enthusiasm and imagination of those two ardent Americans, John Ledyard and John Paul Jones—who had poured many a tale into the ears of Louis XVI and his courtiers—France became interested in the Pacific. The same year that Hanna made his first trip, 1785, Louis sent Comte de La Perouse, the famous navigator, on a scientific trip around the world.

La Perouse was to pay particular attention to two phases of the Northwest coast: he was to look for the Strait of Anian and make a scientific survey of the fur trade. And he was to find the answers to such questions as: How far north did the actual Spanish settlements extend? How far south had the Russians pushed their roots? In what latitudes could the French successfully take pelts and still evade the wrath of the Spaniards to the south and the hate of the Russians to the north? How thoroughly had Cook done his work? What secrets were hidden in those stretches of coast not explored by Cook or Clerke? He was also to investigate and report any lands he thought suitable for colonization.

The French expedition enters the history of the Northwest only when the *Boussole* under La Perouse and the *Astrolabe* under M. de Langle left the Sandwich islands in the early summer of 1786, bound for the North Pacific. The two ships arrived off the Alaska coast, June 23. Though the Frenchman's explorations on the American coast were generally unimportant, he did make several more accurate determinations of latitude and longitude than had previously been made. He spent six weeks on the coast below St. Elias in the vicinity of the Queen Charlotte islands, mostly at Port des Francais, 58° 37'.

La Perouse suspected that the coast north of 48° is almost a continuous chain of islands but neither he nor M. de Langle attempted to test their theories. At first, such a lack of initiative in leaders of a scientific expedition seems inexcusable. On the other hand, science had not yet reached the stage where minute investigations precede conclusions. It is conceivable that had the Frenchmen made such careful examinings, they might have been criticized by their contemporaries for wasting valuable time.

On September 6 the two ships were off 42°. Eight days later they reached Monterey, where they were cordially received by the Spaniards.[1] News that the Russians had several posts far to the north must have irked the gentlemen at Monterey.

Though casual in his search for openings along the coasts he visited, La Perouse was a shrewd observer of what he saw, sometimes looking way beyond the present and interpreting men's actions in terms of their final values. He praised the sincerity and patience of the Spaniards as missionaries, at the same time indicting their system on the ground that in their concern for native souls they too often overlooked the temporal bodies. Such an analysis of the Spanish *reduccions,* or mission villages, was quite accurate.

La Perouse and de Langle next sailed for the Orient, reaching Japan and turning north to Kamchatka. There the Frenchmen landed their journals, dispatching them overland across Siberia to Paris. They then started for New Zealand, Cape of Good Hope, and home. The long journey home was never completed. They reached New Zealand but somewhere out on the South Pacific both ships were lost and nothing has ever been heard of the fate of either ships or crews.

Unimportant in themselves, the La Perouse and de Langle voyages do represent one more step in the conquest of the Pacific.

1.—It is interesting to note the increased speed with which voyages were being made up and down the coast from Mexico to Alaska. Instead of the weary weeks spent by the Spaniards of the seventeenth century in fighting storms, scurvy, and mutiny, Europeans of the eighteenth century were sailing along the same coast with relative ease and without loss of life.

The advent of new types of sailing ships in the next century was to cut the time still more and bring the Northwest coast into the pale of civilization.

JAMES STRANGE GOES TO NOOTKA

BETWEEN THE FIRST AND SECOND VOYAGES of Captain Hanna another Englishman, Captain James Strange, sailed to Nootka at the request of the East India company, now interested in expanding its activities. Strange was fitted at Bombay with two ships, the *Captain Cook* and the *Experiment*. He reached Nootka in June of 1786, where he collected six hundred sea otter skins. Maybe this is why Hanna had such a hard time gathering them on his second trip. Anyhow, the natives admitted to Strange that they had been saving them for someone, presumably Hanna.

Here is a small but amusing discrepancy. Bancroft says that Strange would have got more pelts except that the natives were holding them for Hanna.[1] Yet when Hanna arrived he could get only fifty hides from Nootka and another fifty elsewhere along the coast. Perhaps Hanna had done something on his first voyage which induced the natives—in spite of their explanation to Strange—to withhold their pelts from him when he finally came, either that or they actually had only the fifty and had really sold their main supply to Strange, holding back the smaller number merely to appease any possible anger of Hanna's.

Of course Bancroft's figures might be wrong but what seems more likely is that the natives simply sold their supplies to the earliest comers making no excuse at all for not selling more or offering the first excuse occurring to them. Before many years had passed the Nootka Indians and all their brethren north and south were to become dangerous and treacherous traders against whom the white man had to be constantly on guard.

1.—Bancroft, page 178.

JOHN MEARES, ENGLISH TRADER

FROM 1785 TO 1795 NOOTKA WAS A BUSY LITTLE PORT.*¹* Through common consent it had become the center of all activity on the Northwest coast south of the Russian posts. To its harbors came ships from the Orient, the Sandwich islands and from Mexico.

More and more the world back home realized the potential importance of the Pacific, and that realization sent increasing numbers of traders to Nootka to take out a cargo of furs and lay further claims and plans for even larger operations. Of these the English and Spanish were the most important, but the day was not distant when the Russian and the Boston ships would use Nootka as their terminus. Then the struggle for possession would begin in earnest. Meanwhile there seemed to be pelts for everyone so little open friction occurred. The season from 1785 to 1787—it often took almost two years to complete a voyage from home port to home port—saw several English ships at Nootka. One of the most colorful and significant of these English traders was Captain Meares. Schooled in

---

1.—This was also a vital period on the Atlantic coast. The Articles of Confederation, that pitiable attempt to have a government without either executive or judiciary, had come into being in 1781 and by 1785 was well on the way to collapse. The people were first amazed, then infuriated, as the economic responsibilities attendant on maintaining an independent government began to affect their mode of living. An important western exodus resulted.

This movement in turn brought about the passage of the Ordinance of 1787. That same year the Ohio company organized the town of Marietta and Daniel Shays made his abortive attempt to avoid the new taxes.

Of greater importance than any of these events was the meeting of the Constitutional convention at Philadelphia from May to September, 1787. The adoption of the Constitution was followed by a strenuous nine months' campaign for ratification.

Washington took office on April 30, 1789, and from then until well into his second term he was harassed by such problems as have rarely fallen to an executive—foreign relations, domestic and foreign debts, party bickerings, neutrality proclamations, the federal judiciary appointments, the Whiskey rebellion, Jay's treaty, the Pinckney treaty, and scores of less important matters, each one of which would, as he knew, set a precedent for succeeding presidents.

the difficult Oriental trade, he considered the American Indian an easy prey for his blandishments, and he never permitted his conscience to interfere with a good business deal. Harsh and unyielding in ordinary transactions, when pressed he became an unscrupulous tycoon, willing to bribe, rob, or compromise to achieve a goal. Never in his career did he show any sense of final values nor carry on consistently fair business with the natives or the buying public.

Still he was no erratic plunger, making a fortune one day by dishonest trading and losing it the next by foolish investment. If he was ruthless, he was also shrewd, resourceful, and bold. He neither asked nor gave quarter and would have accepted both bankruptcy and eclipse as new challenges. Such a man easily fits into a competitive society, and Meares left his brave mark in the great annals of maritime fur trade.

He and his first partner, Captain Tipping, were especially favored, having none other than Sir John MacPherson, governor general of India, as patron and co-organizer. Theirs was a business trip to collect furs and ginseng for sale into China. Having outfitted their ships at Bengal, they left in March of 1786, with Meares aboard the *Nootka* and Tipping in command of the *Sea Otter*. They made arrangements to meet at Prince William sound after trading throughout the season along the coast. When Meares landed there in September, he found that both Tipping and the *Otter* had been lost off Kamchatka, en route to the Orient.

This put Meares in complete control of the expedition. He decided to remain on Prince William sound all winter, not leaving for China until the autumn of 1787. That winter on the sound was bitter, more than half of his crew dying from exposure and scurvy. The rest were still sick on their return to China.

In the Orient, Meares had to readjust the technicalities of his sailing papers. He disposed of the *Nootka* and in January, in company with several merchants in the East, fitted out the *Felice* and *Iphigenia*. He himself took charge of the *Felice*, turning the other over to Mr. William Douglas. Meares made this second voyage under the Portuguese flag, though many months later he claimed he had operated under English colors. He could not really defend such a position, for at one time he gave the Spaniard, Martinez, bills of sale drawn on his reputed Portuguese owners; and his own orders called for the capture, if possible, of any Spanish, English, or Russian ships which might interefere with his own trade. That such a course could mean an attack on the ships of his own country, or more especially on those of his benefactor, Sir John MacPherson, did not bother him.

The two vessels left Macao for this second trip to the Northwest coast in January, reaching Nootka in May, 1788.[2] In June Douglas went on to Cook's river with the *Iphigenia,* while Meares secured land for a post from Maquilla, the local chieftain. So far no permanent settlements had been made north of San Francisco or south of Prince William sound, nor does Meares seem to have considered his buildings other than temporary when erecting them. In 1790 he took a more definite stand when he demanded damages for them from the Spaniards. Anyhow, Meares hoisted the English flag, built breastworks, and mounted a three-pounder to defend his holdings. That he was within foreign territory did not deter him.

Having established himself, he began trading operations, the *Iphigenia* going north, the *Felice* south. Later, both Meares and Douglas claimed to have had exclusive trading agreements with the natives.

Before starting on his summer trading cruise, Meares left a force of men at Nootka to build a small boat. This was named *Northwest America* and, with appropriate ceremonies, was launched on September 19, 1788. The first ship built by Europeans on the Northwest coast, it was to play an important part in the quarrel between Meares and the Spaniards.

After ordering the *Iphigenia* and *Northwest America* to winter in the Sandwich islands, Meares left for China, September 23, with the *Felice* and the season's spoils. Arriving in the Orient in December, Meares sold both the furs and the *Felice.* He then made a third financial adjustment—he interested several Englishmen in a loosely-drawn stock company. This organization purchased the *Argonaut,* though already owning two ships. They then

---

2.—During these voyages the United States was rapidly taking shape; Georgia, Connecticut, Massachusetts, New Hampshire, and Maryland all ratified the Federal Constitution about that time.

sent the *Argonaut* and the *Prince of Wales,* under James Colnett, to Nootka.

Meares now entered the fur trade in earnest. When Colnett left the East in the spring of 1789, he took three years' supplies with him. Besides his regular crew he had several Chinamen aboard. This was the beginning of the Oriental labor problem in America.

Meanwhile the *Iphigenia* and *Northwest America* had again left the Sandwich islands, landing at Nootka, April 24, 1789. The vessels were barely able to stay afloat and their supplies were exhausted.[3] At Nootka they found two American ships, the *Columbia* and *Washington* under Robert Gray and John Kendrick. Relations were cordial, and the *Northwest* was dispatched northward for routine pelt collection.

On May 6 a new unrest entered the Nootka trade. Don Stephen Joseph Martinez with the *Princessa* of twenty-six guns arrived from San Blas.[4] Later more Spanish ships came. Martinez had been sent north as a reaction to the publication of Cook's journals and also as a result of La Perouse's report that the Russians had invaded the Northwest territory.[5] On investigation, Martinez found at least 250 Russians trading along the Alaska coast.[6]

From May 6 to 14, Douglas and Martinez seemed friendly, the *Iphigenia's* supplies being supplemented by Martinez as well as by Gray and Kendrick; but, suddenly, on the fourteenth the Spaniards seized both Douglas and the ship. Just what Martinez' motives were has never been clear. After Cook's journal's appeared, Viceroy Florez sent Martinez and Gonzalo Haro north to get information and establish a permanent colony. Having accomplished nothing, the party was sent back the next year, arriving on May 6, 1789.

Though the Martinez-Haro orders were to take positive steps against the Russians, quite likely neither commander cared to distinguish between a Russian settlement and an English or Portuguese trader. Lacking real authority for issuing these or-

---

3.—Snowden, volume 1, page 117.
4.—Less than a week earlier, April 30, George Washington had finally been inaugurated as first President of the United States.
5.—Bancroft. *History of the Northwest Coast,* page 184.
6.—Snowden, volume 1, page 136.

ders, Florez hastily dispatched a letter to the King for necessary sanction. Before this arrived, Revilla-Gigedo relieved Florez of his office and the direction of the later phases of the Nootka affair. It was reasonable for Martinez to consider such trips into the North a mild sort of banishment. Perhaps he decided to wrest what fortune he could out of the voyage and chose the *Iphigenia* as a likely prize.

In his memorial to the British government, Meares states that Douglas claimed Martinez pressured him to sign a document which supposedly reported that Martinez had aided Douglas in every possible way but which actually demanded the amount of the vessel's value, should the Spanish viceroy rule the *Iphigenia* a lawful prize. Such tactics indicate that Martinez doubted the legality of his act. At first, Douglas indignantly refused to sign but, becoming better aware of his position, he later signed the demand note. He was freed and returned to his ship where he found new trouble. He asserted that during his absence the Spanish looted the ship of everything valuable. Yet his very satisfactory trading trip north after his release suggests that the *Iphigenia* was not really seriously damaged.

All this time another intrigue was hatching. Martinez had set his heart on acquiring the *Northwest America* as well as the *Iphigenia,* and Douglas agreed to "sell" her for four hundred dollars, in return for which favor Douglas was to be permitted to proceed to China with the *Iphigenia,* pending settlement by the viceroy of the question as to whether she was a lawful prize.

Martinez must have enjoyed his advantage. Douglas had tacitly agreed to the "prize" status of the *Iphigenia* by signing a demand note to be used in lieu of the ship itself should the viceroy declare the seizure lawful, and he had agreed to a "bill of sale" for the smaller vessel in return for the seemingly unimportant concession of taking the *Iphigenia* to China.

Martinez did not know Douglas. The Englishman had spent too many years aboard trading vessels to be easily duped, but he played his own game. Instead of sailing immediately as was expected, he quietly waited about, hoping the *Northwest* would return to Nootka. He had gone through the motions of issuing orders for her sale and delivery to Martinez in accordance with the Spaniard's wishes but he had also warned the ship of her danger. Suddenly Douglas hoisted canvas and sailed away without actually waiting for the return of the *Northwest*. When out of sight of Nootka, he turned his ship north, proceeding to trade in leisurely fashion but always keeping a sharp lookout for the other ship. He planned to remove the men and supplies of the *Northwest* to the *Iphigenia,* then burn the smaller vessel and sail merrily on to China. Martinez would be left with bills of sale—one of which was undoubtedly fake—for both vessels. The plan was shrewd yet it failed because he missed Mr. Funter in command of the *Northwest*. Nevertheless the Englishman did collect a considerable cargo of furs.

During the weeks Douglas was cruising about the Northwest coast he entered Dixon strait, renaming it after himself. Posterity has disregarded the new name. With a successful summer's trade behind him, Douglas sailed early in the autumn to the Sandwich islands, acquired some iron and fresh supplies, and went on to Macao in October.

In the eighteenth century the Chinese did not take Europeans to their hearts—even as they do not in the twentieth—but they did have an agreement whereby the Portuguese could conduct business within a restricted area at Macao. The Chinese collected a port tax which the Portuguese either paid and grumbled about, or paid and passed on to the consumer, as their successors have learned to do. Because of these restrictions, Meares' associates conceived the idea of taking into the company as a nominal partner Juan Cawalho, a Portuguese, whose nationality was expected to protect the entire English company not only from paying the regular port fees, but also allow them to trade freely in the single Oriental port open to European commerce.

All went well until the governor at Macao, a friend of Cawalho's, died, leaving the bankrupt Cawalho to explain to the suspicious Chinese investigators and worried creditors how so many "Portuguese" gentlemen had English names, spoke the English language, used British boats, and traded in British coin. Cawalho's answers were so unconvincing that the creditors demanded a share of the *Iphigenia* as payment on the debts owed them. The officials calmly took matters into their own hands and ordered the *Iphigenia* to get out—first, however, making sure to collect all the port fees due.

Meanwhile the *Northwest America* had been thrown at the mercy of the Spaniards, for Mr. Funter had missed the warning and sailed into the trap in June. Martinez promptly seized his ship. About the same time he inconsistently permitted the Meares ship, *Princess Royal,* to enter and depart unmolested. He took the *Northwest* on a twenty-day trading trip and shortly after his return Mr. Colnett and the *Argonaut* arrived off the sound. A Mr. Barnett, under arrest from the *Northwest America,* managed to warn Colnett not to enter the harbor lest he be seized by Martinez. The Spanish commander also saw Colnett and so successfully counteracted the Barnett warning that Colnett brought the *Argonaut* into port, where she was promptly captured and Colnett and his crew arrested. Colnett then accused Martinez of treachery, which Martinez countered by claiming that Colnett lost his temper, cursed him roundly, and demanded the right to build a fort at Nootka.

Following his arrest Colnett became mentally deranged and was sent to San Blas. The *Argonaut* was appropriated and used by the Spaniards. Later Viceroy Revilla-Gigedo ordered the crew paid full Spanish wages for the time of their detention, and the ship released to the English.

Spanish-American relations continued cordial. The *Columbia* was about to sail for the Orient to dispose of the cargo of furs it acquired during the summer. This gave Martinez an opportunity to rid himself of the English crew aboard the *Northwest.* Loading his prisoners on board the *Columbia* when she headed for the East, Martinez was free to take his prizes south to San Blas. This he did but he did not return the Chinese to their native land. He attached them, much as if they were cattle, to be used as laborers in the mines.

The positions of both Martinez and Meares were vulnerable. Though acting under orders, Martinez had certainly seized property of another national to which he had very doubtful right and had acted in a high-handed manner characterized by intrigues, falsehoods, and trickeries. Meares' company had deliberately attempted to carry on a trade not only within the areas reserved to the India company but also within a region generally agreed to be either Spanish or Russian domain. In addition, at least one, and probably more, of their ships had illegally sailed under Portuguese colors, a circumstance which even in those early days of international law was a serious breach of maritime custom. Still, England did have sound right to the coast, and had Meares been more consistent in claiming English citizenship, his position would have been strong.

Despite this, Meares as head of the company put in a claim for damages against Spain.[7] That nation immediately and brusquely denied his accusations. Both countries prepared for war, during which time there was a long, bitter diplomatic tangle. Spain offered to arbitrate, England refused. An agreement was finally reached, not because one had convinced the other, but because both nations were suddenly confronted with the French Revolution, far more dangerous to their national safeties than Nootka could ever be. Each promised return of property, signing a preliminary agreement in 1790 and a final treaty in 1795. Terms permitted both nations to trade freely at Nootka, though England was given ownership of the islands along the coast. Meares had asked for 153,000 Spanish dollars as damages from Spain, but was granted 210,000, certainly liberal reparation for any real or fancied losses.

Strangely, both nations withdrew from Nootka almost at once, leaving the once-active little bay to lapse into its customary oblivion. In the twentieth century, Nootka civilization is almost as unknown as it was before Meares and Martinez pushed their respective nations to the verge of war because of it.

Before abandoning Nootka, England drew up a grandiose plan for controlling the New World. Her statesmen and politicians, fired by imperialism, visioned a gigantic British nation extending from Tierra del Fuego to Cape Barrow, save for Brazil and the eastern half of the Mississippi basin. Spain was to be erased from the New World as ruthlessly as France had been a half century earlier, and the Union Jack was to fly undisputed over ten thousand continuous miles of terrain. It was a magnificent dream, even considering the injustice which any such program entailed, and its fruition would probably have brought no more misery to the lives of the millions below the

7.—The outline of the Nootka case to this point has been taken in general from that given by Meares himself when he presented his claim to the British government, April 30, 1790. Despite many exaggerations and evasions, his story in the main seems sound.

Rio Grande than Spanish or home rule. But all such plans were swept aside when the Bastille fell before frenzied mobs and the guillotine began its bloody work. England's dream of a western world empire was dissipated in the havoc of the French Revolution.

Meares' company seems merely a group of ingenious trouble makers, content to profit from the mistakes of others. This is not quite true. John Meares was probably sincere in believing himself to be an amateur explorer, and while his achievements in that field are of no great importance, they do show he had a few instincts beyond the commercial.

On June 11 he and Douglas had taken the *Felice* and *Iphigenia* out of Nootka. Douglas went north to trade and explore, on his return becoming involved in the quarrel with Martinez. Meares coasted southward into Clayoquot sound, which he named Port Cox. He claimed to have discovered and named the Strait of Juan de Fuca on June 29,[8] and to have taken possession in the name of England, at the same time ordering his mate Duffin up that waterway at least a hundred miles. It is amusing that Meares himself spoke of de Fuca as the "original discoverer" and was quite aware of Barclay's voyage which had preceded his own.[9] Furthermore, Duffin did not mention in his records the formalities of taking possession and even admitted that he had never gone more than ten miles up the strait. Such superficial exploring backing up such bold claims have greatly lessened the stature of John Meares.

Continuing southward, Meares named Mt. Olympus on the Fourth of July, and two days later was off the River St. Roc (the Columbia). From earlier maps he knew that the great river should be at that point, but he would not credit the signs of the river and called the estuary Deception bay. It was well named. Meares bitingly referred to the imaginations of earlier men who reported the existence of the St. Roc. The great white breakers completely across the mouth of the Columbia had fooled better explorers than Meares but when a really great explorer ob-

---

8.—The State of Virginia had ratified the new United States Constitution four days previously, to become the tenth state doing so.

9.—Bancroft, volume 1, page 197.

served those same unmistakable signs of a large river, he solved the secret of the Columbia.[10]

By July 26,[11] Meares was back at Nootka where he found a mutiny under way. He quelled this and, August 8, left on another trading excursion. Afterwards, as already mentioned, he took the *Felice* to Macao.

Even in his commercial dealings Meares often did precious little, his commanders frequently carrying most of the responsibility. Besides, he was unsuccessful in most of his relations with the natives. At the time he built his post on the land he secured from the Indians, he made no pretense of building permanently, yet when he came to recite his damage claims he let on that both the Indians and his own party knew the constructions were to be permanent. Bancroft [12] shows that he tried to make excessive profits from the fur trade by forcefully seizing the pelts and making open enemies of people already unfriendly.

Such a policy was tragically shortsighted and doubly foolish considering the fact that repeated voyages to the vicinity of Nootka had actually induced the Indians to work a little on rare occasions in return for a knife or bit of finery. Had Meares possessed Cook's insight, he would have measured the natives' love for iron and ribbons in direct relation to their willingness to work, and by so doing might eventually have induced them to trap systematically and turn their catch over to him for small sums of trade goods. Later the Hudson's Bay company used this very policy, but Meares was too greedy for immediate gain to wait for future profit.

Though he organized many voyages into the outposts of the New World and added some geographical knowledge to the world's store, John Meares was essentially a weak character, ever willing to gain his ends by intrigue or trickery, graft or force. He left an indelible mark on Pacific history, but not an heroic one.

10.—Years later when England and the United States entered their long negotiations over the ownership of *Old Oregon,* one of the British claims rested on "Meares' discovery of the Columbia." To such lengths will diplomacy go for the sake of "national honor." See Snowden, volume 1, page 115.

11.—New York ratified the United States Constitution the same day.

12.—Bancroft, page 190.

LESSER ENGLISH TRADERS

WHILE JOHN MEARES AND HIS SUNDRY CAPTAINS were trading, quarreling, and claiming damages, several other English fur traders sailed into the same waters.

Evidently Captain James Strange, mentioned earlier, discovered and named Queen Charlotte sound.[1] Two others, Portlock and Dixon, carried out a more pretentious venture. Their activities began shortly after those of Captains Hanna and Strange but extended into the year 1787, after the earlier two had dropped out of the race.

Lieutenant Nathaniel Portlock and Captain George Dixon, both of the British Royal navy and ex-subordinates of Cook, left England in 1785 under a license granted by the King George's Sound company, with authority to monopolize the direct trade between the Northwest coast and China and to found whatever colonies would best suit them. Their two ships, the *King George* and the *Queen Charlotte*, safely arrived at the Sandwich islands and hove to for a rest. Then they made a run directly to Cook's river, Alaska, reaching there in July of 1786. Because they had been granted a monopoly in these waters, Portlock and Dixon were disappointed to find the Russians already established.[2] The Englishmen traded the best they could. From September 17 to 28 they worked along the coast from 55° north to Nootka, where they intended to spend the winter. This was something new because traders usually went to the Sandwich group for the winter. As it turned out, Portlock and Dixon did retire to the islands, finding the weather too bad to remain at Nootka.

Hoping to escape rival traders, they sailed in March to

1.—Bancroft, page 178.
2.—Possibly the long voyage to Cook's river under the delusion that they would have free rein there might have been avoided had Captain Cook taken seriously the two Russian notes passed to him by Clerke. These notes may have held information regarding trading privileges north of Nootka.

Prince William sound, but John Meares was already there. It
will be recalled that Meares had wintered on the sound on his
first trip into the north. Half his crew had died from exposure
and the scurvy and the other half was sick. Portlock and Dixon
gave him some assistance but how much is not known. In any
case, Meares accused his countrymen of being niggardly in their
help, and they heatedly replied that they had done all they
could with their meager resources. Since Meares' rivals had a
better reputation for truthfulness, this should be remembered
when choosing sides.

At Prince William sound Lieutenant Portlock and Captain
Dixon separated, Dixon coasting east and south with the *Queen
Charlotte* to Norfolk sound, then at the end of July to the
Queen Charlotte islands, which he named. He also designated
the strait which bears his name. From Captain Barclay he
learned that no furs were to be had at Nootka.

Dixon had already collected 1821 sea otter skins before he
left the North and sailed for Canton. In the Orient he rejoined
Portlock, who had accumulated more than seven hundred skins
in Alaska. The two commanders sold their combined catch for
about $55,000. This price, however, did not represent great
profit because the cost of outfitting two ships was so high. The
first traders to take such a cargo of pelts to China would have
received a rich reward, but succeeding seasons had dumped
more and more furs on the Oriental market until by the time
Portlock and Dixon arrived, it was glutted. Other traders from
the Northwest had collected almost 2500 more skins, causing
prices to drop to a small fraction of what they had been.

While Portlock and Dixon scurried along the coast searching
for a fortune, Captain Barclay and his wife—the first white
woman on the Northwest coast—had left Ostend aboard the
Imperial Eagle, flying the house flag of the Austrian East
India company. Barclay arrived off de Fuca shortly before
Meares and re-discovered the entrance to the strait, giving the
world positive assurance that the waterway really existed.[3]
Though Barclay[4] did not attempt to explore de Fuca, it certainly adds nothing to the brightness of John Meares' name

3.—Snowden, page 107.
4.—Sometimes spelled *Barkley*.

that, when he finally reached de Fuca he not only claimed to have discovered it but also refused to acknowledge Barclay's work. And he surely knew of this inasmuch as Barclay himself had told him of the discovery when the two captains met at Canton in December of 1787.[5]

South of what is now called Cape Flattery the men aboard the *Imperial Eagle* sighted a river which interested them and they ordered the ship's boat ashore to investigate. The spot has been identified with the modern Hoh river, near whose mouth is Destruction island, which received its ominous name because the boatload of men sent to shore by Barclay fell into the hands of the natives. All were murdered as the crew of Heceta's ship had been twelve years before.

Gradually seamen were mapping the maze of islands, headlands, bays, inlets, and straits that make up the Northwest coast beyond 47°. Barclay explored the sound on Vancouver island which bears his name, and in a few more years no maritime secrets were left along those shores. Explorers next turned to the secrets of the interior. But before the epic of the overland explorers took over, there was to be a last attempt by the Spaniards to control the field, and both England and the United States were to write major chapters in the story of the maritime fur trade.

5.—Frontiers of the New World were being invaded from all sides. While Captains Barclay, Portlock, and Dixon exploited the Northwest coast, Congress, acting under authority of the Articles of Confederation, devised the Northwest ordinance for the control of the "Northwest" between the Mississippi and Ohio rivers.

South part of Cape Flattery showing Skagway Rocks and Fuca's Pillar to the right.

24

SPAIN'S LAST TRY FOR POWER

AFTER THE NOOTKA CONTROVERSY, Conde de Revilla-Gigedo succeeded Flores as viceroy. Waiting for no settlement from either Spanish or English foreign offices, the new viceroy determined to occupy Nootka permanently. Immediately he dispatched into the North, Lieutenant Francisco Elisa with the *Conception,* Lieutenant Salvador Fidalgo with the *San Carlos,* and Alferez Manuel Quimper with the *Princesa Real.* All had instructions to explore, erect forts, get along with the natives, and prevent the encroachments of foreigners. On the other hand, they were not to molest traders or attempt to dislodge the Russians.

The fleet left San Blas on February 3, 1790, sailing into northern waters without mishap on April 5.[1] Because of unfavorable winds Elisa did not make a complete study north of Nootka but he did carefully investigate the region about Clayoquot sound and the channels and islands of the Gulf of Georgia. By August the scurvy had become so bad that he turned the *Conception* back to Nootka, doing little more that season.

Early the following May, Fidalgo went north to Prince William sound and Cook's river. Heavy storms barring his return to Nootka, he sailed on to San Blas, November 14.

Quimper had been busy during the late spring and summer exploring de Fuca's waterway as far as the present Victoria. He discovered the Canal de Lopez de Haro and Sequim bay to the south. He surveyed Port Discovery, was first to mention Deception pass, and on August 1 took formal possession of Neah bay on the southern side of de Fuca, east of Flattery. Quimper might have done even more important work had he not been driven south by a storm. The *Princesa* entered Monterey, September 2, and three months later both Quimper and Fidalgo

1.—On the twenty-ninth of May, Rhode Island ratified the Federal Constitution, the last state to do so.

were back in San Blas.[2] Fidalgo was sent north again the next year to found a permanent settlement at Neah Bay.

Final terms in the Nootka dispute not being in force until 1795, the Spaniards meantime made a show of strength by building at Neah bay, across de Fuca and south of Nootka. But they abandoned this early settlement the first year; the era of permanent settlement was to wait almost half a century.

Spanish power in the New World had just about run its course. A generation more and the Spanish flag would be hauled down from staffs over Mexico City. Even as the ministers of Spain and England haggled over the Nootka affair, these minor Spanish and English traders and explorers were giving way to two major ones—George Vancouver and Robert Gray.

2.—Significant events had been happening along the Atlantic during this period. On February 18, 1791, Vermont entered the Union; General St. Clair was defeated by the Indians; Alexander Hamilton established the First National bank, levied an excise tax on whiskey, and spent his remaining energy pleading for assumption by the national government of the state debts incurred in the war against England.

25

GEORGE VANCOUVER MAPS
THE NORTHWEST COAST

OF THE LAST TWO MAJOR EXPLORERS on the Northwest coast, George Vancouver was greater, Robert Gray being great by chance, Vancouver by design.

Vancouver was no haphazard adventurer or uncouth fur trader, stumbling on a geographic mystery and solving it by good luck and the will of the gods. From early boyhood he was trained to think clearly, to work hard, and to consider himself a gentleman fated to be great. And he never forgot this. He felt superior to most men and only inferior in station to some. Actually his childhood scarcely warranted such an elevated personal opinion. His birth is shrouded even in an age unconcerned with vital statistics. Godwin [1] says positively that Vancouver was born on June 22, 1757 at King's Lynn, Norfolk, England, but some historians give it as a year later. The inscription on his gravestone at Petersham states, "Died in the year 1798, age 40 years."

George was the youngest of five children in a family comfortably well-to-do. His father was a Tory deputy collector of customs, a position he held because he was friendly with the person to whom the customs collection had been "farmed out." Not much is known about George's mother except that her name was Bridget. Whatever influence she might have wielded over her brood was short-lived, for she died when George was eleven. The family probably had Dutch ancestry, perhaps even being van Couverdens. However, there is a Dutch town by the same name and the Anglicized family name may have originated indirectly from the town.

George had received all the formal education he was to get before he reached fifteen. At that age he went to sea on Captain

1.—Godwin. *Vancouver, a Life,* pages 1-2.

Cook's *Resolution,* and for the next quarter of a century was a sailor in the best traditions of the British navy.

What sort of young fellow was he? Did he make friends easily and permanently? Was he democratic or pompous? Such questions are answered only by a careful study of his actions. Early environment having given him an exaggerated opinion of his own worth, many an unpleasant scene during his short life resulted. He often resented imaginary infringements on his rights and dignities. His excessive pride in his uniform and rank sometimes cost him valuable subordinates, and in later years he was involved in several undignified rows, originating when some "inferior" dared oppose him.

Yet George Vancouver was far from a naval peacock, strutting about and vaunting; he was rather a conscientious commander and a capable navigator with the right to brag of his own worth—but Vancouver seldom boasted. In some ways he was a modest man. He frequently attributed wisdom and good judgment to his teacher, Captain James Cook. If he made a shrewd maneuver or a farsighted analysis, he often gave Cook credit for having laid its foundation.

Those who study Vancouver as a man over-emphasize his harshness and pride; those who write of him as an explorer permit his feats of exploration to excuse obvious character weaknesses. The ones who berate him accuse him of cold-blooded bestiality, of using cruel and unusual punishments for the slightest infractions of his orders. If a sailor fell overboard, these say that Vancouver tossed him a grating and sailed merrily on his way, deaf to the agonized cries of the drowning man. They point out that the lash was ever around Vancouver's wrist, ready to be laid on bare backs; that he had no use for or sympathy with anyone's ideas but his own, and that a broken head or dank days in the ship's dungeon were the penalties for voicing opposing views.

But, as the record of his life unfolds, many of these faults prove only half-true. He did use the lash freely yet he never exceeded the custom of his time. If he ordered two dozen lashes as punishment for the culprit stealing a hat, and only twelve for the accessory to the crime, then later ordered anyone shot who was caught stealing, it should be remembered that in his day more than two hundred offenses were punishable by death. So Vancouver was no more brutal than the average captain of his day. Trained in a harsh school and dealing with rough men, he took no chance of having his work hindered, as was Bering's, because his men wished to do the opposite of what was essential to their well being. He did sail away from a drowning man; he did leave an insubordinate deckhand stranded on the Sandwich islands; but the drowning sailor could not have been saved even if the ship had been hove to, and to be stranded on the islands was, after all, not a matter of life or death but merely a great inconvenience to be experienced in rather ideal surroundings. Actually Vancouver was capable of both harshness and kindness. His record shows a remarkably even balance.

When he joined the *Resolution* he was listed as an A. B. Seaman; but since the designation was only nominal in those days, he undoubtedly had to take all the hard knocks which any other "young Gentleman" had to encounter. He spent his first four years at sea on the quarter-deck and during the early two of these he visited New Zealand, the Society islands, the Marquesas, New Hebrides, and New Caledonia—considerable globe-trotting for a youngster. In these places he was subjected to sights and impacts which might easily have colored his life. He saw plenty of flogging and watched cannibals boil and eat human heads, yet was not seriously brutalized or coarsened. He remained an English gentleman, with something of the dreamer about him. His blue-gray eyes and delicate features suggested a worthy scion of a stable and dignified society.

He was with Cook on the captain's first and last voyages, taking a personal part in the foray which ended in his commander's death. He studied the rudiments of science and how to treat the scurvy; from Cook he learned that a good commander looks after his men. His years on the *Discovery* also taught young George an unswerving courage and steadfastness. He developed an honesty which, despite his quick temper, eventually made him a good captain and a leader of men.

George Vancouver was an unusual mixture of habit and science. Schooled in the most advanced scientific principles of navigation, at times his intense devotion to his instruments caused him to miss geographic facts easily discernible to the naked eye had he been less engrossed.[2] But this same man carefully followed most of the routine customs of his day, regardless of their values. He "smoked" the sails; he aired the powder; he dieted his men. For him it was sufficient that Cook or some other naval leader had done the same.

On October 19, 1780, he took the examination for a lieutenancy, after which he was appointed to the *Martin*. Later he was transferred aboard the *Flame* under the command of the famous Rodney, with whom he sailed for the West Indies. For another decade Vancouver was in close contact with the best of England's mariners; training, studying, and observing. On the quarter-decks and bridges of the ships stationed in the West Indies he came in contact with such men as Vashon and Whidbey, sailors whose names he never forgot.

In April of 1782, he engaged in the only serious fighting of his career, the Battle of the Saints, when Rodney met and defeated de Grasse who had just given valuable aid to Washington off Yorktown.

After the American Revolution, when England had made her peace with France, Vancouver was chosen for another exploring expedition into the South Seas, where Cook had drawn the bold outlines of the ocean lanes. As the expedition was being planned John Meares presented his memorial to parliament and the Nootka trouble made it imperative for someone to go to the Northwest coast to "receive back" the territory once held by Meares but now by the Spaniards. The English had also planned an extensive New World empire from Cape Horn to Alaska, conceiving Nootka as an important port in that scheme. George Vancouver was selected to execute the Nootka phase of the plan.

By the middle of December, 1790, Vancouver had risen to the rank of commander. The admiralty allowed him the privilege of choosing his own staff of officers and the men he named were the finest the British nation could offer. Mostly he picked men with whom he had associated in the West Indies.[3] He knew their ways and worths; they knew his. If they did not

---

2.—Godwin, page 36.

3.—All the men, including Vancouver himself, were unmarried except one. In this respect the sailor from King's Lynn followed in the footsteps of the pirate from Devonshire, Francis Drake, who always recruited his crews from the unmarried young bloods of the town.

love him as a person, they did respect him as a gentleman and seaman. Still there were clashes in the personnel. Sir Joseph Banks, a powerful figure wherever the admiralty was concerned, had caused Mr. Archibald Menzies to be appointed botanist and assistant surgeon. The commander and Menzies conflicted almost immediately. Both had keen minds, were preeminent in their fields, headstrong, and impatient of restraint. When their interests crossed, they managed to make the situation quite unpleasant for each other. On the whole, though, it was a happy crew.

Vancouver had the *Discovery* of four hundred tons as a flag ship and the new *Chatham* as an armed tender. The first was to carry a crew of a hundred and the other approximately half that number. The admiralty equipped both ships with the best supplies to be had. Because the *Chatham* was new and the admiralty did not know what type of casks would best store in her hold, they ordered that special ones be built to fit whatever peculiarities of space might exist. Everyone seemed tireless. Vancouver wrote almost endless notes, letters, requests, memorials, and just plain suggestions to the officials in charge of the ships' equipment. These granted his requests with laconic notes scratched on the backs of the letters or across the bottoms, "Ordered done. Let him know it."

Occasionally some unusual request would be temporarily held up by the footnote, "Can precedence for such a step be shown?" This was generally followed by "Ordered done." All this acquiescence was highly complementary to Vancouver, and when the expedition drifted slowly down the Thames on January 26, 1791, it was probably the best equipped outfit so far sent to the Northwest coast.

Even then Vancouver was not satisfied. Between January 26 and April 1, he continued to stock his ships with the latest scientific instruments and other likely articles. He left Falmouth on All Fools' Day, 1791. Both he and his men were to remember this day, for when the long task was finished four years later and no Strait of Anian had been found, they recalled how fate had started them out on April 1. Vancouver said, "No small portion of mirth passed amongst the seamen, in consequence of our having sailed from old England on the first of April, for the purpose of discovering a north-west passage."

In addition to his diplomatic services at Nootka and searching for the strait, Vancouver was to determine the number and nature of the settlements along the Northwest coast, and, as proved most important of all, make an accurate survey of the coast from 35° to 60° north.

Because Cook had charged the British mind with the importance of the South Sea islands, the *Discovery* proceeded by way of Cook's old route. This should have simplified the journey but the new *Chatham* was a disappointment. Because she would not sail at normal speed rates, Captain Vancouver had to wait for his tender almost every leg of the journey. The *Chatham's* weakness showed up before they put off from Falmouth, so Vancouver arranged a system of rendezvous between her and the *Discovery* should they become separated. Vancouver grumbled all the while about the erratic tender.

Sailing south from Falmouth he stopped over at Teneriffe, the Canary islands, at that time in the hands of the Spanish. The English were received with as much cordiality as could be expected, and Vancouver with some of his officers paid their respects to the governor while a small detachment of men were allowed shore liberty to visit the local grog shops. The sailors' appetites outran their judgment and on their return they got into a rough and tumble fray with the Spanish marines guarding the dock. Vancouver, with more valor than discretion, defended his crew before investigating. He was promptly thrown into the sea by a Spaniard.

International complications rose at once. The commander demanded satisfaction from the governor for the insult to a British officer and the uniform. The Spaniards quite properly felt that it was not their fault that the British seamen could not "carry their liquor" in the manner of gentlemen. Nor were they to be blamed if the English commander rushed headlong into a fight and got himself mistaken for a common seaman. With that, Vancouver had to be content. Officially, no doubt, the matter was smoothed over in polite phrases, but Vancouver received little apology from the governor. Knowing the temperament of his own crew, their love of liquor, their hatred of the Spaniards, and their tendency to swagger and brawl when drunk, he should not have given them shore leave, especially in any number. He also showed poor sportsmanship by demanding satisfaction as an officer after attempting to play the game according to deck hand rules. But he was young and impetuous and the whole Teneriffe affair is interesting only as an index to Vancouver himself.

The *Discovery* and *Chatham* were on the southwest coast of Australia, September 27, 1791. They spent a month charting those shores, avoiding shipwreck, making minor corrections on previously-drawn charts, and discovering one or two small land bodies. On October 23 they sailed for VanDieman's Land and New Zealand, then to the Society islands, where they remained until January of 1792. Vancouver carried on the good work begun by Cook but left a better impression on the natives than the other. This was particularly true later in the Sandwich islands. The natives there are recorded as feeling that Cook tried to exploit them, whereas Vancouver introduced the rudiments of a modern system of government, trying to convince the islanders that their constant trade wars—in themselves largely caused by "white" theories of commerce — would finally bring only unhappiness.

Vancouver proposed to the natives a uniform and centralized system of government which would permit all to live together in peace and plenty. The significance of such teaching is noteworthy. In that age of Rodney and Frederick the Great, war was taken for granted. Not for a century and a half were the civilized nations of the world even to dream of acquiring new markets except by conquest. When an officer in the royal navy used his time and position to further peace, it was remarkable. Of course, Vancouver could not actually have established such an ideal society on the islands no matter how hard he tried, but the fact that he tried disproves the charge that he was a brutal, soulless person, without human sympathies or understanding. It also helps explain why the islanders preferred him to Cook.

On March 16, sail was run up and the two ships headed for the coast of New Albion, reaching it a month later at 35° north latitude. Two days later they passed Mendocino and on the twenty-fifth were off the Oregon coast, fighting a great storm, and managing to hold their headway only by expert seamanship. Vancouver's immediate task was meeting Don Juan de la Bodega y Quadra at Nootka and formally receiving from him the Spanish cession involved in the Nootka settlement. The commander's pride in his rank and diplomatic mission resulted in his being unfair to Don Quadra. Vancouver regarded the other as an inferior to be "put in his place" by simply making the Spaniard wait until he, Vancouver, was quite ready to see him. Then at the meeting itself the Spaniard was to be asked for more than he would possibly give and Vancouver would then play the diplomat by refusing to accept anything since his pride had been hurt and his high mission compromised.[4] Vancouver thought such a maneuver would place Quadra on the defensive. With these plans, the commander of the *Discovery* approached Nootka leisurely, exploring as he went.

Vancouver believed he had missed nothing between Mendocino and Flattery. Actually he had missed the Columbia. His contempt for theoretical geographers, whom he called "closet philosophers," was to blame. All the signs of a great river were there: drifting logs, discolored water, feeding gulls, cross currents. Yet Vancouver disregarded these signals and theorized himself into thinking no river existed there. "The breakers extending across (the apparent opening) gave us reason to consider (it) inaccessible, and unworthy any loss of time," said Vancouver. Yet the evidence indicating a river was so apparent that a seaman aboard the *Chatham* commented, "The *Discovery* made signal we were standing into danger and we hauled out; this situation is off Cape Disappointment from whence a very extensive shoal stretches out and there was every appearance of an opening actually seen, but it was passed without appreciating the importance of the place." [5]

So plain were the signs of a great river that a common seaman noticed them, yet the commander could find no justification for "wasting time" on them. Vancouver's towering pride is the answer. He had convinced himself that Aguilar's river, the Strait of Anian, and such kindred things were but figments of over-romantic minds, mere old wives' tales. He missed the great rivers of the Northwest—in time he also missed the Fraser and Skeena

4.—Snowden, page 183 and following.
5.—A. C. Laut. *The Conquest of Our Western Empire*, page 67.

—but he amply investigated every minute indentation on Puget sound. Why was he so thorough in one place and so careless in another? His pride forbade his hunting for what he was personally convinced did not exist but drove him to feverish search when he thought it practical.

Leaving Cape Disappointment, Vancouver headed north, sighting and naming Point Grenville at 47° 22′. The next day he was at Destruction island and the historic meeting with Gray took place the following morning at 4 o'clock, April 29, 1792, just off the entrance to de Fuca. Lieutenant Puget and Mr. Menzies were sent off to interview the Yankee. When they brought back their report Vancouver remarked:

"The river Mr. Gray mentioned should from the latitude he assigned to it, have existence in the bay south of Cape Disappointment. This we passed on the forenoon of the 27th; and as I then observed, if any inlet should be found, it will be a very intricate one, and inaccessible to vessels of our burden, owing to the reefs and broken water which appeared in its neighborhood. Mr. Gray stated that he had been several days attempting to enter it, which he at length was unable to effect in consequence of a very strong outset. . . . I was thoroughly convinced, as were also most persons on board, that we could not possibly have passed any safe navigable opening, harbor or place of security for shipping on the coast, from Cape Mendocino to Classet . . . nor had we any reason to alter our opinions."

Vancouver's meeting with Robert Gray is often the *piece de resistance* in any discussion of the work of the two men. The meeting did have its dramatic qualities, though one important question is seldom considered. Just why should Vancouver have believed Gray? What reason had the well-trained, precise British officer to trust the judgment of a Yankee tramp trader? Gray had no information the other lacked, and Vancouver was already convinced that no river existed there. Vancouver may have let his pride cheat him out of a great discovery, but he cannot be blamed for refusing to put much stock in Gray's ideas and beliefs. Since some of the world's tallest tale-bearers are seamen, and tramp seamen the acme of them all, the commander of the *Discovery* quite understandably left Gray's arguments unheeded. Any indictment of the Britisher should be against his unwillingness to credit the river signs which he himself saw. As a result he threw away what might have clinched England's claim to all of Old Oregon.

At twelve o'clock, noon, on April 29, 1792, the *Discovery* was off the entrance to de Fuca and shortly thereafter began cruising eastward along the southern shore of the strait. Vancouver was now in a position to carry out his preconceived scheme for putting Don Quadra on the defensive. From a Spanish exploring party he learned that Quadra was at Nootka waiting to complete the proper formalities. He did not hurry; instead he leisurely explored what is now called Puget sound. Had the positions been reversed and Vancouver the one held up, he would have been furious. Judging by his actions at Teneriffe, he would have demanded proper and official satisfaction for such an insult to his uniform and flag. He apparently overlooked his present discourtesy to the gentleman, Quadra.

Nevertheless Vancouver did attempt to work with the Spanish exploring party; finding their methods too slow for his plans, he went ahead without them. But Godwin says, "He was not pleased by this encounter (with the exploring party) for it meant that his priority as a discoverer might be in jeopardy." [6] If that is correct, probably Vancouver's selfish pride was always foremost and scientific discovery secondary. The testimony suggests that Vancouver treated both Quadra and the exploring party as he did because he would not admit even to himself that they were his equals. Such traits are blemishes on any character, no matter how fine and thorough the work accomplished by the individual.

So all during the summer of 1792 the *Discovery* explored and Don Quadra waited as patiently as he could at Nootka.

On June 4, Vancouver took formal possession of the Strait of Juan de Fuca under the English title, Gulf of Georgia. With such care and accuracy did Vancouver keep his charts that they may be safely used to this day, with proper allowances for natural changes during the lapse of more than a century.

For the crew of the *Discovery*, one day was much like the next, except for an occasional scare when it looked as though the

---

6.—Godwin, page 71.

boats might be wrecked on some hidden rock. Vancouver remained as nearly stationary as possible at night in order to observe minutely from point to point during the day. He would then send out from the ships the exploring crews in the small boats. Altogether Vancouver discovered, or sighted, and named more than two hundred geographic places on the Northwest coast.

Mt. Baker, New Dungeness, Port Discovery, Protection island, Port Townsend, Puget sound, Mt. Rainier, Bellingham bay, Hood canal, Whidbey island, and Vashon island are but a few of the scores of names he scattered along the coast. He remembered and appropriately honored the officers of his ships, the gentlemen who had been influential in backing his ventures, his relatives, both near and distant, and familiar place names from home. He did not forget even the common sailors, naming the island of Betton in honor of one of them who had been hurt there in a brawl with the Indians. Throughout that summer fewer and fewer gaps were left in the coastline of Northwest America and Vancouver was rapidly proving to himself that there was no Strait of Anian near 49° north. Nevertheless he had missed, or was to miss within the next few months, the Columbia, the Fraser, and the Skeena rivers, any of which could have been the Northwest passage had it existed there.

Late in August the *Discovery* sailed for Nootka, where Vancouver met Quadra on the twenty-eighth, not because he was anxious to do so but because he had received word that his supply ship, the *Daedalus,* which failed to meet him at the Sandwich islands, had arrived at Nootka with much-needed replenishments.

The meeting between the commanders was unexpectedly friendly. Quadra, born in Peru and trained in the best traditions of the Spanish dons, was a thorough gentleman and Vancouver quickly fell under the spell of his charms. A lasting friendship sprang up between them.

"If one man may love another without thereby losing something of his masculinity, then Vancouver surely loved Bodega y Quadra." [7] That affection is a tribute to both—to Quadra because he so graciously forgave Vancouver's earlier treatment; to

7.—Godwin, page 77.

Vancouver because he showed that he could sometimes gauge a man on his worth, regardless of birth or station.

Though personal relations were cordial, officially Quadra and Vancouver came to no agreement. The latter demanded that all the Spanish territory north of San Francisco be turned over to him. This was patently unjust. Even if John Meares' property had been as valuable as he pretended, there could be no reason to extend territorial demands south of Juan de Fuca, for neither the British in general nor Meares in particular pretended to any great priority of rights south of 49°. And though Drake had sailed into waters north of 42°, nothing much had been done to follow up the hazy claims thus established between San Francisco and de Fuca. Even work of the English maritime fur traders was only slightly concerned south of de Fuca.

Bodega y Quadra took a more sensible viewpoint. He argued that since the entire controversy grew out of Meares' claims for a reinstatement to his property at Nootka and since neither that property nor the trading activities ever extended as far south as San Francisco, to deliver to the English the territory north of the strait would be complete restoration. Like Vancouver, he used the indefinite wording of his official orders as an excuse for demanding concessions. By day they haggled about what their instructions called for, but at dinner they got together for a pleasant meal and warm toast to each other's health. When it finally became clear that they would never agree, they sent to their respective capitals for further instructions.

Meanwhile important events only indirectly connected with the diplomatic tangle had taken place. Shortly after Vancouver's ship anchored, Maquina, one of the chiefs of the Indian tribe at Nootka, boarded her and was unceremoniously thrown overboard. The chief angrily retired twenty miles up the sound to his own camp. On September 4, at Quadra's suggestion, he and Vancouver visited Maquina as a gesture of friendship. The chief met them with great pomp and palaver. To entertain them he held dances, had the finest tribal drummers beat out barbaric rhythms, and even arranged a sham battle to amuse the two military guests.

Having pacified the native element at Nootka, Vancouver and Quadra turned again to their negotiations, but with no better success. They did agree, though, on a name for the island for which they were contending. In mutual admiration they gave it their own names—Vancouver and Quadra's island, now known simply as Vancouver island. Sentimentally, one might wish that Bodega y Quadra had received a full share of the honor due him as an explorer and gentleman.

Late in September, Quadra left Nootka, returning to New Spain to await further orders from Madrid. Vancouver sent Lieutenant Broughton to Europe with letters for further instructions, but he himself steered the *Discovery* for California and the Sandwich islands where he meant to spend the winter.[8]

Broughton's orders provided that before reporting to England he was to drop down to Disappointment bay and investigate Gray's claim to the discovery of the Columbia. Apparently Vancouver still did not take Gray's reports seriously. Had he done so, he quite likely would have looked into Gray's claims for himself. On the other hand, his pride may have prevented his taking a personal hand in a matter so unpleasant in retrospect.

Broughton safely arrived off the mouth of the Columbia and with only the expected difficulty crossed the bar to the safer waters inside. The *Chatham* proceeded up the river approximately one hundred miles, sounding and observing, and, while yet inside the bar, formally took possession of the river for England. This maneuver was in spite of, even defiance of, Robert Gray's claim a month before. Priority and rights played minor roles in Vancouver's diplomatic tangles. He had unhesitatingly laid absurd claims to Spanish lands far south of any reasonable boundary, and now his lieutenant baldly claimed for England a river which had been discovered by another nation.

Later Vancouver reportedly said, "It does not appear that Gray either saw or was ever within five leagues of its (Columbia river) entrance." [9] It may be that the home officials deliberately misquoted him for diplomatic reasons,[10] but this seems unlikely

---

8.—Year after year the traders and explorers went to the Sandwich islands for the winter instead of remaining on the Northwest coast. It would be interesting to know how much of the long journey was due to a real inability to withstand the conditions of the North and how much to the feminine charms of the island women.

Vancouver could have wintered at Nootka. His supplies had already been replenished, yet he, too, chose the islands.

9.—Laut, page 76.

10.—Same.

because the statement entirely fits Vancouver's character.

Leaving the *Chatham* to investigate the Columbia, Vancouver continued on down the coast to San Francisco, arriving there on November 14, 1792.[11] His reception was cordial. Not only was he treated as a friend, but the ship's supplies which the Spaniards furnished him both at San Francisco and later at Monterey, under the command of Quadra, were termed gifts. Vancouver himself said, "The Spanish officers with whom we had the honor of being acquainted, demanded from us the highest sentiments of esteem and gratitude. Even the common people were entitled to our good opinion and respect, as they uniformly subscribed to the exemplary conduct of their superiors, by a behaviour that was very orderly and obliging." And when Broughton and the *Chatham* finally left the Pacific coast for England, via New South Wales, Quadra gave him twelve cows and six bulls and a like number of ewes and rams to be left at the islands. Such friendliness was doubly significant considering the scarcity of livestock in the New World.

From California Vancouver sailed directly for the Sandwich islands, expecting the former hearty welcome, but conditions there had changed. Mild and peaceful as the natives were, they at last, and effectively, protested against the continual rape and plunder of the white traders. Vancouver himself had done everything he could to foster good relations between whites and natives, going so far as to return to the islands two girls who had been captured and taken to Nootka by a previous trading ship. Such an act was more unusual then than now. To be kind to such unfortunates in the eighteenth century was to be misunderstood as a weakling or worse. Drake invariably took advantage of a pretty face and enticing figure; the redoubtable Captain Cook, though not personally participating in such activities, never pretended to do more than rebuke his men after their amorous conquests, and took few preventive measures.

This practice of abduction and rape often ended in the death of the victims whose desecrated bodies were tossed overboard. So usual was this among the Russians that it seldom caused even comment. Considering the record of other commanders, it

11.—Chapman, page 405.

is not surprising that the natives looked on Vancouver as a friend.

Yet he now found life on the islands much more complicated than before. Aroused by the treatment they had received, the natives plotted to capture all European boats entering their harbors and to hold the crews for ransom. This conspiracy had so far resulted in the execution of two of the crew of the *Daedalus* when she stopped there on her way to Nootka. Vancouver, feeling he should punish the murderers if he could establish their identity, began a determined investigation. Training his guns on the natives, he ordered them to give up the murderers. Finally, two of the islanders were turned over to the English and, after a proper court-martial, were condemned and executed.[12]

These affairs consumed much of the winter but by April of 1793 the *Discovery* was back at Nootka and Vancouver was carefully exploring northward to Sitka. When the ship nosed into Portland canal, his small boat cruised approximately seven hundred miles, yet at no time was it more than sixty or seventy miles from the main waterway. Vancouver accepted no one's word. He re-explored and corrected charts as diligently as he studied unknown shore lines.

Proceeding northward, he encroached on the domains of the Russian fur companies. They retaliated by moving their activities southward. When the Spaniards protested to St. Petersburg and the Czar tried to solve the problem by organizing the independent Russian companies into the Russian American company, neither Spain nor Russia seemed aware that the real threat to their claims in the Far North was a greatly superior power represented by George Vancouver.

When the *Discovery* reached Sitka, winter storms were already in the offing. Vancouver decided to return by way of California for his third and last visit to the Sandwich islands.[13]

12.—Some authors contend that the real murderers were the chiefs and those executed but slaves detailed to pay the penalty in place of their masters. Others say that Vancouver took such pains to find the truth that no question of guilt or innocence remained.

13.—In April of 1793, Citizen Genet, envoy from revolutionary France, landed at Charleston and began stirring up wild enthusiasm among the Republicans and disgust among the Federalists.

At this time Samuel Slater was revolutionizing the textile industry of

On both former occasions when he had stopped at the islands, he had tried to convince the natives that their constant trade wars—which often resulted in the wholesale slaughter of the participants—were unwise and should be replaced by a strong central authority capable of maintaining relative peace and prosperity. The natives had attempted such an organization and now pledged at least nominal allegiance to one chieftain.

Because the island of Owyhee was peaceful and had a fairly stable government, Vancouver decided it would be a good idea to have it ceded to England, without too obvious pressure from the *Discovery's* guns. He persuaded the native chieftain to transfer his holdings to the Crown at London on February 25, 1794. But the English Parliament refused to ratify the cession, and the men from Owyhee were to be "saved" by the civilization of another branch of the Anglo-Saxon race many years later.

With the coming of spring, the *Discovery* again sailed north, this time into the very heart of the Russian fur country, for Vancouver had chosen Cook's river as the place to start his summer's activities.[14] He proved conclusively that Cook's river did not connect with any inlet from the Atlantic or Arctic.

During his weeks in the Russian fur fields, Baranof repeatedly asked Vancouver for a conference but the Britisher refused, showing no particular courtesy. He ignored the Russian's requests, at the same time arranging his sailing schedules to avoid Baranof. Toward both Quadra and Gray this arrogant attitude had been much the same. If Vancouver felt entitled to be in Alaska waters, he should have acceded to Baranof's request and defended himself; if he knew he had no right to be north of Sitka, he should have visited Baranof and defied him in person. Instead, he acted more like a member of the fo'c'sle aboard a ship flying the Jolly Roger.

During that summer Vancouver explored from the north toward those headlands which he had last seen the year before from the south. When he reached them, August 19, 1794, he completed the major English exploring act on the Northwest coast. Realizing this, he called the place Port Conclusion, remarking, "In order that the valuable crews of both vessels

New England by establishing the first cotton mill at Pawtucket, Rhode Island.
14.—On March 14, Eli Whitney had taken out his patent for the cotton gin.

on whom great hardships had fallen, and who had uniformly encountered their difficulties with unremitting exertion, might celebrate the day, that had thus terminated their labours in these regions; they were served with such additional allowance of grog as was fully sufficient to answer every purpose of festivity on the occasion."

Though self-centered, Vancouver was the shrewdest and most thorough Englishman to invade the Northwest before 1800, and he did not permit his love of his own "tight little island" to warp his judgment regarding the Northwest coast: "The serenity of the climate, the innumerable pleasing landscapes, and the abundant fertility that unassisted nature puts forth, require only to be enriched by the industry of man with villages, mansions, cottages, and other buildings, to render it the most lovely country that can be imagined; whilst the labor of the inhabitants would be amply rewarded, in the bounties which nature seems ready to bestow on cultivation."

By September the *Discovery* was back at Nootka with both crew and commander anxious to sail for home. It will be recalled that both Quadra and Vancouver had dispatched messengers to England for further instructions regarding the cessions at Nootka. Having yet received no orders, Vancouver now hastened to California where he was informed that the entire matter had been taken out of his hands and settled by the respective foreign offices under the guidance of a new commission on which he had no place. This came about naturally enough. The preliminary reports sent to Europe might easily have convinced any sane official that it was useless to expect two commanders with such divergent views as Vancouver and Quadra to settle their question so far from their sources of instructions. Consequently a new commission was formed to operate in Europe and in a meeting at Madrid it finally agreed on the following terms:

Meares was to receive 210,000 Spanish dollars as damages; both countries were to be free to use Nootka to erect any temporary buildings needed in their respective activities; no permanent buildings were to be built by either; a British officer was to go through the formality of unfurling a flag as a sign of possession, but neither country was to claim sovereignty. This agreement was duly presented at Whitehall, where it was signed February 12, 1793, and ratified on the same day by the king.[15]

So keenly did Vancouver feel slighted by the new commission that on his return to England he insisted that it be written into the record that no criticism was intended. Indeed, to remove the negotiator in the middle of the negotiation has always been considered an implied censure of his work and Vancouver seemed justified in demanding that the records be kept clear.

His release from further diplomatic duties freed him to start home. Leaving California, he followed down the coast to Valparaiso, where he put in for supplies. The English were as hospitably treated there as they had been at San Francisco or Monterey bay. They sailed from Valparaiso on December 2, 1794, and after rounding the Horn ran for St. Helena.

The entire journey back, once South America was left behind, was unpleasant. The *Discovery* badly needed repair and scurvy had broken out. Vancouver, though still in the prime years of life, had grown prematurely old. He was irascible and often unreasonable in his disciplinary actions. Poor health coupled with great responsibilities often made him a difficult companion and master. He was unwilling to share and thus lighten his burden of authority. In all the weary months in the North he only once called a junta of officers, and that was to confirm his own interpretation of the powers granted him by his commission. This was really a safety move against any adverse criticism by the admiralty. He quarreled with first one then another among his subordinates, the row with the botanist, Archibald Menzies, being the most spectacular and far reaching.

Menzies was born at Stix, Perthshire, in 1754, and received his education at the Weem parish school and Edinburgh. His interests were botanical and surgical, the latter leading him in time to be assistant surgeon in His Majesty's navy. He visited American waters, took part in the "Battle of the Saints" in 1782, and, through the influence of Sir Joseph Banks, eventually was attached to the *Discovery* as botanist.[16] That Sir Joseph was

15.—Bancroft, page 289.

16.—With surprising frequency the botanists on the various Northwest expeditions were storm centers. Cook's epithet of "damned disturbers of the peace" would have been echoed by Bering and Vancouver. One wonders what Lewis and Clark thought about the matter.

aware of the difficulties in store for Menzies, he made clear in his instructions to the botanist. Having sailed with Cook on the *Endeavor,* Sir Joseph had become acquainted with Vancouver. For the guidance of both Vancouver and Menzies he gave these directions:

"As the service which Mr. Menzies has been directed to perform is materially connected with some of the most important objects of the expedition, it is necessary that the Commanding Officer should be instructed generally to afford him on all occasions every degree of assistance in the performance of the duty which the circumstances of the expedition will admit—and particularly with respect to the following points. The Commanding Officer should be directed to accommodate Mr. Menzies with a boat for the purpose of pursuing his researches at the several places which may be visited, at all times when the necessary duties of the Ship will admit of his being spared, and to order that the crew of such Boat may assist him in carrying his heavy luggage, during his excursions on shore, and to cause Mr. Menzies to be supplied from time to time with a due proportion, both in quantity and quality, of the merchandise put on board, in order to enable him, as occasion may require, to obtain any necessary assistance from the Natives in fulfilling the objects of his Mission.

"It will also be necessary that your Lordships should direct the Captain of the *Discovery* to take on board such quantities of Water as may . . . be likely to be wanted, for the nourishment of the plants which Mr. Menzies may collect, and to supply him with the same in such proportion as may be requisite and compatible with the other necessary demands for that Article. That he is also to allow Mr. Menzies to have sole charge and custody of the plants which he may collect, and to direct that care may be taken that neither Dogs or any other animals, or property belonging to any other persons be suffered to be put into the Frame within which the plants are intended to be deposited, and that particular care may be taken, in case the glass of such Frame should from any accident be broken, that the same may immediately be repaired, and that during the time it is necessary to keep the said Frame open, for the convenience of admitting air or rain to the plants, no animals likely to do mischief to them be suffered to be loose in the ship."

In a personal note to Menzies, Sir Joseph said, "How Vancouver will behave to you is more than I can guess, unless I was to judge by his conduct towards me—which was not such as I am used to receive from persons in his situation."

Evidently Vancouver was regarded as a touchy and temperamental commander who not only needed to be restrained from undoing the work of his botanist but whose actions were generally unpredictable. So it came about that on the long, tedious run from Valparaiso to St. Helena the tension between him and Menzies resulted in the arrest of the botanist. Before the expedition had even left England, ill feeling openly flared because of a misunderstanding as to Menzies' rights in the mess. In a letter to his patron, Sir Joseph, on March 14, 1791, Menzies said:

"Sir Joseph,—I wrote to you a few days before we left Portsmouth, but said nothing relative to my mess, as I was then in hopes that Capt. Vancouver's presence might bring the business to a more favourable settlement. On the Contrary, I found he was as averse as any of the rest to submit it to the arbitration of an impartial judge acquainted with the rules of the Navy. In this situation I resolved to mess in my own cabin, but finding that the few utensils and other things necessary to be laid in for so long a voyage would lumber it up so much that the intention of giving me such a good one might be entirely destroyed, I therefore waited on Capt. Vancouver the day we left Spithead, and, situated as I was, submitted the whole business to his own decision (tho' I well knew it would fall heavy upon me unless the Treasury would bear a part).

"In consequence of this I am admitted into the gun room mess on being considered as a member of it from its first establishment, and paying an equal share towards it; that is, I paid £20 to the former mess without receiving the least indulgence for it, & £70 to the present mess before I lived a day in it, which is as equal from its first commencement and for the present supplies laid in for the voyage. As this is an imposition which I never expected I should be obliged to countenance, I must now trust my cause entirely into your hands, & hope the Treasury will allow me for that part of the expense incurred in the present mess before I joined the *Discovery*, which will amount at least to about £20, & may be included in the order for the payment of the arrears of my salary at present in the Treasury, in the same manner as the former was, without much additional trouble, to Mr. Nepean. In so doing you will greatly oblige he who has the honor to be with due respect,

Yours etc.
ARCH'D MENZIES."

Resentment persisted even after the affair of the mess had been adjusted and increased when Vancouver brusquely ordered Menzies to assume the duties of a surgeon aboard the *Discovery*. Before they rounded the Horn on the way home the feud had reached a fever peak, Vancouver seeming to delight in treating Menzies as though he had originally been appointed surgeon instead of botanist, and Menzies retaliating by acting as though being surgeon aboard Vancouver's ship were a degredation in rank. As the miserable, hot days at the equator approached, Vancouver ordered the seaman tending Menzies' specimens back to regular forecastle duty. Many of the valuable plants thus died, some that the botanist had carefully nursed throughout the voyage. Naturally Menzies complained to his commander, who accused him of "insolent and unbecoming behavior." Menzies contended that, on being approached in the matter, Vancouver "immediately flew in a rage, and his passionate behavior and abusive language on the occasion prevented any further explanation, and I was put under arrest because I would not retract expression while my grievance still remained un-redressed."

As the expedition neared the coast of Ireland, Vancouver issued written orders to Menzies to turn over all charts and notes which he had kept in pursuance of his duties. The orders were addressed to Menzies as "surgeon of the *Discovery*." Taking advantage of that, Menzies forwarded his commander the following reply:

Discovery at Sea
Sept. 12th 1795.

"Sir,—I have received your Order of this day's date, addressed to me as Surgeon of His Majesty's Sloop *Discovery;* demanding my Journals, Charts, drawings etc. of the Voyage, but I can assure you, that, in that capacity, I kept no other Journals than the Sick-book, which is ready to be delivered up if you think it necessary.

"I perfectly recollect the orders of the Lords Commissioners of the Admiralty being read on the 2d of July last, and also the conversation which I afterwards had with you, relative to the mode of conveying the Journals, Papers, Drawings etc. I have kept of the Voyage in compliance with my Original Instructions, to the Secretary of State's Office; but situated as I am at present I trust you are not insensible of the necessity which urges me to Act with more caution in this respect, I therefore beg leave to acquaint you that I do not conceive myself authorized to deliver up these Journals etc. to anyone till they are demanded of me, by the Secretary of State for the home department, agreeable to the tenor of my Instructions, of which I believe you have a copy; if not, mine is at Your perusal.

I am

    Sir,

        Your most Obedt Humble Servt

          ARCHIBALD MENZIES."

Vancouver later recommended court-martial for his botanist-surgeon but Menzies apologized for his part in the controversy and the charge was withdrawn.

While this was taking place, another and independent episode occupied some of Vancouver's time. England and Holland were at each other's throats over the age-old questions of commerce and territory. Sighting a Dutch East Indiaman, Vancouver decided to capture her, despite the fact that his crew was ill, he himself far from well, and his ship in a serious condition. After capturing his prize, Captain Vancouver sailed for England, arriving there in October, 1795.

The sea is rarely kind to its commanders and almost never so to its explorers. Though not yet forty years old, Vancouver was an old man, worn out with physical hardships and responsibility. Perhaps he had contracted tuberculosis. Whether or not that is true, certainly he was already a dying man when he retired from the navy and took a little place in Petersham to rest and write his memoirs.

Even in his few remaining years he was constantly embroiled in personal quarrels. Two months after reaching home the Spanish embassy brought serious charges against him, accusing him of having swindled the officials of New Spain while in the Pacific ports. Though the charges were entirely false, fighting them used up a large measure of his remaining vitality. At this time, too, the court-martial was still pending. On top of all this, Vancouver and William Pitt, Lord Camelford, became involved in a bitter and disgraceful personal feud. Pitt's fury was so great that Vancouver was fearful of appearing in public lest he receive physical injury. He appealed for official protection against the irate Camelford. All these affairs prevented the writing of his memoirs.

On May 18, 1789, tired Vancouver permanently laid aside both his temper and his pride, leaving his own name and the names of scores of his fellow Britishers spread along the coasts of the North Pacific.

Some may doubt the greatness of Cortez, or challenge the worth of Francis Drake, but none question the position history has given to George Vancouver. That the Northwest coast of America is today the pleasant abode of more than three million people is due in a large measure to Vancouver's accurate and minute charting of its shores. He sent his men scurrying into every inlet to draw the most detailed maps laid down by an Anglo-Saxon on a voyage of discovery. In the meager number of genuinely great explorers, George Vancouver ranks with the finest.

26

ROBERT GRAY
DISCOVERS THE COLUMBIA RIVER

GEORGE VANCOUVER was great by purpose, Robert Gray by accident. Yet few American seamen have more valid claim to honor than this virile Yankee.

Since the days of the Vikings, no seamen have been more picturesque than the Yankee skippers of the eighteenth century. Hard living and hardheaded, they quarreled, prayed, and labored to the forefront in the world's ports. Fearless for the most part, they nevertheless had high respect for Almighty Jehova and healthy regard for the Hell to which they deemed it altogether too likely they might be relegated when their battles with the New England gales and Barbary pirates were over. Viciously uncouth, they were still sincerely religious, and many a Yankee captain compelled his crew to attend Sunday services aboard ship. He might consider it his inalienable right to clout a deck hand over the head and possibly send him to eternity; but he also considered it his right, even his duty, to save that soul before dispatching it. The fresh saltiness of a Yankee captain's curses and prayers were powerful incentives to action. But his deliberate unwillingness to admit defeat smacked strongly of stubbornness.

Robert Gray belonged in such company. Though shrewd in business to the verge of sharp practice, he honestly attempted to christianize the natives whom he met. Yet he saw no ethical conflict between cheating the Indians with a piece of ribbon and at the same time preaching the gospel to them. He was the direct and positive scion of the business philosophy of his time. Not until the years immediately following World War I did America see trading practices as ruthless as those in the second half of the eighteenth and first part of the nineteenth centuries. Though the day of the great monopolistic combines had not arrived, commerce was equally unprincipled, and the Yankee traders

151

often made their great fortunes by nefarious practices. Slave trade flourished. Puritan New England furnished both the rum and ships to carry the rum to Africa. There it was used to trap the negroes so that they might be more easily shipped, by way of the horrible "middle passage," to the New World to endure slow death in the sugar or cotton fields.

Other Puritans, either from conscience or inability to finance the slave trade, took to smuggling, not because the ports were closed but because they objected to paying their share of import taxes.[1] Still others, finding both the slave trade and smuggling closed for one reason or another, seized upon the Indians of the Pacific Northwest as fair prey for their superior cunning. And the Yankees were as just in their dealings with the natives as the British, Russians, and Spanish. The Yankee talked more, so his shortcomings were more evident. Deeply imbued with democracy, he saw himself as a sort of prophet carrying the torch of human justice into the monarchic wilderness. His acts, though, too often belied his words; under the pretense of trade he tragically plundered the American Indians.

Besides being thoroughly trained in business methods of the time, Robert Gray had the advantage of several years' service in the American navy. His birth in Rhode Island in 1755, just a year before the French and Indian war broke out, precipitated him into those exciting years which culminated in the French being ousted from North America and the English from the fairest part of it. When the Revolution came, Gray, grown to manhood, determined to strike a blow for liberty. At that time an official American navy did not exist but Gray served his country as captain of a fighting ship, likely aboard a privateer.

With the close of the war he had the characteristic desire to turn a dollar quickly and excitingly. The Northwest coast was a new Eldorado for those willing to take the risks and many like Robert Gray were glad to if they could get someone to finance them.

Several Boston merchants, among them, J. Barrell, T. Brown, J. Darby, and C. Culfitch, were anxious to enter the fur trade if they could find captains. Under the circumstances this was easy. These particular merchants first became interested in

1.—A. M. Simons. *Social Forces in United States History*, pages 61-62.

the trade through the descriptions which had filtered into America from the activities of Captain Cook and the adventures of John Ledyard. As early as 1784, the *Empress of China* from New York, with Daniel Parker in command, had sailed around the Horn to Canton, the first American ship to enter Oriental waters. Parker's report quickly intrigued men looking for new routes and new markets.

As commander for their expedition, Barrell and his associates named John Kendrick, a slow, cautious ex-privateer captain of forty-five, father of six children, and without interest in the affair beyond the pay. Not that Kendrick was a dullard, but advancing years and the responsibilities of a large family made him less eager to take chances than a younger man might have been. Robert Gray was chosen to command the smaller of the vessels assigned to the voyage.

Groundwork for Gray's North Pacific venture had been carefully laid by the Spaniards and English; he had no serious geographical problems. The sea route around the Horn to Nootka was a matter of endurance, not exploration. In its main elements at least, the Russians and British had worked out the technique of gathering furs.

The two ships, the *Columbia Rediviva*, 220 tons, and the *Lady Washington*, 90 tons, were finally ready, their holds filled with approved trade goods—worthless junk and trinkets which cost the merchants virtually nothing but were supposed to return big dividends.

Though the venture was a private one, Barrell and his associates must have had some influence with government officials, for they received an official letter as a passport from George Washington,[2] another passport from the State of Massachusetts,

---

2.—President Washington's letter for Gray:

> "To all Emperors, Kings, Sovereign princes, State and Regents and to their respective officers Civil and military, and to all others whom it may concern:
>
> "I, George Washington, President of the United States of America, do make known that Robert Gray, Captain of a ship called the *Columbia*, of the burden of about 230 tons, is a citizen of the United States, and that the said ship which he commands belongs to the citizens of the United States; and as I wish that the said Robert Gray may prosper in all his lawful affairs, I do request all the before mentioned and each of them separately, when the said Robert Gray shall arrive with his vessel and cargo, that they will be pleased to re-

and possibly a similar document from the Spanish minister in the United States. A commemorative medal of the occasion carried on the face the name of Kendrick and a likenesss of the two ships, and on the reverse the names of the merchants who financed the expedition.

Many of the details of Gray's two trips to the Northwest coast are indefinite; a female relative burned the original logs, assuming them to be waste paper. The notes of Robert Haswell, second mate on board the *Washington*, furnished most of the information that exists.

Kendrick and Gray chose a roundabout and formidable route. From Boston they were to cut diagonally the full length and width of the North Atlantic, with the Cape Verde islands the first stop. From there they expected to drift back across the South Atlantic to the Falkland islands, where they would make port before attempting to pass the Strait of Magellan. Once through the strait they would have no rest until they sighted Selkirk islands in the Juan Fernandez group, far up the South American coast. Nootka was to be reached in one nonstop run from Selkirk.

As the two ships dropped down from Boston to Nantucket roads, September 30, 1787,[3] the sponsors held a gay farewell party on board ship. Details of the party have not survived. On Monday, October 1, sail was set and Kendrick and Gray headed for Cape Verde.

Not until the ships were at sea did the marked difference between the two commanders show up. Kendrick was cautious and slow, Gray vigorous and challenging. For the slightest excuse Kendrick would order a delay. Because of this policy, it was April of 1788 before they reached Cape Horn. There they encountered violent storms and often the *Columbia* was on her beam ends with the water pouring in below decks. Scurvy

---

ceive him with kindness and treat him in a becoming manner, &c., and thereby I shall consider myself obliged.

Sept. 16, 1790, New York City
GEO. WASHINGTON

Thomas Jefferson   President"
Secretary of State

3.—This was thirteen days before the new United States Constitution was signed at Philadelphia, but of course Kendrick and Gray left the Atlantic coast without knowing whether the document would be adopted.

broke out and everyone was ill. On August 2, Gray finally got off Mendocino. According to schedule, he had stopped at the island of Juan Fernandez, where Governor Don Blas Gonzales treated him most courteously, supplying the crew with fresh food and aiding Gray in repairing damages done by the storms. The central Spanish authority on the Pacific, strongly opposing such friendly actions, removed Gonzales from office and dispatched a ship from Callao to seize the Americans.[4] The attempt failed. The Spaniards at San Francisco also received orders to halt them, but the Americans did not put in at the California port.[5]

From Mendocino on, interest in the expedition centers around Gray, and an outline of his work is virtually an outline of the entire venture. Although Kendrick did nothing to attract criticism, neither did he do anything to merit investigation.

Gray and the *Washington* spent almost two weeks sailing up from Mendocino to Tillamook, which they reached on August 14. Two days later a small boat and crew were sent ashore for relaxation and to gather grass for the animals on board. The Indians seemed friendly enough, entertaining the Boston men with a war dance and the usual rituals. However, when Lopez, a member of the crew, laid down the cutlass with which he had been cutting grass, a native immediately pounced upon it. Wishing to regain their property without violence, Gray's men offered a reward to the chief for the return of the tool. He replied that if the white men wanted their property, they were free to take it. The Americans accepted the challenge, which resulted in Lopez's losing his life and three others' being wounded. Gray called the place "Murderers' Harbor," but it is generally identified as the modern Tillamook.

After giving what rude honors they could to Lopez, the *Washington* sailed northward, trading as she went, but constant gales and dense fogs handicapped both sailing and trading. Once the ship narrowly escaped shipwreck, and it is surprising that Gray found time to do anything but navigate. Nevertheless he observed the trading habits of the natives and noted the un-

---

4.—Snowden, volume 1, pages 150-151.

5.—According to Chapman (page 403), Arguello, commander at San Francisco, was ordered to take the *Columbia*, "which is said to belong to General Washington." Evidently the significance of Washington's position had not yet penetrated to the Pacific.

mistakable signs of rivers emptying into the sea. These things he was to remember.

The *Washington* was at Nootka by the middle of September, having come by way of Clayoquot. John Meares was there and he detailed men to tow the vessel into port. Gray never forgot this invaluable service, and his relations with Meares were always cordial, even though the other sometimes lied to him regarding such matters as the size of obtainable fur catches. In fact, Meares tried to discourage Gray by maintaining that he, Meares, had managed to get only fifty skins during his stay at Nootka. This was certainly out of line with the damages he later demanded when the Spaniards confiscated his boats and catches. Furthermore, his immediate actions gave the lie to the size of his catch. On September 19, 1788, shortly after Gray arrived, the *Northwest America* was launched, and no intelligent trader would have ordered the ship built if a mere fifty skins were the reward of a season's labor. On the twenty-third, Meares headed for Canton, a voyage he could hardly afford with so small a catch.

Despite the doleful predictions of Meares, Gray decided to keep the *Washington* on the coast and attempt to pick up a satisfactory cargo. Meanwhile the tardy Kendrick arrived with the *Columbia* at Nootka on the same day Meares left for China. Kendrick's trip from the Horn had been stormy and both he and Gray were anxious to send letters to Boston by way of China telling of their safe arrival. At first Meares volunteered this service, but after receiving the dispatches he backed out, returning the mail with a flimsy excuse. Such callous discourtesy keenly disappointed the men, who naturally wished to send word home. In spite of Meares' shabby treatment, the Americans helped his associate Douglas out of the harbor when he left for the Sandwich islands for the winter. The Americans then turned to trading with the natives—if the system of polite robbery then in vogue could be termed "trading."

Though Meares misrepresented the size of his catch, he did have trouble getting the Indians to trade with him. They held back on both furs and food stuffs but as soon as the English vessels were out of sight, the Indians swarmed about Gray, offering to trade for anything he had. Apparently Gray had a better reputation for honesty.

The pleasantness of the harbor and the friendliness of the Indians convinced Kendrick that by wintering at Nootka he could be first in the field in the spring and save the long run to the Sandwich islands and back. The winter passed quietly. Indeed there was very little that could happen when the natives were peaceful. Three thousand miles to the east were the awakening American states; a thousand miles to the south were the scattered Spanish *reduccions,* while to the west and north were barren seas or uninhabited coasts except for the Russians in Alaska.

Spring brought the usual bustle to the camp in preparation for the short trading excursions to the nearby islands and inlets. On March 16, 1789,[6] Gray took the *Washington* to Clayoquot for ten days of trading and fishing. A native chief entertained him with a whale hunt before Gray went on several exploration trips, including a visit to Tatoosh. These journeys continued through April and were important only in that they convinced Haswell, the second mate, that there was probably some sort of water communication to the interior of the continent. On May 6, Martinez and the *Princesa* arrived from San Blas and, after establishing friendly relations with him, Gray headed north to explore and trade about the Queen Charlotte islands. Duncan and Dixon had already visited these islands but had not explored them. The American was the first to investigate their east coast.

Trading was slow, though on one occasion Gray "bought" two hundred sea otter pelts with an old iron chisel,[7] and sold them for eight thousand dollars. Though the total catch was a disappointment, Kendrick decided to send Gray to Canton with the pelts. It was almost impossible to trade direct from Boston to China because America then manufactured very few articles that the Orientals wanted. But they were glad to trade tea for furs.

For some unknown reason, the two captains exchanged ships before Gray left Nootka. Doubtless Gray left a note on the mat-

6.—George Washington was soon struggling along the muddy roads of his native state attempting to get to New York for his inauguration on April 30, 1789.

7.—Bancroft, pages 206-207.

ter in his logs. Whatever the cause, the trade was made and Gray sailed for Canton aboard the *Columbia*.

The Oriental market was another disappointment. Finding it flooded with pelts from his English rivals, Gray had to sell for much less than he anticipated. He disposed of his cargo at the highest price he could, loaded his hold with tea, and set sail for Boston, arriving there in August of 1790—the first American to sail around the world.

The *Columbia* had logged more than fifty thousand miles since she left Boston and was warmly welcomed on her return. John Hancock, governor of Massachusetts, went to the dock to greet Gray personally, though he had previously refused to give a like recognition to George Washington on the President's visit to the city.[8] The immediate enthusiasms, however, did not cover the fact that the sponsors of the trip had made very little money. At first they thought it best to cancel all further plans for trade on the Northwest coast. Later the less interested members withdrew. The rest reorganized the partnership and re-outfitted the *Columbia* for a second voyage. By such a narrow margin did America win the honor of discovering the Columbia.

After quick preparation, anchors were weighed, September 28, 1790, for the second voyage, and the return to Clayoquot began.

In the meantime Kendrick had sailed fifty miles up the Strait of Juan de Fuca and then gone to the South seas, where he picked up a load of sandalwood for Macao. He never came back to his home port of Boston to receive his share of tribute and profit from the Northwest venture; he was killed at Karakakooa bay, Hawaii, by grapeshot from a British boat firing a salute in his honor.

The *Columbia* with its fresh cargo of trade trinkets was once more at Clayoquot, June 5, 1791.[9] Gray spent the summer and autumn trading and exploring to the north, but when the season closed he dropped back to Clayoquot for the winter.[10] There he

---

8.—Snowden, volume 1, page 153.

9.—A month later, July 4, 1791, bids for stock in Hamilton's First United States bank were opened, and all subscribed, in less than two hours.

10.—He probably chose Clayoquot instead of Nootka because Nootka was in dispute between the Spanish and English, and the other was more like a neutral port.

built a tiny defense works, Fort Defiance, and auxiliary schooner which he named the *Adventure*.

Afterwards he tried preaching the gospel to the Indians. Whatever his faults, Robert Gray attempted to be a practical Christian according to his understanding of the term. He instructed the natives and gave them medicine and a few food delicacies. Maybe his kindness partly compensated them for the robberies he committed in the name of commerce. His missionary work was not always practical though. One time he spent much effort persuading a native girl to wash her face, but her tribe ridiculed her and she quickly applied a fresh coat of paint to redeem herself.

The second winter at Clayoquot was strenuous. The Indians were less friendly and the crew often slept fitfully, fearing a night attack. Haswell noted the following in his log: "Oct 7 suddenly awakened (11 oclock) by report musket and every cove full of Indians. Sprang out of bed, armed myself and 7 persons and marched down to beach. Savages turned out to be rocks, which tide ebbing low had left dry."

The case of February, 1792, was not so harmless. Tatoosh, a treacherous and quarrelsome chief, plotted a night attack on Fort Defiance. He attempted to bribe Atoo, a Sandwich island boy, to be accessory from the inside but Atoo remained loyal to his employers and warned them. An uneasy peace resulted.

When the spring of 1792 came, the *Adventure* was sent north to trade with the Queen Charlotte Indians while Gray took the *Columbia* south late in April. Twice he passed the discolored waters at Deception bay; twice he was impressed with the undeniable signs of a great river. It was time to prove either the existence or nonexistence of such a river. At 4 o'clock on the morning of the twenty-ninth the *Columbia* spoke George Vancouver's ship and the Britisher sent Puget aboard to inquire about Gray's supposed trip up Fuca.[11] Gray, of course, could tell him nothing about Fuca, but he could and did tell him about his belief in a river at 46° 53′. The dour Britisher also failed to convince the persistent Yankee who continued southward. On May 7, Gray's harbor was discovered, and three days

11.—Unaware that Kendrick and Gray had exchanged ships, Vancouver thought that Gray had taken the *Columbia* into Fuca.

were spent there in profitable trade. More and more Indians came with pelts but Gray would not linger.

For the first time since the *Washington* and *Columbia* left Boston five years before, furs were no inducement. Was it pique at the attitude Vancouver had taken or was it that stubborn "I will" which has caused most of mankind's major victories in the face of society's scoffings? Probably it was both. The "great river" had challenged Bruno Heceta, August 15, 1775; John Meares, July 5, 1788; and George Vancouver, a scant two weeks before Gray crossed its bar. Yet each of these had forfeited the challenge — Heceta because of the physical weakness of his crew, Meares and Vancouver because of lack of faith. Robert Gray faced the same turbulent waters with no new scientific fact or instrument, but he did have an inner goading which would not be denied.

Call it pique, pride, or stubbornness—there was something that made one sailor succeed where others had failed. Yet the actual feat of discovery as described by Gray himself was simple. He wrote, "Sent up the main top gallant yard and set all sail." It was 8 p. m., May 10, 1792. Leaving Gray's harbor, he sailed south all night and at 4 o'clock "Saw the entrance of our desired port."

Four hours he stood by, studying the possibilities. Then, "At 8 a. m. being a little to the windward of the entrance of the harbor, bore away, and run in east-northeast, between the breakers, having from five to seven fathoms of water. When we were over the bar we found this to be a large river of fresh water, up which we steered. Many canoes came alongside. At 1 p. m. came to with the small bower, in two fathoms, black and white sand. The entrance between the bars bore west- south-west, distant ten miles. The north side of the river a half-mile distant from the ship; the south side of the same, two and a half miles distance; a village on the north side of the river west by north, distance three quarters of a mile. Vast numbers of natives came alongside. People employed in pumping salt water out of our water casks, in order to fill with fresh, while the ship float in. So ends."

It is simple enough to tell, but those four hours changed decades of myth and conjectures to the certainty of knowledge and laid America's first serious claim to the Oregon territory.

One can forgive shortcomings in trade ethics, overlook peculiarities of religious doctrines, and give free praise to a man who could succeed so humbly.

Gray made no attempt to explore the Columbia. He stayed until May 20, then, having completed his trading and calked his ship, he recrossed the bar. The day before he had named the cape on the south, Point Adams, and the one on the north, Cape Hancock. Hancock was long ago changed to Cape Disappointment.

Some contend that had Gray not discovered the Columbia when he did it would have remained hidden for many more years because of Vancouver's adverse reports.   Such was not likely. The day of the overland trapper had come and, regardless of any discovery from the mouth, the Columbia was sure to be found soon by explorers like Lewis and Clark, Lisa, Hunt, or any one of the hundreds who were soon to comb the Far West in search of the beaver.

From the Columbia, Gray again went to the east coast of the Queen Charlottes, where he rammed his ship on a rock and was forced back to Nootka for repairs. There he modestly told Quadra and Vancouver of his discovery. In friendly spirit he showed them his maps. Though pretending to be unimpressed, Vancouver afterwards ordered Lieutenant Broughton up the Columbia with instructions to lay claim to the region for England. The pretext was made of distinguishing between the seven-mile-wide "mouth" which Gray considered, and the narrower one twenty-five miles inland, beyond the point penetrated by Gray. This subterfuge of one great explorer to cheat another of his honors was unworthy of both Broughton and Vancouver.

Gray's second expedition to the Pacific was successful. He discovered an immense river and gathered enough furs to please the most enthusiastic trader. According to Haswell they acquired seven hundred sea otter skins and many thousands of other skins. The voyage should have netted the Boston merchants a handsome profit in spite of any low price existing at Canton. Probably the Chinese price was fair because Gray sold his *Adventure* to Quadra for seventy-five sea otter pelts. This suggests either that the ship was very poor or pelts so valuable that a few would buy her. The second assumption is more likely as Gray would not have tolerated a weak construction job on the ship, and Quadra was too familiar with ships and ship building to buy a worthless vessel.[12]

The rest of Gray's life was uneventful. Returning to Boston, he received the temporary plaudits of a busy people before retiring to Charleston, South Carolina. The country was in the midst of the Jeffersonian revolt against Federalism and had little time for old sea captains.

Not that Gray was neglected, but Lewis and Clark were fighting their way to the Pacific and back; Commander Preble was subduing the Barbary pirates; Jefferson was buying Louisiana for a song; and immigrants were already pushing into the valley whose streams fed the Mississippi instead of the Atlantic. A hearty *huzza* for the deed done yesterday and thoughts were turned to new deeds to be done tomorrow.

Under such circumstances, Robert Gray, America's first great explorer, passed quietly away at Charleston in 1806. More than any other single person, he gave his country that enormous region known as Old Oregon.

12.—These events on the Pacific coincided with Washington's second election on the Atlantic coast.

27

THE END OF THE PACIFIC NORTHWEST
EXPLORATIONS BY SEA

SUCH MEN as Meares, Strange, Portlock and Dixon, Gray, and members of the Russian American company were only a few of those who entered the North Pacific in search of furs. Considering the distances, dangers, and probable profits, the Northwest coast was a busy place during the relatively short heyday of the maritime fur trade. The era began about 1775 and was practically over half a century later. In that brief interval the Russians alone took two hundred thousand sea otter.

And no attempt was made to perpetuate any of the species; each trader tried to get the Indians to kill the greatest number of animals possible, regardless of sex or age. The natives, thirsty for liquor and eager for trinkets, heartily co-operated in wiping out the sea otter and other animals whose pelts would buy a mirror or a dram of whiskey.

Some years many ships came to Nootka; other years, almost none. In 1791, twenty eight dropped anchor there, but between 1810 and 1837 there were only sixty-seven. The peak of production was probably reached from 1799 to 1802, when almost fifty thousand sea otter skins alone were taken to Canton, yet as late as 1804, fifteen thousand pelts were shipped from Sitka. Profits were often fabulous. In 1785, five thousand sea otter sold in China for $160,000 and a trader who invested $50,000 might reasonably expect a yield of $300,000.

These traders were not settlers. When their epoch closed, the Northwest coast might have returned to wilderness had not an era of land exploration opened. Before the last of the fur ships sailed for Canton, new names, new companies, and new forces were trying to solve the riddle of North America from the interior just as the Spaniards, English, and Russians had tried to solve it from the sea. An even mightier struggle was already being launched not only to complete the map of inland North America but to reap the rich harvests of the western lands.

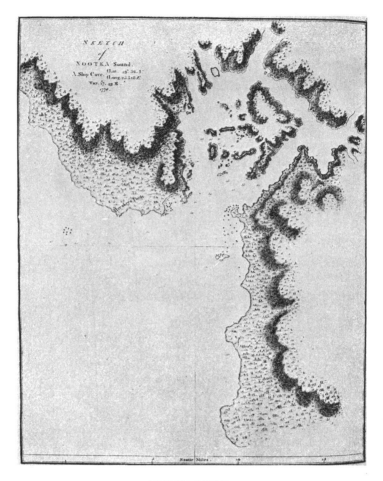

NOOTKA SOUND

Located on the west coast of Vancouver Island, the good harbor of Nootka Sound was sailed into and charted by Captain James Cook in 1778. It soon became the rendezvous for all navigators engaged in discovery, exploration, or trade on the northwest coast of America. Into it in 1788 sailed Captain John Meares aboard the *Felice*, naming it for a former vessel, the *Nootka*. Here he built a fort and traded with the natives.

In the course of the next ten years all of the important explorers, George Vancouver, Robert Gray, W. R. Broughton, and other English, Spanish, and French navigators entered and tarried, some of them establishing colonies. From the harbor they traded or explored. Gray visited the harbor twice in August 1792, following his May discovery of the Columbia river. Returning again in September, he found Vancouver, and here informed him of his discovery and naming of the fabled "River of the West," thus establishing America's claim on the records.

PART TWO —

BY LAND

*ANNO XXVI ·REGNI ·LVDOVICI·XV ·PROREGE

·ILLVSTRISSIMO ·DOMINO ·DOMINO ·MARCHIONI·

· DE ·BEAVHARNOIS ·M·D·CC·XXXXI

· PETRVS ·GAVLTIER ·DE ·LAVERENDRIE ·POSVIT

Face of the lead plate buried near Pierre, South Dakota, by one of the Verendrye sons and uncovered by school children in 1913. Although the inscription carries the date 1741, it is generally agreed that it was not placed until the return trip of the Verendrye sons in 1743. (South Dakota State Historical Society)

JONATHAN CARVER

Jonathan Carver's controversial *Travels*—first published in London in 1778—are still widely read and still warmly disputed by historians and biographers.

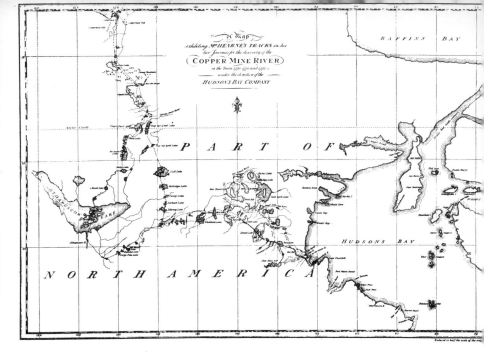

Route of Samuel Hearne, noted English explorer, from Fort Prince of Wales to the Coppermine river and the Arctic ocean. (Hearne's *Journal from Prince of Wales in Hudson's Bay to the Northern Ocean in the Years 1769, 1770, 1771, and 1772*. The Champlain Society, Toronto, 1911)

SAMUEL HEARNE

Hearne proved that there is no Strait of Anian—after three centuries of conjecture and search. He died in the epochal year of 1792, when Captain Gray discovered the Great River of the West.

SIR ALEXANDER MACKENZIE

No Scotsman has a clearer title to honor than Alexander Mackenzie, a canny fur trader and the most indomitable explorer ever to ferret a secret from the interior of North America. His was the honor of discovering the Pacific from the interior. (Radisson Society of Canada, Toronto)

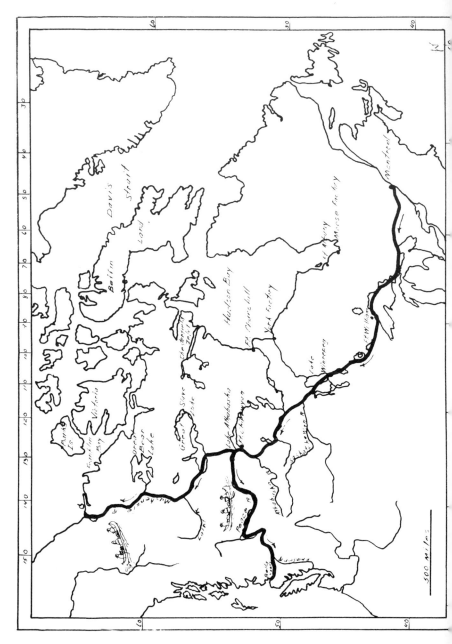

MACKENZIE'S ROUTE TO THE ARCTIC IN 1789 AND TO THE PACIFIC IN 1793.

Above: Indian canoe burial. The dead were interred near water, the body being first wrapped in deerskins and mats. The canoes were pierced with holes so that the rain water would run out and were elevated on posts or in the lower limbs of trees. Personal possessions of the deceased and gifts brought by mourners were placed around the body. (Oregon Historical Society)

Below: This painting of a Chinook mother and her child is credited to George Catlin, who visited the Northwest Coast early in the 1850s when it was common practice to flatten infants' heads in oddly shaped cradleboards. The mother shown here has the classic Chinook profile of the period. (Smithsonian Institution)

William Clark

Meriwether Lewis

President Thomas Jefferson was the vision
ary behind the Lewis and Clark venture
(From a steel engraving by James B. Long
acre from the original painting by Gilbe
Sullivan)

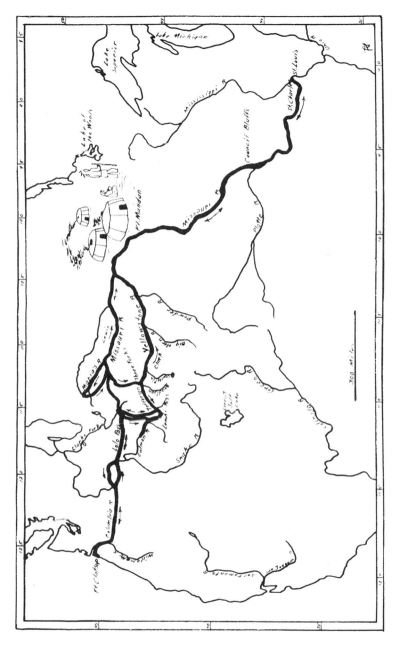

ROUTE OF LEWIS AND CLARK ALONG THE UPPER MISSOURI AND
TO THE PACIFIC IN 1804 AND 1805

WILSON PRICE HUNT

Hunt, explorer and fur trader, engag
in the mercantile business in St. Lo
before being chosen sole Americ
partner in John Jacob Astor's ventu
on the Pacific coast. (From a cray
portrait by O. L. Erickson, Misso
Historical Society, St. Louis)

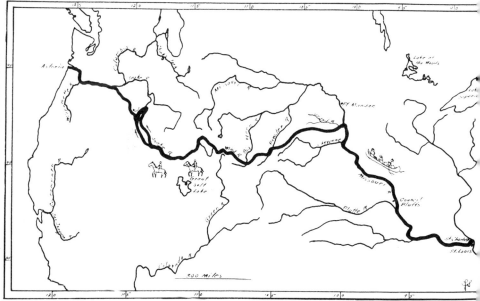

ROUTE OF HUNT AND THE OVERLAND ASTORIANS, 1811-12

Hunt crossed the continent by a route far off the Lewis and Clark trail, making large geographic gains, including the Okanogan region, the Willamette valley, and the upper Snake.

TWO FAMOUS
FUR TRADERS

Manuel Lisa (top) was the dominant figure in the Missouri Fur company. He managed his own forces in the field, drove his
voyagers to staggering labors, but often
paddled the sturdiest canoe himself.
(Missouri Historical Society)

Alexander Henry (right) North West company man—unlike Lisa—was ignorant of both Indian
life and the fur business; yet he knew men. (Huntington Library)

ST. LOUIS, 1832

St. Louis was the base for Manuel Lisa's extensive and colorful fur trade operations.
(Missouri Historical Society)

Manuel Lisa's stone warehouse in St. Louis.

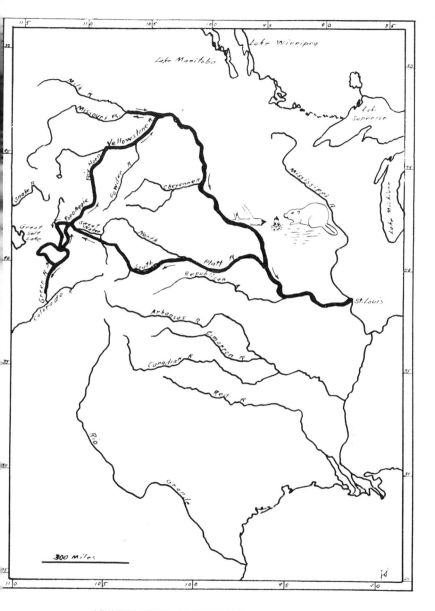

ASHLEY'S ROUTE IN PURSUIT OF BEAVER IN 1825

eneral William Henry Ashley, the Smith-Jackson-Sublette combine, and the Rocky Mountain
Fur company stand out prominently in the mountain fur trade.

JEDEDIAH SMITH

This intrepid Methodist fur trader and trail breaker outranked every other explorer of his period in territory covered. Probably no authentic likeness of him exists, but this bearded figure with Bible and gun is an eloquent image of the most devout and gentle of all the mountain fur men. (Brown Brothers, New York)

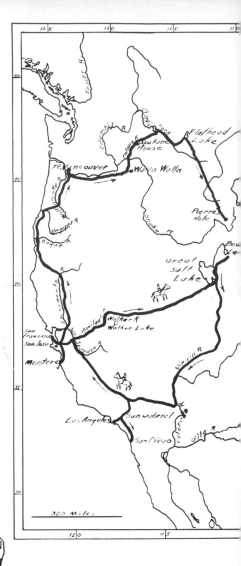

Jedediah Smith leisurely circled the Fc
West from 1826 to 1828.

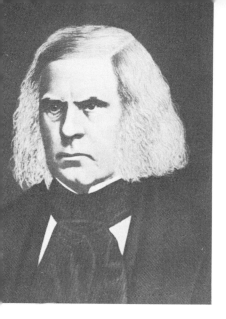

John McLoughlin (left), chief factor at Hudson's Bay company's Fort Vancouver; and Sir George Simpson (right), the company's western governor.

eter Skene Ogden (left), trader, trapper, and brigade leader in the Far West—where Nathaniel Wyeth (right) became famous as a pioneer merchant. (Oregon Historical Society)

Fort Vancouver on the Columbia, from a sketch by Lieutenant Henry J. Warre, first published in London in 1848. Vancouver was headquarters for McLoughlin, and later for Ogden.

S.S. BEAVER

The Hudson's Bay company's *Beaver*, in 1836, was the first steamer to ply the waters of the Columbia.

BLUE MOUNTAINS
Pioneer wagon train en route to the Columbia river valley.

FORT VANCOUVER IN TRANSITION
To the left are the American troops barracks; to the right, the Hudson's Bay company fort, with the Columbia beyond. (Drawing by Gustavus Sohon, U. S. Pacific Railroad Report, 1855)

THE WESTWARD MOVEMENT BY LAND

I

THE SEARCH FOR THE WESTERN SEA

THE FAMED SEARCH for the western sea was actually a search for
a way to that sea. Men were determined to find a practical overland route from one ocean to the other. For almost three centuries, seamen from Spain and Portugal, France and England,
combed both the Atlantic and Pacific coasts for a waterway
through the continent.

These voyages finally outlined the continent except for the
Arctic shore, yet revealed no hoped-for Strait of Anian. Explorers found the great rivers of the New World, yet disclosed
only a hazy idea of the real land mass that is North America.
Despite their vast effort to open the interior, the difficulties they
faced were so great that countless thousands of square miles still
remained unknown to the white man.

Information on distances to be covered was scant; Indians
were often hostile; supply bases uncertain; and knowledge of
natural food sources vague. Nevertheless overland exploration
forged ahead toward its great goal—an overland route. Seldom
a year passed but some new range of hills was recorded or some
tiny river opened to the trapper and hunter. Much of this work
was tiresome and unromantic; all of it was dangerous.

First to command attention in this overland period are the
men Radisson and Groseilliers.

2

RADISSON AND GROSEILLIERS AT HUDSON BAY

HENRY HUDSON discovered Hudson bay in 1611.[1] For several years men hoped that the bay itself opened into the Pacific. When this was disproved, they looked for a strait leading from the bay to the Pacific, but their interest was more than geographic.

Aware of the enormous trade value of pelts, the French had long been active in the fur business. Any number of geographic discoveries were accidental or secondary to the more important job of collecting beaver. Gradually the fur frontier had been pushed westward from Montreal to the Great lakes, reaching Hudson bay by the beginning of the eighteenth century. As pelts dwindled, the circle of activity widened; and when it was finally demonstrated that the bay had no western outlet, several overland expeditions to the Pacific resulted.

Radisson and Groseilliers became prominent while operations were still centered at Hudson bay. The Hudson's Bay company itself was organized as a direct outcome of the work of Pierre Esprit Radisson and his brother-in-law, Medard Chouart, Sieur des Groseilliers. And this company and its competitors were the prime movers in the overland search for the Pacific.

Radisson, always the leader of the pair, was born in St. Malo, France, about 1636,[2] coming to Canada with his family[3] about May of 1651. They settled at the little frontier trading post of Three Rivers on the St. Lawrence. There Pierre's life was one long adventure. At the age of sixteen he found the bodies of two of his massacred friends and while gazing at these, was

---

1.—Champlain was laying the foundations for Montreal at the same time and, two years later, the Dutch began building New Amsterdam.
2.—The year 1636 is, next to 1619, the most important date in the cultural history of America for it brought, through the efforts of Roger Williams at Providence, Rhode Island, the introduction of religious liberty into the New World.
3.—Belief in religious liberty, or at least tolerance, was gaining ground. The Maryland Toleration act was passed two years before the Radisson family moved to Three Rivers.

himself seized by the same Indians. Radisson's valiant struggle against capture won over the Indians and they took him into their tribe. For two years he lived with them as an adopted son. But he was still a prisoner, always watching for a chance to escape.

On one occasion he and another prisoner went hunting with three of their "tribesmen." The two prisoners murdered their captors while they slept, then hurried away toward Three Rivers.[4] Almost in sight of the post, they were recaptured, tortured, and returned to captivity, much wiser in the ways of the aborigines.

Radisson set about convincing the Indians that he was finally willing to be converted to the barbaric life. Unfortunately he felt that the best proof of his conversion would be his participation in some of the worst Indian practices. His months among the Iroquois were perhaps his most shameful. He hunted and fished with them, and once said, "Often have I sunged in French, to which they gave care with a deep silence." This was innocent enough, but he also went on war parties, taking full part in their raids and tortures. He killed women and children with an abandon which brought him the highest honors his savage friends could bestow.

His journal records that he helped load into canoes "10 heads and four prisoners, whom we embarqued in hopes to bring them into our own leasures for the more satisfaction of our wives"; and again, "We plagued those unfortunate. We plucked out their nails one after another."

Some argue that Radisson's *we* meant the Indians, not himself.[5] There is little justification for such a defense. Though he knew English imperfectly, he could clearly distinguish between *they* and *we,* for at another time he used both terms correctly in referring to the Crees when he said they wanted "to gett knives from us (that is, the French) which they love better than we serve God, which should make us blush for shame." [6]

After lulling the suspicions of the natives, Radisson made another attempt to escape, this time successfully. He raced for the

---

4.—William Henry Johnson, *French Pathfinders in North America*, page 196.
5.—Same, page 204.
6.—These particular events were not all a part of his life as a captive but only a phase of it as he lived it from time to time among the Indians. Yet these things do help delineate his character.

Dutch post, Fort Orange (Albany) and, though often barely out of sight of his pursuers, reached the post where he was kindly received. Later he sailed to Manhattan, then Amsterdam. From Amsterdam he journeyed to La Rochelle, France. Wishing to return to Three Rivers as soon as possible, he made the seven-thousand-mile journey to Europe and back—the quickest practical route to reach a home only 250 miles away!

Radisson spent the years following his experience as an Indian captive in and about Three Rivers and the fur country to the west.[7] His trading and exploration around the confluence of the Mississippi and Missouri rivers may have been the factor behind the work of Marquette and La Salle,[8] also searching for a way to the Pacific.

For several years Radisson had been trying to interest his brother-in-law in the fur business. He finally succeeded. At first, this relative was plain Medard Chouart but "he grew wealthy, purchased a title and was afterwards known as 'Sieur des Groseilliers.' "[9] Groseilliers, as he is commonly called by historians, had been involved in the normal life of the frontier at Three Rivers and was alert to the opportunities in the fur trade. About 1660 it became his main interest.

Radisson, not yet thirty, was pleasant and athletic; Groseilliers, older, was not so pleasant, and was heavy.[10] Nevertheless they formed a working association and eventually succeeded in reaching territory beyond the Great lakes; they may even have glimpsed

----

7.—Previous to 1655, Radisson and Groseilliers went on a trading expedition about Lake Superior and south of it. They were waylaid by the Iroquois who murdered thirteen of the party, but the leaders pushed on. Their probable route was up the Ottawa river and its branches, then by a chain of lakes to Simcoe lake, and down Severn river to Georgian bay and Matchedash bay, then to Michilimackinac, where the Jesuits had a post. In the spring of 1655 they started south where they are supposed to have penetrated so deeply that Radisson remarked, "Italy comes short of it," and "the lemons are not so big as ours, and sourer."

The next winter was spent around the western shores of the Great lakes and the following year, 1657, found the adventurers back home ready to begin their fourth trip. (Robert F. Kerr. *The Voyage of Groseilliers and Radisson*, 1652-1684, pages 165-178.)

It is in the matter of the fourth trip that confusion arises. Most authors give 1661 as its date. But this period, like others in Radisson's life, is indistinct. (Johnson, page 199 and following.)

8.—Katherine Coman. *Economic Beginnings of the Far West*, volume 1, page 223.

9.—Snowden, page 384.

10.—Laut, page 101.

the Missouri. Anyhow, they returned to Montreal with a rich cargo of several hundred thousand pelts[11] and promptly laid plans for another expedition. They were determined to strike north toward Hudson bay.

At that time it was the policy to license all traders dealing with the Indians. When Radisson applied for permission to trade into Hudson bay, the governor, D'Avaugour, refused unless he received half the profit. Radisson and Groseilliers decided to go without permission. They were ready probably in 1661.[12] On a night when they were least likely to be seen they slipped away into the wilderness. Their route lay by way of Lake Superior and north to Hudson bay. They built a post at Point Chequamegon on the southern shore of Lake Superior,[13] but it is doubtful if they actually got very far into the Hudson bay country.[14]

During the winter of 1661 and 1662 [15] Radisson spent considerable time with the Crees.[16] Now more careful to guard against any hostile moves of the Indians, he resorted to a simple device to protect himself against a night surprise. He encircled his camp with tiny bells strung on a line, any movement of which would rouse him. He had a sort of humor for he remarked, "During that time we had severall alarums in ye night. . . . The squerels and other small beasts, as well as foxes, came in and assaulted us." But the really dangerous Crees and their neighbors did not molest him.

The winter was severe. Food supplies were exhausted and the dogs and leather tents were eaten to preserve life, but when spring came and the pelts were added together, the French were amply rewarded—the Indians heaped up thousands of skins. When Radisson started homeward, his retinue consisted of 700 Indians and 360 canoes, each laden with the finest pelts the wilderness could produce.[17] During the spring of 1663,[18] these

11.—Laut, page 101.
12.—Same.
13.—Paul Leland Haworth. *Trailmakers of the Northwest,* page 21.
14.—Snowden, page 384.
15.—Massachusetts was now in the midst of her quarrel with England over legislative rights and in 1661 defiantly passed the Declaration of Rights.
16.—It was then that Radisson practiced some of the barbarities already cited.
17.—Johnson, page 219.
18.—Eight English noblemen were struggling at the same time with their first colony in Carolina.

furs were landed at Montreal where the governor promptly laid a fine against them of ten thousand pounds sterling as punishment. This sum, likely not so much a fine as an outright theft by the governor, wiped out the entire profit of the undertaking,

Radisson went to France and appealed to the king, who upheld the governor. Of course Radisson and his partner had deliberately broken the law in making the trip without permission and could offer no legitimate complaint at being caught and punished.

Between the time of this assessment and his appearance at the French court where he took his case, Radisson had an exciting life. He first escaped from the governor's wrath to Cape Breton, where for no apparent reason he roused the anger of the inhabitants who promptly mobbed him. He fled from Cape Breton to escape death. In fact he seems to have spent an impressive portion of his life fleeing from one group or another. He quarreled and made enemies easily and had few compensating or endearing qualities. He was not disliked by all but he was cordially hated by some, merely tolerated or ignored by others.

Still his London home was popular years later. He had a sense of humor and was no prude. He liked to "eat, drink, and be merry." His was an easy, expansive code which he expressed as follows: "What fairer bastion than a good tongue, especially when one sees his own chimney smoke, or when we can kiss our own wives or kiss our neighbor's with ease and delight?" Such standards were acceptable in a society notoriously loose and easy going.

Few men in New France less deserved the treatment Radisson received. His business practices were not one whit sharper or more reprehensible than those of his critics and he had that certain something which marked him indelibly as an adventurer as it did Francis Drake. And—"The adventurer is an outlaw . . . rarely chaste, or merciful, or even law-abiding at all, and any moral peptonizing, or sugaring takes out the interest, with the truth of (his life). The adventurer is an individualist and an egotist, a truant, from obligations. His road is solitary, there is no room for company on it." [19]

So now Radisson, the adventurer, had to flee from Cape

19.—William Bolitho. *Twelve Against the Gods,* pages 3-5.

Breton to Port Royal, Nova Scotia. No welcome awaited him there, and soon he sailed for France, as already mentioned, to appeal directly to the king for a refund of the fine. Though denied the refund after weeks of supplicating first one officer of the court then another, Radisson was finally promised a ship to take into Hudson bay. Jubilant, he left the court to begin preparations, only to be told that the whole thing was a hoax perpetrated to rid the court of him.

For a weaker man this would have ended the whole affair, but it merely challenged Radisson to set about finding someone else to outfit him. That someone was Captain Gillam of Boston, half adventurer, half coward and knave. Eventually Gillam's ship did reach Hudson bay but the terror of the floes overcame the lust for gold and he returned to safer shores. Once more Radisson's plans had gone wrong, and Captain Gillam appears later under even more unattractive circumstances.

Sensing the millions to be had in Hudson bay, Radisson and his less enthusiastic brother-in-law pooled their small remaining cash and chartered two ships. One of these was wrecked while fishing. The charterers, becoming involved in a law suit over its loss, had to relinquish the other ship. Again accident and the courts postponed the conquest of Hudson bay.

Bankrupt but still determined, Radisson got in touch with Sir George Carteret, royal commissioner in Boston. Carteret was so enthusiastic over the Frenchman's proposal that he persuaded Radisson to go to England with him to try to raise the necessary funds. In 1663, every foreign vessel was an enemy, and on the way to England a Dutch armed ship captured the two Frenchmen and Carteret. But instead of taking them to the Low countries, the captain of the Dutch ship landed them in Spain, a natural enough procedure considering Spain's relations with the Low countries. Radisson, Groseilliers, and Carteret now had to escape from Spain. Short of funds, the three pawned and begged their way first to France, then to London. Though King Charles was up at Oxford hiding from the plague, Carteret arranged an audience in which he managed to interest both Charles and Prince Rupert. Within a year Charles ordered the *Eaglet* to prepare for Hudson bay. Rupert and a half dozen friends furnished the money for the trade goods and general expenses.

By this time the Dutch captain, regretting his lack of foresight, asked the Frenchmen to desert their new English friends and go over to the Dutch. Failing in this, he brought a charge of counterfeiting against the two. Unable to prove the charge, his agent was himself imprisoned. It was now the winter of 1667-1668.

Although the *Eaglet* may have appeared adequate, the traders, unwilling to take more chances, chartered the *Nonsuch* from the faint-hearted Gillam. Leading merchants of London who provisioned both ships received shares in the enterprise. Orders were delivered to the two captains—Stannard of the *Eaglet* and Gillam of the *Nonsuch*. Besides building the usual forts and seeking valuable metal deposits, the traders were also to regard themselves as explorers. The order stated:

"You are to saile with the first wind that presents, keeping company with each other to your place of rendezvous (the old mark set up by Radisson when he went overland to the bay.) You are to saile to such place as Mr. Gooseberry (Groseilliers) and Mr. Radisson shall direct to trade with the Indians there, delivering the goods you carry in small parcells no more than fifty pounds worth at a time out of each shipp, the furs in exchange to stowe in each shipp before delivering out any more goods, according to the particular advice of Mr. Gooseberry and Mr. Radisson.

"You are to take notice that the 'Nampumpeage' which you carry with you is part of our joynt cargoes wee having bought it for money for Mr. Gooseberry and Mr. Radisson to be delivered by small quantities with like caution as the other goods.

"You are to have in your thought the discovery of the passage into the South Sea and to attempt it with the advice and directions of Mr. Gooseberry and Mr. Radisson, they having told us that it is only seven daies paddling or sailing from the River where they intend to trade unto the Stinking Lake (the Great lakes) and not above seven daies more to the straight wch. leads into that Sea they call the South Sea, and from thence but forty or fifty leagues to the Sea itselfe.

"Exact journals and maps are to be kept. In case the goods cannot be traded, the ships are to carry their cargoes to Newfoundland and the New England plantations, where Mr. Philip Carteret, who is governor of New Jersey, will assist in disposing of the goods.

"Lastly we advise and require you to use the said Mr. Gooseberry and Mr. Radisson with all manner of civility and courtesy and to take care that all your company doe bear a particular respect unto them, they being the persons upon whose credit wee have undertaken this expedition. 'Which we beseech Almighty God to prosper.'

	RUPERT	ALBERMARLE
(Signed)	CRAVEN	G. CARTERET
	J. HAYES	P. COLLETON"

Radisson went with the *Eaglet* and Groseilliers with the *Nonsuch*. The ships left Gravesend, June 3, 1668. Almost before they were out of sight of land a storm damaged the *Eaglet* so badly that with difficulty she limped back to the Thames, while Captain Gillam—perhaps determined to prove his metal—drove the *Nonsuch* toward Hudson bay. He touched at Baffin land and was off Hudson strait on August 4. This time there was no ice on the strait. By the nineteenth he arrived at Digges' island. Then the *Nonsuch* headed south, making an average of only a hundred miles per week and arriving at the mouth of what was later named Rupert river, September 25. There was not much ice until December so Gillam and Groseilliers built Fort Charles and began trading.[20] Spring came early and by June the *Nonsuch* was loaded and ready to sail for home.

Meanwhile Radisson, having successfully appealed for a new ship to replace the *Eaglet*, was given the *Wavero*. The new ship proving unseaworthy, he had to return to port. There he found the *Nonsuch* with her cargo. No known record of the value of this first shipload of furs exists but it must have been sizable for a secret and immediate application was made to the crown for an exclusive trade franchise into Hudson bay.

On May 2, 1670,[21] a new charter was granted creating the greatest merchant company of modern times, if not of all times—"The

20.—Groseilliers certainly was no novice in driving sharp bargains. A half pound of beads purchased one beaver skin; a gallon of poor brandy, four skins; while one cheap gun was readily exchanged for twelve beavers.
21.—The next year Berkeley, governor of Virginia, said, "I thank God that there are no free schools, or printing presses (in America)."

Government and Company of Adventurers of England Trading into Hudson Bay." It comprised a "monopoly of trade with plenary powers, executive and judicial, in and over all seas, straits, lands, etc., lying within the entrance of Hudson straits, and the rivers entering them, not already occupied by any other English subject or other Christian power or state." [22] "So far as the King could do so, he gave the company a large part of the earth with full power to govern and make whatever use it could of it." [23]

Though this territory was almost as large as Russia, the cost to the company was to be two elk and two black beaver for the king or his heirs whenever they should happen to visit the region. Surely no company ever paid less for such a prize. It would be interesting to know whether the British Crown ever received its elk and black beaver.

The official name, "Rupert's Land," was never popular and was soon replaced by "Hudson bay country." Prince Rupert was the leading figure in the new organization but he put in only 470 pounds of the 10,500 pounds of total capital. Very little of that total was cash; the bulk was credit and "for service." The mighty Hudson's Bay company was firmly launched on a career without parallel in business history. The years have been good to it; and, if its ledgers sometimes tell stories not entirely praiseworthy, they also record tales of rare commercial insight and humanitarianism.

Though the company was primarily concerned with the pursuit of wealth, it spent hundreds of thousands of dollars in geographic research. The conquest of all that vast wilderness which slopes into the Arctic and Hudson bay is largely a monument to the fur men, but most of these were employes of the Hudson's Bay company. Even what was accomplished under another organization, such as the work of Mackenzie, was generally just a reflection of the great company, which either laid the way itself, or had competitors which did.

The company was chartered in May and in June three ships left for the fur fields. At first it looked as though a genuine monopoly had been established but as early as 1674, Father

---

22.—Alexander Begg. *History of British Columbia*, page 111.
23.—Snowden, volume 1, page 386.

Albanel, an English Jesuit but an emissary of New France, seized Fort Charles on the southern shore of James bay. Bayly, the company governor, already disgruntled over a dispute with Radisson and Groseilliers regarding the extension of trade into the interior, accused them of "selling out" to New France. The argument grew so bitter that when William Lyddell, a new governor, arrived, the Frenchmen left for England to present the case to the home offices.

To their chagrin they found that neither had ever been considered a partner, both having been listed merely as employes. The company was willing to pay Radisson a hundred pounds sterling per year but would not grant a partnership. Naturally Radisson felt misused and cast about for some solace to his wounded vanity and flat purse.

The French now offered him four hundred pounds a year and payment of all his debts if he would return to them. Six weeks later he did. His English wife refusing to change allegiance, he left without her. He went back to Hudson bay, apparently under the banner of France but actually with very little French support. Becoming entangled in a sort of free-for-all with his erstwhile English employers, Radisson bluffed them into believing he had a strong force of men "up the river" at his post. He successfully trapped Captain Gillam's own son poaching on Hudson's Bay company preserves, used the knowledge to blackmail the captain, and was himself almost trapped by the English governor, Bridgar, who had been told that young Gillam's camp was Radisson's. Suspicious of the existence of the "force" Radisson pretended to have, the governor sent a party to investigate. They became lost in a blizzard and Radisson rescued them but kept them captive so that Bridgar never again saw them. Radisson captured both the forces of the senior and junior Gillam and after quelling, probably not too nicely, a mutiny of his prisoners, next summer delivered the whole lot of them to Quebec. There all his work was undone; the prisoners were turned loose and Radisson was ordered to France.

Then follows a series of moves and counter moves, the exact details of which seem to conflict. Radisson appears to have been the pawn of a three-pointed diplomatic intrigue among Louis of France, Charles of England, and the company itself. Officially, the British Crown through its minister was demanding the punishment of Radisson while, unofficially, the same forces were trying to bribe him to return to the Hudson's Bay employ.

At the moment Louis was committed to a secret policy of friendliness with Charles, and although he officially criticized Radisson, he secretly ordered him to England.[24] The Frenchman asked for his fair share of the booty, then suddenly and mysteriously slipped away to England, where he took an oath as an Englishman on May 10, 1684.[25] Within a week he was ready to sail once more for Hudson bay. Perhaps it is idle to speculate on the real causes of these sudden changes of allegiance, yet the whole pattern of Pierre Radisson's life exactly fits such actions. He was first and last an adventurer.

Scarcely had he returned to the employ of the English than Louis issued an order for his arrest. Once more he had to dodge official wrath. While this order was in force d'Iberville raided the Hudson bay shores but Radisson's luck held and he was never arrested. During his remaining years he divided his time between the bay and London.

London's social life attracted him and he probably enjoyed it all the more because of his experiences at the bleak fur posts. By occasionally coaxing small sums of money from the company, Radisson lived out his strange career as he began it, vigorously and adventurously. Sometime between March and July of 1710 he passed on to whatever rewards and punishments there are for such souls; and the company which he had done so much to help found had the decency to pay his widow a modest pension for a few more years. Long before, his prosaic brother-in-law Groseilliers had drifted back to peace and security and nonentity at Three Rivers.

Only as a gambler can Pierre Esprit Radisson be called great, yet the sum of his years excites some praise. Chance seldom played into his hands, except in his luck in escaping his enemies. Nevertheless time and again he gambled his life and what wealth

24.—A clear and detailed discussion of this phase of Radisson's affairs is given in Agnes C. Laut's *Conquest of the Great Northwest,* pages 170-190.
25.—Two years before, La Salle had reached the mouth of the Mississippi, proving to his disappointment that it emptied into the Atlantic not the Pacific. In 1684 he was founding a colony near the mouth.
In 1683, William Penn gave the Quakers a home in Philadelphia.

he had, seeming to receive full compensation, not from winning but from the gamble.

Radisson's monument is the Hudson's Bay company, which directly and indirectly motivated that long list of traders and explorers who stopped only when the Pacific and Arctic had been reached, and the Strait of Anian had been erased from the imaginations of men. Such was the work of Radisson and such the reasons why his story has a legitimate place in that next great epoch of the Northwest, the overland search for the western sea.

CREST OF THE HUDSON'S BAY COMPANY

"A skin for a pelt"—or "A pelt for a pelt."

3

THE DE LA VERENDRYES,

AN EXPLORING FAMILY

SOMETIMES IT SEEMS that the little-known crossroads of the world are more often than not the home sites of men whose names are memorized by posterity. Luther and Eisleben, Germany; Bonaparte and Ajaccio, Corsica; Lincoln and Hodgenville, Kentucky —these are typical of the associations of master names with minor places.

Three Rivers, Quebec, belongs to this group. Pierre Radisson spent his boyhood there and Pierre Gaultier de Varennes was born there. Radisson and de Varennes were contemporaries. Though Radisson left Three Rivers and became deeply involved in the life of the Hudson's Bay company before de Varennes was born, villagers must have known both families for their lives overlapped about twenty-five years.

Pierre Gaultier was born on November 17, 1685, the fourth son and eighth child of a family of ten children. His father, Rene Gaultier Sieur de Varennes, was governor of Three Rivers; his maternal grandfather had also held that office. Despite the prominence of the family, few facts are known about Pierre's childhood. He grew up in a comfortably furnished home, and, at the age of twelve, was put to service in the provincial army.

When he was twenty-two he sailed for France, fighting in the War of the Spanish Succession as a lieutenant. He was wounded several times at the battle of Malplaquet and for fifteen months was held prisoner. From here on his life story is clearer. In 1711[1] he returned to Canada and shortly thereafter married. He established a fur post at La Gabelle, near Three Rivers, where he took the name by which he is commonly known, de la Verendrye.

Four sons in four successive years increased his expenses so much that he appealed for a public post to secure himself against want yet leave him free for some money-making activity on the

1.—Mobile, Alabama, was settled by the French the same year.

side. The governorship of a fur post exactly suited his needs inasmuch as such officers were permitted, even expected, to carry on a private trade in addition to their duties as governor.[2] Probably because of his family connections in Three Rivers, Verendrye was given command of a post on Lake Nipigon in 1727. His historical importance dates from this appointment.

In some ways Verendrye was an unusual explorer but there is nothing dramatic or romantic about him. His mind was average and his ambitions intense rather than great. He sensed only a part of the ultimate worths involved in large ventures. Unlike Drake and Radisson, he lacked the color to attract others to his propositions. Without unusual initiative, he instead had endless patience and a stubborn will to achieve whatever vision he saw. Peculiarly mild and plastic, he had none of the driving vitality of Alexander Mackenzie or many lesser men. It is easy to pity Verendrye but he neither wanted nor deserved it; he never whined. All of his record that has survived shows him making a conscientious attempt to do creditable work.

He early determined to be an explorer and his appointment to the Nipigon post placed him in an ideal position for this.

The Canadians had long believed that the Pacific could be reached by ascending the Missouri to its source, crossing over certain heights of land to a westward flowing river, and then following it to the Pacific with relative ease. The plan was feasible as Lewis and Clark were to prove a century later. Verendrye was keenly interested in any project looking toward the west, and he gave the rest of his life to the task of finding some practical solution to the problem of an overland route to the Pacific. Beyond this his imagination never extended.

Meanwhile Father Gonner, also much interested in exploration, had met Verendrye and the two likely talked over the chances of discovering the "westward flowing river" which everyone took for granted existed somewhere.

An Indian by the name of Ochagach had given the Frenchmen a crude bark map showing his conception of the territory west of the Great lakes. This map, plus whatever arguments he could muster about trade advantages, Verendrye presented to

2.—This was not true of the Hudson's Bay company, which forbid such activities by its employes.

Governor Beauharnois with a request for one hundred men and enough supplies to explore west of Nipigon. Beauharnois was the average French governor—more interested in his own comfort than in either geographic knowledge or the glory of France —but he did what he could to aid Verendrye. Because he lacked authority to grant such a request in his own right, he appealed to Paris. The Crown would only grant a monopoly of the fur trade in whatever new regions might be opened.

European crowns seemed to delight in giving monopolies. Either they had no conception of how their numerous grants overlapped or the word held some mystic charm for the trader, making him tractable and easily put off without more substantial help.

Though unimaginative and without much drive, Verendrye knew the practical side of the fur business and clearly understood the difficulties of an explorer. He pointed out that if a man must spend his life swapping pelts, little time would remain for exploration. However he finally accepted such help as a monopoly of a non-existent fur trade would be—it was that or giving up his plans. Doggedly he set about devising a program to fit his financial standing, combining fur trade with exploration and figuring that one would support the other. He intended to build a chain of posts westward from the known region of the French frontier to the Pacific, using each new post as a starting place for further explorations. Impractical as the plan now appears, it was really sound considering the 1730 concept of the size and shape of North America.[3]

Verendrye could not know, any more than anyone else, the distances and hazards west of the Great lakes. Learned geographers were still drawing maps showing a strait through the continent and Vitus Bering had only just laid to rest the equally ancient belief that the New World merely jutted from the old. If the continent were what Verendrye thought, his plan was simple.

Having received the doubtful concession of a monopoly of the fur trade, Verendrye asked the merchants of Montreal to supply trade goods. These gentlemen assumed the risk, at in-

---

3.—Even the so-called settled regions were then very sparsely inhabited. A half century later Washington was just running the first lines in western Virginia and there were fewer than four million persons in all the vast region from the St. Lawrence to Spanish Florida.

terest rates satisfactorily high, and the explorer-trader headed west, June 8, 1731. He took with him three of his sons, Jean Baptiste, Pierre, and Francois; also a nephew, La Jemeraye. Then there was a rough, hardened crew of fifty canoemen—hunters and packers much like the sort of crew that left Montreal regularly. Their route to Michilimackinac was familiar and well traveled.

When Father Mesaiger joined the expedition there, it took on that faintly religious tone of many of the early exploring parties. Verendrye coasted around Lake Superior to the Grand Portage, arriving on August 26, 1731.

So far the trip had been quite peaceful but prospects of a long carry at the portage started a kind of mutiny. Lacking personal strength to meet such a situation, Verendrye relied on appeasement. When the men refused to go forward under his plan, he agreed to alter it. He split the expedition, part under La Jemeraye going ahead to Rainy lake to build Fort St. Pierre, the first of the posts, and the rest staying with the commander.

A year later Verendrye reached the post, which had been duly built on the south side of the lake. Now began the long struggle to get enough pelts to make a profit to finance more posts. Verendrye personally went ahead to Lake of the Woods, where he established Fort Charles, a substantial outpost. Ground was cleared by burning it off, and peas and corn were sowed in May, 1733.[4]

From Fort Charles, Verendrye sent one of his first reports to Maurepas, secretary of state, describing the work done so far. He reported that he had checked a tribal war, Sioux versus Crees, by forbidding them, in the name of the king, to fight, and promising them guns, hatchets, and powder if his orders were obeyed. He should have known that such promises only made matters worse. The two tribes continued to snipe at each other all winter; and because sniping is not war, honor compelled him to bestow the gifts he had offered. But the sniping upset trade almost as much as war would have.

He reported receiving some hazy information about an iron deposit nearby, yet nothing came of it. During January and February he went off to Fort St. Pierre to halt another war,

---

4.—During the 1730s a number of printing presses were set up in the colonies, Rhode Island being the first in 1732.

leaving one of his men with the natives as an observer and hostage for peace.

Verendrye did not have the knack of. reporting things to his superiors which would catch their fancy. His comments on his progress were dull and repetitious. Page after page tiresomely quoted the exact words with which some chief assured the French that his people always had been and always would be friends of the French. Each report ended with a request for aid.

From Fort St. Pierre, Verendrye reminded Maurepas that the whole business was very expensive and voiced the hope that he would not be forgotten. But that was just about what happened. Governor Beauharnois wrote several times to Maurepas requesting funds for the western work, saying that he believed the explorer preferred "the glory of success to the pecuniary advantages which might result," and would Maurepas please "urge upon his Majesty to bestow some consideration upon that officer." Paris was both ignorant of and uninterested in the enormous labors involved in exploring the West. Maurepas replied that Louis and he would be glad to help Verendrye when they saw results, provided these fitted the royal conception of what those results should be. They expected the merchants and the trader to take all the risks, supply all the money, and then find some dazzling and dramatic route from French America to the Pacific. What they intended was a reward, not aid.

Verendrye was often provokingly slow, making little attempts to keep his guides going in a straight line. He fluttered from one Indian camp to another, giving long speeches and passing out presents paid for by Montreal merchants. He returned to his post empty handed or with a "catch" too small to pay the expenses of the trip. More than half of his time he spent trying to manage the intertribal relations of the Indians. Of course such procedure may have been for the best if he were to gain the friendship of the Indians and establish a lasting trade with them.

In 1733, at the end of the first three seasons, Verendrye had spent a total of 43,000 livres [5] but showed no material progress. He was not discouraged though and during the summer of 1734

5.—Reuben Gold Thwaites, *A Brief History of Rocky Mountain Exploration,* page 30.

he went to Montreal to plead personally for more money and supplies.

During this time his son, Jean Baptiste, built Fort Maurepas at Lake Winnipeg. The winter of 1735-1736 [6] was so severe that when spring came Jean and twenty men had to leave the fort to go for supplies. On the way down Lake of the Woods the party was attacked and every man massacred. The Indians decorated the dead with porcupine quills, placing the priest Alneau, in a kneeling position. The elder Verendrye took news of the tragedy calmly. He wrote:

"On the same day (June 22) the sergeant and his men arrived, bringing the sad news of the massacre of the twenty-one men seven leagues from the fort on a little island. Most of the bodies were found, all decapitated, and lying in a circle against one another, which made me conclude they were killed while holding counsel; the heads were wrapped in beaver skins."

Verendrye's calm was not mere callousness; there was just no place on the frontier for hysterics.[7] Certain work had to be done and violent death must not delay it.

He returned from Montreal with a renewal of monopoly rights, new supplies and hopes, and accompanied by his youngest son, now eighteen years old. Verendrye suspended all exploration to collect enough pelts to satisfy his most insistent creditors. Spreading his forces as widely as safety and good business allowed, he called upon his remaining sons to carry double burdens. Fort La Riene was built in 1738 on the Assiniboine river. During October of that year Verendrye himself started for the Pacific. With an Assiniboin guide and fifty men, he planned to go overland to the Mandan villages of Dakota for information about the West.[8] Using the Mandan country as a new base, he wished to

---

6.—In 1735, Peter Zenger carried his famous "freedom of the press" case to court and won for American newspapers the unchecked privilege of printing anything they desired.

7.—The death of Jean Baptiste was all the greater shock because just previous to the massacre the nephew La Jemeraye had died, leaving the administrative department extremely short handed.

8.—The Mandans were different from any other nation in that part of North America, having reached a cultural stage well into barbarism, with some evidence of the beginnings of civilization. Later, they often served as go-betweens for less peaceful groups and the white men. Their part in the Lewis and Clark expedition is common knowledge.

move quickly on to the Pacific, a matter of a few days he supposed.

The French party reached the Dakotas, December 3, having made the 250-mile journey without serious trouble. Verendrye induced the chief of the Mandans to accept a French flag in return for which his nation was claimed as a dependency of the French Crown,[9] but he found that the Mandans either knew nothing about the West or refused to divulge what they did know. That was as far as Pierre Gaultier de la Verendrye ever got toward the Pacific.

By some mischance Verendrye was robbed of every bit of trade goods, the Indians then refusing to act as guides. Even the Assiniboin would go no farther without more pay.

Almost all the explorers of inland America were considerably checked by the Indians' refusal to go far from home. This suggests that the oft-vaunted bravery of the aborigine was somewhat limited to his own campfires and females.

Hoping to find out more through longer acquaintance, two men stayed to learn the Mandan language, the rest of the party returning in midwinter to Fort La Riene, which they reached on February 11, 1739. The five-hundred-mile tramp would have been difficult even in good weather but January in the Dakotas is severe and Verendrye was growing old. When the party arrived at the post he was quite ill. Nevertheless in 1741 [10] he again unsuccessfully attempted to go overland to the West, but his winter trip to the Mandans represented his "farthest west."

The sons now took over westward exploration. On April 29, 1742, Francois, possibly Louis-Joseph, and two others left La Riene for the Mandan country in a third and last attempt at crossing the continent. The father remained behind to tend the post, quiet the Indians and make his reports.

Francois and his companions reached the villages safely, hired two guides and continued on to the Missouri where they lingered until July 23. They then took a generally west-southwest direction until August 2, when they stopped to form a contact with the Indians in that region. During August and September they made little progress. The Verendryes lacked the initiative to

9.—Coman, volume 1, page 224.
10.—Vitus Bering arrived in Alaska at this time.

explore on their own account, relying entirely on the Indians to guide them into new regions. The natives were not only incapable of this but too lazy.

It was October 9 before the exploring party again got under way, and then without the Mandan guides, who had gone home.

Exactly where the explorers now were no one knows. Perhaps they met the Crows who might have passed them on to the Horse Indians who perhaps brought them to the Bows.[11] Maybe three entirely different tribes were involved.[12] In any event the explorers did get some vague news of the Pacific to buoy their spirits, and seeing a few pieces of Spanish leather further convinced them that the Spanish domains were not far away. "All that," said one of the boys, "cooled my ardour considerably for a sea already known; nevertheless, I should greatly have wished to go there had the thing been possible."

Rapidly now the entire project became impossible. The tribe to which the French were attached was headed west on the warpath—possibly against the Snakes. As no enemies were found, the war party became an extended picnic, also the end of the Verendrye project.

On January 1, 1743, the explorers looking westward saw a great range of mountains that they managed to reach by the twelfth. Which mountains these were no one knows. Some say the explorers were as far west as the Yellowstone and were gazing upon the Rockies; others that they never got much beyond the Mandans, probably only to the highlands of the Dakotas.

But like so many seeming failures, the work of the Verendryes actually was very valuable. "Their apparently bootless wanderings opened up the commercial empire from which a wealth of beaver and other peltry was collected and shipped to Montreal,"[13] and they blocked out another whole section of North America in which there was no great waterway and beyond which the Pacific had to lie. Thereafter no intelligent explorer wasted time and money roaming about the Dakotas looking for a route to the Pacific.

Satisfied that to go farther was impossible, the Verendryes

11.—Haworth, page 54.
12.—See also the Champlain edition of the Verendrye Journals, pages 13-15.
13.—Coman, volume 1, page 225.

meandered back to their post, on the way passing through the Saskatchewan region, then dropping down to the Missouri.

Sensing the importance of their work, they buried a plate near Pierre, South Dakota, recording the names of Louis, Beauharnois, and themselves with the date 1741 on the face side. The reverse was scratched with the date, presumably of its burial, March 30, 1743. The plate lay there in the mud until February 16, 1913, when several small boys unearthed it while rooting about in the river bank.

The party reached the Mandan villages on May 18, and La Riene, July 2. Twelve years had passed since the Verendryes, father and sons, put aside the comforts of civilization at Three Rivers to search for the "Western Sea." The father's health was gone and his debts greater than he could ever hope to pay, but he had done his share to help find a way across the continent. In 1744, he asked the governor's permission to retire from active duty, pointing out that he was old, ill, and bankrupt, and should be allowed to withdraw without any reflection on either his ability or his work. The Crown consented because in spite of Beauharnois' defense it had never felt it was getting value received from the Verendrye family.

On the retirement of the old explorer, de Noyelles was placed in charge of the "posts of the Western Sea," as they were romantically called. De Noyelles, proving equally unsatisfactory, was soon removed and Verendrye was told to take up his former duties. The year was 1747.

Meanwhile a little recognition was granted Verendrye. He first received a captaincy in a colonial troop, and, in 1749,[14] after rusuming command in the West, was awarded the "Cross of the Order of St. Louis."

A contradictory strain ran through Pierre de la Verendrye. Ordinarily modest, patient, and faithful, he occasionally acted otherwise, writing letters to his superiors for personal favors. Some of these epistles were strikingly blunt, others naive, yet none were whining. They just repeated simple requests. The "Cross of the Order of St. Louis" is an example.

On August 1, 1731, even before the first post was built and

14.—About now he met Peter Kalm, the Swedish traveler and naturalist. They must have had much to talk about.

while he was still trying to raise cash, Verendrye wrote to Maurepas, "If God grants me the grace to succeed I shall have the honour of going myself to bring the news to Your Highness, and represent to you my thirty-two years of service with five severe wounds on my body; and I venture to flatter myself that you kindly take them into consideration." Six years later he wrote from Quebec, also to Maurepas, "Wherefore, Monseigneur, I beg Your Highness to reward me for my long services by a company, seeing that there are several vacant in this country, and with a Cross of St. Louis for my wounds. Such is the favour that I look for from you, and that of believing me, with most profound respect, Monseigneur, Your very humble and obedient servant."

Direct, this certainly is but it is also dignified. Verendrye did receive his company and the coveted "Cross," but the frontier had already collected its heavy toll. Before he could enjoy his tardy honors he passed away at Montreal, December 5, 1749, at the age of sixty-four just after writing to the minister for the colonies of his plan to lead a new western expedition the following year.

His death did not end a great career but it did end a faithful one. Verendrye remained true to his ideals. When he wrote of the new expedition he gave as one of his reasons that he wished to prove the "disinterestedness and zeal of myself and sons for the glory of the King and the welfare of the colony."

His life was often made miserable by those who hindered when they should have helped.[15] His son Pierre bitterly indicted the officials in a letter dated September 30, 1750. He said his father had been constantly thwarted by the envy of those in power—"envy is still here, more than elsewhere, a prevailing passion against which one has no protection." He further accused the officials of describing the money his father raised from time to time as "dissipation" and his father's narratives as "a pack of lies." His blast went on with, "Envy as it exists in this country, is no half envy; its principle is to calumniate furiously in the hope that if even one half of what is said finds favour it will be enough to injure." The elder Pierre, said the son, was often

---

15.—Beauharnois and, later, la Galissoniere were exceptions.

criticized by the court "because he was more interested in advancing than in talking about it."

This criticism of the Crown, if accepted, is a tribute to the worth of the father that at his advanced age he was willing to undertake another expedition to help prove his devotion to a king incapable of appreciating such loyalty. A lesser man would have taken his comfort and left the problem of the West for another generation.

The sons were urged to continue the work; but, when the father died, Governor La Jonquiere opposed all exploring by this family. The posts already established were confiscated and given to court favorites, the impoverished boys being left to start anew in a land where the fur trade was virtually the only industry. Occasionally their names thereafter appear briefly in some corner of Canada, but their real work was done. The place of Pierre's death is not known.[16] Louis-Joseph was lost in a shipwreck while on his way to France. Francois died in Montreal in 1794.

More than eighty years elapsed between Radisson and the last of the Verendryes, the family which took the second great step in the overland search for the western sea. Only fifteen more years were to pass before the next episode in the cross-continent search. Like its predecessor, this third venture was also abortive. Nevertheless the story of the advance to the Pacific would be incomplete if the tale of Jonathan Carver went untold.

16.—La Verendrye. *Journals and Letters of Pierre Gaultier de Varennes de la Verendrye and His Sons,* pages 30-32.

4

JONATHAN CARVER'S
FAMOUS BOOK OF TRAVELS

WHAT MARCO POLO WAS to the fifteenth century reader, Captain Jonathan Carver was to the eighteenth century reader. Society was never much interested in either man as a human being but it was intrigued by their tales.

Carver copied whole passages from better qualified storytellers than himself, yet his book continues to hold a unique place in the history of American exploration. Because of it, thousands of both Europeans and Americans became curious about the interior of the continent and the overland search for the "Western Sea." In fact, Carver's book rather than Carver himself is more important here. He was one of those delightful literary rogues whose doings annoy historians. Entangled in his mesh of truths and exaggerations, they sometimes call his writings pure nonsense because they do not fit the traditional notion of what an explorer's journals should be. Such characters as Carver charm those who want their heroes human, fallible, and not too conventional.

The facts of Carver's life are unexciting and few. Even his birth date is disputed. That he was born early enough in the eighteenth century to fight in the wars of that period seems certain. Some insist that he was born in Connecticut, probably Canterbury[1]; while others assert the time was 1732, the place, Stillwater,[2] New York.[3] In his younger years he perhaps studied medicine; more likely he practiced shoemaking. Again there is disagreement.

It is certain though that in 1746 he married Abigail Robbins, becoming the father of seven children. But his family never enters into his recorded career. His vivid imagination followed paths quite beyond them. After 1763 he apparently left his family to

1.—Snowden, volume 1, page 224. Lawrence J. Burpee's *The Search for the Western Sea,* page 285.
2.—In any case he was a contemporary of George Washington.
3.—*New International Encyclopedia,* volume 4, page 615.

shift for itself, marrying again in England several years later. He died, January 31, 1780.

Carver may have had important social connections in his home town, for he is supposed to have commanded, under Wolfe, a Massachusetts troop on the Plains of Abraham and to have been with Amherst at the surrender of Montreal. Colonial officers sometimes received their rank by popular vote of the men they were to command. If such were the case with Carver, he was at least well liked among the men of his company.[4] His interests, like his imagination, were unrestrained by that "hobgoblin of little minds," a "foolish consistency." He published a volume on tobacco culture, also *The New Universal Traveler* and *Literary History of the American Revolution.*

When the French wars were over, Carver restlessly determined to go west for adventure but he labeled his project as public service:

"No sooner was the late war with France concluded, and peace established by the Treaty of Versailles in the year 1763, than I began to consider (having rendered my country some services during the war) how I might continue still serviceable, and contribute, as much as lay in my power, to make that vast acquisition of territory, gained by Great Britain in North America advantageous to it."[5]

Three years later he undertook an independent tour into the country west and south of Lakes Michigan and Superior. He made the trip in an open canoe with two companions, an Indian and a French-Canadian. Leaving Boston in June, 1766,[6] he went to Michilimackinac, the farthest post west under British dominion. Appealing there to Governor Rogers for aid, Carver received some supplies and was promised more would be sent ahead to an appointed rendezvous. On September 3, he left the post to paddle across the upper end of Lake Michigan to Green bay, taking two weeks for the trip. From the bay he ascended Fox river, then crossed to the Wisconsin, and by October was on

---

4.—E. G. Bourne says there is no real proof that Carver took any such conspicuous part in the Colonial wars. See his "Travels of Jonathan Carver" in *The American Historical Review,* January, 1906, pages 289-290.

5.—Jonathan Carver. *Three Years Travels through the Interior Parts of North America,* page 1.

6.—March 18 of the same year the Stamp Act had been repealed.

the Mississippi. He turned northward until he reached the Falls of St. Anthony, where he expected but failed to find the additional supplies. While waiting for them, he explored the Elk and Minnesota rivers.

Still without supplies in the spring of 1767,[7] he had to retreat, dropping down first to the falls, then to Prairie du Chien at the junction of the Wisconsin and Mississippi rivers.[8]

Immediately he started plans for another adventure. This time his party ascended the Chippewa and St. Croix rivers, portaging at a small stream flowing into Lake Superior, then paddling around the northern shore toward the mouth of Pigeon river. Shortly thereafter Carver evolved a completely new plan— a trip to the Pacific ocean. The Indians gave him charcoal maps, inaccurate as usual, but these fired him with dreams of wealth and empire. He preferred these rude maps to the French ones, which he claimed were deliberately falsified to keep the English from learning the truth about the interior. On his own, he would proceed to Rainy lake, Lake of the Woods, Lake Winnipeg, and Assiniboine river, then over the divide to the Pacific, studying en route the natives, the soil, and the natural resources. He would build a post, preferably at the mouth of the Strait of Anian, and inaugurate a trans-Pacific trade with the Orient.

When he tried to get adequate supplies for the undertaking he found that traders already in the region could spare none. Thus abruptly a third attempt to cross the continent failed.

Carver returned to Michilimackinac in November of 1767, spending the rest of the winter there.[9] A year later [10] he returned to Boston, having been away almost three years. If he traversed

7.—On June 19, the British laid the tax on tea brought into American ports. During the same year Thomas Jefferson was admitted to the bar in Virginia and began the practice of law.

8.—While north of the Falls of St. Anthony, Carver claims to have entered the Sioux country. His critics question whether he actually got that far. Evidence on both sides is about equal.

9.—It is known that Alexander Henry, the elder, was at Roger's post during the winter and it is possible the two men met. If so, they left no impression on each other strong enough to cause either to mention the other. See Burpee, page 290.

10.—Three interesting events took place in 1768. Galvez left Mexico for the Northwest coast, April 9; General Gage arrived in Boston with the troops which eventually brought on the clash between the townspeople and themselves; and Massachusetts petitioned the king to rescind unjust taxes.

even a major portion of the country he said he did, he paddled and portaged through seven thousand miles of frontier rivers and trails, yet from the standpoint of practical exploration did nothing really important. The region was already partially known; he had added little new definite geographical data; and he had certainly not helped solve the problem of a way to the Pacific. Why then should his name ever appear in a history of the Far West? Why should encyclopedias give space to a wanderer who neither produced an original plan nor proved a new geographic fact?

The answer is simply that Jonathan Carver wrote a book that caught the popular mind.

After arriving at Boston he went on to England where he interested Richard Whitworth, M. P. from Staffordshire, in a proposal to cross the American continent and build a line of ships for the Oriental trade. Just then the American revolt broke out and western exploration had to wait. During this time Carver released his energies by writing the book, the Commissioners of Trade and Plantations having examined him at length and given their permission for him to publish his journals. These were just going to press when the government ordered them turned over to it as part of its permanent records.

Carver was now in a delicate position. He had been hounding the government to recognize his services with a suitable reward. If the Crown took his work at the value assigned by himself and asked him for the precious journals, he could not, while playing the unselfish explorer, refuse them. Of course, in giving up the journals, he would forego the income of publication. Should he insist on keeping them, the government might use some disciplinary measure and deny him any reward for his services. Furthermore, the published book might not be profitable, thus making him the loser on both counts. Carver finally bought the journals back from the printer-bookseller (who apparently had a sharp money sense), made a copy for himself, then turned the originals over to the government.

Later he not only talked the British Crown out of a small pension, but also published, ten years afterwards in Boston,[11]

11.—The volume ran through a surprising number of editions. It was published in London in 1778, a second edition appearing the next year; it was published in Dublin in 1779; in Germany in 1780; in France, two issues, in 1784; in the Netherlands in 1796; and reprints were even more numerous.

his *Three Years Travels through the Interior Parts of North America*. The volume has a style of its own, is easily read, easily believed. The serious sections contain nothing the uninitiated would challenge and the lighter passages intrigue most readers. It is doubtful if any book of American authorship in the eighteenth century achieved quicker or wider international fame than these *Travels*.[12]

Nevertheless few treatises on American exploration have been more controversial. Despite continued bitter criticism, the book is still read. Few defend its authority or champion its author, yet each generation of historians and biographers reads the *Travels* and enjoys tearing the book apart.

It has been called "a compilation from Charlevois, Hennepin, Lahontan, and others."[13] Professor Bourne[14] proves that the author copies whole sections from other writers. One of Carver's supporters, Reuben Thwaites, says the book is "an important contribution to American geography, and it is still held in high regard as a treatise upon the manners and customs of the Indians; for his report is that of an intelligent[15] and discriminating eye witness. "[16]

At the outset Carver comments that his "attention has been employed on giving a just description of a country that promises, in some future period, to be an inexhaustible source of riches to those people who shall be so fortunate as to possess it.[17] . . . I shall in no instance exceed the bounds of truth, nor shall I insert any observations, but such as I have made myself, or from the credibility of those by whom they were related, am enabled to vouch for their authenticity."[18] This statement is enough to make the casual reader hesitate to accept the charge of Carver's ignorance.

Besides telling of his travels, relating tales of Indian life, and

---

12.—Bourne, page 287.
13.—*New International Encyclopedia,* page 615.
14.—Bourne, pages 291-302. Bourne also suggests that Dr. John Coakley is the real compiler of the text.
15.—In quite another vein is the remark that Carver was "too ignorant a man to have written it." See the *New International Encyclopedia,* volume 4, page 615.
16.— Thwaites, page 49.
17.—Carver, pages VIII-IX.
18.—Carver, page 12.

giving a reasonably accurate evaluation of North America, Jonathan Carver did something else in this book—he proposed a geographic theory regarding the drainage of the continent which has since proved to be near the truth:

"I say from these nations (Indian) together with my own observations, I have learned that the four most capital rivers of the Continent of North America, viz. the St. Lawrence, the Mississippi, the Bourbon, and the Oregon [19] or the river of the West . . . have their sources in the same neighborhood. The water of the three former are within thirty miles of each other; the latter however is rather further west." [20]

His near accuracy can easily be proved. If a compass is placed on a map of North America midway between the modern cities of Fargo, North Dakota; and Duluth, Minnesota; and a circle is drawn with the circumference just touching them, it is evident that the headwaters of the Mississippi and Red rivers rise within that circle and that several small rivers emptying into Lake Superior, which is of course drained by the St. Lawrence, also fall within, or just without, the same circle.

All this might easily have been common knowledge to both the Indians and the whites. What was not likely to have been known are several more interesting facts. If the compass is next moved to the west and placed in the center of the triangle formed by the cities, Spokane, Washington; Medicine Hat, Alberta; and Helena, Montana; and a circle drawn embracing them, it will also embrace the headwaters of the Missouri, tributary of the Mississippi; the Clark, tributary of the Columbia; and the Saskatchewan, draining eventually into the Nelson. If the circle is enlarged and Helena becomes the center instead of the periphery and Spokane remains a point on the circumference of the new circle, it will be seen that the headwaters of the Green river, a tributary of the Colorado, will fall on the circumference of the new circle. Furthermore, if Medicine Hat is made the center of an enlarged circle, a considerable portion of the Mackenzie system will also be included.

19.—This is the first known use of the word *Oregon*. So bitter have been the charges against Carver's integrity that his right to use the term is a favorite point of attack. One of his critics indicts him as follows: "The word *Oregon* was in Carver's time as unfamiliar to the Indians as to the white people, and there can be little doubt that he invented it as he invented many of his geographical facts." See Snowden, volume 1, page 227.
20.—Carver, page 48.

It turns out that Carver hit upon a major geographic fact of North America—with the exception of the St. Lawrence, the main springs of the chief drainage systems of North America are to be found in a fairly small area centering in western Montana. These are the Nelson, Mackenzie, Mississippi, Columbia, and Colorado. Basically his knowledge, or theory, regarding drainage of the continent was correct. His error lay in placing the headwaters of the Columbia too close to those of the Mississippi. This error grows less on moving westward and considering the Missouri as the source of the Mississippi. Then, however, the St. Lawrence falls without a reasonably large circle.

In an era when interior transportation followed the rivers almost exclusively, it was important to know, or assume as in this case, that all of the continent might be traversed by merely following any one of the great river systems to its source, thereby being within a few miles of any other of the systems desired. Carver himself realized the value of such information; and the far greater explorers, Mackenzie and Lewis and Clark, used his theory in laying their plans.

In his book Carver included an analysis of the probable value of the Far West, particularly the Rocky mountain regions. "Probably," he wrote, "in future ages they may be found to contain more riches in their bowels, than those of Indostan and Malaba, or that are produced on the golden coast of Guinea; nor will I except even the Peruvian mines. To the west of these mountains, when explored by future Columbuses or Raleighs, may be found other lakes, rivers and countries, full fraught with all the necessaries or luxuries of life." [21]

The facts have outrun his optimistic prophecy and it is fitting that he should be credited with having sensed deeper into the ultimate values of the continent than did one member of the United States Senate, who said Oregon could never be of value, would always be a source of trouble and anxiety and that we might well be rid of it and leave the Rocky mountains as a barrier for our protection on the west. It was, said other so-called leaders of the Congress, impossible to occupy or settle the Far West because of the distances and natural obstacles. [22] Carver

21.—Carver, pages 76-77.
22.—Snowden, volume 1, pages 6-7.

knew better and said so, or at least copied into his book the words of others who thought so.

His interpretations of Indian life are intimate and refreshing. If he digresses to tell a tall tale the reader is usually rewarded. There is the story of the old Indian who had tamed a rattlesnake. The serpent was his "Great Father" and their kinship was such that they would not be separated except for the hibernation period of the reptile. With October the snake was released but when May brought warm winds and sunshine, both would repair to a prearranged meeting place as agreed. A Frenchman, hearing the Indian boast of his pet, laid a sizeable wager that the story was not true and waited a whole season to collect his reward. When the appointed day came, says Carver, the old rattler crawled happily into the Indian's box and the astonished Frenchman paid his wager.

Far different from the author of such tales is that solid character, Samuel Hearne.

FORT PRINCE OF WALES

Forty such guns defended the fort when Samuel Hearne was chief factor there.
(Canadian National)

5

HEARNE LAYS THE GHOST OF ANIAN

WALLS FORTY FEET THICK and twice the height of a man, forty guns staring from as many openings in its thick walls—such was Prince of Wales fort, Hudson bay, when Samuel Hearne in 1782 surrendered it to La Perouse, the Frenchman. It is necessary to know about that fort to understand Samuel Hearne.

In the shadow of that pile of stone at the mouth of the Churchill river occurred many of the romantic and sordid episodes of Hudson bay history. The new stone fort was built by the Hudson's Bay company in 1733[1] and was the center of trading activity to both the west and north. Its story is mainly that of three men: Richard Norton; Moses Norton, his half-breed son; and Hearne.

The elder Norton had helped his son acquire a thin veneer of civilization, thanks to a short sojourn in England and some training at Prince of Wales. The father, long a ruler on the Churchill river, had trained the boy in the ways of the white man; had taught him to sell dear and buy cheap; and had instructed him in the tricks of condescension supposed to make the natives feel the fellowship of the governor and the power of the company. After his father's death Moses found himself absolute governor of an immense region. No longer restrained by his white father, all his dormant primitive instincts and emotions were released and Prince of Wales fort became the scene of appalling orgies. Yet young Norton's critics, including Hearne, credit him with great ability.

His rule was complete and it was firm; but when the blood of his Indian mother rebelled at the restrictions of civilization, the son followed his primitive urges. While preaching morality and sobriety to his men, he himself indulged in every relaxation

---

1.—During the same year James Oglethorpe brought his criminals and debtors to Georgia, attempting to reclaim them for society by improving their economic status.

George Washington was born the preceding year.

which his fertile brain could conjure. He "kept five or six of the finest Indian girls he could get," and did not, like many Hudson's Bay men, pretend that the girls were common-law wives, entitled to a reasonable amount of respect and protection. Nor did he seize or buy them for regular wives as the natives themselves did. Norton kept these girls simply for personal pleasure.

He was fiery tempered and irrational. Frequently his insane jealousy flared into murderous wrath. Hearne relates that when Norton was lying on his deathbed he chanced to see an employe holding the hand of one of his young women. Thereupon the governor, cursing, reared up in bed and promised, if he lived, to murder the offender. Hearne adds that Norton "kept a box of poison to administer to those who refused him their wives or daughters." Once he "actually poisoned two of his women because he thought them partial to other objects more suitable to their ages."

He smuggled constantly but always turned the proceeds in to the company. According to Hearne, he "seldom put a shilling into his own pockets."

In many ways the hinterland bordering Prince of Wales fort is the wildest and most frightful in North America. To the south are inhabitable regions but to the west and north are the seemingly limitless "barren grounds," so desolate of plant and animal life that even the Indians shun them. There is no mystery about the "barren grounds"; they are cold and pitiless and real. There the usual fascination of the North is absent. Elsewhere in the sub-arctic is the constant nearness of immensity. The cold explodes and cannons along the rivers; myriad trees become great, snowy cones when the skies freeze over; and at night a million stars are bright. But in the "barren grounds" it is quite different. There is little or no grass in summer; there are no snow-covered trees in winter to carry one's eyes up to the stars. The distracting perfume of spruce never interrupts the monopoly of frozen space.

The Nortons, father and son, ruled such a country.

Somewhere at its northern extremity was a reputed deposit of copper so pure that the natives pounded out their tools and utensils from it. Naturally tales of this seeped into the Hudson Bay posts and about the beginning of the eighteenth century a few samples of the ore appeared in northern posts. The story reached the Churchill river in 1715. [2]

Among the first factors to attempt to prove or disprove the existence and value of such a copper mine was Captain Knight of York Factory, a man of eighty years. In 1719, in company with Captain Barlow, he set out for the North with two ships, the *Albany* and the *Discovery*, hoping to find the river at the mouth of which the copper mines were said to exist. Both vessels and crews were lost off Marble island.

Even before this ill-fated expedition began, Richard Norton had been interested in finding the Coppermine, but had done nothing more than excite in his son the same curiosity. When Moses Norton became governor, he helped set up the expedition, which finally reached the Arctic by land.

Desire to extend Hudson's Bay domain really began with the Inter-colonial wars. After the fall of Quebec, company profits fell sharply. From ten per cent they slumped to five, then to almost none. The war having scattered the French traders inland beyond the reach of the newly established English law, their trade was lost to the company. When its average yearly catch dropped from a hundred thousand to fifty thousand pelts, the company finally realized it must bestir itself in order not to lose its American empire to rival companies or private traders. Plans took shape for reconquering the lost fur territories and for branching out into new fields, perhaps new industries.

The attempt to locate the Coppermine [3] resulted from this changed policy. Besides, though the Northwest Passage, or Strait of Anian, was still not found, no one had proved it did not exist. The Hudson's Bay company had spent or was to spend, a hundred thousand pounds sterling [4] seeking it. Company scouts sent into a new territory were always cautioned to be on the lookout for it.

Moses Norton was instructed to inaugurate an expedition to achieve three things: increase the territory and trade of the

2.—Three years later at the other end of the continent the French founded New Orleans. Two years earlier they had lost some territory and considerable prestige when the Treaty of Utrecht was signed. Again in the same year the Maryland land grant was restored to Lord Baltimore.

3.—This name was early applied to the river on or near which the deposits were supposed to exist.

4.—Laut, page 381.

company, search for the Northwest Passage, and find the Coppermine. He selected young Samuel Hearne, a clerk aboard a
company brig trading in the river, to lead the expedition. Hearne
had no special qualifications for the task. On the Churchill he
had met Mr. William Wales, an astronomer who had been with
Cook on two of the three Cook voyages, but Hearne himself was
no mathematician and never pretended he could take other than
the rudest observations.

Details of Hearne's early life are vague. His father—a sensible,
respectable man from Somersetshire, and secretary to the water-
works, London bridge—died from a fever at the age of forty,
leaving Samuel, age three, and a daughter, five, in the care of
their mother. The family then moved to the old maternal home
in Dorsetshire, where the children were put in school. But books
failed to attract Samuel. He at last wore down the resistance of
his mother, who wanted a business career for him, and at the age
of eleven joined the navy, serving under Captain Hood during
the Seven Years' war.

Even less is known of his naval career than of his boyhood. He
dropped from sight until several years later when he was noticed
aboard a Hudson's Bay company ship trading with the Eskimos
north of the Churchill river. It was then that Governor Moses
Norton chose him to hunt for the Coppermine.

Hearne's mild, retiring nature often interfered with his efficiency.
Apologists explain that the Hudson's Bay company had sapped
his initiative by demanding absolute obedience to orders, making
him incapable of taking an aggressive position on anything. [5]
Such an analysis is without logic and unfair to the man. Hearne
had hardly been working for the company long enough to have
his spirit broken; he was only twenty-four. Besides, he showed
genuine strength of purpose, a quality rarely related to a broken
spirit. He did seem to flounder in indecision and inaction, not
because he lacked spirit but training, for the task at hand.
Hearne was a student of natural history, not a trained explorer.
Recognizing this, he said that his journals were not for "those
who are critics of geography"; they were for those who may be
"gratified by having the face of a country brought to their view."

5.—See the introduction to the Champlain Society edition of the Hearne
journals.

He saw and remembered easily. If he exaggerated he also analyzed and interpreted observed facts. When urged to publish his journals, he modestly remarked that had he supposed them to be of interest to anyone he would have taken more care with them.

As a recorder of native life Hearne ranks high among early travelers. He started for the Coppermine, light hearted and with little preparation. "I took only the shirt and clothes I then had on, one spare coat, a pair of drawers, and as much cloth as would make me two or three pair of Indian stockings, which, together with a blanket for bedding, composed the whole of my stock of clothing."

Governor Norton's Indian mother belonged to the local "southern" Indians, who were known to be dishonest, but Hearne felt obliged to take two of them as guides when he and his two white companions left Prince of Wales fort for the Coppermine, November 6, 1769.[6] His instructions included orders to study the soil structure of the Arctic plains. If he failed to find the Coppermine he was to depart from the original plans and explore what eventually proved to be nearly all of northern Canada beyond Hudson bay. Even the temperate Hearne was sarcastic at the absurdity of these orders. However, he did not take them seriously, a more intelligent attitude than Bering displayed in similar circumstances.

From the very first the expedition failed. One of the guides deserted the first day and the other became a liability. As he progressed he collected all of his friends and relatives, who ate the food supplies intended for emergency use. And Hearne lacked the will to refuse them.

The explorers covered a bare ten miles a day, in neither a definite nor prearranged direction. By the end of the month the white men had so far lost the respect of the natives that the Indians were openly robbing them of supplies and equipment, even ridiculing Hearne as a weakling. Hearne accepted the situation stoically, trudging back to Prince of Wales where to his

---

6.—There was considerable activity just at this time in other quarters of the continent. The Townshend Acts had been passed two years before and were at the height of their unpopularity with the colonial business men.

Captain Cook was in Pacific waters during 1769; and San Diego, California, was settled the same year. Also, the Spaniard, Portola, unsuccessfully attempted to reach San Francisco bay by land, turning back on November 11.

"own great mortification" he reported his failure to Norton, December 11, 1769.

Governor Norton took the failure calmly and both men started preparations for a second expedition before warmer weather would make sledges useless. By February 23, 1770, [7] everything was again ready. Norton suggested leaving the women and girls at home but Hearne refused. He said they were indispensable but offered no convincing proof.

Three Northern or Chipewyan Indians and two Southern Indians strengthened the guide service for the second expedition. Hearne noted that none of the Indians of his acquaintance had ever been to the Pacific nor did they know much about the Arctic, his guides being of real use only in regions with which they were familiar or in forming connections with other Indians who could supply new information. [8]

The second expedition, with the Seal river as its first goal, was but a prolonged version of the first. Starvation and gluttony alternated. Hearne constantly complained of the Indian habit of wasting food when it was abundant, then starving during scarcity, but he could not change Indian nature. Once he even remarked that the natives "had too much philosophy about them to give themselves much additional trouble by obtaining and preserving food for future use."

Hearne rarely criticized his own fare. When the hunters brought in only half a partridge per man each day he never sulked nor caused trouble, though he knew his Indian "friends" were walking ahead of the white section, killing and devouring what little game they found. On two occasions it was almost three days between meals; another time the white men lived for seven days on a few cranberries, choice pieces of shoe leather, and old burned bones. The women had less because the men were served first. But when the feasts did come they were enormous. One time the hunters killed three musk ox; and, having had no food for some time, the explorers quickly consumed an entire animal. With no material for fire, they ate it raw.

In spite of the experience of the first Coppermine expedition,

7.—Ten days later the Boston Massacre took place.
8.—Because the Northwest Passage was supposed to connect the Pacific with the Atlantic or Hudson bay, an Indian with knowledge of the Pacific would have been invaluable.

the second one was disintegrating. Hearne was caught out on the "barren grounds" with tents but no tent poles, though the Indians had provided themselves with proper equipment. It seems strange that an observant person like Hearne could watch the Indians collect poles and not inquire about their use. Yet, such was the case, and when the storms came he was compelled to dig holes in the snow and turn his sledge edgewise against the wind to get what rest he could.

The party was usually partially lost, Hearne being often three or four degrees latitude in error. Though he devised a simple scheme for marking off "daily courses and distances" on the enlarged section of an outline map of the North—insofar as northern geographic lines were known– it is impossible to do more than trace his general route.

The party had reached the "barren grounds" in April. [9] By that time several detachments of Chipewyans, having unceremoniously attached themselves to the group, began to help themselves not only to the food supplies but to the ammunition and trade goods as well.

August 12 was bitter for Samuel Hearne. Progress had been slow, only two or three miles a day, and on this day his authority was completely flouted. Dividing his personal property among themselves, the natives left him to figure out his own way back home. Because they had previously stolen his gun he could not put up even a token resistance. He had to beg for an awl, a razor, a needle, and a knife, to make his return to the Churchill possible. The natives gave him these simple articles but no sympathy; and, according to the code of the North, he deserved none. He had either broken, or permitted to be broken, most of the laws of self-preservation in the wilderness and should have expected to pay the penalty.

Through all this Hearne kept his good nature which was his greatest strength as well as his greatest weakness. With only a mild outburst of annoyance at his late employes, he started for Prince of Wales, August 19, 1770. The second expedition had failed.

9.—Now and then a bit of trading occurred during the early spring and summer. On July 6, 1770, they purchased a canoe with one knife, "the full value of which did not exceed one penny." What small amounts of iron they gave the Indians often netted the Hudson's Bay company as high as one thousand per cent profit.

A month afterward, while trudging homeward, he met Matonabbee, a Chipewyan chief, leading a party to the Churchill. This hard-headed six-foot barbarian possessed all the practicality that Hearne lacked. He offered to guide Hearne to the Coppermine provided the outfit was rigged in a manner satisfactory to him. Hearne readily agreed. Matonabbee's first rule was that there must be women along to do the slave work. They could be maintained, he said, at very little expense "for as they always stand cook, the very licking of their fingers in scarce times is sufficient for their subsistence."

Matonabbee and Hearne reached the fort on November 25, Hearne having been absent about nine months on what he termed "a fruitless, or at least unsuccessful journey."

Still persistent, he immediately laid plans for a new start. He went through the formality of offering once more to search for the Coppermine. Because his "abilities and approved courage" were well known, Governor Norton accepted his offer. Careless and inefficient as he was, Hearne sincerely liked his work, evading neither its danger nor its disagreeable features.[10] The third Coppermine expedition was ready, December 7, 1770.[11] Since Hearne had returned only two weeks previously, it is obvious that preparations were light. He did have the good sense to put himself in the hands of Matonabbee, who though often brusque, annoying, even deliberately cruel, nevertheless knew his goal and how to win it.

The general plan required working as far north and west as possible each day. Some days they went long distances from the indicated route to contact a new tribe that could give them information or supplies; occasionally they detoured for deer, caribou, firewood, fish, or a portage, but always at the end of a fortnight they were nearer the Coppermine. Some days they made sixteen or eighteen miles; others, only eight or nine. At times they pitched semi-permanent camp where they rested, hunted, dried meat, and repaired equipment.

10.—Among these were the problems of eating and sleeping. Sleeping accommodations were always poor and the food often disgusting, especially its preparation. Nevertheless Hearne refused only one native delicacy, the lice and grubs from the backs of the caribou.

11.—The year 1770 was the "quiet before the storm" period of the American Revolution.

An old bull musk ox was as "intolerable" as on previous trips, but now and then the entire expedition was glad to have a meal from one; or from the filthy remains of an earlier camp. The Christmas of 1770 was foodless. Hearne spent much of the day thinking of the good things his friends in England were eating.

So large had the party become that eight or ten deer supplied only a taste around with a little blood soup added. The scarcity of wood increased as they went farther north, and raw food became more and more their lot. Some of the neighboring tribes even practiced cannibalism. Matonabbee could no more control his appetite than he could his loves, and at least once the expedition had to halt while the old chief recovered from a gorging episode. This usually followed a period of near starvation.

Occasionally they caught a forty-pound lake trout; once in a while their prize was the great wood bison of the North, weighing a ton and a half and with hide an inch thick. [12] Some days were filled with study of the hunting, trapping and hide-curing techniques of the various tribes. When weather and other conditions were right, Hearne took his astronomical observations, but his unreliable instruments along with his personal carelessness made these almost useless.

Matonabbee's fondness for wives, some of whom "would have made good grenadiers," often caused ill feeling. He was physically so powerful and socially so important that he took whom he chose. A sweetheart or husband who challenged him was quickly put in his place. Generally Matonabbee followed the custom of his people, wrestling or fighting for his women; but once having seized another's wife and being reproached for it, he strode into the objector's tent, knifed him savagely, then went placidly back to his own tent, leaving the husband, the tribe, and Hearne to make the best of it.

With all his sins, Matonabbee was a man of immense determination. When Hearne would have lagged, Matonabbee goaded him; when his own wives fell prey to their human ills, he ordered them left behind to catch up as best they could. He joined with the others in ribald ridicule when one of his wives, through a tendency to "belt her clothes so high," froze her buttocks so

---

12.—Haworth, pages 43-44.

severely that great blisters the size of sheep's bladders rose on them when she was thawed out.

"I must acknowledge that I was not in the number who pitied her, as I thought she took too much pains to shew a clean heel and good leg; her garters being always in sight," said Hearne. He seemed unimpressed by the women. Speaking of the young ones in their thirties he remarked that they were a "perfect antidote to love and gallantry. . . . Ask a Northern Indian, what is beauty? he will answer, a broad flat face, small eyes, high cheek bones, three or four broad black lines across each cheek, a low forehead, a large chin, a clumsy hook nose, a tawny hide, and breasts hanging down to the belt."

And so the days passed, some pleasant, some almost intolerable, some monotonous, but always the party made progress toward the Coppermine.

The expedition had left Prince of Wales fort, December 7, 1770. For a few miles Matonabbee led them over the same route used on the previous trips, but before long he branched off. Where Hearne on his second trip turned northwest, Matonabbee held to his westward direction until almost due north of Lake Athabasca, then turned sharply north until arriving at Clinton-Colden lake, after which he bore northwest again until the Coppermine was reached. Only approximations can be made of the directions and distances of the third expedition. Hearne was more careful than before but his observations were still so far off as to be largely unreliable. Some of that region is unexplored even now.

Between December 7 and January 22, the party was more or less in touch with natives of whom they knew something, but on the latter date they met strangers. This meant that the expedition had passed beyond the hazy borders of known land and was finally entering unknown regions where they might discover important geographic facts and economic data.

They reached Pike lake in March. There they encountered a party of Indians going to the Churchill to trade and they seized the chance of sending letters reporting their progress.

In April Matonabbee ordered a long halt to prepare a war party. Up to that time Hearne seems to have been unaware of the bloody intent of his friends. On the other hand, he may have suspected that the chief was not being helpful through mere humanity and have figured that the loss of a few native lives was a cheap price to pay for the Northwest Passage or the Copper-mine. When Matonabbee was satisfied with the pounded meat, repaired equipment and other war supplies, the entire party pushed on to Clowy lake, reaching it in May. Here more warriors joined them and Matonabbee ruled that the women and children were to be left behind. To Hearne the days following the war announcement seemed much like the others. At first he discouraged the preparations but, finding himself regarded as a weakling, he did not press his point.

On May 20, 1771, they came "within a day's walk" of a Captain Keelshies, an old acquaintance trading in the interior. Hearne and the captain got together to exchange news but Matonabbee interrupted their meeting by ruling that the party make ready for a dash to the Arctic and back. The women and children were all to be left behind as planned except for the chief's two girls. The sly, old rascal made a special rule for them.

The party was now well into the unknown North, probably somewhere in the vicinity of 64°, and daylight was almost twenty-four hours long. At 9 o'clock on the night of May 31, Matonabbee with his warriors and Hearne started on the last outward lap of the journey. They made ten miles that evening before halting to rest.

Just about this time Hearne took another of his infrequent observations, reporting they were at 67° 30' north. Of course this calculation too is questionable. On June 21, he said the sun did not sink below the horizon at all. [13] If that were true the expedition had indeed got well into the Arctic. The party consisted of 150 warriors all of whom had to cross lakes and rivers in three small two-man canoes. It would have been unwise, though, to travel with more canoes for they were seldom used.

They first met the Copper Indians on June 22 [14] and Hearne was amused by their reactions to him and his color. He was the

13.—Hearne could not always have been where he claimed. Some authorities challenge his statement regarding the sun. Logic would seem to reverse the criticism. He was surely a careless astronomical observer yet he was no fool. It is hard to believe he could not recognize the sun when he saw it.

14.—Hearne's journals are not clear on this point but he seems to indicate the twenty-second.

first white man the Indians had seen and they were not very enthusiastic. His flesh looked as if ,it had lain too long in the water, they said, and his hair was the color of the "stained hair of the buffaloe's tail." In fact they considered him quite second rate. Hearne thoroughly enjoyed the situation and became fast friends with the natives.

The expedition finally reached the Coppermine river in mid-July. Hearne treated the occasion calmly. He found an insignificant stream and no great copper deposit but he wanted to go on to the mouth of the river to complete his assignment.

Having scouted a five-tent village of Eskimos a short distance ahead, Matonabbee made last-minute preparations for an attack. Wooden shields were painted in grotesque patterns, each warrior having a favorite personal sign intended to bring good fortune in the approaching combat or, rather, massacre. Describing the paintings on the shields, Hearne said, "some few of them conveyed a tolerable idea of the thing intended, yet even these were many degrees worse than our country sign-painting in England." This was no great compliment to the English sign painter.

Hearne now made a final futile attempt to halt the massacre. He was told he could return to the women if he were afraid. He stopped arguing but commented in his journals, "evidently . . . it was the highest folly . . . to attempt to turn the current of a national prejudice which had subsisted between those two nations from the earliest periods."

With the shields painted and Hearne silenced, Matonabbee began the attack at 1 o'clock, the morning of July 17, 1771. True Indians, they crept upon the sleeping and defenseless Eskimos, who ran naked and bewildered from their tents only to be hacked to pieces. No quarter was given. Men, women, and children were killed and mutilated for no crime greater than being Eskimos. In her death struggles one young woman twined her body about Hearne's legs, begging him to save her. He tried to but at slighting remarks about his intentions to the girl he gave up and let the spears and hatchets finish their work. An old man crawled by him to die, his "whole body . . . like a cullender." Women, both living and dead, were subjected to bestial indignities and when the massacre of Bloody Falls was over Hearne was physically and mentally ill. He knew he could not have stopped it but just seeing it made him feel guilty.

Partly to get away from these scenes and partly because there was nothing else to do, he went on north that same night. It was really still daylight and after going but a short distance he looked ahead and saw the marks of the rising and falling tides. [15] One more link in the long chain of geographic knowledge was welded; another myth, the Northwest Passage, had been laid to rest. Never again need any man risk his life and spend his fortune looking for that will-o'-the-wisp.

In the moment of his success Samuel Hearne was peculiarly unemotional, yet he was fully aware of the three-century search for the Strait of Anian, the Northwest Passage. Regarding this he said, "Although my discoveries are not likely to prove of any material advantage to the Nation at large, or indeed to the Hudson's Bay company yet I have the pleasure to think that I have fully complied with the orders of my Masters and that I have put a final end to all disputes concerning a Northwest Passage through Hudson's bay." He was sure his name would be added to the brief list of men who have found the answer to an old riddle but he unceremoniously raised a mark, took possession for his company, then quietly lay down and went to sleep. Six hours later he started home.

Twenty miles south-southeast he found the copper mines which had been the ever-present lodestar. He pocketed a chunk of the ore and continued on his way.[16] On July 25, the reunited party swung south and west to Great Slave and Athabasca lakes. [17] They reached Prince of Wales fort on June 30 of the following year. The return trip took eleven months, uneventful except for several of the women starving to death.

Hearne's last years can be briefly told. His reports were received in London, November, 1772. The following May the Hudson's Bay company sent him to establish a post at Basquia. He went beyond his instructions and built Cumberland house on the Saskatchewan at Sturgeon lake.

15.—There are historians who doubt whether Hearne actually reached the Arctic but his journals leave no such doubt in the minds of most readers.

16.—The specimen is now in the British Museum.

17.—While Hearne was making his dash to the Arctic, Benyowsky was involved in piracy.

At Moses Norton's death in 1775, his place went to Hearne, who was neither administrator nor soldier. When La Perouse, the French admiral, attacked the fort in 1782, "Hearne, mightier with the pen than with the sword, surrendered meekly enough in spite of his massive walls from thirty to forty feet thick. Thus ingloriously he dies out of history." [18, 19] La Perouse treated his captive kindly and was instrumental in getting him to publish his journals.

After the peace Hearne returned to Hudson bay but soon went back to England to live. Meanwhile the company is said to have rewarded him with a gift of two hundred pounds sterling and some small additional amounts as servant's fees. Whatever private funds he had acquired in the fur trade he lost through unsound investments and loans. He died penniless in 1792.

Time has added perspective to the figure of Samuel Hearne and it no longer seems that he passed "ingloriously out of history." He had "a much more exact knowledge of the breadth and character of the continent than was possessed by even the most eminent geographers of his day" [20] and he "deserves a high place in the records of North America exploration; the published account of his remarkable travels shows him to have been a close and enlightened observer, as well as possessed of a remarkable capacity for dealing with savage minds." [21]

Hearne's ability to deal with the savage mind is open to question, but certainly not his right to recognition for the part he played in the discovery of the Northwest. He was a great gentleman and a great explorer, and he laid the centuries-old ghost of the Strait of Anian myth.

18.—Sir Edmund Walker. *Introduction to the Journals of Hearne*, volume 6, page VII.

19.—The French had joined the British colonies in the revolt against George III; thus the struggle for liberty became entangled in the struggle for fur.

20.—Burpee, page 140.

21.—Thwaites, page 51.

6

ALEXANDER MACKENZIE
DISCOVERS A GREAT RIVER

No scotsman has a clearer title to honor than Alexander Mackenzie, a canny fur trader and the most indomitable explorer ever to ferret a secret from the interior of North America. History shows only one Mackenzie, one Drake, one Napoleon. And Mackenzie is unique among overland explorers as Drake is among pirates, and Napoleon among generals. His life was so closely associated with the Canadian Northwest that his birthplace is often forgotten. This was in Stornoway, Lewis, in the Hebrides islands; the year about 1758.[1] He was not a native of the continent on whose map he drew more important lines than any other single person unless possibly Champlain.

Next to Lewis and Clark, Alexander Mackenzie is the most difficult of the overland explorers to humanize. Never dramatic, his journals were rigidly matter-of-fact. He probably never arose in the morning without having the day's activities already mapped out. It must have been a regular evening task to check over the events of the day to see if he had lost a second which might have been used to further his ends. [2] Efficient himself, he detested inefficiency in others, yet he was patient when they failed to accomplish the tasks he set for them.

All his life he was a driver. He drove himself into seemingly impossible achievements and his employes to desertion. Still, most

---

1.—George Washington headed the successful campaign against Fort Duquesne during this year.
2.—He took boyish delight in refuting popular beliefs. One of these was that the swells common to northern lakes presaged a coming storm. Mackenzie checked these swells carefully, concluding that a fine, clear day followed such swells as often as a storm. Once he remeasured the distance between two points and proudly announced that where others found it "a computed one hundred twenty miles . . . I make it only eighty." Referring to the supposed cannibalistic habits of the Chipewyan Indians he said, "I never was acquainted with one instance of that disposition . . . but such as arose from the irresistible necessity which has been known to impel even the most civilized people to eat each other."

men loved him enough to follow him over trails which would have been out of the question under a lesser man.

Sometime before 1778, [3] Mackenzie arrived from Scotland and became an apprentice in a Montreal counting house. In 1779, he entered the employ of John Gregory of Montreal, the chief partner in the "Little Company" of Gregory, McLeod and company, organized to compete with the fur traders in the Great lakes region. Thus, at the age of about twenty, Mackenzie was thrown headlong into the wildest commercial venture the New World has ever seen, not excepting the gold rushes. He never really cared for the fur business, however, always considering it merely a stepping stone to his real career, exploration.

Early in life he learned to control himself as well as his associates and to mold his environment. He did not yield to circumstance; he outwitted it. There were no lulls in his life, no reverses to be recovered. He moved directly and irresistibly to a set goal where he could lay down his tools and rest, secure in the knowledge that those following him would merely map in the details around the major outlines which he himself had drawn.

His attachment to Gregory, McLeod, and company hinged on the explicit understanding that he would be sent into the Northwest of that time to carry on rival trade against those already there. This arrangement was not because he hated these rivals or loved the fur trade. He simply wanted the opportunity of getting a foothold along the frontier where he might better indulge his desire for exploration. In 1784 [4] he went to Detroit. The Gregory-McLeod people were as anxious to have a reliable, aggressive trader at Detroit as Mackenzie was to be there.

He found the western fur fields already held by a hard-fighting crew who gave allegiance to no one and at first refused even to consider sharing their territory with an outsider. Before two seasons had passed these same traders were taking orders from

---

3.—In 1778 the struggling United States concluded an alliance with France, v ich in turn probably threw the scales of war in our favor; although Saratoga, commonly called the turning point in the war, had been fought the year before. A more important event was the signing of the Articles of Confederation in the same year.

4.—On January 14, Congress ratified the Treaty of Paris, closing the American Revolution; and the *American Daily Advertiser,* first daily paper in the United States, began publication.

the Northwest company of which Alexander Mackenzie was a leading figure.[5] The date was July, 1787.[6]

Plans to expand the business went forward at once and the following year Mackenzie ordered Fort Chipewyan built on the southwest shore of Lake Athabasca, [7] seventy days' journey from Lake Superior.

Mackenzie was curious about the destination of the river which flowed away from Athabasca. Two hundred miles to the north lay Great Slave lake, draining into the Mackenzie [8] which wandered away through a pathless 2,500 miles more. This waste fascinated the Scotsman. If the Northwest company were to make a fortune at Fort Chipewyan, it would have to be made by others. Mackenzie was going exploring. The company grudgingly consented. Putting aside all pretense of trading, Mackenzie began the first of the two trips which made him world famous.

Yet he was not indifferent to wealth. Quite the contrary. The British had posted a prize of twenty thousand pounds for anyone who would discover a Northwest Passage. Apparently unaware that Hearne had proved the nonexistence of the strait, Mackenzie was convinced of his own success. He said, "I . . . was confident in the qualifications, as I was animated by the desire, to undertake the enterprise."

At 9 a. m., June 3, 1789,[9] he was ready to leave Fort Chipewyan His party included two canoes, one of which contained four Canadians, the Indian wives of two of these, one German, and the Indian, English Chief, with two of his favorite wives. The other canoe, much smaller, was manned by two young Indian interpreters and hunters. The company clerk, M. Le Roux, accompanied Mackenzie as far as Great Slave lake to carry on trade. Beyond offering pleasant companionship for the first two hundred miles, Le Roux took no part in the project.

5.—An outline of the history of this company appears later.

6.—On July 13, 1787, the Northwest Ordinance was signed; this was the governing criterion for the West for many years. Two months later the Constitutional Convention began deliberating.

7.—Athabasca was immediately adjacent to a huge territory. The lake itself averages thirteen miles wide and stretches more than two hundred miles in length.

8.—For clearness, the name eventually given the river is used throughout.

9.—Early in the spring the electoral college met and cast its votes for Washington for first President. On April 30, seven weeks later, he was inaugurated.

Because midsummer nights north of Athabasca are short, the explorers were almost always on the way by 4 a.m. They often started at 3 or even 2 o'clock, paddling for several hours before halting for breakfast. The day seldom ended before 6 or 7 p.m. and sometimes it was 11:30 p.m. Fifteen and sixteen hours of hard toil was the reward for those who followed Mackenzie to the Arctic. But he was equally active. He would sit up alone all night working over his papers, taking observations, or planning the next day's activities. He was a disciplinarian. He disciplined himself to lead, always doing a margin more than the others, walking a bit faster, taking a few more risks, and resting a little less.[10]

Though the party did not leave Athabasca until 9 o'clock, this was to be the last late start for many days. The following day the canoes were shoved off at 4 a.m., the next at 3 a.m. On June 6, Mackenzie kept his men hard at it from 2:30 in the morning until 6 o'clock at night, in spite of the fact that the day before one of the canoes had gone over a falls and been lost, with all the resulting lowered morale.

On June 9 the ice was too thick to proceed and the explorers waited until the fifteenth to go on. During that week they rested and hunted. Warmer weather brought its evils though, for Mackenzie wrote under the date of the nineteenth, "We were pestered by mosquitoes, though in a great measure, surrounded with ice." The northern mosquito, noisier, stronger, and more vicious than his southern relative, can cause real misery. On June 20 the party was still encompassed by ice but "found abundance of cranberries and small spring onions."

Mackenzie kept up a pace that sometimes exhausted the Indian guides. He wrote, "Toward morning (of the twenty-third), the Indians who had not been able to keep up with us the preceding day, now joined us." He had not even held back for his guides.

From time to time Le Roux did a little trading. On June 24 he obtained eight packs of beaver and marten but his activities centered about Slave lake where the party arrived the following day. Without stopping to help Le Roux establish his trade, Mackenzie at once started searching for the outlet to the lake. The

---

10.—There is only one recorded occasion on which Mackenzie is accused of side-stepping danger or fatigue. On the trip to the Pacific he once ordered a canoe launched in a particularly nasty bit of water. The crew refused to do so until the leader himself entered. This Mackenzie unhesitatingly did.

Indians from Fort Chipewyan and perhaps the whites knew something of the size and relative position of Slave lake. From there on, though, they were all in unknown territory. English Chief, who was to Mackenzie what Matonabbee was to Hearne, secured the services of a local Indian who pretended to know the way from the mouth of Slave river to the outlet of the Mackenzie. Putting themselves in his care, the party set out, confident that they would soon find the river.

The second day after reaching the lake the hunters killed two reindeer but "lost three hours aft wind in going for them." Such was the impatience of Mackenzie. He well knew the necessity of getting food but was jealous of the time it took. In his journal he expressed the annoyance he was too great a commander to voice openly.

English Chief was much less restrained. He was devoted to Mackenzie and did his best to hurry the expedition. When the Red-Knife guide who had pretended to know all about the lake turned out to be totally ignorant of it, English Chief promptly suggested that he be permitted to murder the fellow as a worthless dog. He even threatened to do so on his own authority. Mackenzie narrowly prevented bloodshed.

After three days' search, the source of the lake still eluded them. But at five-thirty on the morning of the fourth day the "object of our search" was found. That is all the journal says about it.

Some days were of course uneventful, some interesting, and a few exciting. On July 1 they concealed a supply of pemmican against their return; the next day "The Indians complained of the perseverance with which we pushed forward"; then the weather turned "extremely cold, which was the more sensibly felt, as it had been very sultry sometime before." On Sunday, July 5, [11] the explorers encountered five families of Slave and Dogrib Indians, who were terrified at the sight of the white men. Tobacco did not appeal to these natives because they knew nothing of its use; but, when grog, knives, beads, and hatchets were offered, greed overcame their fears, and such social interchanges as could be made took place. The Indians entered Mackenzie's tents freely

---

11.—The day before the first protective tariff in our history was passed by the American Congress.

without attempting to steal, probably because of no previous relations with white traders.

Mackenzie had a low opinion of the natives, calling them poor specimens of humanity. Poverty stricken, ugly, dirty, and diseased, they further disfigured themselves by drawing across their cheeks, two black or blue lines from the nose to the ears.

Shortly after meeting the Slave and Dogrib tribes, the party sighted high, snow-capped mountains ahead. The Chipewyan guides from Athabasca began to sulk about, devising plans to slip away and go home. For a time, English Chief and the Scotsman were able to overcome their fears, but from then on there was constant trouble with guides. A new native, hired for a "small kettle, an axe, a knife, and some other articles," tried to renege; Mackenzie, "after delay of an hour, compelled him to embark." Mackenzie does not explain the means used to compel the guide to embark, but firearms settled many disciplinary cases.

The explorers made rapid progress. A month and two days after leaving Fort Chipewyan they passed the mouth of Great Bear Lake river. Two days later they stopped at a four-fire Indian camp, the inhabitants of which at first fled in terror but were coaxed back, becoming friendly and giving the white men some fresh fish and a new guide.

The river became difficult; very deep, and "not above three hundred yards in breadth, but on sounding I found fifty fathoms water." A new guide had to be found and "forced to embark." Just why the Indians of the Far North were so terror stricken at leaving their little localities Mackenzie does not make clear. Of course they had the usual fears of the spirit world about them. For instance the journal dryly records that "there was a Manitoe or spirit, in the river, which swallowed every person that approached it. At it would have employed half a day to have indulged our curiosity in proceeding to examine this phenomenon, we did not deviate from our course."

Such fears are common to all primitive or barbaric peoples and though all of the overland explorers had trouble with their guides, none had so much as Mackenzie. Possibly the fear was not so much of a "Manitoe" as it was of the Scotsman. There was no reason to be happy over the prospect of working twelve, fifteen, or eighteen hours a day for Alexander Mackenzie.

On July 9 another guide deserted and a new one was forced to take his place. Native camps were small and this one had only two canoes. One of them would be used by the new guide. Mackenzie decided to put the other canoe out of commission by taking the paddles, thus preventing a second Indian from following and coaxing his relative to desert.

The explorers were 67° 47′ on July 10, and concern was growing that the return trip could not be made that season. Mackenzie quietly considered an unpleasant winter on the Arctic, for he had now concluded that the river emptied not into the Pacific but "into the Hyperborean Sea." Just then, however, they found another village, from whose inhabitants they learned they were only ten days' journey from the ocean and but three from the first Eskimo huts. Strangely enough this news so frightened the guides that their terror spread to the Chipewyan hunters and Mackenzie found an incipient mutiny on his hands. Taking into account the usual inaccuracies of Indian statistics, he outguessed his people by promising them that if the ocean were not reached within seven days they would return. He then opened a drive to make a ten days' trip in seven.

The margin of safety was not so close as it at first appears. Long practice had taught him that the Indians generally stretched time and distances. Therefore he was reasonably safe in assuming that the actual distance was fewer than ten days' travel. He also knew that ten days' travel to the Indians, unless on the war path, meant ten days of leisurely wandering, and he was sure he could go any distance they chose to name in two-thirds the time they would use. His return offer was just a bit of strategy.

On July 11 the sun did not set [12] and Mackenzie sat up all night observing and thinking about the interesting day just past. He described the igloos, or underground huts, constructed of such materials as happened to be at hand. He had heard of the people who lived on an immense lake to the north and spent their time killing great black fish and huge white bears.

English Chief now became frightened and begged Mackenzie to turn back. Aware of the Indian's excessive fondness for a certain brightly-colored cloak—one which Mackenzie himself was

12.—It will be recalled that Hearne mentions the sun's remaining above the horizon on June 21.

quite partial to—he promised the garment to the guide if he would go on. What a struggle must have taken place in the mind of the savage. In the immediate distance lay the horrors of an unknown spirit world, inhabited by giant beasts and still more giant fish; dangling before his eyes was a tangible and highly-desired piece of finery. The finery won. English Chief swore new allegiance and Mackenzie bound the pledge by giving a moose skin to one of the guides as a token of faith and respect.

By this time the party had reached 69° 1′ north. Solid ice of unknown depth was covered by four inches of cold soil from which sprang short grass and tiny flowers. Maybe the flowers helped, but the same guides who a few hours before had threatened desertion now became so enthusiastic about reaching the Arctic that they agreed to go on no matter how long it took. Sea gulls began appearing overhead and probably this was what really convinced the Indians that salt water was not very far away.

Shortly after retiring on the evening of July 13, 1789, Mackenzie was awakened to move the baggage out of the way of rising water. At the time he attached no special significance to the event. Only later did it occur to him that the rising flood was salt water and that they were at last near the "Hyperborean Sea."

The next day one of the party noticed some whale rolling about offshore. Mackenzie ordered chase in their frail canoes. When the huge mammals had escaped and his judgment cleared, he shamfacedly records that his attempt to catch whale from a canoe "was indeed a very wild and unreflecting enterprise."

The same date bears this simple entry, "This morning I ordered a post to be erected close to our tents, on which I engraved the latitude of the place, my own name, the number of persons which I had with me, and the time we remained there." [13] Any attempt which is made to evaluate Mackenzie's modesty and the magnitude of his accomplishment is open to the charge of attempting to dramatize a simple historical fact, yet his deed was not simple. It took careful planning and ruthless execution to accomplish what he did in such a short time. He had not as he claimed, "settled the dubious point of a practicable North-West

13.—Alexander Mackenzie. *Voyages from Montreal through the Continent of North America to the Frozen and Pacific Oceans* in 1789 *and* 1793, page 271.
14.—Mackenzie, page IX.

passage";[14] that honor goes to Samuel Hearne. But there was honor enough and to spare in being the explorer, as Mackenzie was, of the world's tenth largest river.

He did not linger on the coast. The very next day, failing to find any natives, "We accordingly made for the river, and stemmed the current. At two in the afternoon the water was quite shallow in every part of our course, and we could always find the bottom with the paddle. At seven we landed, encamped, and set the nets," and, the journal records later, fought the usual swarm of mosquitoes.

For the first time and then only briefly, food was scarce and the cooks had to do the best they could with moldy pemmican and an abundance of cranberries. During the third week of July the party of fourteen ate two reindeer, four swan, forty-five geese, [15] and an indefinite number of fish. White fish were the most common; these Mackenzie called "exquisite." There were also lake trout, pike, and carp, the carp often growing as large as salmon.[16] Aside from an overdose of cranberries they feasted extraordinarily well. As delicacies, wild fowl eggs, not always fresh, added variety.

The route home was the same as that going out, the party making equal speed. Ten days after they left the Arctic a wind storm threw rocks in the air so large that "we were obliged to throw ourselves flat on the ground to escape being wounded." Afterwards Mackenzie grumbled about having "lost 1½ hours" along the way. Starts as early as 1:30 a.m. became necessary. It was the first of August and that is the beginning of winter in the Far North. On one day the "heat was insupportable"; the next, "we could not put on clothes enough to keep us warm." The explorers were soon back at Bear Lake river and for the first time since leaving Athabasca it was dark enough for them to see the stars. Here was another sign of winter.

A week later Mackenzie turned off to climb a "nearby" mountain. At the end of three hours' tramping he found the mountain no nearer than it had originally appeared. Disgusted at being so

---

15.—On the outward journey the wild fowl were molting and the hunters often ran them down rather than use ammunition.

16.—The Scotsman tells a yarn about the liveliness of these northern fish. While paddling downstream one day they found the river so full of them that one "of the many which we saw leap out of the water, fell into our canoe."

easily fooled he turned back to the river only to become lost in a swamp, lose his footing and sink to his armpits before help arrived. The accident thoroughly upset the exact and efficient Scotsman. Physically he suffered only a nasty wetting; mentally he suffered far more.

At 4 p.m. on the twenty-fourth they hailed a distant canoe and soon had a pleasant reunion with Le Roux. In another week the party reached the company post on Slave lake. Mackenzie stayed up all night making plans for an early start in the morning.

The first Mackenzie expedition was nearly finished. They returned to Fort Chipewyan 102 days after leaving it. No major accidents occurred, no illness, no deaths, almost no violence, and very few minor mishaps. One canoe was lost over the falls and another was damaged in a scuffle when a native tried to enter uninvited. On one occasion Mackenzie shot a dog.

The greatest American expedition up to 1789 left no rotting bones as did Bering's, witnessed no massacres as did Hearne's. Mackenzie did no senseless wandering; instead, he speedily and accurately delineated a great river. But he was disappoined. "I had come a great way, and at a very considerable expense, without having completed the object of my wishes." To discover and explore an immense river, to write his name forever among the greatest explorers left him "without having completed the object of my wishes."

Mackenzie also produced an extensive record of his travels. He described how the Indians behaved, and gave his opinion of what he saw. His report is a study of the folklore of a primitive people, yet he pretended that he could do little studying on the way. "I was not only without the necessary books and instruments, but also felt myself deficient in the science of astronomy and navigation"; and again, "I could not stop to dig in the earth over whose surface I was compelled to pass with rapid steps."

The long days gave him time for thought and when he published his journals in 1801, he included many of his reflections. These are always clear and fundamental. He observed the foibles and frailties of persons he dealt with, evaluating with ease and justice both the savage and the civilized. He says, "Experience proves that it requires much less time for civilized people to deviate into the manners and customs of savage life, than for savages to rise into a state of civilization."

He was interested in the morality of these primitive people, referring more than once to the sins committed against the Indians by the whites: traders were often a "disgrace to the Christian religion" and when half-civilized Canadians sank to the level of the Indians they only "acquired their (the Indians') contempt rather than their veneration." On the other hand, he probably did not exert himself overmuch to purify the social relationships between reds and whites. Of course the natives, especially the native women, were still considered fair prey for the blandishments of the "superior races."

It was accepted ethics for a white trader to cheat an Indian in a trade or satisfy his sexual desires with the Indian women. These activities were frequently expected and enjoyed as much by the Indians as by the whites. Sharp trading between two Indian men was the accepted mode of business and sexual promiscuity either as a part of the business deal, or independent of it, was equally common. Long generations before the coming of the white men, some of the natives, particularly the Knistenaux, had "a ready way, by use of certain simples, of procuring abortions, which they sometimes practice, from their hatred of the father, or to save themselves the trouble which children occasion."

Mackenzie later noted the habit of the Indian men of lending or hiring their women to the traders with the use of the family hut as a part of the bargain. This custom once considerably delayed a conference with the chiefs. "The sun . . . had risen before they left their leafy bowers, whither they had retired with their children, having most hospitably resigned their beds, and the partners of them, to the solicitations of my young men. [17] To the eye of an European they (the women) certainly were objects of disgust; but there were those among my party who observed some hidden charms in these females which rendered them objects of desire, and means were found, I believe, that very soon dissipated their alarums and subdued their coyness." Sometimes, though, when Mackenzie's own Indians were "very anxious to possess themselves of a woman that was with the natives . . . I interfered, to prevent her being taken by force."

17.—This occurred on Mackenzie's journey to the Pacific, not the Arctic.

Each time he came upon a camp he recorded the number of tents or huts, the number of men, women, and children, now and then remarking on how many were probably away from home at the time. His survey indicates that the valley had always been sparsely inhabited. Often a camp of only two, three, or four dwellings was found, and large villages were never seen. If this information held good for the entire region, the total population could have been counted in hundreds rather than thousands. The people themselves were a lowly lot, their homes generally partly portable, the dog their only domesticated animal, and the art of agriculture almost unknown. [18] The Slave lake natives were without iron of any sort and did their cooking in primitive woven baskets and stone kettles, some of which held two gallons.

They usually wore long leather leggings reaching to the hips, moccasins, and a rough fur shirt or cloak, its hair out for the summer and in for the winter. Ornamentation was simple, for a pair of moose-hide moccasins lasted but a day if the going were rough and the womenfolk were busy enough without bothering with finery. Sometimes a tassel served a double purpose, usefulness and decoration. "They (the women) have no covering on their private parts, except a tassel of leather which dangles from a small cord, as it appears, to keep off the flies which would otherwise be very troublesome." [19]

Disease was not as unknown as the ardent "back to nature" advocate testifies. Smallpox wrought such havoc at times that victims sometimes resorted to suicide to escape a more painful death, and fathers occasionally murdered their entire family rather than have them endure the dread suffering. Frequently the wolves brazenly entered the huts, dragging the dead into the open and devouring them at leisure.

Mackenzie's Second Expedition

Too young and too ambitious to retire after his first expedition, and with only a passing interest in the fur trade, Alexander Mackenzie immediately turned his attention to further exploration. He was sufficiently familiar with the work of the Verendryes to remark that Fort Bourbon "was also a principal post of the

18.—The natives immediately adjacent to the Great lakes were familiar with horses, though they did not use them.
19.—Mackenzie, volume 1, page 235.

French," [20] and he had a general knowledge of the Pacific coast. His next decision was to attempt an overland trip to the Pacific. "Deficient in the sciences of astronomy and navigation," he went to England in 1791 to perfect himself in these. A year later [21] he was back in Canada ready for the Pacific expedition. Once more on Athabasca he laid his plans and he seems to have suspected that the way to the Pacific would be much more difficult than that to the Arctic. Possibly this is the reason he decided to split the venture into two parts, spending the winter of 1792 as far west of Athabasca as possible. The route he mapped only slightly varied from Carver's theory. Mackenzie reasoned that the Peace river, emptying into Athabasca from the west, should, if followed to its source, put the explorer within striking distance of a westward flowing stream. Pursuing this line of thought, he left Fort Chipewyan, October 10, 1792, for the mouth of the Peace river.

Two days later he entered the river, heading west. As on the first trip, he got his crew out at unbelievably early hours and kept them paddling until exhaustion overcame his compulsion for speed. On October 19 the crew was routed and the canoe launched at 3 a.m., for fear the river might soon freeze over and detain them.

To hasten his progress he used any fair, or foul, means. When a slow conference with the natives displeased him, he passed out nine gallons of reduced rum which "strengthened my admonition to them,"and this in spite of his own contention that liquor was an evil for the red men, reducing them below the already low standards they had.

Sometime before Mackenzie left for the West, a trading post, commonly called the "Old Establishment," was built at the falls of the Peace. It was here that the party planned to spend the winter of 1792-1973. [22] On December 7, the explorers began building their cabins, and it was none too soon. Two days after Christmas the cold was so severe "that the axes of the workmen became almost as brittle as glass." Despite this handicap six

---

20.—It seems strange that since he knew of the Verendryes he did not know of Hearne; or, if he did, why he should take credit for settling the Strait of Anian myth.

21.—Gray had discovered the Columbia on May 11.

22.—Vancouver was at Monterey, January 15, 1793.

cabins were finished and surrounded by a stockade, 120 feet square.

The Indians were sent to hunt and Mackenzie was busy keeping peace and administering simple medicines; the natives often fought over their liquor or women. Sometimes his patients died but Mackenzie did the best he could. Once when a combination of rum and soap failed to cure the sufferer, he bled him. The patient recovered and Mackenzie's reputation as a doctor was established. Such a job as dressing the putrefying hand of an Indian three times a day for a month was not pleasant but the hand got well and helped induce the natives to part with their choicest furs.

With the arrival of spring, six canoes were loaded and ready to leave for the fort. On May 8, 1793,[23] they set off and Mackenzie turned toward the Pacific. One large canoe, twenty-five feet long, four feet nine inches at the beam, and twenty-six inches deep, was the only conveyance used on this western trip. It was a masterpiece of canoe building, so light that two men could carry it three or four miles with ease, yet so sturdy that a ton and a half of baggage and ten persons were easily placed inside.

On the Arctic expedition Mackenzie carried full responsibility except for that shared by English Chief; but on his present expedition he was accompanied by Alexander McKay, a trader and explorer of ability who was to figure importantly in the fur business of the Far West.

Mackenzie spent much of his time taking observations.[24] If the weather was too bad, the day's work was delayed an hour or two. On May 15, "rain prevented us from continuing our route till past six in the morning," but two days later the lost time was made up by launching the canoe at 2 a.m. That same day the Rockies appeared in the distance and the first real difficulties began. As Peace river's white water gave way to impassable turbulence, a way had to be found to drag the canoe through a gorge where there was no footing at all along the shore. Steps

23.—Just a month before this, the French envoy, "Citizen" Genet, landed at Charleston and started north, criticizing Washington as he went.
24.—At times, one or both of the commanders would leave the main party and cut across from one bend of the river to another, exploring as they went. On one such tour Mackenzie found a grizzly bear's den, ten feet deep, five high, and six wide. If the animal came anywhere near filling it, he was enormous.

were cut in the rocks, after which, Mackenzie says, "I leaped on a small rock below, where I received those who followed me on my shoulders. In this manner four of us passed and dragged up the canoe." Next morning the commander allowed the men to sleep until "about eight." It was such thoughtfulness that made him not only a great explorer but a great commander.

Parties went out to search for a passage around the rapids and the gorge. They found only one course which seemed practical; this was to cut a way up the sheer side of the gorge, then hack through the bush past the upper end of the rapids and relaunch the canoe. The cutting and slashing was done, with some grumbling from the men, who thought it easier to go back than ahead. Three days later the job was finished and the canoe launched above the rapids.[25]

Several days of torrential rains made work impossible. The men loafed about, getting what rest they could and amusing themselves as they pleased. Mackenzie helped entertain himself by writing a note, sealing it up in a rum keg and sending it off "to the mercy of the current." About this boyish action has grown the legend that Mackenzie habitually sent his reports to headquarters on Athabasca by means of a rum keg. While the Scotsman was as likely as anyone to indulge in a childlike pastime when there was nothing more serious to do, he was too intelligent to use such a fantastic method to report the progress of the expedition.

Up to this date, May 29, 1793, the party had been fighting their way up to the Finlay river, a major tributary of the Peace. Now, though the crew wished to take the other turning, they began ascending the Parsnip. Mackenzie's choice, based on the slight information he had, was logical but it was also unfortunate in that the Parsnip was much harder to navigate than the Finlay. The Finlay would have taken them considerable distance into the Rockies but many hundreds of miles from the Pacific, whereas the Parsnip is the only river except the Laird to cut through the mountains. Soon the men complained, talking of going back. Mackenzie would hear of no such proposals.

On Sunday, June 9, they came upon a relatively large native

25.—The same distance is only a four-hours' walk over the ancient Indian trail which still exists. See Haworth, page 74.

encampment and Mackenzie decided to stop until "the Indians became so familiarized with us as to give all the intelligence which we imagined might be obtained from them." Besides, a rest might raise the morale of the crew. The natives had iron to indicate some knowledge of the Pacific, the only likely place for them to have got it. However, they refused to answer any of the questions the explorers asked.

As the way became increasingly difficult and the men's discontent more pronounced, Mackenzie thought of leaving the river and striking overland. This was a bold idea. One wrong turn and the entire party could be lost. With the river close by, return was always possible; without it, retreat might be impossible. The problem solved itself. On June 12 they were at the source of the Peace river, only 817 paces away from the westward-flowing river. The headwaters of what is now known as the Fraser, called the Tacouche Tesse by the natives, were there under the paddles of the two Scotsmen, Mackenzie and McKay. They did not know where it emptied but they followed the stream.

Previous rough water had made them consider an overland journey; the present river compelled it.

On Thursday the thirteenth the waters seized the canoe and threw the men headlong into the river, icy cold even in summer. Crawling, splashing, and cursing, they finally pulled themselves together on the bank where they surveyed the damage. Valuable equipment, including balls for their rifles, was gone, the canoe wrecked. Grumblings flared into open rebellion. As Mackenzie faced the same situation which had split Verendrye's forces, the Scotsman's genuine leadership showed itself. His men were wet, cold, discouraged, angry with themselves, with him and with fate. Quietly and skillfully he praised their efforts, pointing out that such misfortunes as had come had not been their fault, that they had given their best and he appreciated it. He knew how deeply they were chagrined; how failure rankled; he realized even better than they how really brave and hardy they were, not mere women to cry out and quit because a little water had run down their boot tops.

When the men were dried out and had eaten, Mackenzie told them that he would discuss with them the question of returning. But by that time no one could think of a good reason for going back, so the second expedition repaired their canoe and went on their way.

They reached the north fork of the Fraser on June 17, and the next day the main stream. Proceeding down river, they came shortly upon another Indian encampment whose old men told them that further navigation was impossible. Mackenzie gathered all the information he could. Often nothing of value was learned. Sometimes the questioners became the questioned. One old man caustically asked why, if the whites knew everything as they pretended, they asked so many things.

After 250 miles, Mackenzie had to abandon the river and strike overland to a more navigable stream, or continue by land to the Pacific. On July 4, 1793, he divided the baggage into loads of seventy to ninety pounds, every man being required to carry such a pack besides his own gun and personal effects. [26] Retracing their route for a day, they turned overland by way of the Blackwater river. Within two weeks they reached Friendly village on the Bella Coola river, a small, unimportant stream emptying into the Pacific not far from the present Bentick North Arm. The way down to the sea was easy and soon there were signs of white traders. From time to time Mackenzie could check his notes against those kept by Captain Cook.

Local Indian architecture attracted much of Mackenzie's attention and it is among the carefully reported details of old boxes and chests that the reader must look for the Scotsman's reaction to the discovery of the Pacific from the interior. It is doubtful if history records another great discovery so obscurely. Hidden in a long discussion of native houses are these words, "In the houses there were several chests or boxes containing different articles that belonged to the people whom we had lately passed. If I were to judge by the heaps of filth beneath these buildings, they must have been erected at a more distant period than any which we had passed. From these houses I could perceive the termination of the river, and its discharge into a narrow arm of the sea." [27]

That is all. The next sentence begins a new paragraph on a new topic. It could easily be assumed that the commander failed

26.—The Indian guides' refusal to carry anything lowered the morale of the entire company.

27.—Alexander Mackenzie's *Voyage to the Pacific Ocean in* 1793, pages 298-299.

to realize the importance of his discovery, yet better probably than any other living person he knew the significance of that "termination of the river." He understood the advantages of an overland route between the oceans but he also realized what others did not—how difficult and long that route was. Yet he talked of houses, of dried fish and of filth beneath the steps.

Having thus modestly reported his discovery, he took an "altitude" at the modern Cape Menzies, then coasted along what Vancouver called King's island, where he had a little trouble with the Indians who attached themselves to the party and attempted to steal everything on which they could lay their hands.

Of the record he left of his work on the Pacific he says, "I now mixed up some vermillion in melted grease, and inscribed, in large characters, on the South-East face of the rock on which we had slept last night, this brief memorial—'Alexander Mackenzie from Canada by land, the 22d day of July 1793.'" The next day the party started home.

There is no need to trace the homeward journey. On the trip up the western slope of the Rockies they were short of food, but a buffalo and two elk relieved them. The rest of the trip was uneventful, the expedition reaching the winter post on Peace river, August 24, 1793.

Along the way to the Pacific the Indians had been less friendly than on the way to the Arctic but Mackenzie's good sense and tact made it possible to pass among them again in safety. Fairness with the natives had been his policy throughout: "I paid . . . for everything which we had received, and did not forget the loan of the canoe." He usually agreed to reasonable requests of the Indians but often had to be ingenious in refusals. One old chief insisted on borrowing a canoe which Mackenzie did not wish to lend but had no real reason for not doing so. He resorted to flattery as he often did, explaining that if he were to lend this particular canoe the Indian women would be sure to use it and the chief would not want a canoe also used by women. The chief was satisfied, imagining himself placed in the same category with the white men.

Mackenzie took more observations on his Pacific trip than on the Arctic one but difficulties en route kept him from making a careful study of the natural resources along the route. "I had to encounter perils by land and perils by water; to watch the savage who was our guide, or to guard against those of his tribe who might meditate our destruction. I had, also, the passions and fears of others to control and subdue. Today I had to assuage the rising discontents, and on the morrow to cheer the fainting spirits, of the people who accompanied me. The toil of our navigation was incessant, and oftentimes extreme."

These perils did not keep him from appreciating the beauty of the landscape over which he hurried. "The whole country displayed an exuberant verdure; the trees that bear a blossom were advancing fast to that delightful appearance, and the velvet rind of their branches reflecting the oblique rays of a rising or setting sun, added a splendid gaiety to the scene, which no expressions of mine are qualified to describe." There was something of the artist in this Scotsman.

At the close of the second expedition he wrote, "There my voyages of discovery terminate. Their toils and their dangers . . . have not been exaggerated . . . I received, however, the reward of my labours, for they were crowned with success." But he was not yet ready to retire. In middle life with high spirits and great ambitions, he turned to the fur trade as second choice to further explorations, recommending to the Northwest company that they expand their business to include a transcontinental and trans-Pacific trade in fur and whales.

The supplies would be shipped from Montreal and the skins and whale oil would be sent across to the East India company plants in the Orient. The circle would be completed when the trade goods, bought with the Oriental profits, were ordered and manufactured in England and sent to Montreal for shipment to the fur fields.

"By these waters that discharge themselves into Hudson's Bay at Port Nelson, it is proposed to carry on the trade to their source at the head of the Saskatchewan River, which rises in the Rocky Mountains, not eight degrees of longitude from the Pacific Ocean. The Tacouche Tesse, or Columbia River, flows also from the same mountains and discharges itself likewise into the Pacific in latitude forty-six degrees twenty minutes. Both of them are capable of receiving ships at their mouths, and are navigable throughout for boats.

"The distance between these waters is only known from the report of the Indians. If, however, this communication should prove inaccessible, the route I pursued, though longer, in consequence of the great angle it makes to the north, will answer every necessary purpose. But, whatever course may be taken from the Atlantic, the Columbia is the line of communication from the Pacific Ocean pointed out by nature, as it is the only navigable river in the whole extent of Vancouver's minute survey of the continental coast; its banks also form the first level country in all the southern extent of continental coast from Cook's Entry, and consequently, the most northern situation fit for colonization, and suitable to the residence of civilized people.

"By opening this entire course between the Atlantic and Pacific Oceans, and forming regular establishments through the interior, and at both extremes, as well as along the coasts and islands, the entire command of the fur trade of North America might be obtained, from latitude forty-eight degrees north to the pole, except the portion of it which the Russians have in the Pacific. To this may be added the fishing in both seas, and markets of the four quarters of the globe.

"Such would be the field for commercial enterprises; and incalculable would be the product of it, when supported by the operations of that credit and capital which Great Britain pre-eminently possesses. Then would this country begin to be remunerated for the expenses it has sustained in discovering and surveying the coasts of the Pacific Ocean, which is at present left to American adventurers, who, without regularity or capital, or the desire for conciliating future confidence, look altogether to the interest of the moment. They, therefore, collect all the skins they can procure, and in any manner that suits them, and, having exchanged them at Canton for the produce of China, return to their own country. Such adventurers and many of them, as I have been informed, have been very successful, would instantly disappear from the coast." [28, 29]

28.—Mackenzie is clearly wrong. He himself had found the real Tacouche Tesse, or Fraser, impassable even for his light craft, yet he here insists that the Columbia, which he says is the Tacouche Tesse, is "navigable throughout for boats." He was right in assuming that the headwaters of the Columbia interlock with those of the Peace; his mistake lay only in thinking the Tacouche Tesse referred to the Columbia.

29.—Snowden, volume 1, pages 230-231.

Mackenzie's plan fell through because the Hudson's Bay company, whose directors were very close to the government at London, objected to having so powerful a rival in the fur business, and the necessary permits were refused.[30] Both companies, though, extended their posts beyond the Rockies very shortly after these recommendations were made.

During the winter of 1793-1794, Mackenzie remained at Fort Chipewyan but the following spring the company appointed him agent at Montreal where he stayed until 1805, [31] adding to his already considerable fortune. At this time he was also elected to the provincial parliament.

Mackenzie often went back and forth to London. While there in 1801, he had his journals published. There was abroad at that

---

30.—Coman, volume 1, page 295.

31.—Important events took place in the United States between 1793 and 1805. France and England were at war and the French expected aid from us in return for their aid in our revolt from British power. "Citizen" Genet had been sent to America to negotiate this support but through undiplomatic bungling only succeeded in making himself extremely popular with the people and equally unpopular with the President.

The first cotton mill in America was built by Slater at Pawtucket in 1793; the invention of the cotton gin by Whitney came in 1793; and Jay's Treaty in November of 1795. The Treaty of Greenville in the same year opened the Mississippi for American trade, and the Ohio valley for American settlement.

At this time, too, Mr. Donaldson, United States representative at Algiers, with the aid of Bacri, "the Jew," arranged for exemption of American shipping from the raids of Algierian pirates, provided, of course, the usual tribute money was forthcoming.

On September 17, 1796, Washington delivered his Farewell Address, and early the next year his successor took the oath of office as second President of the United States. Probably the most interesting event of Adams' administration was the X. Y. Z. affair of 1797-1798, in which a French minister tried to bribe the representative of the United States. Several more commercial treaties were consummated during the years 1796-1798 but these could not stop the growing desire in this country for war over the seizure of our merchant men by both France and England. These foreign relations were Adams' greatest problems.

In 1798 the Navy department was organized and Benjamin Stoddard was made first secretary; a new army was provided and Washington was called from retirement to be commander-in-chief in the field. The first direct Federal tax was laid in 1797. In 1798 the Mississippi territory was opened to settlement and the Alien and Sedition Acts were passed. Madison and Jefferson wrote their Virginia Resolutions suggesting nullification of unsatisfactory laws.

On December 14, 1799, Washington died, and a few months later the new capitol at Washington, D. C. was first occupied. John Marshall became Chief Justice of the Supreme Court, to interpret the law for five million men and women living within the United States. After the administration of Adams, the Jeffersonian Republicans elected their leader to the Presidency and the Federalist regime ended.

time a rumor that these had been brought out so late because of earlier suppression by the government. Mackenzie himself gives a much simpler reason, "The delay actually arose from the very active and busy mode of life in which I was engaged since the voyages have been completed." When they were published, he became Sir Alexander Mackenzie, in token of royal appreciation for his services.

About 1805, Sir Alexander decided to retire. With his amassed fortune he now left Canada for good. Back in his native land he seven years later married a kinswoman, Geddes Mackenzie, settling to a life of leisure on his wife's estate in Inverness-shire. He died in 1820, having opened a full quarter of North America to civilization. Even if the trails he followed never became the lanes of commerce he had hoped they would, still the territory he mapped poured out more millions than he ever dreamed possible from such wastes.

As a great explorer Alexander Mackenzie's place is undisputed. As a man, his forcefulness often went beyond mere sturdiness of character to become harsh domination. Pride in his own abilities veered sometimes into jealousy. While he praised his men when this was necessary to make them work harder, his journals give them credit as a group rather than as individuals. Alexander McKay, doubtless a highly valuable lieutenant, receives only passing notice; names or doings of the common canoemen and hunters never appear. And there is considerable evidence that during his earlier years he used unscrupulous methods to gather his pelts.

Yet whatever the personal shortcomings which mar his character, these are overshadowed by his importance as an explorer. With incredible speed and under enormous difficulties, he managed to traverse vast distances. Alexander Mackenzie remains the most phenomenal traveler ever to paddle a canoe on North American waters.

7

LEWIS AND CLARK REACH THE PACIFIC

THOMAS JEFFERSON WAS AS NECESSARY to Lewis and Clark as the half-savage Peter was to Vitus Bering. With all due credit to Lewis and Clark, it was neither their imagination nor their intellect that dreamed and planned their work. These were the product of Jefferson. His idealism rose to heights far above most American statesmen, yet his political machinations often sank to levels he loudly deplored in others.

He readily practiced deceit or trickery if either gained an end advantageous to the "common man." It is here that his character and philosophy bear on the Lewis and Clark expedition.

"Our country is too large to have all its affairs directed by a single government," [1] he said, yet he spent hours scheming to increase the size of that country. He purchased Louisiana under the blind of commercial necessity; Florida he would have seized with the justification of "manifest destiny" and troublesome Indians; and Indian lands were to be acquired by deliberately leading the natives into such debt that only the relinquishment of their free holds could ever liquidate them. In spite of such attitudes and actions, Jefferson's vision for America was deeper and more sincere than that of any other statesman of his time. He saw the new continent as the home of a great and free people and he wished to increase the territorial possessions of those people.

It is easy to think of Jefferson only as an inconsistent politician and philosopher; rarely is he recognized for what he was at heart, an adventurer. Having spent his early life on the Virginia frontier, he knew the enormous lure as well as the drudgery and uncouthness of the hinterlands. And neither Blackstone nor the Federalists could ever quite divorce his mind and heart from that region.

"He was trained in the law, but he was too much the intel-

1.—Taylor and Maury's *Writings*, volume VII, page 451.

lectual, too curious about all sorts of things, to remain a lawyer."[2] "He would not have America follow the trodden paths" [3] in the field of government nor would he be restricted by the beaten paths which led only up and down the Atlantic seaboard.

Long before the Lewis and Clark expedition, he spent his idle moments pondering upon the mysterious regions beyond the Alleghenies; and, as the frontier pushed to the Mississippi, his interests also spread westward. [4] He is reputed to have considered refusing the Presidency of the United States to accept that of a philosophical society in order to indulge in exploration. All the courts of Europe could wait while he and John Ledyard sat about over their glasses, talking and planning of reaching the Pacific coast of North America through the overland back door of Asia. But these men were involved in more than dreams. Ledyard [5] traded his life for exploration and Jefferson never forgot it or gave it up.

Such expeditions as Lewis and Clark's do not spring "full blown from the mind of man" any more than do political philosophies or economic doctrines. In December of 1789, General Knox, Secretary of War, wrote to General Harmar at Cincinnati regarding plans for exploring the upper Missouri river. Harmar chose Captain John Armstrong at Louisville for the work; and Armstrong, pitifully ignorant of the immensity of the task before him, started to the headwaters of the Missouri by himself. Indian hostility alone was enough to doom the attempt but the seed had been planted.

The French botanist, Andre Michaux, had been sent to America by the Old Regime to gather specimens for transplantation to France. The Revolution cut off financial support, leaving Michaux a free-lance scientist in a friendly country. He used his personal fortune to continue his work. In 1793 [6] he proposed to the American Philosophical society—in which Jefferson was a major figure—that it finance a trip to the Pacific. The society

2.—Vernon Louis Parrington. *The Colonial Mind,* page 343.
3.—Parrington, page 349.
4.- On December 4, 1783, he wrote to General George Rogers Clark asking him if he would like to lead an expedition into the Far West, but the old soldier did not accept.
5.—Ledyard's description of Cook's third voyage did much to foster interest in the Pacific.
6.—Eli Whitney introduced the cotton gin the same year.

opened a subscription list with $128.50. Washington added $25, Jefferson and Hamilton each giving $12.50. Michaux left Philadelphia and went to Kentucky, where he became entangled with George Rogers Clark and "Citizen" Genet in a scheme to acquire New Orleans for the French. The trip to the Pacific was forgotten. [7]

The very next year the Commercial company of St. Louis attempted to follow Verendrye's plan and build a chain of posts from the mouth of the Platte to the Pacific. The posts were never built but several traders financed by the company tried to get through and beyond the Sioux country. Each failed.

Ten years passed and Jefferson, the retired Virginia farmer, became the first anti-Federalist President. Just then an old provision, intended to foster trading with the Indians, lapsed and the new President seized the chance to ask Congress for an appropriation supposedly to renew this old act but actually to finance an expedition into the West.

Jefferson sometimes stooped to political maneuvering. For example, on January 18, 1803, [8] he forwarded to Congress a secret message in which he advocated that $2,500 [9] be appropriated for commercial and literary purposes. These were to be achieved by sending a small detachment of the regular army across Louisiana to the Pacific. [10] The project would cost practically nothing for the men could be forced to take their pay in land. The Spaniards, who still governed the region—though the French had title to it at that particular moment—could be quieted by the pretense of a "literary pursuit." Jefferson knew that sending an army into a foreign territory was illegal but by certain verbal maneuvering he suggested they "would cover the undertaking from notice and prevent the obstructions which interested individuals might otherwise previously prepare in its way." [11]

Meriwether Lewis, Jefferson's private secretary, was almost as concerned with exploration as Jefferson himself. The two men

---

7.—Michaux finally returned to France in 1796 and died of a fever contracted while working in his botanical gardens. See Thwaites, page 74 and following.

8.—The treaty of sale on Louisiana was signed, May 2.

9.—Meriwether Lewis supplied the data from which this total was determined.

10.—About the same time, the President suggested the investigation eventually completed by Zebulon Pike.

11.—Edward Channing. *The Jeffersonian System,* page 88.

often discussed the West and the possibilities of exploring it. Probably from the outset Jefferson had Lewis in mind as the logical leader of any such expedition.

Lewis felt that responsibility for the venture should be shared and requested that his old army mate, Clark, be appointed co-commander. When Jefferson agreed, arrangements were completed.

These two men chosen to lead the greatest expedition ever financed by the United States were both exceptional. Meriwether Lewis, a native of Charlottesville, Virginia, was just thirty years old. His parents had been prominent in Colonial and Revolutionary affairs. While still very young, the boy lost his father and his training depended on his mother and an uncle. At eight years of age he was a fearless hunter, going alone at night into the woods after the opossum; and at eighteen he was successfully managing his mother's plantation. On the side, he had picked up a smattering of botany.

Later he volunteered for service in the abortive Whiskey Rebellion and for the rest of his life he was either actively engaged in military affairs or in tasks indirectly connected with that vocation. When the Whiskey Rebellion failed, Lewis transferred to the regular army and rose rapidly. He served under General Wayne and under Captain Guion in a move to take over the Spanish posts on the Mississippi; was appointed paymaster; and, in 1801, was sent on an official tour of inspection to Pittsburgh, Cincinnati, Fort Wayne, and Detroit. Shortly afterwards Jefferson offered him five hundred dollars a year to act as his secretary, with board and lodging at the executive mansion as added inducement.

When Congress at last made the Pacific expedition possible, Lewis was the obvious choice for leader. The President said that he was "brave, prudent, habituated to the woods, & familiar with Indian manners and character. He is not regularly educated, but he possesses a great mass of accurate observation on all subjects of nature which present themselves here, & will therefore readily select those only in his new route which shall be new."

At another time Jefferson spoke even more highly of Lewis, describing him as "of courage undaunted; possessing a firmness and perseverance of purpose which nothing but impossibilities could divert from its direction . . . carefull . . . steady . . . intimate with the Indian character, customs and principles . . . honest, disinterested, liberal, of sound understanding, and a fidelity to truth so scrupulous that whatever he should report would be as certain as if seen by ourselves; with all these qualifications . . . I could have no hesitation in confiding the enterprise to him."

William Clark's career was as interesting as Lewis's. William was John Clark's ninth child, born August 1, 1770. Fourteen years later the family moved to Kentucky, settling at Mulberry Hill, near Louisville, where their home immediately became a center of sociability. Old inhabitants, new arrivals, immigrants going on—all stopped at the Clarks'.

Five years after moving to Mulberry Hill, William left for the Indian wars. In 1794 he was put in charge of seven hundred pack horses carrying supplies to Fort Greenville. The Indians attacked the train and Clark lost five men but delivered his goods intact to the fort. Twice the following year he was sent to negotiate with the Spaniards. Abruptly in 1796 he retired from the army, went home and plunged into the task of straightening out the muddled affairs of his then more famous brother, George Rogers Clark, who was being sued as a result of his Indian campaigns. No more is heard of William until Lewis wrote him, June 19, 1803, asking him if he were interested in the proposed expedition.

Before the Lewis and Clark party was actually organized and on its way Jefferson had purchased Louisiana [12] and the expedition could then proceed openly. Strange as it seems, political opposition, which had not developed while the affair was a secret invasion of a friendly foreign territory, now became bitter. The Federalists especially were caustic about the whole project, some remarking on the hopelessness of such an attempt, others ridiculing it by saying that the men were being sent to look for live mastodons and other freaks of nature. Still others insisted that Jefferson was merely playing politics. [13] The President was, of course, really acting in good faith with both Lewis and Clark and the American people. His questionable activities regarding the diplomatic aspects of the expedition before the purchase are

---

12.—"The Louisiana Purchase came in the nick of time to save Jefferson from violating the code of international ethics. Whether the expedition was planned partly with a view to possible seizure of the country cannot be stated; the conjunction date is remarkable." See Channing, page 88.

13.—Snowden, pages 259-260.

quite beside the point in this good faith. Louisiana once owned, the whole affair was ethical.

The two men were given joint command, though Clark's commission had lower military rank than Lewis's. This fact rankled but Clark did not let it affect their friendship.

Lewis headed the scientific phases of the work; Clark, the military. Before his partner arrived, Lewis had gone to Harpers Ferry for special rifles, scientific instruments, and miscellaneous supplies. From there he went on to Philadelphia to learn the rudiments of astronomical observations, a science about which he knew next to nothing.

Early in May, Jefferson sent him a rough draft of his instructions, shortly followed by a complete one. The main purpose of the expedition was to explore the Missouri river and find a way to the Pacific in order to establish commerce with the Indians. On the way, the party was to obtain accurate and thorough information about the natives and conciliate them as much as possible. "Kine-pox" was to be introduced to them "as a preservative from the small pox." The explorers were to collect natural history specimens, note the sources and courses of rivers and the location of lakes, observe the routes of Canadian traders, chart strategic military points, and list the visible resources of the country.

The lives of all the members of the expedition were to be safeguarded, for the loss of the men, Jefferson pointed out, meant the loss of the valuable information they possessed. Official permission for the "literary" party to travel in their domains had already been issued by the Spanish and French authorities. The commanders were given ample letters of credit and told that the American agents at Batavia, Isles of France, and Cape of Good Hope had been instructed to aid them should their return trip include any of those ports. With one exception, Jefferson provided every safety factor practicable. He failed to order an American ship to meet the explorers, yet he did instruct that at least two men with copies of the reports be sent home by sea.

The commanders were to encourage other members of the party to keep journals and, if any information of a dangerous nature were discovered, they had orders to "put into cypher whatever might do injury if betrayed."

Knowledge of the frontier and the nature of their orders kept

Lewis and Clark from attempting a hurried push to the Pacific. Compared with Mackenzie they seemed to loiter, yet their routine proved sound. It was August 30, 1803, before the party left Pittsburgh with a partially completed crew, and Lewis's journal from there to the Mississippi is packed with all sorts of delays. The "fogg" detained him until 8 o'clock. He had to pay a dollar to have a horse drag the boats across some riffles, remarking as he did so, "I find them the most efficient sailors in the present state of the navigation of this river." The local people held him up because they were "generally lazy, charge extravagantly when they are called on for assistance and have no filanthrophy or contience."

The party stopped to catch the giant catfish of the Ohio. Some member of the crew, unable to carry his liquor, had to be forcibly brought aboard boat to sober up; and at least once the entire expedition stopped to watch the "uncivilized backwoodsmen" from Kentucky race their horses, a pastime not to be missed if the West were never explored. The race promoters were "almost entirely emegrants from the fronteers of Kentucky & Tennesee, and are the most dessolute and abandoned even among these people." In such manner did the leaders progress from Pittsburgh to the Mississippi and then to the mouth of the River Dubois to establish a winter camp, almost opposite St. Louis.

At Kaskaskia, Lewis left the party, heading overland to St. Louis. Clark stayed behind in command of the expedition and journal. On December 11, he wrote, "a Verry rainey morning. . . . Capt. Lewis detain for to acquire information of the Countrey." The men built cabins and, until spring, drilled, collected new supplies and information, and received last-minute instructions from the President.

At the formal transfer of Louisiana to American ownership on March 9, Lewis acted as the official representative. The old Federalist leaders were infuriated at the turn of events in national affairs and Jefferson reported tartly to Lewis, "The acquisition of the country through which you are to pass has inspired the country generally with a great deal of interest in your enterprise. The inquiries are perpetual as to your progress. The Feds alone treat it as a philosophism, and would rejoice at its failure. Their bitterness increases with the diminution of their numbers and despair of a resurrection. I hope you will take care of yourself, and be a living witness of their malice and folly."

The exploring company as finally organized consisted of forty-five persons, including Clark's huge negro servant, York, six feet two inches tall and coal black. All were in fine health, most of them unmarried and foot-loose. During the winter the men built a batteau or flatboat, fifty-five feet long and carrying twenty-two oars and a square sail; also several pirogues or keel boats, much lighter and more flexible.

At 4 p.m., May 14, 1804, [14] Clark ordered the expedition to start. Lewis, across the river at St. Louis tending to the final details, did not expect Clark to embark until the next day. The expedition waited for Lewis at St. Charles, where it arrived the following noon, then waited around until the twenty-first.

The lower Missouri was known to the French and Spanish as well as to the Americans and English. For the past ten years the Spaniards had been going as far as the Mandans in North Dakota and the English had traded with these natives for about twenty years. The French, at times, had ventured to the Black Hills, perhaps even to the Yellowstone river. All St. Louis traders were familiar with the general facts regarding the Mandans, had exchanged trade lore with the North West and Hudson's Bay men, and most of them knew a little about the Rocky Mountain region. Though the journey from St. Louis to the Mandans was in no way an exploration, this did not simplify reaching the Dakotas. The unpredictable Missouri was as temperamental as ever; what was a channel one day became a sand island the next. It was forever cutting corners, gouging new angles, and piling up fresh islands of sand and silt. Lewis, writing to his mother from Fort Mandan, March 31, 1805, told of the hazards of this river:

"So far we have experienced more difficulties from the navigation of the Missouri than danger from the savages. The difficulties which oppose themselves to the navigation of this immense river arise from the rapidity of its current, its falling banks, sandbars and timber, which remains wholly or partially concealed in its bed, usually called by the navigators of the Missouri and the Mississippi 'sawyer' or 'planter.' Such is the velocity of the current

14.—Three months earlier, Preble, the American naval commander, had bombarded Tripoli as part of the so-called Tripolitan war.

at all seasons of the year, from the entrance of the Missouri to the mouth of the great river Platte, that it is impossible to resist its force by means of oars or poles in the main channel of the river; the eddies which therefore generally exist on one side or the other of the river, are sought by the navigators, but these are almost universally encumbered with concealed timber, or within reach of the falling banks."

The explorers also found many of the natives hostile, because of their past experiences with white men.

The party did considerable hunting, living "off the country" as much as they could. Lewis himself spent whole days walking along the shore gathering natural specimens for Jefferson.[15] Many conferences were held with the various tribes. [16]

Punishment from "ticks" and "musquiters" and "knats" was constantly mentioned in the party journals. [17] On June 19, Sergeant Ordway wrote, "The Musquetoes are verry troublesome. Got Musquetoes bears from Capt Lewis to sleep in." And Lewis himself, writing after the party left the Mandans, said, "Our trio of pests still invade and obstruct us on all occasions, these are the Musquetoes eye knats and prickly pears, equal to any three curses that ever poor Egypt laiboured under, except the Mohometant yoke." He may have been somewhat mistaken regarding the great plagues of Egypt, but he knew how he himself was plagued.

Lewis and Clark had other kinds of trouble. George Shannon, a boy hired as a hunter, was constantly getting lost. When he left

---

15.—Ordway also noted many of the plants and animals: "Jo Fields & Reuben went hunting   Jo killed & brought in an animal which the French call a brarow . . . this animal Resembles our Ground hogs in colour & Shape nearly but the head like a dogs.   four feet like a bear especially the claws. Inside like a hog   long teeth   they live on flys & bugs . . . and dig in the Ground like a G. Hog   they Say they gravel like a possom.

16.—Two possessions of the whites amazed the Indians: an air gun which they considered very powerful "medicine" and York, Clark's servant. This fellow entered readily into the sport and "made himself more turribal than we wished him to doe," says Clark.   York told the Indians that he had originally been a wild animal but that he had been caught and tamed by his master.

After these exhibitions Lewis took care to make the Indians "sensible of their dependence on the will of our government for every species of merchandise as well as for their defence & comfort."

17.—Besides the joint official journal of Lewis and Clark, the following members of the expedition kept private records of the days' events: Sergeants Floyd, Ordway, Pryor, and Gass; and Privates Whitehouse and Frazier. This was the best-documented expedition attempted up to that time.

camp in the morning, no one knew, he least of all, whether he would find his way back or not. Time after time he became lost, once for sixteen days. He had hunted ahead of the river party and kept going faster and faster to catch up with those already far behind him.

The land party often accidentally got out of contact with those in the boats and Lewis and Clark would then have to dispatch two or three men to search for the hunters. Such conditions should not have existed. Some signal system could have been devised to inform the land party whether or not the boats were ahead or below. For centuries the Indians used smoke. This expedition could have done likewise, considering the distance covered each day—from ten to twenty miles.

Much speed was lost because of specimen collecting,[18] much more by having no definite hours of travel. When the weather was excessively warm, they would rest for two or three hours at mid-day, stopping or starting any time that suited the commanders' fancy. As a result of this the men never knew when their day's labor was finished. Several times they either deserted or attempted to, and military court-martial was used to discipline them. Many of the journalists mention these court-martials but none give details. Ordway, under the date of June 28, states that two men were court-martialed for stealing whiskey and that one of them received a hundred lashes on his bare back; the other, fifty.

When Moses B. Reed attempted to desert, orders went out for his capture "dead or alive." He was returned and sentenced to run the gauntlet four times and thereafter was not considered a member of the party. Joseph Barter was sent on an errand to an Indian camp. He never came back. John Newman was court-martialed as a deserter on October 13, given seventy-five lashes and dismissed from the party. La Liberty, a deserter, was caught "but he decived them and got away," Clark says. Bratton claimed that the men forming the gauntlet laid the blows on vigorously, fearing a like punishment if they seemed lenient. [19]

18.—Nothing was too ordinary to attract Lewis's attention. He stuffed and sent to Jefferson the above-mentioned "G. Hog." Shortly after killing it he also shot a pelican whose pouch-like bill could hold five gallons of water. He crated alive "Magpyes and prarie hens" to be sent to the President.

19.—Milo M. Quaife, *Journals of Captain Meriwether Lewis and Sergeant John Ordway*, page 112, note.

Why did the journals admit the desertions, thefts, and court-martials and uniformly give no details about them? Lack of space cannot possibly be the reason for many pages recorded merely items like the size of the catfish, the expedition's camps and stopping places, the temperature of the water, the amount of rain, why squirrels always crossed the river in one direction, or how a particular Indian looked.

Men stole from or deserted Vitus Bering because they were starving; they deserted Mackenzie because they misunderstood what "a day's work" meant. But none of Lewis and Clark's men were starving; from St. Louis to the Mandans there was no food shortage. Black-tailed deer, antelope, bear, buffalo, and many kinds of fish were so abundant that Clark said he saw ten thousand buffalo at one time; and Lewis noted, "When we have plenty of fresh meat, I find it impossible to make the men take any care of it." Corn, pumpkins, squash, wild onions, garlic, and watermelons were easily obtained from natives along the way. Horses lightened the labor of dragging the heavy boats over the riffles. Nor can desertions be blamed on the usual discontent with army life because Clark hand picked every man for his particular ability, robustness, and good faith.

There are only two clues to the cause of the desertions. These desertions ceased abruptly after the party reached the Mandans; and Newman, sentenced to seventy-five lashes for desertion, was highly recommended by Lewis when the party got back home. Similarly, a soldier sentenced to fifty lashes for scaling the post walls in sight of the Indians was, according to Ordway, "laid to the mercy of the commanding officer who was pleased to forgive him the punishment awarded by the court." Perhaps Lewis and Clark realized that too many otherwise great expeditions had been wrecked by commanders who spared the lash when it was most needed. Whatever the facts, they kept their party on the move and discipline at a high point.

The expedition made satisfactory progress from St. Louis to the Mandans, and on May 14, 1804, fired one gun of farewell to frontier civilization. The twenty-third was devoted to arms inspection. Two days later they passed La Charette, the last white settlement. On June 16, the Frenchman, Dorion, who had spent twenty years with the Sioux, was hired to return with the Americans in the hope of inducing a delegation of those Indians to go to Washington. [20] On July 12, the party stopped, apparently because of illness, for Ordway said, "We lay by for to Rest and wash our cloaths." Floyd, under the date of July 11, wrote, "the men is all sick." Clark, on the same day, wrote that the men were "much fatigued." [21] They celebrated July 4 by fighting one of those sudden, brief storms in the Missouri valley. "The Storm Suddenly Seased, and the river became Instancetaniously as Smoth as Glass," said Clark. One journal records that on Sunday, August 19. Sergeant Floyd died with a "Biliouse Chorlick." Probably he had an acute attack of appendicitis. He was buried near the present Sioux City, Iowa, with "the usal Serrymony," wrote Ordway.

By July 22 they had reached the Platte,[22] where they stopped several days to confer with the Indians. From August 26 until September 11, Shannon was lost from the party. A more startling occurrence came on the night of the twentieth when the sand bar on which they had camped suddenly collapsed under them. Five days later they had their first serious dispute with the Sioux, but Clark bluffed them out of their warlike notions and the party proceeded. On the twenty-eighth the Sioux once more tried to stop them but again Clark's coolness [23] and Lewis's diplomacy triumphed. On October 8, the expedition met the friendly Arikaras [24] whom Clark described as "both pore and Durety," but whom Gass reported as "the best looking Indians I have ever seen—the most cleanly Indians I have ever seen on the voyage."

On August 26, the Americans had met Hugh McCracken of the North West company, and the following day, two or three Frenchmen with their native wives. They had passed any number of independent traders going down to St. Louis with their season's catch of furs. By this time the expedition was in the country of

---

20.—Though a party of Mandans did come down the river, the Americans did not have much success getting the natives to make the journey.

21.—This was the date of the famous duel between Alexander Hamilton and Aaron Burr.

22.—The Platte was to the fur men of the Missouri what the equator is to sailors. When the novice crossed the river mouth the first time, his head was shaved and such other initiatory actions were inflicted upon him as would cause him to remember the occasion.

23.—Clark was cool enough outwardly but he recorded, "I felt MySelf warm & spoke in verry possitive terms."

24.—These Indians refused liquor on the grounds that it made fools of them.

the Grosventres, or Big Bellies as they were popularly called. By the last of October they reached the Mandans, sixteen hundred miles above St. Louis.

Clark and eight men now selected a site for a winter camp, about eight miles below the mouth of Knife river. There on the east side [25] they built Fort Mandan, consisting of two rows of huts of four rooms each, the rows joined at an angle, and the open end closed with pickets, thus forming an enclosed area within which the whites would have some freedom of action and still be protected from any hostile maneuvers by the natives.

The winter at Fort Mandan was quiet. Lewis persuaded the Indian and Canadian traders that the American expedition was a friendly commercial venture, in no way intended to interfere with their mode of living and trading. He charged the British with bad faith in circulating the feeling that the coming of the Americans forecast the end of wilderness life and the inroads of civilization. Lewis was annoyed, not at the bad faith of the British, but at the fact that they saw through the American pretenses. Clark, less sensitive in the matter, was friendly with all the other traders, helping to counteract whatever ill will Lewis caused. In defense of Lewis, it may be said that the British were really doing all they could to hold their monopoly with the natives.

During the winter the men were busy getting food and fire-wood and repairing tools for themselves and the Indians. An old Grosventre chief said that the only two sensible people in the whole American contingent were the "worker of iron and mender of guns."

Toward the end of February crews went into the timber to cut logs for the building of new dugouts and canoes. Crates and boxes were constructed for the specimens collected en route. Spring would soon open the river, then all furs, specimens, reports, letters, and discharged men would be sent to St. Louis, and eventually to Washington.

During the winter, a Frenchman, Charboneau, was hired as an interpreter and guide. Though he tried to be useful, his

---

25.—In 1831, Fort Clark of the American Fur company was built almost opposite **Fort Mandan.**

Indian wife Sacajawea proved more valuable. Hers was the task of interpreting. She repeated a native message to Charboneau who translated to a mulatto who in turn told Lewis and Clark.

Sacajawea gave birth to a son on February 11, and the little fellow rode to and from the Pacific on his mother's person. Some say that Sacajawea carried the child in her arms rather than strapped to her back Indian fashion. Such a tradition is interesting but unlikely. The journals constantly refer to the usefulness of the Indian woman in manual tasks. Sacajawea would have needed her hands free to perform these tasks.

A barge and canoe laden with all the paraphernalia gathered so far set off down the river to St. Louis on April 7.[26] That same afternoon at 4 o'clock Clark ordered his two dugouts and six canoes to move up the Missouri toward the Pacific. Lewis wrote:

"Our vessels consisted of six small canoes, and two large perogues. This little fleet altho' not quite so rispectable as thos of Columbus or Capt. Cook, were still viewed by us with as much pleasure as those deservedly famed adventurers ever beheld theirs; and I dare say with quite as much anxiety for their safety and preservation. we were now about to penetrate a country at least two thousand miles in width, on which the foot of civilized man had never trodden; the good or evil it had in store for us was for experiment yet to determine, and these little vessels contained every article by which we were to expect to subsist or defend ourselves.

"however as the state of mind in which we are, generally gives the colouring to events, when the imagination is suffered to wander into futurity, the picture which now presented itself to me was a most pleasing one. entertaining as I do the most confident hope of succeeding in a voyage which had formed a darling project of mine for the last ten years, I could but esteem this moment of our departure as among the most happy of my life."

The rest of the men doubtless felt much the same, though were less inclined to put the feeling into words.

One week after leaving the villages the expedition reached the point beyond which white men seldom went. Two weeks later they arrived at the mouth of the Yellowstone. Lewis, at once rec-

26.—The trial, after impeachment, of Justice Chase of the United States Supreme Court was then in progress.

ognizing its strategic importance as a trading center, recommended that the American people set up a post there. On June 3, the explorers came to the forks of the Missouri. There they faced their first serious choice of routes. A wrong turn could spell disaster. The men measured the water velocity and the depth and width of each branch, concluding that the right fork was the proper one. The commanders disagreed, wisely as it proved. They overruled the men and, after naming the right branch Maria's river, headed their prows up the left-hand stream. Before leaving, they cached part of their goods against their return, pulled the larger of the dugouts to a place of safety and hid it; then jerked a quantity of bear and elk meat.

While tramping ahead of the main party on June 13, Lewis came upon the Great Falls of the Missouri. This confirmed some of the information gathered from the natives regarding a possible route to the Pacific. Clark spent two days portaging around the falls, only to find he had to build new canoes because the old ones could not be used above the falls in the present state of the river.

Twelve days later the explorers were at Three Forks of the Missouri, again facing a choice of routes.[27] This time all agreed on the southwest branch as the logical route. They named the southwest river branch, the Jefferson; the middle fork, the Madison; and the southeast, the Galatin.

Snake and Shoshone Indians ranged the territories near the headwaters of the Missouri. The commanders contacted some of these people to learn a possible route through the mountains and to get horses to carry supplies when the river was no longer navigable.

In these negotiations Sacajawea was invaluable. Five years before, she had been seized as a prisoner by the Minnetarees and taken to the lower Missouri where she was "united to the interpreter Charboneau, who frequently maltreated her."[28] On the lookout for a native hunting party or encampment, Lewis hoped to profit by Sacajawea's relationship with the Shoshones.

27.—While the explorers were traversing this part of the country, Jefferson was struggling with the increasing complexity of the French-British-American trade tangle which finally resulted in the War of 1812.

28.—Thwaites, page 146.

He reached the three forks of the Jefferson river, August 4, left a note for Clark, then ascended the middle branch. Because the beavers cut down the pole on which the note had been posted, Clark failed to get it. He went up the northwest fork, Big Hole, but returned on finding it unnavigable. When the two commanders finally rejoined each other, they proceeded up the middle fork, the modern Beaver Head river. As soon as it became evident that they could not follow the river much longer, Lewis announced that he was going ahead of the main party to try to cross the divide to get aid from someone, somewhere. On the eleventh even the light Indian trail failed him. Just as he seemed to be in completely uninhabited territory he caught sight of a Shoshone warrior on horseback. When Lewis tried to approach him, the Indian raced away.

The following day ended the long quest for the headwaters of the Missouri. Lewis found the spring, August 12, 1805. Flow from it went unbroken to the delta below New Orleans, four thousand miles away.[29] Later the same day he tramped on ahead, crossed the divide and came upon the Lemhi, or Lewis river, a tributary of the Columbia. For the first time an American could predict with some certainty the probable course of the Columbia. Next day Lewis suddenly encountered three squaws, two of whom ran away at once, while the third, too feeble to run, bowed her head to receive the death stroke which she thought would fall. When Lewis gave her a few beads, a pewter mirror, and a little paint as friendly tokens, she called the other women back. The three then conducted the Americans to their camp where Lewis found about sixty warriors. He remarked, "we wer all carressed and besmeared with their grease and paint till I was heartily tired of the national hug."

Diplomacy was nevertheless the rule of the moment and he persuaded the Shoshones,[30] for such they were, to supply him with enough horses to return to the other side of the mountains and connect with Clark, who was still dragging his heavy canoes up the little creek which the Missouri had now become. When

29.—Three days earlier, Zebulon Pike began his trip to the headwaters of the Mississippi.

30.—Some idea of the extent of trade relations of the North American Indians is evident in the fact that these Shoshones possessed Spanish bridles and mules.

the Americans and a small group of Shoshones reached the head of navigation, August 14, Clark had not yet arrived. The Indians suspected a trap, Lewis having promised them that more whites would await them there. Lewis needed all his tact to hold his advantage until Clark came up three days later.

Here the meeting between Sacajawea and her brother Cameawhait, the Shoshone chief, took place. Most of the eyewitnesses agreed that it was a joyful reunion but Ordway makes no special mention of it, and Lewis says, "I cannot discover that she shews any immotation of sorrow in recollecting this event (her capture), or of joy in being again restored to her native country; if she has enough to eat and a few trinkets to wear I believe she would be perfectly content anywhere."[31]

The reunion helped get horses from the Shoshones, though the bargaining was sharp even with Sacajawea's help. The Indians asked prices which the whites considered far too high yet were not half what the whites were asking in proportion for their cheap goods. The real trouble was that the Indians were demanding a fair price for their services. Finally the Americans bought twenty-nine horses for "merchandise which cost us originally about six dollars," said Lewis.

Clark now went ahead of the main party to help bring the horses back while Lewis supervised the unloading of canoes and the arrangement of baggage to fit the new mode of travel. Supplies not immediately needed were cached.

Clark had trouble with the Indians. They had haggled over prices and now threatened to desert after the bargain had been struck. Cameawhait had trouble keeping his men in line. When the party finally started down the Lemhi, this proved a poor route, and the commanders decided to go overland to another fork. They took the Nez Perce trail through the Lolo pass of the Bitter Roots, a trail which generally follows the watershed between the north and middle forks of the Clearwater river. So tortuous was their route that it is uncertain just where they did go. On at least one occasion, because of the mistakes of their guides, they were forced to back track. Each "authority" on the

31.—In an emergency though, Sacajawea acted with great dispatch, saving valuable articles from being lost overboard. Lewis praised her by saying she had "equal fortitude and resolution with any person on board."

expedition has traced the route to his own satisfaction but unfortunately they do not agree among themselves.

As the party struggled through the mountains, food became short, for the first time, yet never on the entire journey to the Pacific and return did the men show a finer spirit. Of course they were disheartened but there were no mutinies or desertions. They killed and ate their recently acquired horses and Clark went ahead to forage for food.

Remarkably often Clark got the disagreeable tasks. Time after time he was left behind to pull boats and build camps while Lewis went on to reconnoiter and hunt. When half-wild horses were to be brought to camp, the task was Clark's. So now, faced with starvation, it was Clark who accepted the responsibility while Lewis had the easier job of staying with the main party. There are two probable explanations. Lewis by nature was inclined to assume leadership and with it less difficult physical duties. Besides, he recognized the practical qualities of Clark, and in serious difficulties tended to rely on him. In spite of appearances, Lewis likely did not intend to slough any work on the other.

Little by little the American expedition worked its way down to the Weippe plain, where, on September 22, a party of Nez Perce Indians welcomed them. At the confluence of the north and south forks of the Kooskooskee, or Clearwater, the explorers stopped for a badly needed rest. Food was still scant. There were only inferior fish and the camas root, imported by the Nez Perces from down river.

Clark turned doctor and administered his crude remedies whenever he could, relying on "Rushes Pills" to accomplish all sorts of medicinal miracles.

New canoes had to be built before the expedition could once more get under way, October 7, 1805. The voyage from the Clearwater to the sea was uneventful. A diet of fish soon growing tiresome, dogs were substituted. At first the men objected but later admitted that once they got used to the idea the dogs were quite satisfactory. The leaders themselves were less easily pleased with the new diet.

The party arrived, October 16, at the junction of the Snake and Columbia rivers. They took the occasion calmly. Some were unaware that they had not been on the Columbia but only on its main tributary, the Snake.[32] Ordway wrote, "towards evening we arrived at the big forks. The large River which is wider than the Columbia River comes in from a northly direction." Below the Snake, the Columbia is broad and deep and navigation of it is a simple matter except for an infrequent bit of white water and the so-called great falls. As the party hurried west they passed the mouths of the modern Umatilla and John Day rivers, then the Deschutes, below which the falls at Celilo caused some delay. Farther down they passed the Dalles and more rough water.[33]

The Americans were at tide water, November 1, 1805, and four days later met the first natives decked out in European finery. These fellows thieved and swaggered but Lewis and Clark treated them kindly, knowing they must go that way again. If there were to be any violence, it would be better to have it on the homeward journey.

"Great joy in camp, we are in view of the Ocian . . . this great Pacific Octean, which we have been so long anxious to See, and the roreing of noise made by the waves brakeing on the rockey shores . . . may be heard distictly," wrote Clark under the date of November 7. Actually the party was still many miles up the Columbia. They did not reach the ocean proper for eight more days.

A vote decided the winter camp site. They had only the vaguest notion of what sort of weather to expect, though the journals abound in uncomplimentary notes on its tendency. In addition to shelter, two other problems were involved. They wanted to be close enough to the ocean and river to sight any arriving ship, and to be able to manufacture salt. A temporary camp was set up at Baker's bay. Young's bay down the coast a few miles became the permanent camp. There the men went to work to construct log houses and a palisade. The natives were not openly hostile but they had dealt with white traders enough

32.—So thoroughly had Carver's geographical theories been accepted that Lewis and Clark never doubted that the river which they found so close to the headwaters of the Missouri was the Columbia.

33.—The explorers missed the Willamette on their westward trip but discovered it on their return in the spring.

to have acquired many of their vices though surprisingly few of their virtues. Clark finally issued strict rules and posted a sentry to control the natives.

The party spent the winter making salt, hunting elk and deer, and fighting fleas. The persistent fleas accented their other troubles. It was difficult to find enough food to keep the men alive. Dog was a staple and as Lewis grew reconciled to it he wrote, "I have learned to think that if the chord be sufficiently strong, which binds the soul and body together, it does not so much matter about the materials which compose it." But Clark never agreed that a good fat dog could take the place of the more usual cuts of meat.

They chose a location thirty-five miles from camp for salt production and after months of tiresome work obtained twenty gallons, enough to keep the thirty-seven men and Sacajawea in good health. When Christmas came there were few physical enjoyments to be thankful for except their health. After complaining of the continual rain and "poore Elk meat," Ordway specifically mentions the blessings of feeling well. Clark says they would have feasted "had we anything either to raise our Sperits or even gratify our appetites; our Diner consisted of pore Elk, so much Spoiled that we eate it thro' mere necessity, Some Spoiled pounded fish and a fiew roots." Among the men who smoked, the commanders divided the remaining tobacco, a small handful apiece. To the others they gave a silk kerchief as a remembrance of the dreariest Christmas any of them had ever experienced.

Largely because of the poor diet, by the first of March, Lewis and Clark were anxious to start home. Then, too, they were almost out of trade goods, the Indians having "charged extravagantly for their small supplies of dogs, roots and dried fish."[34] Since neither ships nor traders had come during the winter, the letters of credit from the President were worthless.

The commanders left the Indians a list of their names[35] and their accomplishments to date, with instructions to give this list

---

34.—Thwaites, page 168.
35.—Some sailor had already left a record of his name, J. Bowman, tattooed on the arm of a native woman.

to the first vessel which stopped there.[36] To this report they attached rude maps of the route they followed. Patterning after Mackenzie, Clark scratched on a tree the legend:

"Wm. Clark, December 3d 1805 By Land from the U.States in 1804 & 5."

Preparations for the homeward journey were simple. The remaining trade goods could be wrapped in two handkerchiefs, and there was no surplus food or personal luggage. The clothes with which the men had originally left St. Louis had long since worn out and been replaced by rough garments fashioned from skins.

On March 23, 1806, the party headed for St. Louis and home. They purchased horses by turning brass buttons from old uniforms into trade goods. Both Lewis and Clark practiced primitive forms of healing in return for food and horses. According to Lewis, eye water was in great demand and he had traded a small vial of it for an "eligant gray mare." But as he himself said, the explorers had to eat.[37]

At the mouth of the Walla Walla, the commanders exchanged their canoes for beads and more horses, the beads to be used of course for further bartering when the expedition entered the Rockies.

The route home was not an exact retracing of the outward journey. When they reached what is now Eastern Washington they left the river, traveling overland to the Clearwater. On May 8, they arrived at Twisted Hair's camp, where they collected the horses which they had branded and left there the year before. Some authorities say the animals were in excellent condition; others that they showed hard useage.[38] At the camp they now built on the Clearwater the Americans settled to await melted snows and warmer weather. They moved ten miles up the Weippe flats on June 10. Five days afterwards they attempted to

---

36.—One of these many copies at last did get back to the United States. Captain Hill of the *Lydia* took it to Canton with him in January of 1807, and from there it was forwarded to Philadelphia.

37.—They were never in imminent danger of starvation, nor did they "at any time go long hungry," according to Snowden, page 302. The explorers themselves expressed a different view. At one time Clark was so weak from hunger that when he again tasted food, he became quite ill.

38.—Coman, volume 1, page 278, says "the horses left with him were in good condition." According to Thwaites, page 172, "Many of the animals had strayed afar, while others bore evidence of hard treatment."

get through the mountains but, finding too much snow, returned. The weather soon moderated and the expedition continued.

In order to investigate those regions they had neglected on the outward trip, Lewis and Clark now split their forces. Lewis took nine men, crossed the divide to the Medicine river country and Great falls, and explored Maria's river. Meanwhile Clark, with the rest of the men, went by way of the Big Hole to Wisdom river, then down the Jefferson and up the Gallatin to the Yellowstone and Missouri. Such explorations opened all the vast headwater system of the Missouri to American traders and trappers. Except for a single brush with the Minnetarees[39, 40]—probably the popularly-called Blackfeet—the exploring parties had no serious mishaps before arriving at the mouth of the Yellowstone. Lewis got there on August 7, and found a note from Clark saying he had gone ahead a week before. Lewis caught up with him on the twelfth.

The day before, Lewis had been accidentally shot in the leg by Crusatte. With considerable relief he turned to Clark for dressings and attention. Even with the best of care Lewis was disabled for a month.

The commanders reached the Mandans on August 14. There they released Charboneau and Sacajawea. The Frenchman having determined to settle among the Mandans, Lewis and Clark gave him a set of blacksmith's tools, hoping he would use these to advance the civilization of his chosen people.

About three weeks later the returning explorers met a trader, Aird, who gave them their first news from home. The political world was buzzing with the tragic duel between Alexander Hamilton and Aaron Burr. The travelers were no doubt thrilled

---

39.—Thwaites says, "In the scuffle, Reuben Fields stabbed one of the savages to the heart . . . the only Indian killed by the expedition." See page 177.

40.— Coman says, "and in the scuffle that ensued, in spite of Lewis' endeavor to avoid bloodshed, two of the Indians were killed." See page 280.

Coman and Thwaites often disagree over details. Of the condition of the cached goods on the return trail, Coman says, "The caches were found in good condition and the supplies of powder, salt and medicine fortunately re-enforced." (page 279.) Thwaites remarks that Lewis "found that much of the material in the caches had been destroyed by moisture." (page 176.)

Such minor disagreements are important only in showing the difficulty of tracing exactly the work of Lewis and Clark.

if not shocked, considering their political faiths.[41] On September 6, three days after meeting Aird, they encountered "outgoing" traders with whom they made the first exchanges for supplies. To celebrate the advent of civilization, they drank a gallon of whiskey.

On September 9 the party again crossed the mouth of the Platte, receiving next day their first news of Pike's successful work. They paid eight dollars for two quarts of whiskey on the twentieth to observe the event.

And at high noon, September 28, 1806, Lewis and Clark dramatically entered the amazed village of St. Louis. The welcome they met is known to every reader of American frontier lore. "They had," says Channing, "performed a feat without parallel in the history of exploration."[42] However that may be, there is no question regarding the importance to the United States of the work they did.[43]

After their western trips, the lives of the commanders were peculiarly unsatisfactory. Clark, raised to the rank of brigadier general, engaged in the fur trade and served as governor of Missouri territory until 1820. He was appointed superintendent

41.—Hamilton was the most reactionary of all the Federalists, who had with great gusto ridiculed Jefferson and his entire work, particularly his interest in the West.

42.—Channing, page 94.

43.—While Lewis and Clark were journeying to the Pacific and back, the United States was in the midst of a critical period of national development. Most of the events of such long standing that they could not be compared with specific dates in the trip of Lewis and Clark.

Jefferson had asked for the Lewis and Clark appropriation in January of 1803 but the expedition was not ready to leave St. Louis until May of 1804. Meanwhile Samuel Chase, Justice of the Supreme Court, had been impeached and plans were afoot to do likewise with John Marshall. Gallatin, Secretary of the Treasury, in honor of whom Lewis named one fork of the Missouri, was striving to liquidate the national debt.

The Tripolitan war dragged on until Lewis and Clark were just about to reach the Pacific in 1805. As early as 1803, the famous Yazoo claims, concerning the ownership of lands in Western Georgia, began to interest the public, but this controversy was not settled until long after Lewis and Clark were back in St. Louis.

The War of 1812 was developing rapidly. American ships were being seized by England and France, the *Essex* in 1805 being an example of this. In April of 1806, nine days before Lewis and Clark reached the Walla Wallas on their return trip, the First Importation Act was passed by Congress. England laid down the paper blockade of the northern coast of Europe, May 16, 1806. Events were thus smoldering through the summer and autumn that Lewis and Clark were exploring Maria's river and the Yellowstone.

of Indian affairs from 1822 to 1838. As the years went by, he became self-centered and crusty, feeling that his services and abilities had not been properly appreciated either by his fellow citizens or by his government. He died in St. Louis, September 1, 1838.

Lewis was appointed governor of Louisiana but did not serve long. While going to Philadelphia in 1810 to edit his journals,[44] he met a violent death in a log tavern in Tennessee. There has always been suspicion that he was murdered. Whether it was murder or suicide, the mystery remains as to why Lewis should want to do away with himself or why anyone else should seek his death.[45]

As with other genuinely great explorers, all the journals of this expedition are more than mere outlines of the route. Their pages offer manifold pictures of human interest—cabins of white-dressed buffalo hide; of canoes fashioned from skins; of dogs used as beasts of burden; of the Grosventres who disposed of their dead "Roped up in a Buffalow Robe" on a scaffold above ground; of "squars" carrying a hundred pounds of baggage besides their babies; of ropes made of elk skin, if a French trapper who entertained the Indians by dancing "on his head & C."; of drinks of "toffee" (a cheap rum) after cold hunts. They tell of sentries being relieved every half-hour when the thermometer dropped to seventy-four degrees below zero; of lonesome men dancing with each other in place of more pleasant partners; of trying to sleep in a crevice filled with fleas, alkali dust, and alkali water; of fires made of "buffalo chips"; of sweat houses used to cure all manner of human ailments; of great Tillamook canoes fifty feet long and capable of carrying ten thousand pounds of baggage.

The journals contain even more careful descriptions of natural phenomena, exciting adventures, and native habits. When the Americans arrived at the falls of the Missouri, there was the strange noise "made by the mountains" which they at first discredited but were later forced to admit existed.

"Since our arrival at the falls we have repeatedly heard a

44.—Nicholas Biddle finally gave the journals to the public in 1814.

45.—Lewis was in difficulty with the Federal Government over his financial accounts. Hints of graft were leveled at him but not proved.

strange noise coming from the mountains in a direction a little to the north of west. It is heard at different periods of the day and night (sometimes when the air is perfectly still and without a cloud), and consists of one stroke only, or of five or six discharges in quick succession. It is loud, and resembles precisely the sound of a six-pound piece of ordnance at the distance of three miles. The Minnetarees frequently mentioned this noise, like thunder, which they said the mountains made; but we had paid no attention to it, believing it to have been some superstition, or perhaps a falsehood. The watermen also of the party say that the Pawnees and Ricaras give the same account of a noise heard in the Black Mountains to the westward of them. The solution of the mystery given by the philosophy of the watermen is, that it is occasioned by the bursting of the rich mines of silver confined within the bosom of the mountains."

These peculiar noises have many explanations, the most likely being that they are caused by the explosion of the species of stone known as the geode, fragments of which are frequently found among the mountains. The geode has a hollow shell lined with beautiful crystals of many colors.[46]

The explorers had plenty of adventure. The official journal records the following:

"Last night we were alarmed by a new sort of enemy. A Buffalo swam over from the opposite side, and to the spot where lay one of our canoes, over which he clambered to shore: then, taking fright, he ran full speed up the bank towards our fires, and passed within eighteen inches of the heads of some of the men before the sentinel could make him change his course.

"Still more alarmed, he ran down between four fires, and within a few inches of the heads of a second row of the men, and would have broken into our lodge if the barking of the dog had not stopped him. He suddenly turned to the right, and was out of sight in a moment, leaving us all in confusion, every one seizing his rifle and inquiring the cause of the alarm. On learning what had happened, we had to rejoice at suffering no more injury than some damage to the guns that were in the canoe which the buffalo crossed."

Sometimes these wildlife encounters along the shores were not

46.—Noah Brooks. *First Across the Continent,* pages 122-123.

so pleasant, as when Captain Lewis came upon the grizzly bears:

"We proceeded early, with a moderate wind. Captain Lewis, who was on shore with one hunter, met, about eight o'clock, two white (grizzly) bears. Of the strength and ferocity of this animal the Indians had given us dreadful accounts. They never attack him but in parties of six or eight persons, and even then are often defeated with a loss of one or more of their party. Having no weapons but bows and arrows, and the bad guns with which the traders supply them, they are obliged to approach very near to the bear; and as no wound except through the head or heart is mortal, they frequently fall a sacrifice if they miss their aim.

"He rather attacks than avoids a man, and such is the terror which he has inspired, that the Indians who go in quest of him paint themselves and perform all the superstitious rites customary when they make war on a neighboring nation. Hitherto, those bears we had seen did not appear desirous of encountering us; but although to a skilful rifleman the danger is very much diminished, yet the white bear is still a terrible animal.

"On approaching these two, both Captain Lewis and the hunter fired, and each wounded a bear. One of them made his escape; the other turned upon Captain Lewis and pursued him seventy or eighty yards, but being badly wounded the bear could not run so fast as to prevent him from reloading his piece, which he again aimed at him, and a third shot from the hunter brought him to the ground. He was a male, not quite full grown, and weighed about three hundred pounds. The legs are somewhat longer than those of the black bear, and the talons and tusks much larger and longer.

"Its color is a yellowish brown; the eyes are small, black, and piercing; the front of the forelegs near the feet is usually black, and the fur is finer, thicker, and deeper than that of the black bear. Add to which, it is a more furious animal, and very remarkable for the wounds which it will bear without dying."

The disgusting habits of the natives were sometimes adventures. Drewyer, one of Lewis's most valuable men, had killed a deer. An Indian, thinking he might be cheated of his share, ran ahead. Lewis stopped to see what the Indians would do.

"Captain Lewis slackened his pace, and followed at a sufficient distance to observe them. When they reached the place where

Drewyer had thrown out the intestines, they all dismounted in confusion and ran tumbling over each other like famished dogs. Each tore away whatever part he could, and instantly began to eat it. Some had the liver, some the kidneys—in short, no part on which we are accustomed to look with disgust escaped them. One of them who had seized about nine feet of the entrails, was chewing at one end, while with his hand he was diligently clearing his way by discharging the contents at the other.

"It was indeed impossible to see these wretches ravenously feeding on the filth of animals, the blood streaming from their mouths, without deploring how nearly the condition of savages approaches that of the brute creation. Yet, though suffering from hunger, they did not attempt, as they might have done, to take by force the whole deer, but contented themselves with what had been thrown away by the hunter."

With the completion of the Lewis and Clark expedition the way was clear for the final epoch in the exploration of the Northwest coast. Spaniards had opened the earliest sea lanes. Englishmen, Russians, and Spaniards renewed those activities a century and a half later, drawing in most of the remaining lines of the coast. Frenchmen, Englishmen, and Americans proved there is no Strait of Anian. In its stead they had searched out the overland route to the Pacific.

But one period remained—the conquest of the Pacific Northwest by the white men and for the white men. That work was to be undertaken and largely fulfilled by that astonishing breed of men, the fur traders. Theirs is a stirring story, an epoch in itself. When they had finished with their traps and canoes, there was no longer any real western wilderness.

8

FUR TRADE AND EXPLORATION

THE FINAL CHAPTER in the discovery of the Northwest is the story of an era as well as of men. It is the saga of the moutain fur trade from 1800 to 1840, a period unique in the history of exploration. Amazing adventures took place among more bizarre scenes than those commonly found in the realm of fiction.

Before and after this time, Englishmen and Canadians generally confined themselves to the fields about the Great lakes and Hudson bay.

St. Louis was the main source of this new activity. Reckless and lewd, the city faced civilization on one side, the edge of the frontier on the other. As late as 1810 it had no bank, no school, no Protestant church, no resident Catholic priest. Only a newspaper and post office served as links with the Atlantic seaboard.

In 1764, long before Lewis and Clark's expedition, even earlier than Jefferson's dreams of exploration, Pierre Laclede Liguest, a member of the trading firm of Maxent, Laclede and company of New Orleans, chose the site and broke ground for the village of St. Louis. He planned a haven for the French refugees expatriated by the Treaty of Paris of 1763. He hoped for, and achieved, a city which drew tribute from all the trade on the great river. St. Louis became the only city to furnish the needs and pleasures of a host of men who spent their lives west of the Mississippi. Up and down its dusty streets tramped every sort of human being from savages to crown princes. Soft-spoken Creoles rubbed elbows with hard-eyed Yankee gamblers who found the frontier a safer place than the boardwalks of Boston. Spaniards from the pass at Taos and south of Santa Fe spoke a language little understood by the aristocracy of Europe who came to outfit a buffalo hunt. Greasy, fierce chiefs cared nothing about what dignified, Virginia gentlemen thought of their hairdress or their fleas. Crafty, middle-class traders worshipped at a different shrine from godly missionaries striving to bring the story of the Nativity to barbarians. Yet all these men breathed the same dust, paddled the same river, feared and fought the same Indians.

Even before the Declaration of Independence, St. Louis had become the crossroads of America. Every conceivable kind of goods was piled high on its docks and in its warehouses. For half a century it was the most important inland city in the New World, building for itself a legend which places it with the great fair towns of Samarkand and Khiva. If it was less than these in years and background, it vies with them in color and intrigue. St. Louis thrived on violence, sudden death, outlawry, and cutthroat business methods until encroaching civilization gradually eclipsed them.

French voyageurs brought the finest furs to St. Louis, and their songs were rivaled only by the boatmen of the Don, the Volga, and the Grand canal.[1]

The number of traders working the region west of the Mississippi and south of 50° north probably never exceeded a thousand, and when the labors of five organizations have been recorded, the history of the period has been told. Manuel Lisa and the Missouri Fur company, John Jacob Astor and his American Fur company and Pacific Fur company, the North West company, the Rocky Mountain Fur company, and last and greatest, the Hudson's Bay company—these comprised the field. And because Astor's American Fur company neither covered new ground nor explored new territory, only the other companies are significant in the story of Northwest exploration.

1.—Sung in corrupted Canadian French, many of them are difficult to translate into English, some impossible, yet their vitality and rhythm are apparent in spite of translation. One of them goes:

> **On my way I met**
> Three cavaliers well mounted
> One, your, (Cavalier?) a Danish robber
> One, your, (Cavalier?) a Danish robber
>
> Three cavaliers well mounted
> One on horseback, the other on foot.
> One, your, (?) a Danish robber.
> One, your, (?) a Danish robber.

9

MANUEL LISA, THE INDIANS' FRIEND

FEW MOUNTAIN FUR MEN were more colorful than the Spaniard, Manuel Lisa. Obscure son of an obscure father, Lisa came to St. Louis from New Orleans about 1790.[1] By 1802 he had grown so important in the river trade that the government granted him exclusive trade with the Osages. By that time too, he was already building up that long list of enemies who never ceased to attack him while he lived and to blacken his reputation when he died.[2]

The following letter written by Berthold to Pierre Chouteau, August 20, 1819, shows the kind of abuse so often hurled against Lisa:

"From Mr. Dent I learn that Manuel decided to bring his wife to F. Lisa so that he might draw to his home the protection of the officers, since he has found out that they expect to watch his conduct. He does well to treat them so kindly since he hopes to get considerable advantage from it.

"In case you might have decided to make a visit there, I believe that some good letters of introduction to the superior officers might be of value.

"The snail has always been a boaster and in advance has claimed to predict what he would do. This year he claims to be firmer than ever. For my part I believe that as for himself, he is the least capable of the traitors."

Though Manuel Lisa acquired these enemies partly through his own fault, he was more sinned against than sinning. Of all the traders to penetrate the mountains, he was the ablest; and, unlike many company stockholders, he managed his own forces in the field. His business code was as ethical as others of his time and he won his place by initiative, daring, and energy. Because he smoked the pipe of peace and kept his guns handy, in the

1.—Lisa is supposed to have been born in New Orleans, September 8, 1772. Nothing important is known about his boyhood or early life though a vague tale exists that for a time he followed the sea.

2.—W. J. Ghent. *Early Far West*, pages 73-74.

many thousands of miles he traveled among the Indians he never had a serious personal brush with them. Like Mackenzie, he drove his voyageurs to staggering labors but he often paddled the sturdiest stroke himself. In a letter written in 1817 to General Clark, governor of the territory of Missouri, he analyzed his own strength:

"But I have had some success as a trader; and this gives rise to many reports.

" 'Manuel must cheat the government, and Manuel must cheat the Indians, otherwise Manuel could not bring down every summer so many boats loaded with rich furs.'

"Good. My accounts with the government will show whether I receive anything out of which to cheat it. A poor five hundred dollars, as sub-agent salary, does not buy the tobacco which I annually give to those who call me father.

"Cheat the Indians! The respect and friendship which they have for me, the security of my possessions in the heart of their country, respond to this charge, and declare with voices louder than the tongues of men that it cannot be true.

" 'But Manuel gets so much rich fur!'

"Well, I will explain how I get it. First, I put into my operations great activity; I go a great distance, while some are considering whether they will start today or tomorrow. I impose upon myself great privations; ten months in a year I am buried in the forest, at a vast distance from my own house. I appear as the benefactor, and not as the pillager, of the Indians. I carried among them the seed of the large pompion [pumpkin], from which I have seen in their possession the fruit weighing 160 pounds. Also the large bean, the potato, the turnip; and these vegetables now make a comfortable part of their subsistence, and this year I have promised to carry the plough. Besides, my blacksmiths work incessantly for them, charging nothing. I lend them traps, only demanding preference in their trade. My establishments are the refuge of the weak and of the old men no longer able to follow their lodges; and by these means I have acquired the confidence and friendship of these nations, and the consequent choice of their trade."

Even Lisa's enemies did not deny these claims, for though they hated him they admitted his efficiency.

After the Lewis and Clark expedition Lisa formed a partnership with two merchants from Kaskaskia, Pierre Menard and William Morrison, in order to trade farther west than anyone had yet done in the territory now within the United States. As aides, Lisa chose three men who had just returned with Lewis and Clark: George Drewyer, perhaps the most valuable man on that other expedition; John Potts, and Peter Wiser. With these as a nucleus, Lisa gathered a company to go to the mouth of the Big Horn river, erect a post, and barter with the natives. The men themselves were also to set and tend traps, a new policy.

With forty-two men Lisa left St. Louis, April 19, 1807,[3] for the upper Missouri. Acting Governor Bates tried to induce him to wait until safe conduct could be furnished but Lisa slipped away on his own responsibility. When the party reached the Arikaras in August, they found these people at war with the Mandans. The Arikaras ordered the whites to give up their expedition because from them the Mandans would buy articles leading to a successful war. Though aware that refusal meant trouble, Lisa had been among the Indians too long to give in to such demands. The Arikaras promptly retaliated by robbing him of a large portion of his trade goods, after which they assumed he would return to St. Louis. Instead, he ordered his crew to push ahead. He reached the Big Horn, November 21.

Here he built a post, set out traps, and opened trade with the Crows. These trapping and trading parties carried on the work of exploring, winning for their employers and themselves a place among the discoverers of routes to the Northwest. Since the best furs were always found farthest "in," each trader searched deeper and deeper into unknown valleys.

Having completed their post, Lisa and his men split into various parties. Lisa himself intended to return to St. Louis as soon as summer arrived. Meanwhile he sent John Colter in an important expedition. Colter had also been with Lewis and Clark and had spent the preceding winter trapping on his own, probably at the Yellowstone.[4] Now he was to go to the Grosventres of the Prairies —commonly called the Blackfeet—to persuade them to trade with

3.—Fulton sent the *Claremont* up to Albany in August, establishing the steamboat as a new mode of travel.

4.—Hiram Martin Chittenden. *The American Fur Trade of the Far West,* volume 2, page 713.

Lisa. It was a delicate mission. The Blackfeet were hereditary enemies of the Crows and it was a Blackfoot who had been killed by the Lewis and Clark expedition on its way back from the Pacific. That alone tended to make them unfriendly to all whites. Yet, according to reports, they were temporarily inclined to be friendly; and Colter, with a thirty-pound pack, a gun, and ammunition, started out by himself toward the southwest.

As with most early travelers, Colter's exact route is unknown, but he probably proceeded to Pierre's hole by way of Jackson hole, then Union pass through the Wind River mountains, and Teton pass through the range of that name. In Pierre's hole a fight took place between the Crows, with whom Colter was then allied, and the Blackfeet. The Blackfeet were defeated and Colter had certainly not helped his relations with them, the very tribe he had been sent out to pacify. Furthermore he was several hundred miles from home, and wounded. He gave up his project, striking off directly toward Lisa's post. Happily, his route lay through that great natural wonder, Yellowstone park. Colter traversed it diagonally from the southwest. His enthusiastic report on its beauty and magnificence immediately labeled him as a notorious liar. Unfortunately, later adventures added fuel to this reputation. Nevertheless, to Manuel Lisa's skill and John Colter's energy must go the credit for the discovery of Yellowstone park.

The following spring Lisa again sent Colter to the Blackfeet. In company with John Potts, he arrived in their territory, tending traps at night and sleeping during the day for greater safety. All went well until Potts became careless. One morning he accused Colter of cowardice, then paid with his life for the taunt. Indians, that Potts vowed were only buffalo, killed him and seized Colter, who was stripped naked and asked if he could run well. Realizing the ordeal ahead, Colter said he was a very poor runner. This lie saved his life. The Blackfoot method was to allow the intended victim to race with their warriors as a fox races with the hounds, death being the penalty for slowness. They made it a sporting event by allowing a handicap to poor runners.

Colter was led some distance beyond the assembled warriors. Then, with a war whoop as signal, the race was on. Entirely naked and without a weapon, Colter dashed madly for the river six miles away across a plain completely filled with prickly pear. He ran until the blood spurted from his nostrils. Glancing over his shoulder he spied one of the Indians not twenty yards behind. The savage stumbled in the very act of throwing the spear. Its point lodged in the earth and the shaft cracked in his hand. The Blackfoot fell and Colter, turning, grabbed the lance head, pinning the warrior to the ground with it.

The rest of the warriors were closing in fast but Colter reached the river a few yards ahead of his nearest pursuer, plunged in and swam toward a small island. Near its shores he found an old raft partly covered with driftwood and brush. Diving under this he discovered a crevice for his head. There, with the Indians swarming about him all day, he waited until night, then swam silently downstream. He landed out of sight of the natives and traveled all night toward his post. Seven days later he was back at Lisa's fort, having had nothing but roots to eat the entire way. For the second time, he unintentionally helped make the Blackfeet even more hostile.[5]

During the summer of 1808,[6] Lisa and Drewyer left for St. Louis to bring out the next year's supplies. Though unimportant in themselves, each of these seasonal trips for supplies drove another wedge into the wilderness barrier. Already the day was near when this barrier was to topple and wagons were to begin rolling across the passes to Oregon.

A new company was being organized in St. Louis and, on February 24, 1809,[7] the St. Louis Missouri Fur company was established.

Most of the important names in and near St. Louis appeared in this new organization: Lisa, Menard, Morrison, General Clark, Chouteau—both father and son—, members of the Wilkinson and

---

5.—See Chittenden, volume 2, pages 717-721; also Washington Irving's *Astoria*.
6.—During the latter part of 1807 and until March of 1808, the Federal Congress debated and finally passed the Embargo Acts in an attempt to force England to meet its terms in the three-cornered quarrel with Napoleon, the United States, and Great Britain.
7.—Americans did not take kindly to the Embargo Act and, in January of 1809, an Enforcement Act was passed. In March the Non-Intercourse Act followed the Embargo law but, on April 19, 1809, Madison renewed trade relations with England.

Lewis families, Labadie, and Major Andrew Henry.[8] Negotiations with the government were already under way for the return of Chief Big White and his Mandans to their home, following their visit to civilization. The government agreed to pay seven thousand dollars for this service; and the new company, with their charges, set out about the middle of June, 1809, for the upper Missouri. Except for Morrison, Clark, and Wilkinson, all of whom remained behind, every member of the new company was in the party, totaling close to two hundred.

The Mandans were returned the last of September and Lisa began constructing Fort Mandan at the mouth of Knife river. Trapping parties were dispatched; then Lisa either went on to his post on the Big Horn or returned to St. Louis, there being some doubt which course he took.[9] Anyhow, about March of 1810, he once more headed for the Three Forks of the Missouri, where he established a post. During the winter of 1810-1811, he again journeyed to St. Louis.[10]

Not having heard from Major Henry, who had been left on the upper Missouri, Lisa decided to go to his aid. The Blackfeet having made business on the Three Forks impossible, the post there was abandoned. Before that, eight men had been killed and all traps and pelts stolen by the Indians. Colter and one companion constructed a canoe and reached St. Louis only thirty days after leaving the post. Others of the crew arrived later. A few determined to stay on but, by July 1, they also gave up and returned.

Major Henry now decided to go up the Madison river to Henry's lake, cross the mountains to a fork of the Snake, and built Fort Henry, near the present town of Elgin, Idaho. This

---

8.—These fur companies were not elaborately organized commerical affairs comparable to present-day companies. They were loosely-drawn partnerships, arranged to run for only one, two, or three years.

9.—"Lisa, Pierre Chouteau, and some others of the company thereupon returned to St. Louis, arriving about November 20." See Ghent, page 121.
"He ascended the river again in the spring of 1809 to his post on the Bighorn, which he transferred to the new company. He returned to St. Louis in October, 1809." See Chittenden, volume 1, page 126.

10.—Meanwhile John Jacob Astor had organized his Pacific Fur company. Wilson Price Hunt, in charge of the overland Astorians, was then at St. Louis organizing his crew.
Napoleon and England were fast raising the war fever in the United States. The Rambouillet Decree and Macon's Bill Number Two only made matters worse.

fort is supposed to have been the first American post west of the Rocky mountains, although a Lieutenant Pinch may have had one earlier on the Columbia.[11] Early in the spring of 1811, just about the time Lisa decided to look for him, Henry left the region.

While Manuel Lisa was enlarging his activities, John Jacob Astor's American Fur company was already firmly established in the Mississippi region and expanding toward the Rocky mountains. Astor was not popular with the rank and file of St. Louis traders and if he were allowed to merge his Mississippi and mountain holdings into one business the combine would threaten others. Lisa took the initiative in checking Astor. He was the logical leader for the campaign, knowing as he did the country and Indians better than Wilson Price Hunt, Astor's commander at St. Louis. Besides, he had as much at stake as anyone else in St. Louis.

Some have sharply criticized Lisa for his attack on Hunt and the Astor project, arguing that this great venture would never endanger the smaller traders' domain.[12] Such an assumption is not logical. Astor's trading methods up to 1811 were well known and Lisa and the other St. Louis traders realized their danger. After the disastrous expedition to the Three Forks, Lisa planned a new post with the Arikaras and was collecting his goods for it when Hunt arrived in the city. Naturally Lisa did not want Hunt to get into the Arikara country at all, especially not ahead of Lisa himself. Since Hunt could not be stopped entirely Lisa delayed him as much as he could.

Hunt had as guide and interpreter a man by the name of Dorion, once employed by Lisa and still indebted to him. Lisa got a warrant for Dorion's arrest. Too old a hand to be caught by a simple ruse, Hunt merely had the guide leave the party, make a wide detour inland, and avoid service of the warrant.

Both Lisa and Hunt were rushing preparations to beat each other to the Arikaras. Hunt's party left first. The long race which followed was one of the oddest ever run: here were two great combinations of men, out of sight of each other for the entire distance and separated at the beginning by Hunt's three

11.—Ghent, page 123.
12.—Chittenden, volume 1, pages 183-184.

weeks' head start and 240 miles of turbulent river. Their finish line would be that day when the canoe behind caught up with the boats in front. More than a thousand miles were covered before the shouts of one party were heard by the other. Over each mile Lisa drove his men by every trick at his command. He praised their robustness, cursed their cowardice, taunted their weaknesses, and plied the mightiest paddle himself.

Crude, crafty, and unethical though he may have been, Lisa was a shrewd judge of men and what they could be forced to do. On May 19, he was opposite the Omaha villages with Hunt so far in the lead that Lisa, believing himself beaten, sent a note to his rival, who was then on the Niobrara. He asked Hunt to wait so that the combined parties would offer greater protection through hostile territory. Hunt supposedly agreed but whether he deliberately lied, or changed his mind, or never made any such promise, will probably never be known. Whatever the answer, he hurried on, leaving Lisa with twenty-five men and a single canoe to do the best he could through enemy country. According to the favored version, Lisa was so angered that he redoubled his efforts to catch his rival.

Two traders with Hunt, McClellan and Crooks, are said to have helped convince Hunt that Lisa would only deliver them by trickery into the hands of the savages. There is no evidence that Lisa intended any such thing but such were the tactics of the fur men.

Pushing his men ever harder, Lisa overtook the others just at the edge of the Sioux country, June 2, exactly two [13] months after Hunt left St. Louis.[14] Now Lisa had realized two of the three objectives of his struggle with Hunt: he had forestalled Hunt's entry into the Arikara country before his own party and had practically forced his protection through the dangerous Sioux lands.

If the Hunt and Lisa quarrel was such a bitter affair, it is strange that Franchere, a contemporary authority on the Astoria enterprise, does not mention any trouble of the sort. He even dismisses in a few lines the Hunt expedition as far as the Mandans.

13.—On November 7, 1811, Harrison struck a death blow at Indian power in the Old West in his victory at Tippecanoe.

14.—With Lisa in this race were Charboneau and Sacajawea.

Anyhow, the two leaders stayed together until they reached the Arikaras, where Lisa turned to his trade and Hunt bargained for horses.

Learning there that Andrew Henry was safe, Lisa was relieved of the responsibility of searching for his partner.

He took the season's catch down the river early in the autumn of 1811, reorganizing the company during the winter. The new title, and the one most commonly connected with Lisa's name, was the Missouri Fur company. Though the general public was urged to put up the money for it, investors were skeptical. The directors themselves finally had to finance it.

The new company launched an aggressive trade. About the first of May, 1812,[15] they sent eighty-five men to the upper Missouri. On the way they built a new post, Fort Manuel, among the Arikaras, later dispatching trapping parties to the Little Bighorn in southern Montana, to the Wind river in Wyoming, and even sending three men south to the Arkansas river.[16] Lisa himself stayed at the Mandan post until spring, returning to St. Louis, June 1, 1813.[17]

Meanwhile the War of 1812 broke out and the government was looking for some one who could keep the Missouri river Indians neutral or perhaps induce them to join the Americans. The choice fell on Manuel Lisa. All the men who eventually earned a niche in the mountain fur trade were in and out of St. Louis at the time of his appointment, but were passed over by Governor Clark.

Lisa not only kept the Indians from joining the British but organized them into bands operating for the Americans. Nor did he maneuver these actions from St. Louis. Immediately on being named sub-Indian agent he went to Fort Lisa, near the

---

15.—On March 9, the famous "Henry Letters," for which Congress had been duped into paying fifty thousand dollars in the belief that they contained sensational information, were read to the lawmakers.
War was finally declared against England, June 18.

16.—This is not the first time Lisa tried to enter the South. In a letter to Pike in 1806, Wilkinson declared that Lisa "and a society . . . have determined on a project to open some commercial intercourse with Santa Fe." See R. L. Duffus, *Santa Fe Trail*, page 55.
Two years before the party of 1812, Lisa had also attempted to make a contact with the Arapahoes, directly west of St. Louis, but failed as he did in his Santa Fe venture.

17.—On September 10, 1813, Perry won his victory on Lake Erie.

present Omaha, taking personal charge. After the war he acted as Indian agent until 1817, when he resigned his commission to General Clark. He returned to the fur trade, going up and down the Missouri as he had wanted to do before the interruption, but his work during the three remaining years of his life is unimportant. On reaching St. Louis from his posts in April of 1820, he was well and energetic as ever. Then suddenly on August 12 he passed away.[18]

Manuel Lisa's career was short yet into it he crowded an amazing amount of activity. In thirteen years he had personally ascended the Missouri river twelve or thirteen times, each trip covering at least 650 miles. In all, he traversed more than twenty-five thousand miles by canoe and boat. His men penetrated to the upper Missouri; explored and trapped large sections of Montana, Idaho, and Wyoming; and discovered Yellowstone park. He sent out two or three unsuccessful parties to tap the wealth he felt certain lay along the route to Santa Fe. He took time to do more than his share in the War of 1812.

Nor was his private life less busy. Three times he was married, once to a native girl strictly for business reasons, twice to women of his own race. The Indian girl inconvenienced Lisa by falling in love with him and following him to St. Louis where his second white wife was expected. He had trouble persuading the native that there was no place for her in the new scheme of things.

Few try to defend these affairs which the fur men had with the Indians, but at least Manuel Lisa made it clear when he formed the union with the native that he already had a white wife. Furthermore, he did not desert his children as so many of the traders did. The fact that he took them away from their mother and tried to educate them accounted for part of his trouble. His will instructed his executors to give two thousand dollars to each of his two half-breed children when they should reach their majority. [19] There is no record that this provision was carried out.

On Lisa's death, Joshua Pilcher became the leader of the Mis-

18.—Even as Lisa died, the drama of the extension of slavery into the territories was unfolding. The admission of Maine and Missouri to the Union with or without slavery ended in the Missouri Compromise of 1820.
19.—Chittenden, volume 1, pages 133-135.

souri Fur company. The organization struggled on for a few years but the old fire was gone. Lisa had been the dominant figure; his was the intellect and drive behind each major move. When these were absent from the organization, little but the shell was left. Remaining members could neither visualize nor carry out the rugged policies necessary to success in the fur fields. Though Pilcher at first reported some progress, disaster followed disaster until, by 1830, the Missouri Fur company was part of the past.

FORT CLATSOP

The reconstructed camp of Lewis and Clark, just south of Astoria, Oregon.
(Oregon State Highway Dept.)

10

ASTOR AND THE PACIFIC FUR COMPANY

THE MEDICI OF ITALY and the Fuggers of Germany have long since given way to the Mellons, the Morgans, and the Deterings, but the clans have only changed their names. Business and business ethics today are much as they were when the first financial barons collected toll from king and peasant alike.

Among trade tycoons there have been two classes, those who allowed the purchaser a reasonable return for his money and those who allowed the least possible. Among the greatest American fortunes built on the second of these philosophies was that of John Jacob Astor, immigrant from the village of Waldorf, Duchy of Baden, Germany. He seldom pretended to be other than he was, a pirate in the fur markets, "and by keeping always in view the object of giving the least, and getting the most in every transaction, he readily acquired enormous wealth." [1] At seventeen years of age he went to London. Four years later, in 1784, he arrived in Baltimore with seven cheap flutes which in his lifetime grew to a fortune of millions of dollars, all saturated with the hate of men cheated along the way.

Before the boat bearing him docked at Baltimore, young Astor had already decided to enter the fur trade. Hastening to New York, where his older brother was a prosperous butcher, he got a job in a fur store to learn the business. Soon he himself went among the Indians, buying as cheaply and selling as dearly as he could. By 1800 [2] he was the leading New York dealer. "John Jacob Astor was to the New York of 1825 what Robert Morris had been to Philadelphia a generation before—an evidence of the wealth that was to be got by those who would boldly exploit the vast resources of America." [3]

1.—Ghent, page 135.
2.—The Federal Government moved from Philadelphia to the new capital during July of 1800.
3.—Vernon Louis Parrington. *The Romantic Revolution in America*, page 195.

Astor intended to enter the fur fields about the headwaters of the Mississippi. He had the attention of the government in the person of that important politician, Thomas H. Benton. Federal Government stores had been set here and there among the tribes but there was no chance for private exploitation under such a system. Astor and Benton fought these government posts persistently and savagely. For them, no lie was too big, no ruse too mean, if either speeded the day when the government would relinquish the red men to the gods of trade. Eventually Astor won. On May 6, 1822, Congress refused to appropriate further money, the stores were closed, and private traders were free to rob by unfair weights and measures and to corrupt by diluted-liquor sales.[4]

Astor had entered the territory before the government. Between the years 1784 and 1808, he built a fortune large enough to permit him to organize the American Fur company with a capital of one million dollars. This was on April 6, 1808. The story of the company is not important here except for the fact that it finally drove out all competitors who seriously endangered its monopoly.

Two years later,[5] on June 23, Astor organized the Pacific Fur company with $400,000, under the terms of which he meant to go to the mouth of the Columbia to compete with all traders west of the Rockies.

Astor never invaded a territory until others had cleared the way and proved its worth. Though not very romantic, this policy was mainly responsible for Astor's successes. Thus, after Manuel Lisa and others had demonstrated the possibility of ascending the Missouri and descending to the Pacific by way of the Columbia, Astor laid his plans for the Pacific Fur company. "It was a grandiose conception worthy of a feudal baron of commerce. It was knit up with dreams of conquest." [6] Practical, experienced fur men were to handle every phase of the work—traders who had

---

4.—The liquor was even unfairly measured, the vendor often holding his thumb well inside the small cup used as a standard, in order to lessen the amount needed to fill it. When the customer was sufficiently drunk, plain water was substituted for the already diluted rum but the price was the same.

5.—The Wilkinson-Burr scandal had reached Congress in April and an official committee had been appointed to investigate the affair.

6.—Parrington, page 195.

gathered pelts all the way from the Great lakes to Hudson bay and the Arctic. The ultimate failure of the company was due to entirely different causes from those ordinarily associated with the fur trade.

Pacific Fur company stock was divided into one hundred shares, half of which Astor himself kept and half of which he parceled out among various partners.

From the first, the company intended to do more than gather beaver hides along the Columbia. Far to the north old Baranof growled and drove his Russians; away to the south, the Spaniards still pretended to control a dominion as large as central Europe. Astor would carry food stuffs and manufactured supplies to the Russians and push the Spaniards as sharply as possible. The fur wealth from all this vast region he meant to dump onto the markets at Canton, and he expected to make a double profit: one on goods supplied the Indians and Russians, another on the pelts they sold to him. The scheme was "a grandiose conception" but also a gigantic gamble. It was all very well for Lisa to risk a paltry forty thousand dollars; it was quite another matter for Astor to risk ten times that amount.

On the other hand, those who pretend that Astor entered the Columbia trade in a sporting frame of mind, willing to win, lose, or draw, do not appreciate the commercial shrewdness of the man. Organizing the Pacific Fur company as a separate enterprise may easily have been an intelligent step to remove the risk of undermining the capital of the American Fur company should the Pacific venture fail. But to assume that Astor believed he had no more than an even chance to win on the Columbia is to deny the principle upon which he founded his fortune. His assurance of success is proved by his guarantee to stand all losses for the first five years, and certainly nothing in his past suggests he would enjoy the role of loser.

Astor was actually practicing shrewd business psychology. By such promises he could lure into his organization traders who otherwise might have hesitated to risk their time, energies, and what money they had. Alexander Ross said that Astor led every employe "to believe that his fortune was made."

So confident was Astor that the papers of partnership stipulated that no new additions were to be made to the company without the consent of all concerned. He further underwrote success by offering one-third interest in the Pacific Fur company to his rival, the North West company of Canada, but that organization was not interested. Probably it did not fear competition.

Two separate divisions of men undertook the actual building of the posts and organization of the trade. Astor had dealt in furs long enough to realize that there were certain things he could not control. To cancel these as far as possible, he split his forces, sending one section to the Columbia by sea, the other overland.

ASTORIA, OREGON, 1813

This sketch was made two years after Astoria's founding by the men of the *Tonquin*. Alexander Ross, critic of the venture, wrote, "It would have made a cynic smile to see this pioneer corps, composed of traders, shopkeepers, voyageurs, and Owyhees, all ignorant alike in this new walk of life, and the most ignorant of all, the leader." (Sketched from Franchere's *Narrative of a Voyage to the Northwest Coast of America.*)

11

THE *TONQUIN* GOES TO THE COLUMBIA

ASTOR'S FIRST SHIP, the *Tonquin*, was ready to sail from New York in August of 1810, a trifle more than two months after he organized the Pacific Fur company. Captain Jonathan Thorn was in command. On board were sailors, clerks, partners, and sundry employes between these grades, totaling thirty-three men.

Important passengers included Gabriel Franchere, a clerk whose journal gives a restrained statement of all that took place at Astoria; the two Stuarts, Robert and his Uncle David, both partners; Duncan McDougal and Alexander McKay, partners [1]; and Alexander Ross, another clerk-journalist but one who left a very expressive account and vivid interpretation of the happenings on the Columbia.[2]

The ship was packed with the usual tawdry baubles incident to "conquering the wilderness" from the natives, and everything seemed set for a successful voyage. The now famous *Constitution* was detailed by the Navy department to watch the *Tonquin* clear of the coast, lest her seamen be impressed. This alone shows how deep Astor had sunk his power into the Federal government.

Unfortunately the *Tonquin* carried men completely incapable of co-operation, many of them holding exaggerated opinions of their own authority. Over them all was the explosive Jonathan Thorn. Astor could hardly have picked a man less fitted to command a ship to the Columbia. A veteran of the Tripolitan war, Thorn was used to handling conscript sailors between ports of civilized nations, where in an emergency he could rely on one of two alternatives to enforce his will—either discharge one crew for another or call in the police power. Since on the Pacific

1.—McKay had been with Mackenzie on his second expedition.
2.—The enormous amount of material available on Astor's activities, including numerous journals, early histories, and independent analyses, makes it almost impossible to incorporate all such interpretations.
    The two journalists, Franchere and Ross, both reliable, have furnished much of the information used here. Their records are, of course, supplemented by other authorities.

neither of these solutions was practical, Thorn faced a problem he neither understood nor wished to understand. Added to these weaknesses was his unstable temperament. At the slightest provocation he flew into unmanageable rages, threatening death to anyone within sound of his voice. Time after time he put his chief assistants in irons because they dared to oppose his judgment. Permeating his character were a meanness and brutality which under ordinary circumstances would have made him merely unpleasant but in his present position made him dangerous.

Before the *Tonquin* got outside of American waters, Thorn and some of the mechanics crossed swords. Several of these craftsmen were hired on condition that officially they be considered clerks. Thorn treated them with contempt, not only refusing to recognize them as clerks but compelling them, under threat of being shot, to go forward, live with the crew, and act as common deck hands throughout the voyage. They threatened to use force in defense. Though Thorn had his way without violence, that fact did not lessen his irritability.

When the *Tonquin* reached the Falkland islands she hove to for fresh water because the next logical stop was the Juan Fernandez group far up the coast. Everyone who could hastened ashore. Several stumbled upon two old graves. The head boards needing repair, the men set about the task. Just then Captain Thorn hoisted canvas and sailed away, leaving eight of his passengers on the unfriendly and partly barren islands. The shore party being divided, fully a half hour was lost before the men could start out after the ship in their small boat. They knew Captain Thorn and were not at all confident that he would relent and turn back to pick them up. It was growing dark and the men pulled mightily at the oars, hoping through their own efforts to overtake the ship. They steadily lost distance. Then just as they gave up and were debating going back to the island, Thorn suddenly hauled about and soon picked them up.

Their rescue did not result from the captain's humanity. Young Robert Stuart, whose uncle was with the land party, seized a pistol, pointed it at Thorn's head and "threatened to blow his brains out unless he hove to and took us on board," according to Franchere who was also among the land party. In Ross's report,

Stuart said that Thorn was "a dead man this instant" if he refused to go back. Regardless of the exact words, the men owed their lives to young Stuart. Thorn's deliberate and vicious cruelty increased the hatred of the men.

Nor did the shortage of water on the way up the Pacific improve tempers. It became so scarce, says Ross, that some of the men offered a gallon of brandy for a pint of water; but, he added, when fresh water was obtained next day, a "hogshead of it was in turn offered for a pint of brandy." [3]

As the Sandwich islands loomed on the horizon, a boy named Perrault [4] climbed the rigging to see better but lost his hold and fell overboard. Chairs, hencoops, and other loose wooden articles were thrown to him, yet he would have been lost "but for a wide pair of canvas overalls full of tar and grease, which operated like a life preserver." The captain seemed annoyed that the boy's life had been saved. He became even more difficult to get along with. When his ship finally dropped anchor, some of the crew deserted rather than serve longer under such a man. One of them, Aymes, who meant to go back aboard, missed the returning ship's boat so hired a native canoe to take him out to the *Tonquin*. Franchere describes the scene:

"The captain immediately missed the man, and, on being informed that he had strolled away from the boat on leave, flew into a violent passion. Aymes soon made his appearance alongside, having hired some natives to take him on board; on perceiving him, the captain ordered him to stay in the long-boat, then lashed to the side with its load of sugar-cane. The captain himself got into the boat, and, taking one of the canes, beat the poor fellow most unmercifully with it; after which, not satisfied with this brutality, he seized his victim and threw him overboard!

"Aymes, however, being an excellent swimmer, made for the nearest native canoe, of which there were, as usual, a great number around the ship. The islanders, more humane than our captain, took in the poor fellow, who, in spite of his entreaties

3.—A curious incident took place just as the *Tonquin* rounded the Horn. Ross says that as they turned into the Pacific a fairly small fish was seen swimming ahead of the ship and that, "During a run of upwards of five thousand miles, our little piscatory pilot was never known, by day or night, to intermit preceding the ship's bow."
4.—Ross gives the name as Joseph la Pierre.

to be received on board, could only succeed in getting his clothes, which were thrown into the canoe. At parting, he told Captain Thorn that he knew enough of the laws of his country, to obtain redress, should they ever meet in the territory of the American Union." [5]

During the stop-over at the islands, Captain Thorn was in a bestial mood though possibly he was happiest in this state. The island king came aboard with his wives who "were of an extraordinary corpulence, and of unmeasured size," says Franchere, adding that the native women were "very lascivious, and far from observing a modest reserve, especially toward strangers."

As the ship left the islands and pounded northward, the nerves of all became more and more chafed. Thorn was unbearable, the partners peremptory, the crew sullen. By the time they reached the Columbia another act in the Astoria tragedy was ready for staging.

Until recent years a great bar obstructed the mouth of the river. Crossing this required expert seamanship. The most efficient captains, respecting its dangers, frankly waited for favorable conditions; but by the time he had brought his quarreling cargo from the Hawaiian islands to the Columbia, Thorn was unwilling to wait for anything. He arrived, March 25, 1811. [6]

"The wind was blowing in heavy squalls, and the sea ran very high; in spite of that, the captain caused a boat to be lowered, and Mr. Fox (first mate), Basile Lapensee, Ignace Lapensee, Jos. Nadeau, and John Martin, got into her, taking some provisions and firearms, with orders to sound the channel and report themselves on board as soon as possible. The boat was not even supplied with a good sail, or a mast, but one of the partners gave Mr. Fox a pair of bed sheets to serve for the former. Messrs. M'Kay and M'Dougall could not help remonstrating with the captain on the imprudence of sending the boat ashore in such weather; but they could not move his obstinacy.

"The boat's crew pulled away from the ship; alas! we were never to see her again; and we already had a foreboding of her fate. The next day the wind seemed to moderate, and we ap-

5.—Reuben Gold Thwaites. *Early Western Travels,* volume 6, page 227.
6.—Two months later the U. S. frigate *President* defeated the British sloop *Little Belt.*

proached very near the coast. The entrance of the river, which we plainly distinguished with the naked eye, appeared but a confused and agitated sea: the waves, impelled by a wind from the offing, broke upon the bar, and left no perceptible passage. We got no sign of the boat; and toward evening, for our own safety, we hauled off to sea, with all countenances extremely sad, not excepting the captain's, who appeared to me as much afflicted as the rest, and who had reason to be so." [7]

This is Franchere's version of the loss of the **first** boat. Ross says that Mr. Fox, the first mate, remonstrated with Thorn on the impossibility of a boat's living in such a sea and was told, "Mr. Fox, if you are afraid of water, you should have remained in Boston." Fox is then said to have shaken hands with those left on board remarking, "Farewell, my friends! We will perhaps meet again in the next world."

After pulling out to sea the *Tonquin* was brought back to the bar and Thorn sent the second boat to sound a passage. While this boat struggled desperately with the swift current, the ship herself was hurled, quite by accident, inside the bar. Just then the ship's boat was seen drifting rapidly downstream. Those on board both the small boat and the *Tonquin* expected Thorn to order the men picked up. But with night at hand, the ship went on to safety, leaving the deserted men to fight against wind, and tide, and terror.

The *Tonquin* had no more than plunged over the bar when the surf capsized the little boat. Steven Weeks, one of the survivors of this second tragedy, told Ross:

"After the ship passed us we pulled hard to follow her, thinking every moment you would take us on board; but when we saw her enter the breakers we considered ourselves as lost. We tried to pull back again, but in vain; for we were drawn into the breakers in spite of all we could do. We saw the ship make two or three heavy plunges; but just at that time we ourselves were struck with the boiling surf, and the boat went reeling in every direction; in an instant a heavy sea swamped her—poor Mr. Aikens and John Coles were never seen after. As soon as I got above the surface of the water, I kept tossing about at the mercy of the waves.

7.—Thwaites. *Early Western Travels*, volume 6, page 230.

"While in this state I saw the two Sandwich islanders struggling through the surf to get hold of the boat, and being expert swimmers they succeeded. After long struggles they got her turned upon her keel, bailed out some of the water, and recovered one of the oars. I made several attempts to get near them, but the weight of my clothes and the rough sea had almost exhausted me. I could scarcely keep myself above water, and the Owyhees were so much occupied about the boat, that they seeemed to take no notice of anything else. In vain I tried to make signs, and to call out; every effort only sank me more and more. The tide had drawn the boat by this time out to sea, and almost free of the breakers, when the two islanders saw me, now supporting myself by a floating oar, and made for me.

"The poor fellows tried to haul me into the boat, but their strength failed them. At last, taking hold of my clothes in their teeth, they fortunately succeeded. We then stood out to sea as night set in, and a darker one I never saw. The Owyhees, overcome with wet and cold, began to lose hope, and their fortitude forsook them, so that they lay down despairingly in the boat, nor could I arouse them from their drowsy stupor. When I saw that I had nothing to expect from them, I set to sculling the boat myself, and yet it was with much ado I could stand on my legs. During the night one of the Indians died in despair, and the other seemed to court death, for he lost all heart, and would not utter a single word.

"When the tide began to flow I was roused by the sense of my danger, for the sound of the breakers grew louder and louder, and I knew if I got entangled in them in my exhausted state all was lost; I, therefore, set to with might and main, as a last effort, to keep the boat out to sea, and at daylight I was within a quarter of a mile of the breakers, and about double that distance short of the Cape.

"I paused for a moment, 'What is to be done?' I said to myself; 'death itself is preferable to this protracted struggle.'

"So, turning the head of my boat for shore, I determined to reach the land or die in the attempt. Providence favoured my resolution; the breakers seemed to aid in hurrying me out of the watery element; and the sun had scarcely risen when the boat was thrown up high and dry on the beach. I had much ado to extricate myself from her, and to drag my benumbed limbs along. On seeing myself once more on dry land, I sat down and felt a momentary relief; but this was followed by gloomy reflections. I then got into the boat again, and seeing the poor islander still alive, but insensible, I hauled him out of the boat, and with much ado carried him to the border of the wood, when covering him with leaves I left him to die. While gathering the leaves I happened to come upon a beaten path, which brought me here." [8]

Meanwhile Thorn had evidently been recalling those acts which had already sent one boatload of men to their deaths and, for all he knew, a second. Bestirring himself sufficiently to make a half-hearted search for survivors of either boat, by mere luck he came upon Weeks. Eight other men had been lost at the mouth of the river.

After investigating first one place then another as a site for their post, the partners finally moved over to the south side of the river to Point George. They immediately began clearing for Astoria.

For all his astuteness as a fur trader, in many ways Astor failed to provide for his infant colony. Intent on profits, he overlooked some of the practical techniques necessary to achieve these profits; nor did he give any others enough authority to supply these shortcomings. He had engaged fur men and factors, clerks and seamen, but had not provided for their safety. The *Tonquin* carried twelve guns but Thorn had no orders to use them to protect the land party, once he had delivered the guns at the mouth of the Columbia. And he refused to use them without definite word from Astor.

No physician or medical man was in the party, though Astor surely could not have supposed there would be need for none. Woodsmen, essential to any large building program, were also missing. Alexander Ross, the critic of the venture, tells of the difficulties encountered while constructing houses and other needed buildings:

"It would have made a cynic smile to see this pioneer corps, composed of traders, shopkeepers, voyageurs, and Owyhees, all ignorant alike in this new walk of life, and the most ignorant of

---

8.—Thwaites, volume 7, pages 83-85.

all, the leader. Many of the party had never handled an axe before, and but few of them knew how to use a gun, but necessity, the mother of invention, soon taught us both. After placing our guns in some secure place at hand, and viewing the height and the breadth of the tree to be cut down, the party, with some labour, would erect a scaffold around it; this done, four men—for that was the number appointed to each of those huge trees—would then mount the scaffold and commence cutting, at the height of eight or ten feet from the ground, the handles of our axes varying, according to circumstances, from two and a half to five feet in length.

"At every other stroke, a look was cast round, to see that all was safe; but the least rustling among the bushes caused a general stop; more or less time was thus lost in anxious suspense. After listening and looking round, the party resumed their labour, cutting and looking about alternately. In this manner the day would be spent, and often to little purpose: as night often set in before the tree begun with in the morning was half cut down. Indeed, it sometimes required two days, or more, to fell one tree; but when nearly cut through, it would be viewed fifty different times, and from as many different positions, to ascertain where it was likely to fall, and to warn parties of the danger.

"There is an art in felling a tree, as well as in planting one; but unfortunately none of us had learned that art, and hours together would be spent in conjectures and discussions; one calling out that it would fall here; another, there; in short, there were as many opinions as there were individuals about it; and, at last, when all hands were assembled to witness the fall, how often were we disappointed! The tree would still stand erect, bidding defiance to our efforts, while every now and then some of the most impatient or fool-hardy would venture to jump on the scaffold and give a blow or two more. Much time was often spent in this desultory manner, before the mighty tree gave away, but it seldom came to the ground.

"So thick was the forest, and so close the trees together, that in its fall it would often rest its ponderous top on some other friendly tree; sometimes a number of them would hang together, keeping us in awful suspense, and giving us double labour to extricate the one from the other, and when we had so far succeeded, the removal of the monster stump was the work of days. The tearing up of the roots was equally arduous, although less dangerous; and when this last operation was got through, both tree and stump had to be blown to pieces by gunpowder before either could be removed from the spot.

"Nearly two months of this laborious and incessant toil had passed, and we had scarcely yet an acre of ground cleared. In the meantime three of our men were killed by the natives, two more wounded by the falling of trees, and one had his hand blown off by gunpowder." [9]

In spite of these troubles, some sort of post was finally achieved. Besides the usual residences for the men, there were shops, powder houses, and a storehouse, sixty-two by twenty feet. All were completed by late September.

As their work progressed, the men made constant peace overtures to that old rascal, Concomly, the local native chief. He was an unpredictable person, always professing friendship yet forever being caught in some unfriendly intrigue. Occasionally a few arrows would fly harmlessly. Now and then the whites would ransom someone, or hold an important Indian until certain property had been restored, but they rarely killed a native. In fact, if Astor's partners had guarded their own men's safety as well as they did the natives', the death toll of the party would not have reached sixty-one.

Sometimes an Indian hired to do a particular job played his own kind of trick on his employers. One, after carrying a load of tobacco the length of the portage, pitched it down a two-hundred foot bank. A similar act caused an Astorian to suggest that the culprit's ears be cut off as a reminder to his fellows, but such punishments never happened. There was the more subtle penalty of trading four or five leaves of cheap tobacco for a fine beaver skin.

While the buildings were going up and the Indians were being pacified, the partners sent several parties into the interior. One of these went up the Columbia to verify a report regarding the penetration of the lower part of the river by the North West company. They left Astoria, May 2, but had not gone far before

9.—Thwaites, volume 7, pages 90-92.

they discovered the mouth of the Cowlitz. Heading upstream, they found the natives totally ignorant of white men. Franchere says they were constantly "lifting the legs of our trousers and opening our shirts" to see if the pale hue of the skin extended over the entire body. After getting on friendly terms with the Cowlitz Indians, the party returned to the main stream, continuing their search for the North West company agents. For several days they voyaged up the Columbia, making contacts with the natives whenever they could but learning nothing of the rival company. They did, though, sight three mountains—St. Helens, Hood, and Jefferson. Jefferson they mistakenly called Mount Washington.[10]

At home, a crew went to work putting together a small vessel, its frame having been brought from New York. But again the Astorians were deprived of an item important to their success— the boat was not large enough to use outside the bar.

On June 5, 1811, the *Tonquin* started on the trading expedition from which she never returned. Her final days are obscure. It is known that Captain Thorn was anxious to get away from Astoria as soon as possible; and that McKay,[11] perhaps the most valuable man of all those aboard, was induced to go along because of previous trading experience, which no one else had. This fact alone should have made him indispensable at Astoria,

---

10.—While on this trip they came upon a blind man who told them he was the son of a Spaniard wrecked on the Columbia years before.

11.—McKay was an intriguing character; Mackenzie had found him invaluable. But McKay's responsibilities never completely sobered him. In many ways he remained a boy, playing practical jokes which he often carried to extremes. Ross tells how he almost caused the death of a boatman by one of these pranks:

"On Mr. McKay's return from his reconnoitering expedition up the river, he ordered one of his men to climb a lofty tree and dress it for a May-pole. The man very willingly undertook the job, expecting, as usual on these occasions, to get a dram; but he had no sooner reached the top than his master, through love of mischief, lighting a fire at the bottom, set the tree in a blaze. The poor fellow was instantly enveloped in a cloud of smoke, and called out for mercy.

"Water was dashed on the tree; but this only increased the danger by augmenting the smoke, for the fire ran up the bark of the gummy pine like gunpowder, and was soon beyond our reach, so that all hope of saving the man's life was at an end. Descending a little, however, he leaped, in despair, on to a branch of another tree, which fortunately offered him a chance of safety; and there he hung between earth and heaven, like a squirrel on a twig, till another man, at no small risk, got up and rescued him from his perilous situation." (Thwaites, volume 7, page 96.)

which was to be the central depot of all operations. Furthermore, McKay had not had any sea experience, his activities having been limited to the overland trade.

It is known that Captain Thorn intended going to Newtee harbor (Nootka), Vancouver island, and trading there until he had a satisfactory cargo; and that soon after the *Tonquin* passed out of the Columbia, disquieting rumors of her fate began drifting back to Astoria.

All other information about the *Tonquin's* fate is from a single source, an Indian claiming to be a survivor and persuaded by Concomly to tell his tale to the whites. Because the Indian was not convincing as to his own part in the tragedy, many persons have challenged his report. However, Franchere considered it seriously enough to record the whole story as nearly as possible in the native's own words:

"After I had embarked on the *Tonquin,* that vessel sailed for Nootka. Having arrived opposite a large village called Newity, we dropped anchor. The natives having invited Mr. McKay to land, he did so, and was received in the most cordial manner; they even kept him several days at their village, and made him lie, every night, on a couch of sea-otter skins. Meanwhile the captain was engaged in trading with such of the natives as resorted to his ship: but having had a difficulty with one of the principal chiefs in regard to the price of certain goods, he ended by putting the latter out of the ship, and in the act of so repelling him, struck him on the face with the roll of furs which he had brought to trade. This act was regarded by that chief and his followers as the most grievous insult, and they resolved to take vengeance for it.

"To arrive more surely at their purpose, they dissembled their resentment, and came, as usual, on board the ship. One day, very early in the morning, a large pirogue, containing about a score of natives, came alongside; every man had in his hand a packet of furs, and held it over his head as a sign that they came to trade. The watch let them come on deck. A little after, arrived a second pirogue, carrying about as many men as the other. The sailors believed that these also came to exchange their furs, and allowed them to mount the ship's side like the first. Very soon, the pirogues thus succeeding one another, the crew saw themselves surrounded by a multitude of savages, who came upon the deck from all sides. Becoming alarmed at the appearance of things, they went to apprize the captain and Mr. M'Kay, who hastened to the poop.

"I was with them, and fearing, from the great multitude of Indians whom I saw already on the deck, and from the movements of those on shore, who were hurrying to embark in their canoes, to approach the vessel, and from the women being left in charge of the canoes of those who had arrived, that some evil design was on foot, I communicated my suspicions to Mr. M'Kay, who himself spoke to the captain. The latter affected an air of security, and said that with the firearms on board, there was no reason to fear even a greater number of Indians. Meanwhile these gentlemen had come on deck unarmed, without even their sidearms. The trade, nevertheless, did not advance; the Indians offered less than was asked, and pressing with their furs close to the captain, Mr. M'Kay and Mr. Lewis, repeated the word *Makoke! Makoke!* (Trade! Trade!)

"I urged the gentlemen to put to sea, and the captain, at last, seeing the number of Indians increase every moment, allowed himself to be persuaded: he ordered a part of the crew to raise the anchor, and the rest to go aloft and unfurl the sails. At the same time he warned the natives to withdraw, as the ship was going to sea. A fresh breeze was then springing up; and, in a few moments more, their prey would have escaped them; but immediately on receiving this notice, by a preconcerted signal, the Indians, with a terrific yell, drew forth the knives and war bludgeons they had concealed in their bundles of furs, and rushed upon the crew of the ship. Mr. Lewis was struck, and fell over a bale of blankets. Mr. M'Kay, however, was the first victim whom they sacrificed to their fury. Two savages, whom, from the crown of the poop, where I was seated, I had seen follow this gentleman step by step, now cast themselves upon him, and having given him a blow on the head with a *potumagan—*felled him to the deck, then took him up and flung him into the sea, where the women left in charge of the canoes, quickly finished him with their paddles.

"Another set flung themselves upon the captain, who defended himself for a long time with his pocket-knife, but, overpowered by numbers, perished also under the blows of these murderers. I next saw—and that was the last occurrence of which I was witness before quitting the ship—the sailors who were aloft slip down by the rigging, and get below through the steerage hatchway. They were five, I think, in number, and one of them, in descending, received a knife-stab in the back. I then jumped overboard, to escape a similar fate to that of the captain and Mr. M'Kay: the women in the canoes, to whom I surrendered myself as a slave, took me in, and bade me hide myself under some mats which were in the pirogues; which I did.

"Soon after, I heard the discharge of firearms, immediately upon which the Indians fled from the vessel, and pulled for the shore as fast as possible, nor did they venture to go alongside the ship again the whole of that day. The next day, having seen four men lower a boat, and pull away from the ship, they sent some pirogues in chase: but whether those men were overtaken and murdered, or gained the open sea and perished there, I could never learn. Nothing more was seen stirring on board the *Tonquin;* the natives pulled cautiously around her, and some of the more daring went on board; at last, the savages, finding themselves absolute masters of the ship, rushed on board in a crowd to pillage her. But very soon when there were about four or five hundred either huddled together on deck, or clinging to the sides, all eager for plunder, the ship blew up with a horrible noise. I saw the great volume of smoke burst forth in the spot where the ship had been, and high in the air above, arms, legs, heads and bodies, flying in every direction.

"The tribe acknowledged a loss of over two hundred of their people on that occasion. As for me, I remained their prisoner, and have been their slave for two years. It is but now that I have been ransomed by my friends. I have told you the truth, and hope you will acquit me of having in any way participated in that bloody affair." [12]

The Indian's report cannot now be proved or disproved. Anyway, the *Tonquin* was gone and the Astorians must get along without such support as the evil genius of the ship could give.

On June 15, ten days after the ship left, two Indians, not

12.—Thwaites, volume 6, pages 288-292.

native to the mouth of the Columbia, arrived with information causing the partners to order another expedition into the interior to settle the status of the North West company there and to establish such posts as seemed advisable. Though they had beaten the Canadians to the Pacific, apparently the Astorians were not going to enjoy a monopoly. The investigating party intended to leave July 15. About noon on that day, David Thompson came gaily paddling down the Columbia. He was probably the most important member of the western department of the North West company. His arrival at Astoria resulted in mixed feelings. The Scotsman, McDougal, himself an old Nor'-Wester, was most cordial; but Alexander Ross, disgusted at the excessive courtesy shown a supposed rival, said:

"Mr. Thompson, northwest-like, came dashing down the Columbia in a light canoe, manned with eight Iroquois and an interpreter, chiefly men from the vicinity of Montreal. M'Dougall received him like a brother; nothing was too good for Mr. Thompson; he had access everywhere; saw and examined everything; and whatever he asked for he got, as if he had been one of ourselves." [13]

Thompson painted a dark picture of conditions in the interior, saying that it was inhabited by vicious savages constantly on the warpath; that the pelts were few and far between, and too inferior to make the cost of gathering them worth while. He even told the Astorians their only hope of making a profit on their venture was by staying at the mouth of the Columbia and leaving the interior alone—presumably for the exclusive use of the North Westers.

Obviously there was no need to go into the interior to find out about a rival company if those rivals, whom Ross called the "strutting and plumed bullies of the north," were willing to bring that information to Astoria. On the other hand, McDougal was confident that Thompson had been sent to seize the region for his company. Thereupon McDougal determined to complete the original plan by establishing posts on the upper Columbia which would best reach the Indians and serve the Americans. Canoes were loaded and, on July 23, a party under David Stuart and accompanied by the returning Thompson, started up the

13.—Thwaites, volume 7, page 101.

river. The rivals went together as far as the Cascades, where Thompson left the Astorians and hurried on ahead. Stuart worked his way leisurely upstream until he reached the mouth of the Okanogan river where he erected a post.[14]

Stuart then pushed on to the headwaters of the Okanogan, leaving the unhappy Alexander Ross to spend the winter alone at the new fort, his "only civilized companion being a little Spanish pet dog." Ross wrote:

"Picture to yourself, gentle reader, how I must have felt, alone in this unhallowed wilderness, without friend or white man within hundreds of miles of me, and surrounded by savages who had never seen a white man before. Every day seemed a week, every night a month. I pined, I languished, my head turned gray, and in a brief space ten years were added to my age. Yet man is born to endure, and my only consolation was in my Bible."

This pious activity did not keep him from carrying on a lucrative trade. He said that "During Mr. Stuart's absence of 188 days I had procured 1,550 beavers, besides other peltries, worth in the Canton market 2,250 l. sterling, and which on an average stood the concern in but 5½d, apiece, valuing the merchandise at sterling cost, or in round numbers 35 l. sterling; a specimen of our trade among the Indians!"

As a matter of business, and probably inclination, Ross formed an alliance with a native girl. He also spent much time studying the customs and institutions of the Okanogans. Of the native doctors he said: "When the *tla-quill-augh* enters the wigwam or lodge, he views the patient with an air of affected gravity, such as we see some of our own doctors assume on entering the dwelling of a sick person, and tells bystanders, with a shake of the head and a groan, that the case is a very bad one, and that without him the patient would have surely died."

He filled page after page of his journals with the folklore of his adopted people, all of it interesting, some of it simply and beautifully told, like the account of the Okanogan legend of the creation of the world:

"The origin of the Oakinackens is thus related:—Long ago, when the sun was young, to use their own expression, and not

14.—About this time, rumors about the *Tonquin* began filtering into the post.

bigger than a star, there was an island far off in the middle of the ocean, called *Samahtuma-whoolah,* or White Man's island. The island was full of inhabitants of gigantic stature, and very white, and it was governed by a tall white woman, called Scomalt. The good woman Scomalt, possessing the attributes of deity, could create whatever she pleased. The white people on this island quarreled among themselves, and many were killed in the affray, which conduct so enraged Scomalt that she drove all the wicked to one end of the island, then broke off the part on which they stood, and pushed it adrift to the mercy of the winds and waves.

"There they floated about for a length of time, not knowing whither they went. They tossed about on the face of the deep till all died but one man and woman; and this couple, finding the island beginning to sink with them, made a canoe, and paddling for many days and nights, going in a westerly direction, they came to a group of islands, and kept steering through them till they made the main land—the land which they now inhabit —but they say that it has grown much larger since that time. This couple, when first expelled from the island of their forefathers, were very white, like the other inhabitants of the island; but they suffered so much while floating on the ocean that they became dark and dingy from the exposure, and their skins have retained that colour ever since.

"From this man and woman all the Indians of the continent have their origin; and as a punishment for their original wickedness, they were condemned by the great Scomalt to poverty, degradation, and nakedness, and to be called Skyloo, or Indians.

"They believe that this world will have an end, as it had a beginning; and their reason is this, that the rivers and lakes must eventually undermine the earth, and set the land afloat again, like the island of their forefathers, and then all must perish. Frequently they have asked us when it would take place—the *its-owl-eigh,* or end of the world." [15]

Probably Alexander Ross, in his turn, told his Indian neighbors another story of the creation.

Ross sometimes left his post at the mouth of the Okanogan to visit with John Clarke on the Spokane, after that post was

---

15.—Thwaites, volume 7, pages 273-275.

built.[16] One of these trips nearly cost him his life. Having finished his visit he started back, following along the river as usual. The exertion made him remove his coat, which held his fire steel. He placed both the garment and his gun on the back of one of his horses. Man and horses were scrambling up the steep bank when a terrific snow storm suddenly struck. The horses bolted, leaving Ross afoot and thinly clad. With a wild effort he caught a horse but not the one carrying his coat and gun. He mounted the animal and started looking for shelter. The horse soon grew exhausted and the cold sapped Ross's strength. He tried walking and leading the horse. His own words best describe the next thirty-six hours:

"Night came on; the storm increased in violence; my horse gave up; and I myself was so exhausted, wandering through the deep snow, that I could go no further. Here I halted, unable to decide what to do. My situation appeared desperate: without my coat; without my gun; without even a fire-steel. In such a situation I must perish. At last I resolved on digging a hole in the snow, but in trying to do so, I was several times in danger of being suffocated with the drift and eddy. In this dilemma I unsaddled my horse, which stood motionless as a statue in the snow. I put the saddle under me, and the saddle-cloth, about the size of a handkerchief, round my shoulders, then squatted down in the dismal hole, more likely to prove my grave than a shelter.

"On entering the hole I said to myself, 'Keep awake and live; sleep and die.' I had not been long, however, in this dismal burrow before the cold, notwithstanding my utmost exertions to keep my feet warm, gained so fast upon me that I was obliged to take off my shoes, then pull my trousers, by little and little, over my feet, till at last I had the waistband round my toes; and all would not do. I was now reduced to the last shift, and tried to keep my feet warm at the risk of freezing my body. At last I had scarcely strength to move a limb; the cold was gaining fast upon me; and the inclination to sleep almost overcame me. In this condition I passed the whole night; nor did the morning promise me much relief; yet I thought it offered me a glimpse of

---

16.—The Spokane post, intended to offset any Canadian or English competition in that vicinity, was erected a year after the Okanogan house, by Clarke, who had come overland with the Hunt party.

hope, and that hope induced me to endeavor to break out of my snowy prison.

"I tried, but in vain, to put on my frozen shoes; I tried again and again before I could succeed. I then dug my saddle out of the snow, and after repeated efforts, reached the horse and put the saddle on; but could not get myself into the saddle. Ten o'clock next day came before there was any abatement of the storm, and when it did clear up a little I knew not where I was; still it was cheering to see the storm abate. I tried again to get into the saddle; and when I at last succeeded, my half-frozen horse refused to carry me, for he could scarcely lift a leg. I then alighted and tried to walk; but the storm broke out again with redoubled violence.

"I saw no hope of saving myself but to kill the horse, open him, and get into his body, and I drew my hunting-knife for the purpose; but then it occurred to me that the body would freeze, and that I could not, in that case, extricate myself. I therefore abandoned the idea, laid my knife by, and tried again to walk, and again got into the saddle. The storm now abating a little, my horse began to move; and I kept wandering about through the snow till three o'clock in the afternoon, when the storm abated altogether; and the sun coming out, I recognized my position.

"I was then not two miles from my own house, where I arrived at dusk; and it was high time, for I could not have gone much farther; and, after all, it was my poor horse that saved me, for had I set out on foot, I should never, in my exhausted condition, have reached the house." [17]

Ross did not spend the second of his two winters alone at Okanogan. An additional force of men permitted him to trade farther into the interior. He crossed what is now the international boundary line, traveling a considerable distance north to Thompson's river, a major tributary of the Fraser. There were two profits in such expeditions, financial and geographic. A glance at the map shows that he was crisscrossing the region opened up by the great Mackenzie and Stuart and Fraser. The natives were friendly, about the only trouble coming from the fondness of his own men for the native women. One of the men, Boullard, be-

---

17.—Thwaites, volume 7, pages 202-204.

came enamored of a Thompson river woman. Ross says that by the time they were ready to go home:

"Boullard, my trusty second, got involved in a love affair, which had nearly involved us all in a disagreeable scrape with the Indians. This was the very man Mr. Stuart got from Mr. Thompson in exchange for Cox, the Owyhee. He was as full of latent tricks as a serpent is of guile. Unknown to me, the old fellow had been teasing the Indians for a wife, and had already an old squaw at his heels, but could not raise the wind to pay the whole purchase-money. With an air of effrontery he asked me to unload one of my horses to satisfy the demands of the father-in-law, and because I refused him, he threatened to leave me and to remain with the savages. Provoked at his conduct, I suddenly turned round and horsewhipped the fellow, and fortunately, the Indians did not interfere. The castigation had a good effect: it brought the amorous gallant to his senses—the squaw was left behind."[18]

Carelessness now and then endangered the lives of one or more of the party. Attempting to start a fire, a Canadian took his powder horn, as was the custom, and sprinkled its contents on the tiny blaze. Misjudging the amount needed, both he and Ross were blown six feet away, flat on the ground. Neither was seriously injured and such episodes were only minor in an otherwise important phase of the Astorians' work. After two years on the Okanogan and one at Spokane, the men had collected 140 packs of furs and grown familiar with all that vast territory now comprising eastern Washington, the edge of northern Idaho, and the southeast corner of British Columbia.

Some of the other inland activities of the Astorians should be mentioned here, though these extended beyond the present date and were occasionally undertaken by men who did not reach the Columbia until Wilson Price Hunt brought them through.

The Columbia river makes a great bend to the north just where the Snake river empties into it, and the Snake eventually cuts deep into the Rocky mountains, completely crossing the southern portion of the present state of Idaho. This region was assumed to be rich in pelts but had been practically untouched by traders. The Astorians decided to send Donald McKenzie

18.—Thwaites, volume 7, page 200.

there to trap, trade, and strengthen the company position against possible interlopers. Though a splendid fellow personally, Mc-Kenzie was unsuccessful on the upper Snake. [19] His post, Flat-head, was not popular with the natives, who stole his goods and cut off his food supplies. While he generally got his goods back [20] and was never close to starvation, these conditions were not profitable. Still, the Astor men deserve credit for opening up that particular field to white trade. Neither the Lewis and Clark expedition, nor Hunt at a later date did more than hastily cross it.

To return to the post at Astoria and the events taking place there while Ross, Clarke, Stuart, and McKenzie were in the interior: [21]

With the *Tonquin* gone and Stuart up the river, Astoria was considerably weakened, a fact which led to several plots by the Indians. Old Concomly, pleading a sore throat, attempted to get Franchere and McDougal into his camp to treat his throat. He hoped to seize them while his warriors attacked their post. The attempt might have succeeded had not an Indian woman warned the Astorians. Actually, good results came from the plot because the stockade was strengthened and additional precautions taken against surprise.

To the fear of attack, uncertainty about the *Tonquin,* and worries of active competition from the North West people was now added the problem of food. Astor had provided for an annual supply ship but crises on the Columbia had depleted stocks below normal, and the Indians, following practices per-

---

19.—Chittenden says that Hunt, McDougal and McKenzie all proved poor choices for their respective positions. In another place though, he suggests that the St. Louis traders were unwise in not permitting Astor a hand in their affairs. (volume 1, pages 231-232.)

On the basis of Astor's choices for his Pacific company, apparently the St. Louis men exercised good judgment in excluding him from their enterprises. At the same time it must be admitted that Astor's American Fur company was quite successful.

20.—The goods which Hunt was later to cache on his overland trip were all stolen by the Indians. McKenzie regained them by a single-handed raid on the native camp. Reasoning that the goods would be secreted here and there among the various dwellings, without warning he dashed into first one, then another, ripping and tearing and upsetting everything in his wild search. After a few moments of this havoc the Indians promised to restore everything if McKenzie would only stop.

21.—More or less regular communication was kept up between these interior forces and the main staff at Astoria.

fected by the whites, raised their prices outrageously. One stag cost a blanket, a knife, some tobacco, a quantity of powder and ball, and—what was more unusual—the loan of a gun with which to kill the animal.

The only good news in a long while came to Astoria on October 5,[22] with the first reports from Stuart's party. These,[23] contrary to Thompson's earlier description, gave a glowing account of conditions up the river.

The first year of the Astor enterprise was about to close with little regret at its passing; 1811 had been unpleasant for all, tragic for some.

22.—On November 7, William H. Harrison crushed Indian power in the Middle West at the Battle of Tippecanoe.

23.—Such news did not stop several men from deserting on November 10. They did not improve their lot. When overtaken, they had already been captured and made slaves by the natives.

Two unforgettable Astor men: Lieutenant Jonathan Thorn (left), who commanded the *Tonquin* on her fatal voyage to the Northwest in 1810 and 1811; and Robert Stuart (right), who commanded the second return expedition of the Hunt overland party. (Oregon Historical Society)

12

HUNT AND THE OVERLAND ASTORIANS

THE TONQUIN REACHED THE COLUMBIA on March 25, 1811. Nine
months later no word had yet come from Wilson Price Hunt, in
charge of Astor's land party. Anxiety was growing concerning
him and the badly needed supplies which he was to bring.

According to Ross, Hunt was "bred to mercantile pursuits
but unacquainted with this new mode of travelling," a "conscientious and upright man," and "a person every way qualified
for the arduous undertaking." Despite this estimate, on almost
every important occasion, Hunt made the wrong move. He
should have known that the best subordinates for the company's
Canadian-Scots officers would be the French-Canadian voyageurs
with whom they had worked for so many years. Astor himself
had chosen these officers because of their extensive knowledge
of the fur business. But Hunt, instead of recruiting his party at
Montreal, where he had gone from New York, decided to wait
until reaching the frontier post at Michilimackinac to hire the
boatmen. There, Ross said, he found an entirely different scene
from what he had expected:

"Hunt and M'Kenzie in vain sought recruits, at least such as
would suit their purpose; for in the morning they were found
drinking, at noon drunk, in the evening dead drunk, and in the
night seldom sober. Hogarth's drunkards in Gin Lake and Beer
Alley were nothing compared to the drunkards of Mackina at
this time. Every nook and corner in the whole island swarmed,
at all hours of the day and night, with motley groups of up-
roarious tipplers and whiskey-hunters. Mackina . . . resembled a
great bedlam, the frantic inmates running to and fro in wild
forgetfulness.

"These different parties visit Mackina but once a year, and
on these occasions make up for their dangers and privations
among the Indians by rioting, carousing, drinking, and spending
all their gains in a few weeks, sometimes in a few days; and then

300

they return again to the Indians and the wilderness. In this manner these dissolute spendthrifts spin out, in feasting and debauchery, a miserable existence, neither fearing God nor regarding man, till the knife of the savage, or some other violent death, despatches them unpitied." [1]

Hunt dropped down to St. Louis to complete his crew from the American hangers-on there. These did not help matters much. Some deserted as soon as they received an advance on their wages. Others stirred up trouble among themselves and the Canadians. Still others knew little and cared less about their new tasks. They quarreled over the quality and variety of food, and the Canadians were already angry because the Americans had sugar and were better fed. When Hunt tried to cut all his people down to the rations allowed the Canadians, more desertions followed.

On top of all this, Lisa was in St. Louis, doing his best to hinder the Astor party from making a satisfactory start.[2] But finally Hunt and his partners, Donald McKenzie and Ramsay Crooks, got together some sort of company and set off up the river, October 21, 1810. On November 16, they arrived on the Nodaway, near the present St. Joseph, Missouri, where they established winter quarters. Hunt returned to St. Louis, took two new partners, Joseph Miller and Robert McClellan, and made final arrangements for the spring.

Meantime Astor changed his mind regarding the command of the overland party, removing McKenzie from partial control and giving complete authority to Hunt. Of course McKenzie was annoyed, and Hunt was not the kind of person to benefit from having unlimited power. The Astorians left St. Louis for their Nodaway camp, March 12, 1811. With them were Joseph Bradbury and Thomas Nuttall, English botanists; Pierre Dorion, interpreter; and Edward Rose, ex-Lisa man and friend of the Crows, the guide. A final start from Nodaway was made, April 22.

Though Hunt intended to follow as nearly as possible the Lewis and Clark route, his friction with Lisa later on caused him to change this plan as well as several more.

1.—Thwaites, volume 7, pages 176-177.
2.—It would be interesting to know how much of the trouble Hunt was having with his men could be traced to Lisa's influence.

The hate between Lisa on the one hand and McClellan and Crooks on the other was deep and persistent. McClellan had once threatened to shoot Lisa on sight, an intention not carried out when the time came. Nevertheless Hunt's failure to wait for Lisa so that both might travel with greater safety has been blamed on McClellan and Crooks. Their tales and insinuations may have convinced Hunt of Lisa's treachery.[3] According to one story Lisa got his revenge on Hunt by exaggerating the savagery of the Blackfeet and persuading Hunt that his only hope of reaching the Pacific was to quit the Missouri, buy horses from the Arikaras, or other Indians, and proceed overland. Lisa knew quite well that to attempt to reach the Columbia without going up the Missouri invited death.

The story seems poorly founded and probably just another of the many efforts to slander Lisa. No one better understood than Lisa himself the savagery of the Blackfeet. They had robbed his own posts. Colter had found the entire region dangerous and other St. Louis traders were regularly robbed along the Lewis and Clark trail.

Whatever his reasons, Hunt did purchase horses from the Arikaras. With a party of sixty-four persons, including Dorion's squaw and two children, and eighty-two horses, he started overland, July 18, 1811. Only six of the horses were used for saddle purposes. The rest carried freight, indicating the considerable amount of trade goods and supplies bound for the Pacific division.

Hunt now made another mistake. He became suspicious that Rose, the ex-Lisa guide, was plotting to betray the entire party to the Crows when they should be reached. So the inexperienced Hunt struggled and blundered along, never asking for advice. He might easily have benefited by Lisa's company had he chosen to co-operate, and he might have been relieved of untold anxiety on the overland road had he trusted Rose, who apparently had no intention of breaking his trust.

By the first part of August the party was skirting the Black Hills, as unfriendly a bit of country as can be found north of the Cimarron; but they had no trouble there and on the seventeenth sighted the Big Horn mountains. There Rose was pleased

3.—Chittenden, volume 1, pages 186-187.

to find old friends, the Crows. The Astorians rested two days, then with the help of the Indians crossed the mountains to the Shoshones, who in their turn aided the travelers along to Wind river, where they arrived, September 9. Hunt followed up this stream till the fifteenth when he took his men across the Wind River mountains, probably by way of Union pass, into the valley of the Green. From the pass, the Teton range could be seen.

Because food was short, Hunt rested for a week to kill buffalo. Still without serious mishap, the party progressed over the divide between the Green and Snake rivers, going swiftly down the Hoback to its junction with the Snake. It was now September 26 and the trip seemed nearly over. They were on the Snake, the Snake discharged into the Columbia, and the mouth of the Columbia was their goal. The men clamored to leave the horses and take to the river but were temporarily restrained.

Four men were detached from the main party to trap and trade, the rest heading for Henry's deserted post. Hunt now made another blunder. He gave in to his men, abandoning the horses for the river. Having turned the animals loose, the party spent several days building canoes. These they loaded with freight, the men took their places, and the expedition again started off. But on October 28, the Crooks' canoe was wrecked and one of the men, Antoine Clappine, drowned. Still they kept to the river, struggling down it for 350 miles, but it was far too turbulent for any canoeman to navigate, regardless of his efficiency. Mishap followed mishap. Canoe after canoe was destroyed. Hunt lost all sense of leadership and. initiative. The entire expedition became disorganized and demoralized.

Just at the time of year when they should have been pushing swiftly ahead, Hunt ordered a halt. He split his command into several sections, sending one detachment in search of food, another back to try to round up the horses, and a third ahead to explore the river. Others were commissioned to look for a camp of friendly Indians. The situation seemed hopeless. The overland Astorians were on foot in the heart of the Northwest, hundreds of miles from their goal and hundreds more from their starting place, equally unable to return or go forward.

Hunt divided the last of his force into two groups. One, consisting of twenty-two persons including the Dorion family, started on foot down the right-hand bank of the Snake. Crooks with eighteen men went down the other side. By November 9 neither group had made any noticeable progress, nor had they a month later. On December 6,[4] Crooks hailed Hunt across the stream, begging him for food. Hunt willingly shared his own inadequate supply. Starvation now threatening, Hunt ordered retreat. They were, says Ross, eating "putrid and rotten skins of animals." [5] A single beaver served the entire party for three days.[6] Franchere describes their suffering:

"The rocks between which the river flows being so steep and abrupt as to prevent their descending to quench their thirst (so that even their dogs died of it), they suffered the torments of Tantalus, with this difference, that he had the water which he could not reach above his head, while our travelers had it beneath their feet. Several, not to die of this raging thirst, drank their own urine: all, to appease the cravings of hunger, ate beaver skins roasted in the evening at the campfire. They even were at last constrained to eat their moccasins." [7]

Hunt could not know that he was nearing the western edge of Idaho and that his men had already crossed the worst part of the way. He ordered a general retreat while he himself left their main route and went into the Weiser river valley where he found some friendly Indians. He stayed with them until December 21, when he went back down the Weiser to the Snake.

In the northeastern corner of Oregon is a region known as the Grande Ronde, more or less hemmed in on the west by the Blue mountains and on the south by the Powder River mountains. Hunt worked his way overland into that valley, crossed the Blue mountains—which he might have skirted quite easily—and, on January 8, 1812, reached the Umatilla river. Shortly he came upon the Umatilla tribe and remained with them a week, then set off down the river. The next day he reached the Columbia. For some reason not now clear, he crossed the Columbia near the mouth

4.—On December 25, General Wilkinson was tried by army court-martial and acquitted of treasonable acts in connection with Burr's attempts to create a new nation west of the Mississippi.

5.—Thwaites, volume 2, page 183.

6.—Same, volume 7, page 184.

7.—Same, volume 6, page 269.

of the Umatilla and proceeded down the right-hand bank to the Dalles, getting there about the end of the month. Canoes were again obtained and, February 5, the Hunt detachment left the Dalles, reaching the mouth of the Columbia, February 15. Several of the smaller parties had made better time than either Hunt or Crooks and had arrived ahead of their leaders.[8] The one under McKenzie arrived as early as January 10.

Crooks followed his commander as far as the Grande Ronde valley where he ordered winter quarters set up. Late in March his group started once more, Crooks and John Day going ahead of the main party. They made it to the Columbia safely but there the Indians seized, robbed, and stripped them. They were miserably struggling along when David Stuart, coming down from the Okanogan, picked them up, May 1.[9] Ten days later they were in Astoria.

Other straggling members of the original party did not arrive on the lower Columbia until January 15, 1813. In all, the overland venture had been a dismal failure, relieved only by the endurance and bravery of the men.

As soon as Hunt reached Astoria he determined to send an overland party to report to Astor. Again his judgment was poor. He could not pretend the return trip would be much easier than the outward journey, despite the knowledge now of the routes. Besides, he knew that Astor meant to send an annual supply ship. Nevertheless he organized the return party, placing John Reed in command. The men left Astoria, March 22, 1812, but at the Dalles they were attacked and robbed of everything, even the shiny tin box which held their reports. They returned to Astoria.

Before Hunt could prepare a second expedition, Captain Sowles and the *Beaver* were on the Columbia, May 9, with the year's supply of trade goods. Sowles confirmed the report of the loss of the *Tonquin,* news he had picked up in far-off Hawaii.

Robert Stuart was given command of the second return expedition. With him, in addition to the regular helpers, were McClellan and Crooks, both eager to return east. All told,

---

8.—Chittenden, volume 1, pages 194-195.

9.—Two weeks earlier, the United States added West Florida to Louisiana.

Stuart had a party of only seven men. They left, June 29,[10] and except for the sudden insanity of John Day—who had to be left with some friendly Indians on their promise to return him to Astoria—Stuart's party reached the Walla Walla Indians without trouble. There they traded for some horses, then followed up the Snake by land. On August 20,[11] they met four of Hunt's old party who had been trapping. One of these, Miller, joined Stuart, but the others continued with their traps.

Near the present Pocatello, Idaho, Stuart turned north to Henry's old fort. This was unfortunate, for about the middle of September the Crows stole all of their horses, leaving them afoot in the same general region where Hunt had been. Going by way of Teton pass, Jackson hole, and Green river, Stuart led his men through the famous South pass late in October. Two months later, January 2, 1813,[12] they were on the North Platte, south of Casper, Wyoming. Hardships had been frightful and starvation more acute than it had been for Hunt. Le Clerc, one of the men, suggested they cast lots and one of them sacrifice himself for the good of the rest. Apparently nothing came from the proposal.

Stuart built a small fort on the North Platte, where he intended to spend what was left of the winter; but, for some reason, possibly fear of the Indians, abandoned it almost immediately and hurried east until near the present Henry, Nebraska. He halted there to await spring.[13] Late in March the little party slipped down the North Platte to the Platte, then to the Missouri and St. Louis, arriving, April 30.

Hunt's report delighted Astor, who is said to have exclaimed that they had hit upon the right idea when they decided to establish Astoria.

Meanwhile affairs on the Pacific had grown worse. Astor showed an actual talent in picking the wrong men for his Pacific post. Captain Thorn had been quarrelsome and over bold. Captain Sowles of the *Beaver* was the extreme opposite; he feared the

10.—Three days previously Congress increased the army to 36,000 men to prosecute the war with England.
11.—The day before, *Old Ironsides* captured the *Guerriere*.
12.—On the same day, Congress appropriated $2,500,000 to build ten new ships for the American navy.
13.—Ghent, page 142.

Columbia bar as he would have Scylla or Charybdis, once re-marking that he would never cross it again.[14] He had, though, managed to get the *Beaver* up to Astoria where the goods were unloaded and the furs already collected placed aboard to be taken to Canton. Then Hunt made a foolish decision. Just when he was most needed on the Columbia he went with Sowles and the *Beaver* on a trading trip, intending ultimately to go as far as Baranof's colony in Alaska to establish trade. He was to return to Astoria before the *Beaver* sailed for Canton. Sowles left for the north about the first of July and the men at Astoria settled down to routine affairs, awaiting Hunt's return. Franchere says the weather was unusually bad and that they amused themselves "with music and reading."

Sowles and Hunt found trade brisk, and on arriving at Bar-anof's post learned he was anxious for the Americans to supply him with all the goods necessary to a comfortable living. And he was willing to pay a handsome price for it.

When this business was over, Sowles, to the surprise of Hunt, refused to return to the Columbia on the grounds that the *Beaver* was in such disrepair that she could not safely be taken over the bar again. He insisted on going to the Hawaiian islands for repairs, leaving the other to catch the next annual ship to Astoria, while he himself would go on to Canton.[15]

When the *Beaver* was finally at Canton, Sowles heard definite word of the War of 1812. Always cautious, he now would not go back to Astoria for fear of falling in with the enemy. At first he even objected to selling the pelts, which could have brought him a profit of a quarter of a million dollars.[16] Too late he changed his mind, disposing of his furs for only a little above their actual cost.

Hunt had meanwhile been fretting away time waiting for a ship to take him to Astoria.

Astor had indeed dispatched his third ship, the *Lark*. By good luck and seamanship she escaped the British, arriving off the Hawaiian coast only to be caught in a sudden squall with all hatches open. She filled with water until her superstructure alone

---

14.—Thwaites, volume 7, page 233.
15.—The *Beaver* was not expected to return to New York but was to remain on the Pacific carrying on trade with the Orient and Alaska.
16.—Chittenden, volume 1, pages 219-220.

was above water. For four days and nights the crew, lashed to the bowsprit, had neither food nor water. Finally they rigged up a piece of canvas, and, twelve days after the squall, sighted land. Six days later they abandoned their hulk, making for the shore where the Hawaiians promptly stripped them and carried away all the ship's goods. The crew appealed to the king of the islands for the return of these; but the king, applying the whites' own laws of salvage, ruled that the goods of an abandoned ship belongs to anyone who can get it.

On hearing of the *Lark's* fate, Hunt chartered the *Albatross*, filled her with what he could obtain on the island, and headed for Astoria.[17] Captain Smith was in command.

While Hunt and Sowles were at sea, several North West men under J. G. McTavish [18] arrived on the lower Columbia. From time to time more Nor'Westers came down. Duncan McDougal, in charge at Astoria, knew of the War of 1812, as did the Canadians. Astor's men realized that their post was fair prey for any British ship in that area; also that, because of the war, Astor might not send out the annual ship. In this case their position would be extremely dangerous. The Canadians patiently waited about, tongues in cheeks, for time to deliver the entire American project to them. Privately at first, but with growing boldness, there was talk of abandoning the post:

"When we learned this news, all of us at Astoria who were British subjects and Canadians wished ourselves in Canada; but we could not entertain even the thought of transporting ourselves thither, at least immediately: we were separated from our country by an immense space, and the difficulties of the journey at this season were insuperable: besides, Mr. Astor's interests had to be consulted first. We held, therefore, a sort of council of war. . . . Having maturely weighed our situation; after having seriously considered that being almost to a man British subjects, we were trading, notwithstanding, under the American flag: and foreseeing the improbability . . . that Mr. Astor could send us

---

17.—The *Albatross* was one of the two ships which, during 1809 and 1810 under the sponsoring of the Winships, had attempted to found a colony at Oak Point on the Columbia. High water and Indian hostility prevented this.

18.—McTavish had been at Athabasca. After the purchase of Astoria, he went down the coast where he collected a valuable cargo of furs.

further supplies or reinforcements while the war lasted, as most of the ports of the United States would inevitably be blockaded by the British; [19] we concluded to abandon the establishment in the ensuing spring, or at latest, in the beginning of the summer.

"We did not communicate these resolutions to the men, lest they should in consequence abandon their labor; but we discontinued, from that moment, our trade with the natives, except for provisions; as well because we had no longer a large stock of goods on hand, as for the reason that we had already more furs than we could carry away overland." [20]

Still more Canadians drifted into Astoria, many camping just outside the stockade in full view of those within, as if to remind the Americans of their plight and fate. Yet the Canadians themselves were insecure.

"As the season advanced, and their ship did not arrive, our new neighbors found themselves in a very disagreeable situation, without food, or merchandise wherewith to procure it from the natives; viewed by the latter with a distrustful and hostile eye, as being our enemies and therefore exposed to attack and plunder on their part with impunity; supplied with good hunters, indeed, but wanting ammunition to render their skill available. Weary, at length, of applying to us incessantly for food (which we furnished them with a sparing hand), unable either to retrace their steps through the wilderness or to remain in their present position, they came to the conclusion of proposing to buy of us the whole establishment.

"Placed, as it were, in the situation of expecting, day by day, the arrival of an English ship-of-war to seize upon all we possessed, we listened to their propositions. . . . At length the price of the goods and furs in the factory was agreed upon, and the bargain was signed by both parties on the 23rd of October. The gentlemen of the North West company took possession of Astoria, agreeing to pay the servants of the Pacific Fur Company . . . the arrears of their wages, to be deducted from the price of the goods which we delivered, to supply them with provisions,

19.—This reasoning is a splendid example of the invincible faith of a Britisher in His Majesty's navy, a faith to be sadly shaken before the war was over. This unpleasant experience was repeated a century later.
20.—Thwaites, volume 6, page 280.

and give a free passage to those who wished to return to Canada over land." [21]

The sale of Astoria was easily consummated for several reasons. There were the national ties with other Scotsmen, personal conflicts between the Astor partners; and, above all, a general feeling that Astor had insulted them, played them false, and would readily sacrifice them to the British, if he could thereby save some of his investment.

McDougal wanted an immediate sale. Clarke and Stuart, more loyal to Astor, opposed this. After many heated discussions McKenzie, at first neutral, finally sided with McDougal and "poured forth such a torrent of persuasive eloquence, backed by facts, that the opposite party were reduced to silence.

" 'Gentlemen,' said he, 'why do you hesitate so long between two opinions? Your eyes ought to have been opened before now to your own interests. In the present critical conjuncture, there is no time to be lost: let us then, by a timely measure, save what we can, lest a British ship of war enter the river and seize all. We have been long enough the dupes of a vacillating policy—a policy which showed itself at Montreal on our first outset, in refusing to engage at once a sufficient number of able hands.

" 'At Nodowa that policy was equally conspicuous. Did not Astor's private missive to Mr. Hunt at that place give umbrage to all? Did not his pen, over the heads of all the clerks in the concern add to that umbrage? Could there be anything more impolitic and unjust? Could there be any measure more at variance with the letter and spirit of the articles of agreement? Did not his private instructions to his captains annihilate the power and authority of the partners? When the unfortunate *Tonquin* left this, what did she leave behind? Did she not, by virtue of Astor's private instructions to her captain, carry everything off that was worth carrying off? Has not the same line of policy been pursued in the case of the *Beaver?* And this year there is no ship at all! Has it not been obvious from the beginning, that under Astor's policy we can never prosper? And, besides, there are other untoward matters over which Mr. Astor had no control, such as the delay of the *Beaver,* the absence of Mr. Hunt, our formidable

---

21.—Thwaites, volume 6, pages 296-297.

rivals in the North West Company, and, to crown all, the declaration of war.

" 'Now, gentlemen, all these inauspicious circumstances taken together point out, in my opinion, the absolute necessity of abandoning the enterprise as soon as possible. We owe it to Astor—we owe it to ourselves; and our authority for adopting such a course is based on the 15th and 16th articles of co-partnership, which authorize us at any time within a period of five years to abandon the undertaking, should it prove impracticable or unprofitable. Not, gentlemen, that there is any fault in the country—no country, as to valuable furs, can hold out better prospects; but Astor's policy, and a chain of misfortunes, have ruined all. Astor, with all his sagacity, either does not or will not understand the business. The system we were bound to follow was bad, and that system we cannot alter; so that we are bound in honour to deliver the whole back into the hands from which we received it—and the sooner the better.' " 22

Nor were these indictments peculiar to the men on the Columbia. Chittenden, the historian of the western fur trade, says that all of Astor's old employes grumbled at his treatment of them; while a federal Indian agent called his American Fur company "the most corrupt institution ever tolerated in our country," saying "They have involved the government in their speculations and schemes; they have enslaved the Indians; kept them in ignorance; taken from them year after year their pitiful earning." 23

News of McKenzie's tirade 24 surely leaked out to the Nor'-

22.—Thwaites, volume 7, pages 237-238.
23.—Chittenden, volume 1, page 377, and note, page 381.
24.—Ross felt much the same way. "But these we might have overlooked, had we not felt aggrieved in other matters closely connected with the general interest. The articles of agreement entered into, and the promises of promotion held out, when the company was formed, were violated, and that without a blush, by the very man at the head of the concern,— that man who held its destinies in his hand.

"This perhaps may be rendered a little more intelligent by stating, that according to the articles of co-partnership made at New York, two of the clerks were to be promoted to an interest in the concern, or, in other words, to become partners, after two years' service, and on that express condition they joined the enterprise; but what will the reader say, or the world think, when it is told that a young man who had never seen the country was, by a dash of the pen, put over their heads, and this young man was no other than Mr. Astor's nephew.

"Although a little out of place, we shall just mention another cir-

Westers hovering about, and final papers had not yet been signed. Ross says that each side was playing for time, the Canadians hoping a British ship would soon arrive and seize the post as a war prize, the Americans urging that the papers be signed before such a vessel should arrive so that they might save the purchase price for themselves.

Hunt had meanwhile reached Astoria with Captain Smith and the *Albatross*, August 4. Though annoyed at the decision to sell, being in the minority he could not change this. He had to witness all the byplays and maneuvers incident to the actual transfer, each of which brought him closer to a crisis in his own financial career.

The price for Astoria finally agreed upon seems to have been but $58,000,[25] an absurd sum, considering all the advantages the buyer was getting. The Russian trade was in itself worth many times that amount. Even so, McTavish delayed signing the papers until, Ross says, McDougal became so provoked that he and McKenzie trained the post's guns on the Nor'Westers' camp, giving them two hours to sign the papers or get off Astor's property.[26] Franchere says nothing of any such warlike moves, but then he often overlooked the unpleasant side of the Columbia story. Papers were at last signed, October 23, 1813,[27] making the Pacific Fur company a part of the past as far as Astor was concerned.

On November 15, Alexander Stuart and Alexander Henry, famous North West company men, arrived at Astoria in time to welcome the British war vessel *Racoon,* under Captain Black. Black had come to seize the post. According to Franchere, the captain exclaimed:

---

cumstance which may show how deeply and how sincerely Mr. Astor was interested in the success and prosperity of his Columbia colony. When the war broke out between Great Britain and the United States, the Boston merchants sent out, at a great expense, intelligence of the event to their shipping on the Northwest coast, and applied to Astor for his quota of that expense, as he too had people and property there at stake. What was his reply? 'Let the United States' flag protect them.' Need it then be told that we were left to shift for ourselves. So much did Mr. Astor care about our safety." (Thwaites volume 7, page 162.)

25.—Ghent, page 150.

26.—Thwaites, volume 7, page 246.

27.—During the summer, New England business interests openly began to object to the continuation of the War of 1812, arguing that it interfered with their profits.

"What, is this the fort which was represented to me as so formidable! Good God! I could batter it down in two hours with a four-pounder." [28]

Ross has it that Black closed the matter lightly with, "The Yankees are always beforehand with us." [29]

The name of Astoria was formally changed to that of Fort George,[30] December 12. As for the personnel, Franchere agreed to stay on for four or five months to help the new owners become acquainted with their property, though he manifestly did not approve the sale. He left the Columbia the following April. Alexander Ross, always favorable to the Nor' Westers and one of McDougal's stanchest defenders, joined the Canadian company. When it merged with its rival, the Hudson's Bay company, he rose rapidly. He was still young when he retired to a hundred-acre Winnipeg farm given him by the company.[31]

McDougal, key man in the transaction, soon became a partner in the North West company. This has led many historians to believe there was some treason in his conduct toward Astor. Certainly the sale was unnecessary. Even Franchere confided to his journal how easily the post might have been saved:

"It was only necessary to get rid of the land party of the North West Company—who were completely in our power—then remove our effects up the river upon some small stream, and await the result. The sloop-of-war arrived, it is true; but as, in the case I suppose, she would have found nothing, she would have left, after setting fire to our deserted houses. None of their boats would have dared follow us, even if the Indians had betrayed to them our lurking-place. Those at the head of affairs had their own fortunes to seek, and thought it more for their interest, doubtless, to act as they did, but that will not clear them in the eyes of the world, and the charge of treason to Mr. Astor's interests will always be attached to their characters." [32]

Cox, McClellan, and McKenzie also stayed with the North

28.—Thwaites, volume 6, page 302.
29.—Thwaites, volume 7, page 250.
30.—The North West company moved the actual post from the site used by McDougal to Tongue Point, which they considered more advantageous.
31.—The fur business brought him wealth and influence. He entered politics in 1835. In 1849 he published the journals quoted here.
32.—Thwaites, volume 6, page 303.

West company, as did John Day, who had been returned, insane, from Stuart's St. Louis party. Hunt, Halsey, Seaton, Clapp, and Farnham all went back to New York on the *Pedlar,* which left the Columbia, April 3, 1814.[33] The next day the remaining Astorians started home overland.[34]

So ended the great Pacific Fur company. Despite Washington Irving's case to prove that Astor was in a patriotic race for empire, Astoria was founded for mercenary reasons only. Astor had set aside $400,000 for his Columbia venture; most of it was doubtless gone and the $58,000 which one Scotsman got from another at the sale was a small remnant of the larger sum. Altogether sixty-one men lost their lives trying to establish the Pacific company. Thorn threw away eight crossing the Columbia bar; Hunt lost five; twenty-seven went down with the *Tonquin;* three lost their lives at Astoria; the *Lark* took eight more; the Snake country claimed nine men, and one final victim lost his life just as the Americans were leaving for home after the sale. This is a pitiful record, if not an indictment of those charged with the responsibility.

Yet there were gains, especially geographically. Two parties, Hunt's and Stuart's, had crossed the continent by routes far off the Lewis and Clark trail. The immense region, of which the Okanogan country is the center, had been thoroughly explored. The Willamette valley had been opened to the whites; and the upper Snake, though still hostile, was slowly coming into the dominion of the fur men.

Journalists left a wealth of information about the natives, much of which would soon have become lost. Very shortly these simple folk with their waterproof cheapool, or conical hat, would change. Their cedar-bark petticoat would be replaced. This petticoat, Ross said, "might deserve praise for its simplicity," though it did "not screen nature from the prying eye" since "in a calm the sails lie close to the mast, metaphorically speaking, but when the wind blows the bare poles are seen." These skirts

33.—Hunt entered the fur business at St. Louis and apparently got into politics, for President Monroe appointed him postmaster there in 1822.

34.—Robert Stuart and Ramsay Crooks both served Astor in and about the Great lakes region after their return from Astoria.

would vanish with the coming of civilization's less comfortable, less picturesque clothing.

Soon natives would no longer tie a stone about the neck of a dead slave and cast his body into the water or drag that body out to be devoured by wolves and vultures; or place their own dead in consecrated woodlands. No longer would they believe that "he is a religious man, who honors the divinity by making use of his benefits (and) contributes, as much as lies in his power, to avert from his fellow-man the scourge of famine."

They would change their practice in warfare of removing women and children to places of safety, of giving advance notice of attack, and of attempting peaceful settlement before striking a blow. The medicine man—reported as curing venereal diseases with his simples—would give way to patent medicine and quackery. The hard, but often surprisingly efficient primitive life would shortly surrender to civilization's peculiar ruthlessness.

Jackson Hole and the Teton range. Wilson Price Hunt crossed the valley in 1811, and it became a favorite area of the mountain men. (Wyoming Travel Commission)

13

THE NORTH WEST COMPANY OF CANADA

FOR A HUNDRED YEARS the "Governor and Adventurers of England Trading into Hudson Bay" were supreme. Their ships came and went with monotonous regularity. Their profits soared to astounding heights. In fact, the governors resorted to "stock watering" so that these would seem less fabulous. But still the percentages climbed—past the hundred-per-cent mark, then the two-hundred, then the three- and four-, until they finally reached the unbelievable figure of six hundred per cent a year.

For three generations the Hudson's Bay company rule held. For ten decades they had cooped their factors inside coastal stockades, refusing to move one inch toward the interior, which, if it wished civilized trade, could come to civilization—the Hudson's Bay post. Nor would the company permit anyone else to penetrate the interior. It continued to reign over one third of North America, with power to coin money, regulate commerce, set up and administer courts of justice, and wage war with non-Christian peoples.

Suddenly this security was challenged by traders and trappers more ruthless than the company men themselves. Some of these invaders had learned their cutthroat methods from the old company. About 1770 there opened fifty years of struggle, running the gamut from petty trade stratagems to cold-blooded murder and even warfare.

The work of all those owing allegiance at one time or another to the Nor'Westers becomes clear only when it is broken down into its various organizations, routines of trade, and geographic explorings. And some of these overlapped. Any attempt to trace the wanderings of most of the individual traders is idle. These men came and went, crossed and recrossed their own routes with such speed and industry that they are soon lost in a maze of trails and portages. It seems best to select a few of the most important and to see their work as representative of the others.

Company Organization

Just when the men who formed the North West company originally entered the fur trade is uncertain. A number of the business records are lost and the company went through many reorganizations with resulting shifts in partners. Besides, there were several names for the one organization.[1] There was a loose company of some sort even before 1770.[2] In that year a Thomas Curry, or Corry, went west to the farthest French post, Fort Bourbon, to forestall the Hudson's Bay company in that region. Though this was not the first attempt, from Curry's activities on, the trail is rather definite, so his work offers a convenient starting place for the story of the North West company. Curry himself collected enough furs in a single season to retire.

The next year, one of the numerous Finlays, probably James, went west to La Corne (Nipawee).[3] In 1772, Joseph and Thomas Frobisher founded Cumberland house on the Saskatchewan river, Joseph going on over to the Churchill river and intercepting the furs being brought down to the Hudson's Bay post. This called for the building of Fort La Traite as a storage place. The Frobishers were followed by others and the lethargic company on Hudson bay was finally stirred to action.

Samuel Hearne, recently returned from the Coppermine, was sent to build a post on Cumberland lake in 1774.

By 1775,[4] opposition to the Hudson's Bay people was serious. Alexander Henry and Peter Pond entered the struggle. Henry was one of the earliest Englishmen to invade the French fur domains; and, though ignorant of both Indian life and the fur business, he could judge men and opportunities. As his adviser he chose the clever old French trader, Etienne Campion. To him Henry owed most of his success. Going northwest by way of Sault Ste. Marie, Grand Portage, Lake of the Woods, Winnepeg river, and Saskatchewan, Henry arrived at Cumberland house, October 26, 1775.

1.—*Documents Relating to the North West Company*, edited by Wallace W. Stewart, volume 22, page 4.
2.—Hearne was in the midst of his exploring activities at the same time.
3.—For a brief discussion of the difficulties of tracing the activities of the Finlays, see the *Oregon Historical Quarterly*, volume 26, pages 273-275.
4.—The first battles of the American Revolution were fought in the spring of 1775.

Pooling his stock with the Frobishers, these two and a few others encircled the Hudson's Bay company preserves far enough up the rivers so that they could intercept and divert all furs destined for the older company. Meanwhile the more astute traders were frantically smoothing out their difficulties among themselves, not because they loved each other but because they hated the Hudson's Bay company and wanted to build strength against it.

In 1775, James McGill, Benjamin Frobisher, and Maurice Blondeau were licensed to trade beyond Grand Portage. Though their partnership applied only to the West, some pressure was nevertheless felt in Montreal, and in 1779 eight distinct groups formed a one-year agreement regulating themselves. These took, or perhaps merely continued to use, the already popular term, North West company. The concern was divided into sixteen shares, two shares going to each of the little companies making up the combine. For instance, Benjamin and Joseph Frobisher received two; McTavish and company, a like number; Todd and McGill, the same, and so on for all sixteen shares. Most of the five to eight hundred men engaged in the northern trade, exclusive of the Hudson's Bay company, were connected in some way with these eight companies.

The combination of 1779 was renewed for a period of three years but there was a third reorganization before that time expired. Benjamin Frobisher, Joseph Frobisher, and Simon McTavish, crowding out the smaller partners, organized a new company operating under the same name. These conducted a deadlier and wider-scaled competition.

The Nor'Westers had 25,000 pounds of property inland by 1780.[5] They constructed the *Beaver,* one of the innumerable ships of that name, placing her on Lake Superior to vie with the King's vessels. About this time they applied for a monopoly of the trade between 55° and 65°, from Hudson bay to the Pacific, in return for which they promised to explore that country, which

5.—In 1779, Alexander Mackenzie had entered the employ of the "Little Company," organized just previously to compete with the Nor'Westers. He was instrumental in forcing the consolidation of Gregory-McLeod with the North West company in 1783.

of course included a sizable chunk of the Hudson's Bay territory.

Between 1783 and 1791,[6] several minor changes occurred in the company's fiscal affairs, another reorganization taking place at the end of this period. The new agreement was to run for seven years with twenty shares divided among the stockholders. Possibly these constant readjustments were a deliberate attempt to eliminate the small holders, thus tightening the monopoly the others hoped for.

In 1795,[7] the Nor'Westers quarreled among themselves. A few of the partners withdrew under the firm-name of Forsyth, Richardson and company. Though Alexander Mackenzie stayed on with the older group, his dislike of Simon McTavish caused still another change in 1798, when Mackenzie announced his retirement from the fur trade. He went to England, remained there several months, then returned to Canada to organize a rival company, the New North West company, or the Sir Alexander Mackenzie company; or, as it is better known, the X. Y. company. Bitter trade rivalry and fighting resulted. Mackenzie cut heavily into the business of his former partners. McTavish, determined to prove he was the better man, pushed more deeply into Hudson's Bay territory. In 1803,[8] McTavish actually sent the *Beaver* into Hudson bay to trade. Canadian courts were now forced to extend their jurisdiction to settle the quarrels of the rivals, though for every case taken to court there were dozens more settled by fist or gun.

When Simon McTavish died in 1804, the way opened for another reorganization of the Nor'Westers. Mackenzie's X. Y. company had given heavy competition and almost before McTavish's burial was completed, a movement began to get the Scotsman back into the fold. On November 5, 1804, the X. Y. company broke up, its officers and men joining the North West group. The outcome was less violence among the whites and less liquor consumption among the natives.

Nine years later the North West traders bought out the Astor

6.—This period embraced and overlapped the so-called "critical period" in American history.

7.—Jay's Treaty, which tried to settle America's post-Revolutionary problems with England, was ratified, June 8, 1795.

8.—The year of the Louisiana Purchase.

people at the mouth of the Columbia,[9] then turned on Lord Selkirk's Red river colony which, as an agricultural subsidiary to the Hudson's Bay company, would cut off the North West company from their Montreal supplies. The Selkirk affair developed into a civil war, but the fierceness and bloodshed did some good. Officials of both companies began to see that their mutual interests demanded peace if there were to be profit for anyone.

Exactly when the two companies first considered merging is not known but, in 1819, Sir Alexander Mackenzie said the business was paying him nothing. Terms under which the company was then operating were due to expire in 1822. It is likely that about 1819 or 1820 some of the more dissatisfied partners were thinking of combining. Yet, at the annual stockholders' meeting at Fort William in 1820,[10] the existing organization was extended for another ten years.[11]

Not all of the delegates were present at this meeting though. Two had gone to London on some pretext, Dr. John McLoughlin probably being one of these. Simon McGillivray, the other, seems responsible for opening negotiations toward a consolidation in December of 1820.[12] Agreement was reached the following March, with a formal deed dated April 6 of the same year. Parliament granted a charter to the new combine in 1821. Davidson [13] says there is no sound reason known for the merger. Others credit the move to the government. "The union was brought about by intercession of government officials," says

9.—After this transaction the company continued a certain amount of local expansion and entered the trans-Pacific trade. They sent the *Isaac Todd* to Canton in 1814. During the two years following, the *Columbia* and *Colonel Allen* entered this trade, never profitable because of opposition from the East India company, which refused to allow the North West ships a return cargo.

Boston merchants were engaged to carry the company's goods both ways between Canton and Boston, an arrangement continuing until the union of the Nor'Westers and Hudson's Bay company, when British ships took over the trans-Pacific trade.

10.—While the fur trade was going through this phase north of the Great lakes, Americans were greatly agitated over the admission of Missouri as a slave-holding state.

11.—Gordon Charles Davidson. *The North West Company*, pages 174-175.

12.—Same, page 176.

13.—Same, page 180.

Professor Schafer.[14] Miss Coman [15] puts the case much stronger, "The home government was forced to interfere at last, and the only feasible solution, the consolidation of the two companies, was reached in 1821."

So involved had the business affairs of the Nor'Westers become that even after uniting there were countless legal squabbles. Minority stockholders felt they had been unfairly squeezed out, as no doubt they were. Some of these had been put off with vague promises of "adjustments" which never materialized and as late as 1830 there were still cases in the courts involving charges of graft and collusion. Several possible litigants were quieted only by receiving large sums of money in place of taking their claims to court.

14.—Joseph Schafer. *A History of the Pacific Northwest*, page 80 note.
15.—Coman, volume 1, page 298.

TRADE AND TRADING METHODS

THE NOR'WESTERS WERE VERY DIFFERENT from the Hudson's Bay people. The Bay company never even pretended to send its trappers into the wilderness. They relied on the natives to bring their catches to them at any of their numerous posts scattered along the shores of the bays and lakes or at the mouths of the important rivers. Because of this the Nor'Westers believed they could deal a fatal blow to their rivals by sending traders and trappers into the interior. In this way they would have two chances to get to the pelts first, by trapping them themselves and by purchasing them from the natives. Such a policy at last forced the Hudson's men into the interior. When the two groups met there was violence.

The Canadian personnel was like that generally found in the industry. There were the coureurs du bois, French whites who had lived so long with the Indians that they were often indistinguishable from them; the Montreal and Three Rivers merchants, who furnished the supplies; the "pork-eaters," canoemen who doubled back and forth over the "settled up" lap of the route; French Creoles, who willingly held all kinds of positions; and, finally, the factors, partners, and clerks—all generally Scotsmen—whose interest in the organization was genuine for each had a share in the earnings.

Transportation methods resembled those used for generations, two general classes of canoes being favored. The first, thirty-five feet long and six feet wide, was built of the thinnest yellow birch bark but could carry four tons. This craft with its "grand perch" —four poles lengthwise in the bottom with all goods carefully stored so as not to touch the frail bark—was used from Lachine to Fort William, the first lap of the westward journey. A definite schedule determined the load of every canoe. Each took sixty-five packages of goods, six hundred pounds of biscuit, two hundred of pork, three bushels of peas, two oilcloths, a sail, an ax, a towing line, a kettle, a sponge for bailing, and gum, bark, and *watape* for repairing the craft.[1]

A second class, the "north canoes," were about half the size of the others, manned by four or five men, and used from Fort William on as far as the fur men went. Actually this meant almost as far as the continent stretched because Fort Good Hope, three days below the confluence of Bear Lake river with the Mackenzie, was the most northerly of the company's posts.

The trade was well organized with regular routes and schedules even before consolidation with the Hudson's Bay company. There were two annual expresses, the winter express leaving the posts in November and reaching Sault Ste. Marie in March. At that time of year canoes were useless, snow shoes and sledges taking their place. The summer express was different.[2] It left the posts ahead of the regular canoes, carrying news of the winter trade, dispatches to the officials, and letters home. After the Pacific became part of the company domains, the fastest and finest expresses of all were instituted. The Columbia brigade left the Pacific promptly on the first of April every year and just as promptly arrived at Fort William, July 1. For twenty days the men celebrated their return from exile, then, on July 20, took up their paddles and started west again. Sometime during the day, October 20, the men on the Columbia could be sure they would see their comrades come singing and shouting downstream. The expresses never failed.

On special occasions small parties traversed the continent. A light canoe would reach Montreal from the Columbia in one hundred days, though on shorter runs it could make even more remarkable time. Simon McTavish probably held the record when his boatmen took him from St. Josephs, southeast of the Sault, to Montreal in seven and three-quarter days.

Distance was measured in terms of "pipes" rather than of miles or time, for the men smoked incessantly. From one point to another easily became so many "pipes." They worked incredible hours. For three weeks at a stretch they would paddle twenty hours daily except for five- or ten-minute rests every two hours.

1.—During good seasons the average value of the return load of pelts of these canoes was $2,640, of which $640 represented overhead expense.
2.—As inland trade developed, the companies, wherever practicable, used a huge, wooden-wheeled cart pulled by a pony.

Such labors demanded enormous food supplies, each man being allowed eight pounds of meat per day in addition to such delicacies as were acquired from time to time. Occasionally a very hearty eater would demand, and get, a double ration. No record reports whether the last morsel of the sixteenth pound was always consumed.

On reaching the portages every man loaded himself with two packs of ninety pounds each, carried by a sling around his forehead. "I have known some of them set off with two packages of ninety pounds each, and return with two others of the same weight, in the course of six hours, being a distance of eighteen miles over hills and mountains." [3] When a suitable portage offered the opportunity, all such light loads were forgotten and the French-Canadian showed his real metal. "This portage is near a half league in length. . . . There have been examples of men taking seven packages of ninety pounds each, at one end of the portage, and putting them down at the other without stopping." [4]

Such a record makes eight pounds of meat a day seem little enough. But then the whole tribe of fur men ate and drank in huge quantities.

"Perhaps never were there assemblages of men who feasted more heartily when the work was done. The Christmas week was a holiday, and sometimes the jollity went to a considerable excess, which was entirely to be expected when the hard life of the voyage was taken into consideration. Whether at Fort William, or in the North West Company's house in St. Gabriel Street, Montreal, or in later days at Lachine, the festive gatherings of the Nor'Westers were characterized by extravagance and often hilarious mirth. The luxuries of the East and West were gathered for these occasions, and offerings to Bacchus were neither of poor quality nor limited in extent. With Scotch story and Jacobite song, intermingled with *La Claire Fontaine* or *Malbrouck S'en Va*, those lively songs of French Canada, the hours of evening and night passed merrily away.

"At times when they had been feasting long into the morning, the traders and clerks would sit down upon the feast-room floor, when one would take the tongs, another the shovel, another the

---

3.—Alexander Mackenzie, in the foreword to his journals.
4.—Same.

poker, and so on. They would arrange themselves in a regular order, as in a boat, and, vigorously rowing, sing a song of the voyage; and loud and long till the early streaks of the East were seen would the rout continue. When the merriment reached such a height as this, ceremony was relaxed, and voyageurs, servants, and attendants were admitted to witness the wild carouse of the wine-heated partners." [5]

For many years the Beaver club was maintained at Montreal for the private enjoyment of nineteen favored members who had spent a lonely winter together in the interior, and these gentlemen sometimes put on gargantuan feasts and drinking bouts. Alexander Mackenzie loved to entertain, his private dinners often rivaling the Beaver club's in magnificence. At one such meal twenty guests began eating and drinking at 4 o'clock in the afternoon and, twelve hours later when the party broke up, had consumed 120 bottles of choice wine.[6]

There was a much different side to the fur trade. As competition between companies grew more strenuous, the business ethics of each dropped to the level of savages. Liquor became the standard method for enticing the natives to surrender furs which rightfully belonged to another company.[7] The Indian often resisted at first because he was still in debt to his original creditor, but liquor generally brought him around.

The companies not only charged outrageous prices but cheated in quality and quantity. A rum, with proof as low as four per cent, would be diluted fifty or seventy-five per cent with water, then measured out to the Indians. Even so, huge quantities of liquor were used. By 1773, more than 10,000 gallons of brandy were annually taken into the Hudson's Bay territory, while, in 1803, the North West people used 16,299 gallons, and other independents sold 5,000 more. In 1805, the North West people used 13,500 gallons of wine besides their distilled liquors.

5.—George Bryce. *Remarkable History of Hudson's Bay Company*, pages 158-159.

6.—Davidson, page 243, note.

7.—The Indian was generally outfitted a year in advance. For instance, he might be given a blanket, a cheap gun, a little powder and shot, and charged with forty or fifty dollars' debt to the company. This meant an outlay in cash of only half that amount or less, the difference representing profit. At the end of the season the Indian's catch was supposed to liquidate his debt.

The yearly average between 1806 and 1810 was 9,700 gallons. These amounts consumed by a population of around 60,000 resulted in a terrible degeneracy. Natives commonly bought liquor with their meager earnings though their families were starving. Often the drinking parties became wild melees where the savages killed friends and foes alike.

Sometimes the whites, endangered by these sprees, resorted to powerful remedies. If a brave became extremely unruly, either because he was sober enough to understand he had been cheated or drunk enough not to care whom he killed, the trader gave him laudanum or opium, drugs which quickly produced a more cooperative attitude, providing the dose was not too large. In that case the vender left at once, for even the drunken Indians sensed murder and were quick to revenge.

Liquor profits could be enormous and the company even cheated its own men. Once the interior was reached, rum which cost one dollar a gallon in Montreal was sold to employes at eight dollars a quart. Such practices were not restricted to liquor. The "company store" system of exploitation was practiced full scale, and the illiterate voyageur was encouraged to buy large amounts of finery for his native female friends. The cost was charged against his annual wages, which averaged only forty pounds. The company knew these simple men could neither add nor subtract and so would have no idea of the size of their bill or what was due them at the end of the season.

This dishonesty was topped by other practices. Prices were trebled and quadrupled, and a system of company money was used. The divisions of this money corresponded in name to coins issued by the Montreal government but were double in value, thus an article costing the voyageur two units of North West money represented a huge profit over the Montreal cost to the company. The employe, thinking in terms of Canadian money, soon became hopelessly confused and relied entirely on the company clerk to keep his accounts straight, with obvious results.

As the struggle over territory increased, so did the violence. In 1743, peltries from New France amounted to 120,000 pounds; in 1780, imports to Hudson bay totaled only 3,600 pounds; but, by 1794, they had jumped to 83,200 pounds, representing export values in terms of pelts purchased of many thousands over that. Imports to England in 1789, exclusive of Hudson bay, Nova Scotia, and Newfoundland, amounted to 191,000 pounds. In 1801, the furs exported from Quebec reached 371,139; and even in 1815, when the country was just emerging from the Napoleonic and American wars, the North West people sold 101,000 dollars' worth of furs on the Canton market alone. These were worthy prizes, and any means taken to intercept a rich shipment was regarded as fair business. About 1776, the government complied with a request from the companies to station a body of troops at the Grand Portage to preserve order, the companies agreeing to pay a proper share of the cost of such service.

The violence was often personal as well as general. On October 11, 1818, Mr. Robertson, a Hudson's Bay man, while attending the funeral of a colleague, was arrested by the Nor'Westers and brought to Fort Chipewyan. From there he was taken toward Canada, but on the way the canoe upset, his captors were drowned, and Robertson escaped to England, charging there that the North West men had tried to drown him at Pin Portage. But he was not very convincing in proving that he did not help bring on the accident which cost his captors their lives. Out of such episodes as these grew duels, arrests, and counter-arrests, kidnappings and ambushes, in fact all manner of feudal warfare and some not so feudal.

When the Hudson's Bay men were caught and ringed about by the Nor'Westers in the Athabasca region, eighteen of them starved to death because their rivals would neither feed them nor permit the Indians to sell to them. Others were starved for a few days until they became "reasonable" and joined the North West company. Such tactics resulted in great trade advantages. The Nor'Westers took out 400 packs of furs in one season from one region while the Hudson's Bay men acquired but five; and, in 1818, the aggressors took out 430 packs from Athabasca while the English company shipped none at all. These tactics also caused the death of half of the men engaged by the great company in that region.[8] Posts were attacked and pillaged with as much savagery as if some civilized principle were at stake. When the Hudson's Bay company was reported preparing a ball-proof

8.—Davidson, page 157.

barge to be used in blocking the Grand Rapids, naturally every fur ship either on the Great lakes or in the overseas trade was armed. Despite these struggles a wealth of beautiful furs poured into Europe to be sold at public auction.[9]

As for the final fate of these warring voyageurs, clerks, and factors, the Nor'Westers provided for that; and therein lay the strength of the company. Traders either were or could become shareholders. When their usefulness was over or they decided to retire or enter another industry, they could sell their share and go to Montreal. A native wife and children might be included as a part of this deal.

On the other hand, if old age overtook an employe still in the service of the company, he often cleared a piece of ground near some post where he settled down to spend his remaining years watching the sleek north canoes come and go. He grew a few vegetables in a scrubby garden, and spun tall yarns of how much cleverer voyageurs were in the old days. He boasted of the past silkiness of furs, of drinking bouts, of battles and of victories. Bragging and exaggerating, he played an interesting though ever less important part in the drama of the fur trade.

9.—Beaver, bed-feathers, whale fins, and castoreum were sold by the pound; goose quills went by the thousand; while such skins as wolverine, bear, mink, squirrel, elk, marten, otter, and fox, were sold by the single pelt. The lowly cony (rabbit) came in lots of a dozen.

15

NOR'WESTERS AS EXPLORERS

THE NORTH WEST COMPANY required its clerks and other officials to keep a journal of their doings. Most of these records have long since been lost. Many in existence use place names unknown to modern readers, while others are so fragmentary they have no value geographically. Still, they help sketch in the main outlines of the company's work as an exploring agency.

Alexander Mackenzie and David Thompson were the brightest stars in the galaxy of the Nor'Westers. Mackenzie has already been discussed as a major figure in the overland search for the Pacific. And Thompson deserves more than passing mention. Besides these are others, men who spent their entire adult lives on the wilderness trails and whose combined wanderings deserve at least a word or so.

There was Alexander Henry, who, with old Etienne Campion, entered the fur trade ignorant of both the trade and the Indians, but successfuly worked his way up to Cumberland house in 1775. In 1792 he was a Nor'Wester though his journal does not begin until 1799 at Riviere Terre Blanche, thirty-five miles west-northwest of Portage la Prairie. The following year Henry was among the Dakotas, in 1801 building a post on Red river. For the next seven years he traded about Lake Superior, Red river, and Kaministikwia river, adding nothing important to the sum of geographic knowledge. In 1805,[1] he issued a report, supposedly for the North West company, that in this year his company had 1,090 men, 368 women, and 69 children under its jurisdiction; and that Mackenzie's X. Y. company had about half as many, 520 men, 37 women, and 31 children.[2]

In May of 1808, Henry left his post for the Saskatchewan. Within two years he was at Rocky Mountain house; and, when the North West company took over Astoria, he was there to enjoy

1.—Lewis and Clark were on the Pacific at this time.
2.—Davidson, page 88.

the ceremonies, November 13, 1813. Six months later he drowned there. His individual contributions were not large when measured by such standards as Mackenzie's or Thompson's but his small role helped ease the work of those who followed him.[3]

Peter Pond, perhaps the least reliable of all the great, or near great, names on the rosters of the Nor'Westers, was remarkable mainly because of his violence. He was forever being mixed up in some serious business involving murder or robbery, and proof of his guilt or innocence is equally difficult to establish. It is probable that he went as far north as Great Slave lake; he may have sent C. Grant and Laurent Leroux there in 1786. He was particularly interested in map making and peltries, often acquiring furs by using opium on the natives.[4] As a map maker, Pond was famous far beyond his desert, for his map of the West was mostly wrong.[5]

The Canadian Northwest was rapidly explored following Mackenzie's return from the Arctic. Several traders, either independently or as members of a combine, entered the territory. In 1789, Angus Shaw established a post northeast of the present Edmonton, Alberta, only to find the Hudson's Bay men ahead of him. Two years afterwards he built Fort George on the Saskatchewan. In 1797, James Finlay got as far west as the headwaters of the Peace river, then turned north to examine the Finlay river west of the mountains. James McDougal went up the Peace and Parsnip rivers and built Fort McLeod on McLeod's lake in 1805.

The next year, Simon Fraser and his clerk, John Stuart, a civil engineer, entered the Rockies on a combined trading and exploring trip to strengthen the British claim to the Northwest. They hoped that a grateful government would grant them a charter as a reward, but were disappointed. Just who was the leader in this partnership is not known. Fraser has generally been named but Stuart's friends insist that he really carried the burden.

Fraser, the son of an American loyalist, entered the North

3.—Henry was essentially a trader, not an explorer; and the regions in which he worked were not always new. It is sometimes said that his history and that of Thompson are inseparable; that where one explored, the other traded. While this is not quite fair to Henry, who occasionally preceded Thompson, yet, in final judgment, Henry was the barterer, and Thompson, the explorer and geographer.

4.—Davidson, page 46.

5.—Same, pages 36-46.

West company at the age of sixteen. By the time he was twenty-six he was a partner. He was appointed agent at Grand Portage in 1797 and was, says Thwaites, "One of the most daring fur traders of his day." [6] But Haworth, while admitting he was a restless adventurer, says he was "without much education or special mental endowments." [7] He apparently served satisfactorily at the Portage because he later gained command of the always important post on Athabasca. In 1806, he and Stuart established a post at McLeod's lake, west of the mountains, and thoroughly explored all the regions, naming it New Caledonia. Later Fort St. James was built at Stuart lake and Fort Fraser at Fraser lake. The two men spent the winter in New Caledonia, trading and trapping.

Sometime in the spring of 1807,[8] they received word to go on to the Pacific by way of the Tacouche Tesse. Fraser was delighted. He and Stuart, accompanied by a well-informed trapper, Quesnel, and twenty-one men in four canoes, set off for the Pacific, May 22, 1808. From first-hand experience they knew much of the route. When they reached the Tacouche Tesse, they tried using Mackenzie's route, hoping to extend it to the sea, but found, as the other had, that the Fraser river is poorly suited to navigation. Rapids and whirlpools, encased in sheer rocky walls, follow each other in rapid succession. Fraser aptly describes their difficulties:

"Leaving Mr. Stuart and the two men at the lower end of the rapid, in order to watch the motion of the natives, I returned with the other four men to the camp. Immediately on my arrival I ordered the five men out of the crews into a canoe lightly loaded, and the canoe was in a moment under way. After passing the first cascade she lost her course and was drawn into an eddy, whirled about for a considerable time, seemingly in suspense whether to sink or swim, the men having no power over her. However, she took a favorable turn, and by degrees was led from this dangerous vortex again into the stream. In this manner she continued, flying from one danger to another, until the last cascade but one, where in spite of every effort, the whirlpools forced her against a low projecting rock. Upon this the men

6.—Thwaites, page 192.
7.—Haworth, page 187.
8.—Robert Fulton sent the *Claremont* up to Albany that year.

debarked, saved their own lives, and continued to save the property, but the greatest difficulty was still ahead, and to continue by water would be the way to certain destruction.

"During this distressing scene, we were on the shore looking on and anxiously concerned; seeing our poor fellows once more safe afforded us as much satisfaction as themselves, and we hastened to their assistance; but their situation rendered our approach perilous and difficult. The bank was exceedingly high and steep, and we had to plunge our daggers at intervals into the ground to check our speed, as otherwise we were exposed to slide into the river.

"We cut steps in the declivity, fastened a line to the front of the canoe, with which some of the men ascended in order to haul it up, while the others supported it upon their arms. In this manner our situation was most precarious; our lives hung, as it were, upon a thread, as the failure of our line, or a false step of one of the men, might have hurled the whole of us into eternity. However, we fortunately cleared the bank before dark." [9]

When the stream became unnavigable the men left their canoes and proceeded by land. Here their difficulties were at least as dangerous as on the stream itself:

"As for the road by land, we could scarcely make our way with even only our guns. I have been for a long period among the Rocky mountains,. but have never seen anything like this country. It is so wild that I cannot find words to describe our situation at times. We had to pass where no human being should venture; yet in those places there is a regular footpath impressed, or rather indented upon the very rocks by frequent travelling. Besides this, steps which are formed like a ladder by poles hanging to one another, crossed at certain distances with twigs, the whole suspended from the top, furnish a safe and convenient passage to the natives down these precipices; but we, who had not had the advantage of their education and experience, were often in imminent danger, when obliged to follow their example." [10]

The party never actually reached the ocean proper though they

9.—Snowden, volume 1, pages 233-234.
10.—Same.

came at last to an arm of the sea, about the present New Westminster; but the hostility of the natives forced them to return. The lower Fraser was probably not explored until 1824, when James McMillan of the Hudson's Bay company completed the work. These others proved that the Tacouche Tesse was not the Columbia, as Mackenzie thought.[11]

Another trader of more than passing importance was D. W. Harmon, who entered the North West company about 1800 and spent nineteen years in the West. In 1810, he took charge of Fraser's New Caledonia, wintering at Fort Fraser. Early in 1811 he returned to Stuart's lake, his headquarters for six years. Harmon was genuinely interested in the Indians, carefully studying their customs and languages. In 1812 he went north to the Babine range, doubtless the first white man to approach the tribe of that name. Possibly he was the one who discovered the headwaters of the Skeena.

These few names only suggest the long list of secondary explorers operating under the North West banner, but their achievements are a fair indication of the kind of work done by the company for half a century.

11.—Fraser returned to the Red river of the North and continued to serve the North West people for several years in and about the Lake Superior region.

Mandan Village, from a painting by Karl Bodmer.
(North Dakota State Historical Society)

16

DAVID THOMPSON
DISCOVERS ATHABASCA PASS

NEXT TO MACKENZIE, David Thompson was the most important Nor'Wester. His work must be understood to get anything like a clear picture of a company whose unfair business policies make it easy to forget the splendid work of their explorers.

Unlike most of the great names associated with the Nor'Westers, David Thompson was not a Scotsman. He was born in Westminster, England, of Welsh parents in 1770. At fourteen he entered the employ of the Hudson's Bay company, being assigned to Fort Churchill in 1784. Samuel Hearne was in command there. Possibly Thompson's remarkable spirit of exploration was fostered by Hearne's recital of his three trips toward the Arctic. After the first winter at Churchill, Thompson was sent down the bay to York Factory, and, in July of 1786, was ordered west to establish posts on the Saskatchewan.

From 1786 to 1797, he left no mark to distinguish himself from any other Hudson's Bay man, but he was a natural explorer. Time after time he endeavored to interest his employers in explorations; but as long as the musty ledgers showed an annual profit of ten or fifteen or twenty per cent, the "adventurers into Hudson bay" could not be moved. David Thompson stood it as long as he could, then on May 23, 1797,[1] he left this company to sign up with the Nor'Westers. After recording the change of companies in his journals he adds, "May God almighty prosper me." The change proved a happy one for he became the official explorer and geographer for the North West company.

It is difficult to understand this company's attitude on exploration. Their business ethics were evidently more ruthless than those of any other organization that had done business in North America up to that day. They lied, committed murder, starved their enemies, and cheated the Indians and their own men with an

---

1.—Washington had just finished his second term as President.

unmatched viciousness. Their rivals could only imitate their barbarities. Whenever a beaver skin was involved, the Nor'Westers were more anxious to make money than any of their competitors, yet they were the ones who seemed most seriously interested in exploration. Of course exploration and new fields meant larger profits, but such an interpretation does not account for all the instructions given to David Thompson. His commission provided that he determine the 49° parallel,[2] visit the Missouri country and the "ancient agricultural nations," seek fossils of large animals, and search for old monuments as clues to the past history of the country.[3] Now there was not likely to be much profit in old bones, decaying monuments, and histories of a long-dead people. Naturally his company hoped to receive a charter in return for any extensive explorations, but they were too shrewd to suppose this could be had by delivering ancient skeletons to Whitehall. Some day the Hudson's Bay company file may give the answer.

Thompson became immediately active as the official geographer. From Grand Portage to the mouth of the Winnipeg river he accompanied the August brigade of Hugh McGillis. Leaving the express there he went on to Dauphin, Swan, and Stone Indian rivers, and the Assiniboine. So far he had not added much to general knowledge.

From the Assiniboine, he went down to the Mandans, arriving November 28, 1797. He remained with these semi-civilized people until January, then decided to explore the entire headwater system of the Mississippi. On January 26, he started for the Red river, from which stream he entered Red lake, crossed over to the Sand Lake river, and by way of St. Louis river arrived at Lake Superior in May, 1798. He had made the first careful survey of the upper Mississippi, though the French and Canadians had previously been in and out of the country. Not content with contemporary opinions regarding Lake Superior, he explored its south shore and was back at the Grand Portage by June 7.[4]

Seven days later, Thompson set off for the Saskatchewan. On this trip he got west as far as Lesser Slave lake but, by the sum-

2.—He had learned a little mathematics at Grey Coat school and picked up practical astronomy under Mr. Philip Turner at Cumberland house.
3.—Davidson, page 92.
4.—The day before, the American Congress had abolished the ancient practice of imprisonment for debt.

mer of 1799, was again back at the Grand Portage. During this traveling he had married. The poor girl must have found her husband a most unsatisfactory fellow, for he would not stay home, and to keep up with him would have been impossible.

In September Thompson was at Fort George where he stayed until March of 1800, when he went to Fort Augustus and then Rocky Mountain house, a mile above the mouth of the Clear-water in the Saskatchewan basin. At this "farthest in" permanent post of the North West company, he found a convenient head-quarters for his work.

The time of the season did not much interest the Welshman, and, on October 5, 1800, he left Rocky Mountain house for the mountains. Older traders were already planning to go to safer quarters, but Thompson went ahead, proceeding as far as upper Red Deer river, directly west of which—but on the other side of the Rockies—lay the upper Columbia. He turned to the Bow river [5] before going back to Rocky Mountain house for the winter. The native Piegan tribe was not unfriendly to Thomp-son. The tribe's chief, Kootanae Appee, was his friend, but the Piegans, like all of the Blackfeet confederacy, were arrogant and suspicious. They were willing to trade with Thompson but they never stopped watching him. Over the Rockies to the west were their mortal enemies, the Kootenay, and the Piegans knew that if Thompson should penetrate the other side, as Indian rumor said he intended doing, he would take firearms to them. The Piegans would then lose their present military superiority. Under such circumstances they can hardly be blamed for secretly plan-ning to block any move Thompson might make to cross the mountains. This was the situation when the Nor'Wester re-turned to his post to spend the winter of 1800.

With spring, Thompson explored into the Rockies as far as latitude 51°, longitude 116°; and, during 1802 to 1804, he traded widely over territories adjacent to Hudson's Bay company lands. Because this region was already fairly well known, his travels there have no special geographic importance.

On June 14, 1806, Thompson left Cumberland house for Fort William, spending the following year in the East. The time had

---

5.—Thompson says that Duncan McGillivray went through Howse pass at this time.

now come for him to execute his long-dreamed of plan, to cross the mountains and explore the upper waters of the Columbia and by that stream reach the Pacific. He was off, May 10 of the following year. The Piegans meanwhile had become even more opposed to the whites' going over the mountains. They set a watch on Howse pass and let Thompson know that neither he nor any of his men would be permitted to cross.

Thompson had certain alternatives. He could wait until his friendly enemies became tired of patrolling the pass and then slip through. He could trust that some urgency would attract their attention, leaving him free to cross. Or he could find a new pass. The second of these possibilities occurred. A small party of Piegans had become embroiled with white traders on the Missouri and the Rocky Mountain division of the tribe turned its attention from Thompson to avenge fancied insults on the Missouri. Their war party was hardly out of sight before Thompson collected his goods and men for a dash over Howse pass. By June 22, he was at the summit of the Rockies; on the thirteenth he was down the other side on the Columbia.

Instead of following the stream toward the Pacific, he turned upstream, establishing his first transmountain post, Fort Kootenay, a mile below Lake Windemere in 1807.[6] He built the post with exceptional care, making it as stout as possible with the materials at hand, for he knew the Piegans, furious at his success, would attempt to punish him. He was right.

Soon a party of forty braves arrived outside the fort, settling down for a siege. There were seven white men and ten guns inside the post but food was short and there was no water. During the first night the men attached two kettles to cords, letting them down to the river and pulling them up full. They could now afford to wait. The siege was brought to a sudden halt, though, by the approach of a considerable body of Kootenay Indians. The Piegans forgot Thompson and hurried home, probably making up a likely story to explain their temporary failure to the home folks.

The Indians immediately formed a new party of three hundred braves led by Kootanae Appee himself, who, against his

6.—On March 2, 1807, the President signed the law prohibiting the importation of slaves after January 1, 1808.

will, took up arms against his friend Thompson. The warriors arrived west of the mountains, taking a position some distance away from the fort. As was their custom they sent two men to the post to spy out the land. Thompson at once recognized them, inviting them in and showing them about the post. He pointed out its strength, then played his best card. He bribed the entire party with their most cherished article, tobacco. Thompson was using a sacred rule of the Piegans—not warring with one from whom they had accepted a gift—and the Welshman had carefully offered a gift which he knew the natives could not easily refuse. Again he escaped punishment from the Indians.[7]

Thompson once more gave his attention to exploration. In April of 1808, he went eastward to Kootenay river, descending it to Kootenay lake. He returned to Fort Kootenay before leaving for Rainy Lake house with his pelts, arriving there, August 2. By the end of October he was back on the Columbia.

He now delegated Finan McDonald, one of the most intriguing personalities ever engaged by the Nor'Westers, to establish a post at Kootenay falls while he himself spent the winter at Fort Kootenay. The season's catch was good and, in April of 1809, Thompson took forty packs to Augustus, which he reached, June 24.[8] On his return to the Pacific side of the divide he went up the Columbia and down the Kootenay, then through the Cabinet range to Lake Pend d'Oreille where he built Kullyspell house before continuing to explore the lake. In November he put up Saleesh house not far from Ashley creek, Montana, spending the winter of 1809-1810 there. In the spring of 1810 he again went east to Rainy lake.

Three years now having passed since the Piegans first blocked Howse pass, Thompson could assume that their hostility had vanished. Re-entering their lands late in 1810, he found the reverse. No longer pretending friendship, they were openly warlike. His way was completely cut off and no simple trickery would work this time.

Thompson came up the Saskatchewan with his annual supply of trade goods for Kootenay house and had gone well beyond

---

7.—For this interpretation of how Thompson outwitted the Piegans in 1807, see Lawrence J. Burpee's *On the Old Athabasca Trail*, pages 32-44.

8.—Returning to the mountains, Thompson met Joseph Howse, who had also been exploring in the West.

Rocky Mountain house before being checked. On the way west he met Alexander Henry, who co-operated in every way to help get the goods through the mountains. Midnight baggage trains, secret comings and goings, false starts—all were tried in a futile attempt to outguess the Piegans.

Because the Indians were trailing them closely, Thompson and his small party had to dash off one morning at daybreak, their enemies at their heels. Finally a friendly snowstorm having blotted out their trail, the whites sat down to discuss their plight. In their extremity Thompson fell back on the third of the three choices he had when the Indians were hostile in 1807: he searched for a new pass. The first step was to reunite the separated forces. These were forty miles away at a trader's old shack. Following "much consultation we fully perceived we had no further hopes of passing in safety by the defiles of the Saskatchewan river." They changed their route to the Athabasca, trusting that it might lead through the mountains.

Some of the men went after the horses which had been left near Howse pass. On their return the explorers set off, October 28. In his party Thompson had twenty-four men and a like number of horses loaded with trade goods, but no food. Indeed, the men were starving before they ever left on that winter's expedition to find a new pass through the Rockies.

Day after day the hunters came back with little or no game, and the weather grew increasingly unpleasant, but on they went. By November 29 they reached the Athabasca, then turned west up that stream into the mountains. On December 3, they were at Brule lake where the guide wanted to set up a winter camp. Thompson refused because of lack of food for the horses. They settled on a place a few miles farther on, stopping for nearly a month. The men built winter quarters and made snow shoes and dog sleds.

Thompson divided his forces into two nearly equal groups. One, under William Henry, he left to take care of the horses. He himself started with the other division on a final dash over the mountains, December 29. Deep snows and want of food took their toll of men and beasts. Thompson became annoyed at the amount of food his men ate, complaining unreasonably about the eight pounds of meat they demanded each day. He seemed to forget that that was the standard ration and that the men were risking their lives just as he was, yet without any hope of reward which success might bring. At best they would receive a few extra pennies at the end of the fiscal year. There would be no promotions for them, no retirements in comfort and plenty, no record of their names in the annals of the Far West. On his part, Thompson carried serious responsibility and probably the stress of the moment made him criticize his men for what he himself might have done in their position.

The thermometer showed 26° below zero on January 5, but the men struggled on. By the tenth they reached the height of land down whose western side lay the Pacific. Seven feet of snow made hard going for the dogs—the last horses had been left behind—but the warmer winds from the Pacific eliminated the danger of freezing to death. The voyageurs were terrified at the avalanches from the melting snows, and their fears were justified. On a return trip they found one of their camps completely buried under such a slide.

The party found the descent toward the Pacific much easier and they reached the Columbia safely, making Thompson the first white man to effectively discover Athabasca pass; though others, his Iroquois guide for one, had been through before him.

Once over the mountains, Thompson explored around the upper Columbia, later blocking off the Middle Columbia region and exploring it. Starting at Spokane house, he went down the river of that name, then up the Columbia to Kettle falls. Satisfied that there was nothing important north of the falls, he retraced his steps. He passed the mouth of the Spokane and kept on until he reached the confluence of the Snake and Columbia, where he halted long enough to take formal possession of the country for the British Crown. On July 15 he paddled into Astoria just as the American company was ready to leave for the interior to search for the Nor'Westers. A few days later he accompanied the Stuart party as far as the Dalles on his return trip. The Astorians seemed uninterested in why Thompson wished to hurry on ahead after that. Actually he wanted to investigate the lower reaches of the Snake river.

Near latitude 46° and longitude 118° he left the Snake and headed overland for Spokane house, bisecting the only corner of the Columbia valley still unfamiliar to his company. From Spokane house he retraced his earlier way down the Spokane and up the Columbia to Arrow lakes and from there on to the mouth of Canoe river. During the rest of the winter of 1811 and the year of 1812, Thompson, having decided to retire, was busy arranging for his successor. On August 12, 1812, he was at Fort William.

He settled down in the country of Terrebonne, Quebec,[9] where he drew his map of the Northwest, a work so detailed and accurate that, until recent years, it remained a source of information about the region.

The explorations of David Thompson do not, of course, rival those of Sir Alexander Mackenzie. Thompson did much of his work on routes and in territories already roughly outlined by others. Still, he was the first white man to trace the Columbia from its source to its mouth. He opened Athabasca pass for use. He left a map which served for a generation as the only safe guide to the Canadian West; and he carried many fortunes in pelts to the eastern posts of his company. If such a record places him just below the greatest explorers, it also elevates him far above the average.

9.—Thompson died at Longeuil, February 16, 1857, and was buried in the Mount Royal cemetery, Montreal.

17

ROCKY MOUNTAIN MEN

THE FUR TRADE inevitably attracted self-sufficient men, but their total was never large. One thousand persons would easily cover the number in the average year.

In the Rocky mountains as in the North West company, certain men's names appear first as partners in one concern, then in another, and three of the major combinations will show the pattern of all. There were dozens of others, a few as important as Lisa, who took out a load of trade goods and brought back a fortune in pelts. Men like William Becknell and Richens Wootton considered the mountains secondary to the Santa Fe trade. But General William Henry Ashley, the Smith-Jackson-Sublette combine, and the Rocky Mountain Fur company stand out prominently in this mountain trade, really forming the kernel of the whole business, with the exception of the various Astor companies.

William Henry Ashley

As with so many men important on the frontier, the early years of William Henry Ashley are almost unknown. The democratic American West cared nothing about a man's heritage; performance was what mattered.

Ashley was born in Virginia about 1778, came to St. Louis about the time of the Louisiana Purchase, probably in 1802; was a merchant and manufacturer of sorts; dabbled in real estate and evidently operated a powder factory; and there is reason to believe that he did some mining. These occupations supplied him with money to enter the fur business. When he first moved to the West, he settled at Ste. Genevieve, where he made his initial fortune. From here on details of his life are better known.

In 1822, he entered partnership with Major Andrew Henry, an ex-Lisa man, and together they outlined an expedition to the source of the Missouri. They hired a hundred men, setting off up the river, April 15, 1822. Eighteen-year-old Jim Bridger
342

and Etienne Provost were among the crew. At Fort Osage one of the keel boats and ten thousand dollars in goods were lost. In the Assiniboine country of the upper Dakotas, Indians attacked the traders, robbing them of fifty horses. Because of this bad luck the partners abandoned their scheme for reaching the Three Forks of the Missouri, deciding, instead, to build a stockade at the mouth of the Yellowstone.

More than a decade had elapsed since Lisa, Lewis and Clark, and Hunt had gone that way but the natives' hostility was still strong in spite of the luxuries the white men now brought them.

Ashley established the Yellowstone post, then returned to St. Louis to recruit a new and more formidable company of men, leaving Henry to carry on business. This new party was "both for the character of its personnel and for the results it achieved . . . the most notable company that ever set out from St. Louis for the interior." [1] There were Thomas Fitzpatrick; William L. Sublette, a native of Kentucky; Hugh Glass; Jedediah Strong Smith, the strangest character of them all; David E. Jackson, whose past was unknown; and the mulatto Ed Rose, who had been with Lisa and Hunt. These were the leaders but others brought the total to about a hundred.

Ashley acquired two new keel boats, the *Yellowstone Packet* and *Rocky Mountain*. These he loaded with thousands of dollars' worth of goods and, on March 10, 1823,[2] left St. Louis for the Yellowstone.

It is surprising that neither Ashley nor the other mountain men ever used the steamboat to avoid the drudgery of the tow line, especially since these boats had been used east of the Alleghenies for fifteen years and on the Missouri itself for more than two years. Almost every boat taken up throughout the fur-gathering period was propelled by one or another of the ancient methods. There was the old pole practice by which mere human power edged the heavy craft inch by inch up the current. Another method was the use of a small patch of square sail when wind and river permitted. The most common technique, though, was the tow line. This line was fastened to a high mast, to clear

---

1.—Ghent, page 206.

2.—During the spring of 1823, the Austin family was attempting to colonize **Texas**.

the branches along the shore, and powered by the boatmen who tugged and hauled over rocks, through shallow water and over high banks. No wonder ten miles a day represented good time, or that Indians thought such craft and forces easy prey.

By early May the Ashley party reached Fort Atkinson, a few miles above the mouth of the Platte. They passed Fort Kiowa, belonging to the American Fur company, and by the latter part of the month were among the Arikaras. On the thirty-first the *Yellowstone Packet* and the *Rocky Mountain* were hauled up opposite one of the fortified, and apparently friendly, Arikara villages. Perhaps Ashley, knowing the ways of these people, should have been more suspicious of this friendliness, but they had been cordial the year before. On June 1, trade for horses opened and Ashley easily bought forty head. Still unsuspecting, he made no attempt to protect the men herding these animals.

All was quiet during the night of June 1, except a report, about 3 a. m., that trouble was brewing, but it was too late to do much. At daylight the Arikaras opened fire. Before Ashley could do more than realize what was happening, the savages had killed fourteen of his men and wounded eleven others, one quarter of his entire crew. Extricating his forces the best he could, he dropped down the river a safe distance and halted. He urged his men to proceed but most of them refused without better safeguards. Ashley then appealed for help to Henry on the Yellowstone, and sent a fast courier to Colonel Leavenworth, commanding the federal troops in that district. He also broadcast a general request for assistance from all independent trappers in the vicinity and from the momentarily friendly Sioux.

Henry himself was deep in trouble with the Blackfeet but he took about fifty men to aid his partner. Leavenworth sent a detachment of soldiers. Sixty trappers under Mr. Pilcher answered the call, and seven hundred Sioux turned out to chastise the Arikaras—in all, a force of eleven hundred men. Such an exhibition on the Missouri in 1823 would have been an impressive show of military strength, and the culprits should have been speedily subdued, and Ashley on his way. Instead, the Leavenworth forces made only a half-hearted assault on the enemy, who solemnly pledged good behavior, then scampered off to plan new deviltries. The Sioux braves were disgusted at the timidity of the whites who, they thought, should have attacked and massacred their enemies.

Pilcher withdrew his trappers, Henry returned to the Yellowstone, and Ashley himself moved to Fort Kiowa. The Arikara battle resulted in no decisive advantage to any of the traders and caused Ashley enormous losses, besides seriously hurting his credit.

More trouble was to follow. Could his own fortune have stood the losses of 1822 and 1823, Ashley might have made a third attempt to get up the Missouri, regardless of how others viewed such a venture. Forced to borrow for a new supply of goods, he had to please his creditors and attack the problem from a different angle. He decided to relinquish the upper Missouri to the natives and the Missouri Fur company and dispatch an overland party of traders directly west, while he stayed behind to administer the business details at St. Louis.

He chose the Green river as the most likely field and placed Jedediah Strong Smith in charge of the expedition. Thomas Fitzpatrick was given second command, William L. Sublette and the others filling in lesser positions. Rose was to act as guide and interpreter. Probably no other man, except perhaps Jim Bridger, acted as guide to so many important parties as Ed Rose. Even though his employers were not always satisfied with him, his services were constantly demanded.

Smith got his supplies together and left Fort Kiowa toward the end of September, heading due west. He circled around the Black Hills; reached a party of Crows, Rose's old friends, early in November; then crossed the Big Horn range to the confluence of Wind river and Popo Agie. The party next hurried up Wind river, where they found the main village of the Crows. By crossing a wide stretch of the interior and into the mountains, they proved that the headwaters of the Missouri could be reached without going through the hostile Arikara and Blackfeet territories.

Ashley's men took this discovery calmly enough. Their minds were on beaver, not geographic achievement. After resting two months with the Crows, from whom they learned about South pass, the party started south in the dead of winter, February, 1824,[3] reaching the Sweetwater safely. Smith led his party over South pass, descending to the Green shortly after the middle of March. They were the first white men consciously to use this pass, though possibly Colter, returning from his adventures under Lisa, may have gone that way. Robert Stuart might have stumbled over the same route as he struggled along toward St. Louis with his reports for Astor.[4]

When Smith arrived on the Green he divided his trappers into parties and set them working the main stream and its tributaries. Furs were plentiful and of good quality. When all the men gathered at the prearranged rendezvous over on the Sweetwater in June, there was a most satisfactory catch. Fitzpatrick was to deliver the furs to Ashley at St. Louis while Smith was to remain in the mountains to organize the following season's work.[5]

Meanwhile Andrew Henry, who had moved his posts from the Yellowstone to the mouth of the Big Horn, had left this post in the spring of 1824 and moved south to follow Smith and Fitzpatrick onto the Green. He too had been successful, and, after collecting the pelts from his men, personally took the entire crop to St. Louis by way of the Missouri river.

The story of the mountain fur trade everywhere points out the startling bravery of these men. Without hesitation they re-entered regions and used routes from which they had barely escaped with their lives. And no one knew better than Henry the dangers that lurked along the Missouri, yet he boldly took a season's catch of fine furs through the exact territory from which he had just been compelled to withdraw. Henry delivered his cargo to Ashley who, immediately got ready to return to the mountains, leaving St. Louis, October 21, 1824. Jedediah Smith replaced him in the partnership.

"This departure, strange to say, is the very last word which we have of Andrew Henry in the fur trade." [6] Years afterwards, Henry married a young French girl and still later lost his fortune by endorsing bad notes. When urged to dodge his responsibility

3.—In the same month Congress officially invited Lafayette to visit the United States, offering a government ship for his use. Lafayette accepted the invitation but declined the ship.

4.—Ghent, page 211. Chittenden, volume 1, 271.

5.—Under normal conditions there were two catches a year, fall and spring. Smith would thus be getting ready for the autumn of 1824.

6.—Chittenden, volume 1, page 272.

by putting his fortune in his wife's name, he is said to have indignantly refused.

While Andrew Henry dropped out as a fur trader, Fitzpatrick got into trouble. Shortly after leaving the mountains, one of his men, James Clyman, became lost. Alone and on foot, Clyman struggled for six hundred miles to reach Fort Atkinson. Fitzpatrick himself lost many of his furs, caching what was left not far from Independence Rock, just above where the Sweetwater empties into the North Platte. He struck out eastward, not reaching Fort Atkinson until September. He wrote of his troubles to Ashley in St. Louis, acquired a horse, and back tracked for his cached pelts. On October 26, 1824, he returned with his goods. Almost immediately he again started for the mountains, being overtaken by Ashley who decided to have a personal hand in affairs.

The two partners intended going up the Platte but, warned by the Pawnees of the danger, they cut off and took the South Platte, heading into the present Colorado. Soon deep snows and blizzards struck them, shutting off whatever natural food supplies might have appeared along the way. Starvation and intense cold threatened them hourly. Their horses, less robust than they, froze to death. When near the present Greeley, Colorado, Ashley and Fitzpatrick swung north toward the Medicine Bow mountains. Fighting desperately for life, they managed to skirt around the northern edge of the range and cross to the Green river by way of Bridger's pass.

After recovering, Ashley split his company and, with a few men, explored the canyon of the Green. The remaining men he instructed to scatter widely and carry on their trapping. Also they were to tell others they met of a great rendezvous scheduled at Henry's fork the coming summer.[7]

Ashley investigated the Green downstream about as far as the present Wyoming-Utah boundary, then took horse and traveled almost due west overland to the valley of the small Weber river, north and slightly east of the present Park City, Utah. He arrived there in June and began assembling his trappers.[8]

During all this time Smith had wandered north to the Hud-

7.—These activities took place during the second decade of the nineteenth century. Ashley had about one hundred men under him. The Hudson's Bay company had also penetrated the region with about sixty trappers.

8.—Chittenden has a different version of this phase of Ashley's trip. He says

son's Bay post on Flathead lake, Montana, where he met Peter Skene Ogden, chief factor. He and Smith started south together. Smith began coaxing Ogden's men over to the Ashley-Fitzpatrick payroll, promising them higher prices for their furs. When the expedition was about forty miles north of the present Ogden, Utah, Smith had won twenty-nine of the Hudson's Bay men. Such methods were contrary to the religious principles Smith so devoutly preached but were regular "mountain practice."

Ashley was now in a position to make up most of his 1822-1823 losses. Furs were plentiful and good; experienced traders and trappers had joined his forces; and he had opened several new fields. One of his men reached Utah lake, while Jim Bridger, using a primitive bull boat,[9] went down Bear river and discovered Great Salt lake. Ashley was in high spirits. About this time he jockeyed Ogden into selling him $75,000 worth of furs for next to nothing. No one knows why. With these in hand he took all his men and trade goods and tramped to the meeting at Henry's fork. Assembled there were 150 whites: Ashley men, Hudson's Bay men, and independent trappers from Santa Fe and Taos; in addition to some 800 Indians, men, women, and children.

These mountain rendezvous were unique in the history of the fur trade and had few counterparts in the world. They harked back to the days when the great caravans from western Europe stopped at Khiva or Nizhni-Novgorod and set out their wares for traders from the distant Orient.[10] But those ancient fairs were held in cities where the dust from thousands of feet filled the air and the sound of trade was sometimes drowned by the tolling of chapel bells or the mumblings of evening prayers.

The background for the mountain meetings was very different. Behind were the gigantic Tetons or some smaller range; in front, a sweet and well-watered valley. Gathered there were savages of of all degrees; naked children playing at their everlasting game of war; skulking dogs; half-wild horses and mules tethered to

Ashley's boat was wrecked and that in returning he fell in with Provost, possibly by prearrangement and that the combined party then went back to Salt Lake valley. (volume 1, pages 274-275.)

9.—These craft were made of hides stretched tight around a crude framework. They were neither very sturdy nor manageable, their chief advantage being their availability in the buffalo country.

10.—This system was taken over bodily by the traders who made the tiny mountain town of Taos for many years the center of southwestern trade.

stakes; traders from every sort of company and from no company; Jedediah Smith with his Bible and his gun; halfbreeds with their native squaws; educated gentlemen out to see the West at first hand; traders who, gamblers at heart, prided themselves on spending a year's earnings in an evening's play; frontiersmen who had throttled the throats of savages; partners with such deep mutual faith that, as they rushed into battle with the Indians, they had been known to shout their wills to each other, well aware that the survivor would execute them as faithfully as if they were written in legal phrase.

They drank and gambled, raced their horses, slept little, ate much, talked long and boastfully, fought, swaggered, lied, cheated the Indians, their own people, and each other. When the occasion had finally spent itself, and all the beads and baubles had been exchanged for hides and pelts, each trader went his way to labor and fight for another year, so that for a few days he could again live through these wild scenes. Yet with all their debauchery and even filth, these mountain rendezvous were brilliant pages in the story of the American fur trade.

Ashley opened trade on July 1, and by the next morning the first of the great annual mountain fairs was over. He had sold out. With Smith and fifty trappers he left for the East, picking up an additional cache on the Sweetwater. Because of returning by the water route they had a brief though light skirmish with the Blackfeet and the Crows. Arriving at the navigable waters of the Big Horn, they built enough boats to handle the freight. Dismissing most of the men, Ashley and Smith took the rest and started floating down to the mouth of the Yellowstone. There they were met by General Atkinson, who was just then making a series of treaties with the Indians along the Missouri. Ashley reached St. Louis with huge gains and no serious losses. He cleared himself of debt and had enough left to outfit two new expeditions, not, however, before promising himself that if these were successful he would retire from the fur trade.

The first of these new ventures he sent west, October 30. He himself led the second one which started the following March, 1826.[11] This was to be his last trip into the moutains. At the end

---

[11].—The first Panama Congress was called about this time, debate over which resulted in the notorious duel between Henry Clay and John Randolph, April 8.

of the season he sold his pelts, clearing eighty thousand dollars, enough for him to retire from active mountain work.[12] He sold his interests to his partners, Jedediah Strong Smith, David E. Jackson, and William L. Sublette.

The prices which the new partners paid Ashley indicate what happened to values when supplies got a few miles west of the Missouri. The bill of sale was dated, July 18, 1826, and among other items was the following price list for invoiced goods: calicoes, $1.00 per yard; thread, $3.00 per pound; rings, $5.00 per gross; cheap beads and cheaper files, $2.50 per pound; horse shoes, nails, and tin pans, $2.00 per pound. Bridles were listed at $7.00 each. Four-proof, reduced rum was $13.50 per gallon, and handkerchiefs, $1.50 each. Considering that these prices would be doubled and trebled, even quadrupled, when quoted to the Indian, it is easy to see how fortunes were made in a single season. Chittenden [13] says that an outlay of two thousand dollars could net around seven or eight times the amount, and that Ashley later entered and left the business again all within a six-months period. But in that short time he managed to net seventy per cent on his investment.

Apparently once Ashley left the Missouri and began carrying his trade overland, his severe losses stopped and his profits began. The care and skill he used in organizing his overland parties explain their general success. Instead of horses, he relied on mules to carry freight. They could more easily stand the long hours, short food, and heavy loads. Their work was often so severe that one observer wrote of them as having "scarcely any skin on their backs; they are peeled from withers to tail, raw underneath from the use of the surcingle," [14] yet each day they were compelled to do their full allotment of work. Unfortunately there was seldom need for such treatment. It could have been avoided by a few more pennies being spent for proper pack equipment or by a little more careful loading.

12.—Neither before nor after his fur-trading days did Ashley confine his interests to money making. Politics always intrigued him and, during his lifetime, he was at various times congressman, first lieutenant governor of Missouri, and adjutant-general of militia, some of these duties being carried on while he was in the fur business.

13.—Chittenden, volume 1, pages 6-7.

14.—Charles Larpenteur. *Forty Years a Fur Trader*, volume 1, page 7.

Often the men were downright brutal to the animals, especially when heavy freighting came to be done with mule-drawn wagons. Then the muleteers exercised their wrath and profanity to their heart's content, unless they worked for such a person as Alexander Majors, the great Santa Fe trader, who made every employe take a signed oath that he would neither swear, get drunk nor mistreat his animals while in his service. The penalty was immediate discharge without any pay for services rendered.

In Ashley's routine, each employe was assigned two mules and a saddle horse. These animals were outfitted with standard and specific equipment including two bridles, a light one for regular use and a heavy one for tethering, made of hide or tarred rope and strong enough "to hold the horse under any circumstances." There was a hardwood pin, two feet long with a swivel ring in the top. Driven into the ground this became the tethering post.

All animals and equipment were charged against the man they were issued to, and he was strictly accountable for them.

If the party consisted of sixty or more men, four were made sub-commanders, the others being divided into messes of eight or ten men each. One from each mess acted as a supply and disbursement officer. On the march, camps were formed in squares with one side being a river or lake shore if possible. As soon as a halt was made, saddles and packs were used to make a breastwork around the camp. Horses and mules were delivered to a special guard outside the square to graze until sundown, when they were brought inside the camp. Every man was required to stake his own charges, giving thirty feet of range to each animal. Regular night watches were set until sunrise when two or more mounted scouts were sent to search for hostile Indians. Not until these had reported favorably were the horses again taken outside to graze as the men breakfasted.

When the party was ready to move, they lined up, mess by mess, retaining that order throughout the day. The mess which was ready to move first was allowed front place in the line, a choice position when the dust was bad. After the train started, scouts were kept several miles ahead, on the flanks, and in the rear, to protect the main party against any sort of surprise.

"In this way I have marched parties of men the whole way from St. Louis to the vicinity of the Grand lake, which is situated about one hundred and fifty miles down the waters of the Pacific ocean, in 78 days. In the month of March, 1827, I fitted out a party of 60 men, mounted a piece of artillery (a four pounder) on a carriage which was drawn by two mules; the party marched to or near the Grand Salt lake beyond the Rocky mountains, remained there one month, stopped on the way back fifteen days, and returned to Lexington, in the western part of Missouri, in September, where the party was met with everything necessary for another outfit, and did return (using the same horses and mules) to the mountains by the last of November, in the same year." [15]

In St. Louis, Ashley continued to supply the goods which his old partners needed, making a liberal profit from them. Granting the rightness of the whole fur trade setup, there was nothing to criticize in this. Yet Ashley was not above certain shady business tricks, very close to bribery. It seems that Astor paid Ashley a liberal sum each year not to re-enter the mountains in competition.[16]

As for William Henry Ashley's historic achievements, he did several things of lasting importance. He proved that it was relatively easy to reach the Rocky mountains by going directly west overland, leaving the upper Missouri to the Arikaras, Sioux, and Blackfeet. His men worked the full length of the continental divide from South pass, which they discovered, to western Montana. Ashley himself explored a considerable portion of Green River canyon. One of his men discovered Great Salt lake and they had all gone over the immense region around it many times. Though these explorations were secondary to their trading, they still entitle the Ashley-Fitzpatrick party to an enviable place in the ranks of discoverers of the Pacific Northwest.

15.—Chittenden, volume 3, pages 940-941.
16.—Same, volume 1, page 930; Ghent, page 216, note.

18

JEDEDIAH SMITH DEFIES THE SPANIARDS

JEDEDIAH STRONG SMITH and William L. Sublette were the most important members of the combination of Smith-Jackson-Sublette. Of the two, Smith was by far the more interesting.

Sublette, one of four brothers, was a normal fellow, neither more nor less remarkable than the average good fur trader of his day, but Smith was quite another sort. A recent historian of the West calls him "one of the most noteworthy explorers and fur traders of his time." [1] He was a native of New York and moderately well educated. At about eighteen years of age he went to St. Louis and took service with Ashley and Henry. Engaged in the most lawless "legitimate" trade ever to run its course in America, Smith always remained a devout and sincere Christian gentleman; yet how he reconciled fur trading tactics with the teachings of the Nazarene is puzzling. He carried his Bible with his gun, and was as untiring in the study of one as in the use of the other. He took the Book to the Flatheads but brought back their pelts, no doubt paying as little as he could for each hide.

After Ashley left the business, Smith sought to explore the region south of Salt Lake. With fifteen men he left Cache valley northeast of the lake, August, 1826.[2]

He skirted around the eastern shore, went down past Ashley's old post on Utah lake, worked up the valley of the Sevier river, keeping well to the east of that stream, then headed for the Virgin river, going down to its confluence with the Colorado. Not far south of there his party crossed the larger stream and with much suffering worked its way across southern California to San Diego. The governor was quite unfriendly, and Smith avoided arrest only by lying to him, saying that a shortage of food compelled him to enter California.

1.—R. L. Duffus. *The Santa Fe Trail*, page 125.
2.—In the early part of the following month, William Morgan was abducted from Canandaigua, New York, and possibly murdered by his political enemies, the "Morgan Killers" as they were popularly called. The affair resulted in the anti-Masons' rise to national importance.

Whether the governor believed this tale is not known but he did permit Smith to set off upstate in February of 1827, probably with the understanding that he would leave the country as fast as possible. Whether Smith specifically agreed to this is uncertain but he made no attempt to hurry away. Moving well toward the middle of the state, he trapped and hunted leisurely throughout the winter. Only after reaching the Stanislaus river did he show any intention of getting out of Spanish territory. There he did try to cross the Sierras but deep snows blocked his way. Without hunting for another pass, he moved his men into a friendly, warm valley and left them.

Smith knew he would have to return eventually to American territory and, on May 20, with two companions and seven horses he went over the mountains into the Nevada desert. He could hardly have chosen a more unfortunate place to cross the range. On the one side was fresh water and green grass, abundance of food and game; on the other, a sagebrush desert with almost no animal or vegetable life fit for human consumption, a region in which even the natives found meager living. Six of the seven horses were killed but Smith and his companions struggled on across the desert, reaching Salt lake, June 17, 1827.[3]

The rendezvous having been called for Bear lake, Utah, that year, Smith proceeded there at once. Jackson and Sublette had had a profitable season and Smith thought the California region so promising that he was off again on July 13, this time accompanied by nineteen men and two women. The second California expedition followed the same route as the first until they came to the Mojaves, just where their route crossed the Colorado and turned westward toward the coast. These Indians had been very friendly the year before and still seemed to be. With nine of his men, Smith crossed the river on a raft and was starting to assist the rest of the party over when the Mojaves, possibly at the instigation of the Spaniards, turned upon those still on the east side of the river, massacring everyone, except the two women, whom they took as slaves. The Indians reduced the American forces approximately one-half, then helped themselves to all the property they could lay hold of.

3.—The British-American Treaty of Joint Occupancy of Oregon which was to expire in 1828 was renewed on August 6, the new treaty to run indefinitely.

This was August of 1827. Ten days later, Smith had moved directly over to San Gabriel instead of chancing a meeting with the unfriendly authorities at San Diego. At San Gabriel, Smith was given supplies and courteously helped along his way to the valley where he had left his men the previous May. Had he followed his earlier route when leaving San Gabriel, the story of his second California venture might have been quite different, but his insatiable curiosity made him deliberately seek out the Spanish settlements. Not particularly modest, Smith may have felt capable of taking care of himself in any situation the Spaniards could devise, or sure that his last year's experience was an exception and that the bulk of Spanish authorities were genuinely friendly to strangers. Whatever his thoughts, he digressed from his previous route and stopped at San Jose where he was promptly arrested and thrown into prison.

The future looked dark for the Methodist fur trader. There was no good reason why he should have been a second time in Spanish territory without a permit. He could not hope to make the thin excuse which he used the first time serve him again. Shortly after his arrest he was taken to Monterey. There he appealed to an American ship captain for aid. Just what tale these two put up to convince the authorities this time of Smith's innocence is not recorded, but Smith was released after having definitely bound himself to leave the country. He now exerted some effort to keep that promise. Uniting with his men at San Francisco, he tried to cross the Sierras, then decided they were too dangerous. Without a second attempt he turned still farther away from home, heading toward Oregon.

From San Francisco to the northern end of the Spanish domains was a good four hundred miles, and at that point, roughly the 42° parallel, he would in no sense have been closer home. Actually his line of travel was at a tangent away from home, and Smith was far too well educated, both in book learning and frontier lore, to be unaware of this. He must have chosen the route he did to cover as much Spanish territory as possible and to collect as many pelts as he could along the way.

Smith had been moving northward through the Sacramento valley but just where that stream swings in from the northeast he turned toward the coast, crossing the mountains and following the shore north to the Umpqua. Because the natives all seemed cordial, the American party may have grown careless. Early in the morning of July 4, 1828, while Smith was away, the savages attacked the camp, killing all but two, John Turner and Arthur Black. Turner and Black escaped to the woods, though not together. Back at camp, Smith found the bodies of his men. The Indians had stolen all his property. To save their own lives, he and Turner, whom he chanced to meet, started out on foot for the Hudson's Bay post at Vancouver. They met Black wandering about and the three went to McLoughlin's post by way of the Willamette.[4]

McLoughlin received them kindly, doing what no rule of the fur trade or his own company required: he sent a powerful party of his own men to punish the Umpquas and regain his competitor's property. Taken unaware, the Indians were properly punished and most of Smith's pelts restored. McLoughlin then did another surprising thing: he gave Smith full market value for the entire lot, in the sum of twenty thousand dollars;[5] nor did he charge Smith an exorbitant price for the expedition in a trumped-up effort to wipe out the value of the furs. He merely asked the Americans to stand the cost of the men's time at the same rate the Hudson's Bay company paid them, and to pay four dollars per animal for each horse lost on the trip. Smith fully appreciated McLoughlin's generosity.

During the winter of 1828-1829[6] the Rocky Mountain men enjoyed the hospitality at Vancouver but by March they were ready to re-enter the game. On the twelfth they started back for the Popo Agie, hoping to be in time for the rendezvous of 1829.

Jedediah Smith must have had real wanderlust for just as he took the long way out of Spanish California, so now did he traverse almost the entire Columbia watershed claimed by the Hudson's Bay company. Leaving Vancouver, he went over to the south side of the river, following it to the Umatilla Indian territory where he should logically have turned southeast, crossing

---

4.—Historians disagree as to whether only Black and Smith escaped the massacre and also whether Smith wandered to Vancouver alone or with the other survivor or survivors.

5.—Some place this amount at a much lower figure, as little as three thousand dollars.

6.—These are the years of Jackson's election and inauguration to the Presidency, ushering in the second so-called "revolution" in American politics.

the Grande Ronde and Blue mountains, then up the Snake to Henry's fort and his partners. Instead, he headed away from home, going almost due north overland to Spokane house by way of Walla Walla and the Palouse river. His curiosity satisfied on the Spokane, he turned east, skirted well to the north of Coeur d'Alene lake, went around the northern end of the Bitter Roots, through the valley between them and Lake Pend d'Oreille, and then up Clark's fork to Flathead post in Montana, where he had been several seasons before. Not until he reached that post did he decide to join his partners. Using the most direct overland route, he went straight south to Pierre's hole, meeting on the way, August 5,[7] Jackson and Sublette, who were looking for him.

In speed and endurance Alexander Mackenzie was the greatest overland explorer in North America, but in territory covered, Jedediah Smith outranked every other explorer of his period. A close second might be that persistent mountaineer, James Bridger. Smith traversed every important valley from the Rockies to the Pacific and from the Mexican border to 49° north. Twice he went to California; three times he traveled over the Great Basin; and he was probably the first white man to cross the Sierras. Still not content, he was to shift his attentions away from the Rockies for the fairs at Taos and the Santa Fe trail and finally, lose his life on the Cimarron.

Before these events though, others occurred in the mountains. Smith had already withdrawn his share of the men from Hudson's Bay preserves on the upper Snake, out of gratitude for McLoughlin's treatment. Though David Jackson re-entered the region in 1830, Smith's action did cut short their work there. At the start of the 1830 season there was talk of selling out. The best days of the mountain fur trade were over and the richest pelts for the smallest prices had been taken. Such men as these wanted to move on to more profitable fields. Besides, they sought a change, restlessly demanding new scenes and new faces regardless of financial profit. The three partners decided to sell their interests after the rendezvous of 1830 on Wind river.[8]

7.—Three days later the "Stourbridge Lion," first locomotive in the United States, was given a trial run at Honesdale, New York.

8.—This rendezvous was important in another way. Sublette proved it was possible to use wagons in the overland trade by taking ten of them, five mules per wagon, and two dearborns, one mule each, from St. Louis to Wind river and back. The coming of wheels over the mountains doomed the wilderness and all wilderness industries, though the transition was slow.

On August 4, the Smith-Jackson-Sublette combination released their interests to Thomas Fitzpatrick, Milton G. Sublette—younger brother of William L.—, James Bridger, Henry Fraeb, and Jean Baptiste Gervais. These five organized themselves into the Rocky Mountain Fur company. This was a general name often before used to indicate the major company doing business in the mountains at any given moment.[9]

9.—William L. Sublette and Robert Campbell later went into partnership, giving the American Fur Company the only serious competition it had for ten years. They built two posts, one at the mouth of the Laramie, the other on the Missouri near Fort Union. Laramie became an important government post, as many as forty thousand animals a year passing it on the way to and from the West.

Pueblo of Taos, New Mexico, mecca of Spanish-American-Indian trade during the fur-trade era. The pueblo is about 800 years old. (New Mexico Department of Development)

19

THE ROCKY MOUNTAIN FUR COMPANY

COMPETITION IN THE MOUNTAIN TRADE was now assuming alarming proportions. Tales of Ashley's amazing success fired the imagination of dozens of independent trappers who made a formidable hole in the total amount of pelts available. Besides, the Hudson's Bay people and the American Fur company were trying to drive from the region all smaller traders. These large companies were more to be feared than the unorganized independents because they could operate almost indefinitely at a loss, if in the end they could be sure of winning a certain field for themselves. The independents could not survive such warfare. The result was that from 1830 on, the great combinations constantly pressed the lesser ones, driving them from valley to valley until the day finally came when they were wiped out and their only choice in the fur trade was to work for one of the larger combines.

Before that day arrived the Rocky Mountain Fur company was to see some accomplishments. The new organization started an energetic campaign. Fraeb and Gervais took a small party into the Colorado mountains where they remained a year. Fitzpatrick, Milton Sublette, and Bridger went north into Montana and for once succeeded in coaxing the Blackfeet into profitable trade. The partners then turned south again into Utah. Finding that Ogden had already entered the particular valleys they intended to trap, they moved on to their old ground, the Green, spending the winter on Powder river.

Early in 1831 Fitzpatrick started for St. Louis to pick up the goods for that season's rendezvous. En route he met his old friends, Smith, Jackson, and Sublette, now plying the Santa Fe trade. These gentlemen persuaded Fitzpatrick to accompany them to Santa Fe, promising to supply his needs from the south.

Wagons were just beginning to be used in the Santa Fe trade and the Smith-Jackson-Sublette company was taking twenty new ones with them. The party consisted of eighty men, enough to guarantee safety under normally dangerous conditions. The trail to Taos and Santa Fe, so famous a few years later, was not well known in the spring of 1831.[1] Smith lost his way and for three days the entire expedition wandered in the desert. Their water was gone, eyes ached, tongues became thick, and speech difficult. The animals suffered even more than the men. Smith left his command to find water by himself. Following a buffalo trail he came to the dry bed of the Cimarron. Aware of the nature of these desert streams, he dug a hole and saw the water seep and rise. But while on the verge of saving the lives of his men he lost his own life. He was attacked and killed by Indians, probably the Comanches, though there is no proof of this.

Before expiring, Smith managed to kill two of his assassins. "So with blood on his hands, died one of the gentlest of men and one of the best friends the Indians ever had." [2] Smith fulfilled the prediction he made for all fur traders, that once the lure of beaver, marten, and buffalo got into a man's veins he would never be good for much else, but would always wish to live the life of the semi-savage.[3]

The tragedy of Jedediah Smith took valuable time and, though Fitzpatrick hurried, one delay after another kept him in Santa Fe. Finally taking what goods he had, he started for Taos. There he rounded up a few trappers, among them the now famous Kit Carson, and headed north to find his partners. These had been carrying on their routine work, covering nearly the same ground as in past seasons. They had all gone to the rendezvous without Fitzpatrick, who was too late to be of any use. They sent Fraeb to search for him, the rest returning to their traps to await the winter fair on Powder river. Fraeb and Fitzpatrick met near the mouth of the Laramie.

When the Rocky Mountain men reached Powder river valley they found the Astor men already there. Disgusted, they slipped

---

1.—Nat Turner's negro insurrection occurred in August of 1831.

2.—Duffus, pages 126-127.

3.—Josiah Gregg, an early trader into Santa Fe, expressed the same philosophy in a different way: "It will hardly be a matter of surprise when I add that this passion for prairie life will be very apt to lead me upon the plains again, to spread my bed with the mustang and the buffalo under the broad canopy of heaven; there to seek to maintain undisturbed my confidence in man by fraternizing with the little prairie dog and wild colts, and the wilder Indians."

away to another field, only to be followed relentlessly by the American Fur company. Throughout the winter this hide-and-seek trade war continued. All signs of it were present at the rendezvous in June of 1832 at Pierre's hole. In addition to the Rocky Mountain men, whose fair it was in theory, were free trappers, Indians, Nathaniel Wyeth and his New England immigrants, Astor's men, and Benjamin Bonneville's trappers. These last were probably a subsidiary company financed by Astor, though they pretended independence.

Fitzpatrick now had his back to the wall. All through the preceding winter he had futilely tried to escape his rivals. Now he made the mistake of offering to compromise with the interlopers by dividing the territory with them. Astor's men, knowing that an offer of compromise meant a weakened rival, declined, and the battle for streams went on. At the time of these negotiations all three companies anxiously awaited their trade goods so that buying and selling could open.

Sensing that he was making a last stand, Fitzpatrick planned to steal a march on his competitors by getting his goods in first and thereby purchasing the best of the pelts. He set out alone to find Sublette, in charge of the supply train, and to urge him to hurry. He easily found his partner and was going back to Pierre's hole when the Grosventres ambushed him. He had provided for such an emergency by leading, as always, a fresh horse ready saddled. On sighting the Grosventres he mounted the horse and dashed for the hills, hiding there three days. In trying to slip out secretly he again fell in with the enemy, lost his second horse, and was on foot without even a blanket in a hostile mountain country. Still hopeful, Fitzpatrick set out for his camp, subsisting on whatever he could find along the way. The terrible conditions under which he had lived the past three or four days had completely sapped his strength. He was finally discovered by a friendly half-breed who took him to Pierre's hole. Some say that as a result of these experiences his hair had turned white by the time he reached camp.

The Rocky Mountain supply train did beat the Astor goods to the rendezvous. By July 15, when trade was over,[4] the Rocky

---

4.—Three days later the Battle of Pierre's hole occurred, during which traders who remained after the rendezvous were attacked by the Grosventres.

Mountain Fur company could boast of a season of 168 packs of furs worth $85,000.[5] William Sublette, still acting as agent for his old partners, took these to St. Louis.

Rivalry between the Rocky Mountain people and the American Fur company grew increasingly bitter. During 1833,[6] all the traders were in the field and one or two new combinations had entered. During this year there was a dastardly attack on Fitzpatrick. The Crows robbed him of all his furs and equipment, even taking his watch and clothes. He openly accused Astor's local representative of instigating the attack. Surprisingly both the Indians and the American Fur company agent admitted their guilt. Nevertheless the crowning shame appears in an excerpt from a communication which McKenzie, representing the company, sent to Tulloch, the agent:

"The 43 beaver skins traded, marked, 'R. M. F. Co.,' I would in the present instance give up if Mr. Fitzpatrick wishes to have them, on his paying the price the articles traded for them were worth on their arrival in the Crow village, and the expense of bringing the beaver in and securing it. . . . I make this proposal as a favor, not as a matter of right, for I consider the Indians entitled to trade any beaver in their possession to me or to any other trader." [7]

What a favor, indeed! Astor would rob his rival, then "permit" him to buy back his own furs if he would further give tribute to the gentleman from New York by paying the transportation cost incurred by those who instigated the robbery. That the American Fur company was not punished for such piracy shows how thoroughly Astor dominated the government, or at least that division dealing with Indian affairs. All such atrocities might have been avoided had the government itself remained in the Indian trade. But Crooks, president of the American Fur company, was the implacable foe of such "interference" and was, as stated earlier, finally successful in closing the government stores.

5.—Ordinarily one pack consisted of sixty beaver weighing a total of about a hundred pounds with a market value somewhere near seven or eight dollars per pound.

6.—The years 1832 and 1833 were vital for the United States. South Carolina, following the philosophy of secession laid down in 1814 by her New England cousins, had passed and later repealed ordinances of nullification and had threatened secession over the tariff proposals of 1832.

7.—Chittenden, volume 1, page 302.

Ashley recognized the drift of affairs when he said, "If there is not some alteration made in the system of business in this country very soon it will become a nuisance and a disgrace to the United States."

Competition was so keen the year following these disgraceful proceedings that Milton Sublette actually got into open rivalry with his own brother William. The year 1832 had the last important rendezvous. After the 1834 fiasco the Rocky Mountain company dissolved its rendezvous system,[8] agreeing thereafter to market its furs through the offices of the American Fur company. This move only prolonged for a year or two the time when Astor would have driven every independent trader from the field, for he arranged that the Rocky Mountain men receive nothing beyond daily wages.

Fur trade was a cutthroat business in which quarter was neither asked nor given. Yet it supplied a romantic era in American life with its pageantry, its wars, and half-savage, wholly self-reliant mountain men. When these men passed, taking the rendezvous system with them, something went out of American frontier life which even Sutter's fort, Hell's gulch, Last Chance, and Carson City could not replace—something big and wholehearted in spite of its obvious wickedness.

What had been the geographic importance of these traders? They wandered over practically every foot of the West. Some like Jim Bridger became so famous that when the government sent out official explorations it hired these mountain men to show the way and get the federal divisions safely back home. Bridger was only eighteen when he entered the West and of him Chittenden says, "It would be an endless task to trace the ubiquitous wanderings of this restless mountaineer during the next forty years of his life." [9] The same could be said for most of the other mountain fur traders.

"That they discovered every important geographic fact of the West is quite as certain as it is that their discoveries were often barren . . . and exercised little influence upon subsequent set-

8.—In 1834, Nathaniel Wyeth went into competition with the Rocky Mountain company, building Fort Hall in July of 1834. The Hudson's Bay company at once erected Fort Boise to offset Fort Hall.
9.—Chittenden, volume 1, page 258.

tlement and discovery." [10]   Yet, when the last rendezvous was held in 1840, not a major section of the route to the Northwest was unexplored; and Old Oregon, though generally untouched by the mountain men, was being crossed and recrossed in every direction by Hudson's Bay trappers and expresses.

10.—Frederic Logan Paxson. *Last American Frontier,* page 71.

Northeast corner of Fort Vancouver as it looked a few years after Dr. John McLoughlin ruled there. (Oregon Historical Society)

20

DR. JOHN McLOUGHLIN, AMERICAN CITIZEN

THE ROUTES TO THE PACIFIC NORTHWEST had been searched out and mapped. Ships had come and gone. Traders who made fortunes from the otter and beaver had retired to luxury and unctuous respectability. Others had fallen to bankruptcy and despair. All had helped open the Pacific Northwest.

By 1835, the age of explorers was almost over. But one era cannot pass before its successor is full blown. There must inevitably be an overlapping of events, a transition period when the old and the new struggle for power. In this period there must be also a transition vehicle, some Columbus or Galileo to stumble on a new truth, some critical social upheaval, some French or Russian revolution to upset the smug contentment of a world and force it, against its will, into a different cycle.

When the Nor'Westers and Rocky Mountain men had fought their last battle and held their final rendezvous, the Pacific Northwest was ready to emerge from a wilderness into a civilized commonwealth. The role of agent was to be played by the Hudson's Bay company, though against its will. For a hundred years the stockholders on Fenchurch street had kept their kingly grant all to themselves. But the Nor'Westers, challenging this right to hold such an enormous domain alone, prodded the company protestingly westward until it unwittingly became the factor which closed the era of exploration and opened the age of settlement.

It has been seen how Radisson and Groseilliers helped found the Hudson's Bay company; how critical pressure, after a century of inactivity, forced it to send Samuel Hearne to the Arctic; how the North West company made it change its system of trade and establish posts in the interior; how warfare between these two powerful companies almost ruined both and resulted in their combining in 1821. Details of their business between the time Hearne returned from the Arctic and 1821 do not concern

365

the Pacific Northwest. Their importance here properly begins in 1824 after the Nor'Westers' flag was hauled down on the Columbia and the Hudson's Bay pennant was run up.

Sir George Simpson, company governor in North America, aggressively campaigned to strengthen and expand the business. The fur country had four main divisions, Montreal, the Southern, Northern, and Western. Over each was a chief factor and under him were chief traders, chief clerks, apprenticed clerks, postmasters, interpreters, voyageurs, and laborers.

From the outset, three men assumed prime importance on the Columbia, Sir George Simpson, Dr. John McLoughlin, and James Douglas. Simpson was as reactionary and money loving as any man ever to pull a ball of lifeless fur from a trap. Proud and overbearing, he had but two interests in life, the Hudson's Bay company and Sir George Simpson. Not that he was an unpleasant boor; far from it. No man was suaver in turning a pound sterling, but he was less interested in human relationships than most men and never hesitated to send friends or members of families to widely separated posts if such moves pleased his fancy or notions of discipline.

A man by the name of McLean, a Hudson's Bay employe for forty years, typifies the difficulties of serving under Simpson. He says:

"The history of my career may serve as a warning to those who may be disposed to enter the Hudson Bay Company service. They may learn that from the moment they embark in the Company's canoes at Lachine or in their ships at Gravesend, they bid *adieu* to all that civilized man most values on earth. They bid *adieu* to their families and friends, probably forever, for if they remain long enough to attain the promotion that allows them the privilege of revisiting their native land (twenty or twenty-five years), what changes does not this life exhibit in a much shorter time?

"They bid *adieu* to all the comforts and conveniences of civilization to vegetate at some solitary post, hundreds of miles perhaps from any other human habitation, save the wigwam of the savage, without any society other than that of their own thoughts or of the two or three humble persons who share their exile. They bid *adieu* to all refinement and cultivation, not infrequently becoming semi-barbarians, so altered in habits and sentiments, that they not only become attached to savage life, but lose all relish for any other." [1]

Dr. John McLoughlin, ex-Nor'Wester, was banished to the Columbia because he dared contend for better terms for his company in the union of 1821. Simpson could not abide men who asserted themselves. He felt his position automatically validated any statement or proposition he made. John McLoughlin, though like Simpson in many ways, had a much higher concept of duty to his fellow men, sometimes disagreeing violently with his superior. For this he was appointed chief factor of the western division, a position generally considered a banishment. In effect, Simpson merely removed his problem. He did not solve it because the Scotsman's will and business principles remained unchanged. Though when they chanced to meet, both respected the civilities of social and business life, neither time nor distance diminished their mutual ill will.

McLoughlin was born at Riviere de Loup on the St. Lawrence in the autumn of 1784. His father was drowned while John was still a boy; and his mother, a Fraser before her marriage, took John and his brother David to the old Fraser home. Just as the Napoleonic wars broke out, the sons were sent to Europe to study medicine. From then on they grew apart. David joined in the wars to defeat the Corsican while John refused on the grounds that he admired him too much to fight him. But John McLoughlin certainly never used Napoleon as a model; two more unlike careers are hard to imagine.

After finishing his studies John returned to Canada, got into a petty quarrel with an officer while defending a pretty girl from military rudeness; and, to escape punishment, was forced to give up medicine and run away to relatives in the North West company. He rose rapidly and was soon in command of a post but he did not distinguish himself until after his assignment to the Columbia.[2]

1.—Charles B. Reed. *The Masters of the Wilderness*, page 150.

2.—The Nor'Westers took over Astoria in 1813. The summer following the sale of Astoria the British entered Washington and burned the capitol buildings, August 24. Four months later, the Treaty of Ghent ended the War of 1812.

In April of 1816, the Second United States bank was chartered. In 1817

McLoughlin entered his new western duties with the same vigor which characterized every act of his life. In 1825, he and James Douglas began erecting Fort Vancouver almost opposite where the Willamette empties into the Columbia. A stockade measuring 750 by 500 feet, enclosed with twenty-foot pickets, formed the main defense against attack. Inside were two courts, forty wooden houses for the men, a church, a brick powder house, stores and shops, and, in the center facing the great gates, a two-story house for the chief factor himself. Outside the palisades, were sixty more houses for unimportant employes and visitors.

Soon the total population of the fort rose to eight hundred, a significant note in the grand pathos of McLoughlin's career. He saw that he would be the instrument to change the Columbia from a great fur preserve into a settled community. He had a duty of loyalty to his company but humanity often compelled him to follow policies hostile to the fur trade. No one in all the "Great Company" knew better than he that eight hundred people could be fed and clothed and housed most efficiently if they furnished their own needs as far as possible. And no one knew better that to encourage the industries necessary for such self-support meant the end of the fur era.

— But McLoughlin was a humanitarian and paternalist so he went ahead and encouraged the planting of gardens, the promotion of home life and of domestic industries, even though these meant defeat for the company. He obeyed a higher code than that of beaver and sterling. For twenty-two years he ruled at Vancouver, each of these years bringing closer the day when the mountain fur trade south of 49° should become a thing of the past.

Seed grain was brought in 1825; cattle were purchased and

James Monroe became the fifth president. That same year William Cullen Bryant wrote "Thanatopsis," causing a little stir in cultural circles. During 1818 Great Britain and the United States agreed to extend the forty-ninth parallel from the Lake of the Woods to the Stony mountains, and to occupy Old Oregon jointly for a period of ten years, the treaty to be renewed if agreeable to both parties. On February 22, 1819, Spain ceded Florida to the United States for five million dollars.

Cotton was rapidly becoming the most important export and immigrants the most vital import. On the Mississippi river sixty or more regular steamers were in service. In 1823 President Monroe issued his famous doctrine.

In the autumn of 1824, John Quincy Adams was chosen President. The following year Clinton had the satisfaction of seeing his Big Ditch, the Erie canal, completed and open for business.

allowed to multiply.[3] The Dalles Indians came down to drive out the King George men but McLoughlin's pipers calmed them. The *Cadboro* was sent to help occupy the lower Fraser in 1827; Jedediah Smith staggered into the fort in 1828, finding a gracious welcome; a sawmill was built on the Willamette the following year.

Then bad luck came. For three years a strange fever racked the natives and McLoughlin tended them as if they were his own kin. Many died and the doctor himself was sick but he sent his clerks with quinine to do the best they could. With his own hands Peter Skene Ogden lighted the pyres and watched the flames purify and devour the diseased bodies of the dead. A rival Boston ship ran aground in 1828 and Hudson's Bay men saved the crew from massacre and pulled the ship free; poor business practice, surely, but very humane. Old traders were encouraged to settle on farms at Champoeg on the Willamette, even though the company had its own fifteen-hundred-acre farm near Vancouver. In 1832 and again in 1834, when Nathaniel Wyeth came west to drive the company out of business, the chief factor treated him as a rival until he was bankrupt, then helped him return safely to the United States.

That amazing frontiersman, Ewing Young, and the erratic Hall Jackson Kelley arrived in 1834. Though McLoughlin received them coolly because a Spanish report charged them with horse-thieving, he saw that they received food and clothes. Young long resented this attack on his good name but he took a farm in the Willamette valley, gladly benefitting from the peaceful rule of the old factor down the river. Kelley also found it easier to receive than to give, accepting passage to the Hawaiian islands on a company boat.

When the half-starved Jason Lee and Marcus Whitman missionary parties reached the Columbia, it was McLoughlin who sent them canoes loaded with relief goods. In 1841, Sir George Simpson stormed into Vancouver on his way around the world, accusing McLoughlin of losing the Willamette valley for the company by feeding and clothing the missionaries and settlers, and generally treating them like human beings. The Scotsman's blood ran

---

3.—In the earlier days of the fort he would only lend the cattle to the settlers, knowing that if he sold them the offspring might be butchered. It was imperative to build up large herds if the valley were to be self-supporting.

hot and for a second time Sir George found that he could neither frighten his subordinate nor impress him with his position. McLoughlin bluntly informed Simpson that his, McLoughlin's, acts of kindness were the dictates of a Christian conscience and that Sir George need not expect his chief factor to conduct himself otherwise. Furthermore, McLoughlin reminded him that the Treaty of Joint Occupancy gave American missionaries and settlers on the Columbia the same rights as British fur traders and governors.

Later McLoughlin found time to establish new posts until there were a dozen or more under his care. He erected flour mills, built sawmills, planted orchards, established trade with Alaska, caught and exported salmon, and introduced agricultural necessities.

With military discipline he ruled his half-breed employes, but he kept them loyal. He governed the Indians justly and wisely. He forbade the sale of liquor to the natives, allowing his own men only what he knew they could use without losing their self-control. He treated friends and foes with equal humanity and fairness, if not like cordiality. But he was repaid with ingratitude and hate. His own company accused him of treason, forcing him to resign in 1846. Americans criticized him for autocracy and ulterior motives; and, after Oregon became American territory, they refused to legalize his honest claims to personal property on the Willamette. Yet he seemed not to care greatly.

For half a lifetime McLoughlin labored to make the Oregon country a home for his fellow men. Against his judgment as a fur trader he set up all the agricultural and domestic machinery needed by a landed people. He saw trappers and adventurers settle down and become farmers and tradesmen; he witnessed excess crops being exported to an unbelieving world; and through his gates he watched pass the first missionaries, the first settlers from home, the first wagons. And finally he saw his own unlimited power yield to provisional governments, with a new flag and a new code of laws on the Columbia.

For two decades Dr. John McLoughlin poured millions into the vaults of his company, but he always knew what his superiors could never comprehend, that he was serving as the link betwen the mountain fur trade and the period of settlement. Already the dust of the buffalo trails had given way to the dust from immigrant wheels. That simple change marked the close of two great ages—McLoughlin's empire and the exploration of the Pacific Northwest.

Dr. John McLoughlin house in Oregon City. McLoughlin built the house in 1846, following his retirement from the Hudson's Bay Company. (Oregon State Highway Department)

BIBLIOGRAPHY

Bancroft, Hubert Howe. *History of the Northwest Coast.* San Francisco: A. L. Bancroft Co., 1884.
 History of Alaska. Same, 1889.
Bechdolt, Frederick Ritchie. *Giants of the Old West.* New York: Century Co., 1930.
Begg, Alexander. *History of British Columbia.* Toronto: William Briggs, 1894.
Benson, E. F. *Sir Francis Drake.* New York: Harper and Brothers, 1927.
Beniowsky, Moriz August. *Memoirs and Travels of Maurilius Augustus, Count de Benyosky.* Translated by William Nicholson. Dublin: P. Wogan, 1790.
 Same. Introduction by Captain S. Pasfield Oliver. London: K. Pavl, Trench, Trvbner and Co., 1904.
Bolitho, William. *Twelve Against the Gods.* New York: Garden City Publishing Co., 1930.
Bourne, E. G. "Travels of Jonathan Carver." *American Historical Review,* January, 1906.
Brooks, Noah. *First Across the Continent.* New York: Charles Scribner's Sons, 1915.
Bryce, George. *Remarkable History of the Hudson's Bay Company.* New York: Charles Scribner's Sons, 1910.
Burpee, Lawrence J. *On the Old Athabasca Trail.* New York: Frederick A. Stokes Co., 1927.
 The Search for the Western Sea. Toronto: The Musson Book Co., 1908.
Carver, Jonathan. *Three Years Travels Through the Interior Parts of North America.* Philadelphia: Key and Simpson, 1796.
Channing, Edward. *The Jeffersonian System.* New York: Harper and Brothers, 1906.
Chapman, Charles E. *History of California, the Spanish Period.* New York: Macmillan Co., 1921.
Chevigny, Hector. *Lord of Alaska.* Portland, Oregon: Binfords and Mort, 1951.
Chittenden, Hiram Martin. *The American Fur Trade of the Far West.* New York: F. P. Harper, 1902.
Coman, Katherine. *Economic Beginnings of the Far West.* New York: Macmillan Co., 1912.

Cook, James. *Voyages of Captain James Cook.* London: Richard Phillips, 1809.

> *The Voyages of Captain Cook Round the World.* Edited by Christopher Lloyd. London: Cresset Press, 1949.

Coues, Elliot. *History of the Expedition Under the Command of Lewis and Clark.* New York: Francis P. Harper, 1893.

Dale, Harrison Clifford. *The Ashley-Smith Explorations and the Discovery of a Central Route to the Pacific.* Cleveland: Arthur A. Clark, 1918.

Davidson, Gordon Charles. *The North West Company.* Berkeley: University of California Press, 1918.

De Voto, Bernard Augustine. *Across the Wide Missouri.* New York: Houghton, Mifflin Co., 1947.

Documents Relating to the North West Company. Edited by William Stewart Wallace. Toronto: Champlain Society, 1934.

Drake, Sir Francis. *The World Encompassed.* Boston: Old South Leaflets, 1902.

> Same. London: Argonaut Press, 1926.

Duffus, R. L. *The Santa Fe Trail.* New York: Longmans-Green and Co., 1931.

Dye, Eva E. *McLoughlin and Old Oregon.* Portland, Oregon: Binfords and Mort, 1938.

Elliott, T. C. "Peter Skene Ogden, Fur Trader." *Historical Papers and Addresses.* Portland, Oregon: Ivy Press, 1910-1932.

Fiske, John. *Discovery of America.* New York: Houghton, Mifflin Co., 1892.

Franchere, Gabriel. "Franchere's Narrative of a Voyage to the Northwest Coast" in R. G. Thwaite's *Early Western Travels.* Cleveland: A. H. Clarke Co., 1904.

Gass, Patrick. *A Journal of the Voyages and Travels of a Corps of Discovery under the Command of Captain Lewis and Captain Clarke,* 1804, 1805 & 1806. Pittsburgh: David M'Keehan, 1808.

Ghent, W. J. *The Early Far West.* New York: Longmans-Green and Co., 1931.

Godwin, George. *Vancouver, a Life.* New York: D. Appleton and Co., 1931.

Golder: F. A. *Russian Expansion on the Pacific.* Cleveland: Arthur H. Clark Co., 1914.

Goodhue, Cornelia. *Journey into the Fog; the Story of Vitus Bering and the Bering Sea.* New York: Doubleday-Doran and Co., 1944.

Gregg, Josiah. *Commerce of the Prairies.* New York: H. G. Langley, 1844.

Greenhow, Robert. *The History of Oregon and California.* Boston: C. C. Little and J. Brown, 1844.

Hallenbeck, Cleve. *Alvar Nunez de Vaca.* Glendale, California: Arthur H. Clark Co., 1940.

Haworth, Paul Leland. *Trailmakers of the Northwest.* New York: Harcourt, Brace and Co., 1921.

Hearne, Samuel. *Journey from Prince of Wales Fort on Hudson's Bay to the Northern Ocean.* Edited by J. B. Tyrrell. Toronto: Champlain Society, 1911.

Henry, Alexander. *New Light on the Early History of the Greater Northwest.* Edited by Elliot Coues. New York: F. P. Harper, 1897.

Howay, Frederic William. *The Dixon-Meares Controversy.* Toronto: Ryerson Press, 1929.

    Voyages of the "Columbia" to the Northwest Coast, 1787-1790 and 1790-1793. Boston. Massachusetts Historical Society, 1941.

Hudson's Bay Company. Toronto: Champlain Society, 1938-1949.

Hulley, Dr. Clarence C. *Alaska 1741-1953.* Portland, Oregon: Binfords and Mort, 1953.

Irving, Washington. *Astoria.* Portland, Oregon: Binfords and Mort, 1950.

Jefferson, Thomas. *Writings.* Washington: Taylor and Maury, 1853.

Johnson, William Henry. *The French Pathfinders in North America.* Boston: Little, Brown and Co., 1905.

Judson, Katherine Berry. *The British Side of the Restoration of Fort Astoria.* Portland, Oregon: Ivy Press, 1920.

Kerr, Robert F. *The Voyage of Groseillers and Radisson, 1632-1684.* Aberdeen, S. D.: News Printing Co., 1902.

Kippis, Andrew. *The Authentic and Complete Narrative of Captain Cook's Voyage Around the World.* (Originally published in England, 1788). Porter and Coates' reprint quoted here. New York: A. Knopf, 1924.

Lamb, Peter O. *The Sin of the Buffalo Skull, the Story of Jim Bridger.* New York: Frederick A. Stokes, 1932.

Larpenteur, Charles. *Forty Years a Fur Trader.* New York: Francis P. Harper, 1898.

Lauridsen, Peter. *Vitus Bering, the Discoverer of Bering Strait.* Chicago: S. C. Griggs and Co., 1898.

Laut, Agnes C. *Conquest of the Great Northwest.* New York: Outing Publishing Co., 1908.

    The Conquest of Our Western Empire. New York: Robert M. McBride and Co., 1927.

    Vikings of the Pacific. New York: Macmillan Co., 1905.

Lyman, Horace S. *History of Oregon.* New York: North Pacific Publishing Society, 1903.

McCurdy, James G. *By Juan de Fuca's Strait.* Portland, Oregon: Binfords and Mort, 1949.

McLoughlin, Dr. John. *Financial Papers of Dr. John McLoughlin*. Edited by Burt Brown Barker. Portland, Oregon: Oregon Historical Society, 1949.
    Letters of Dr. John McLoughlin Written at Fort Vancouver, 1829-1832. Edited by Burt Brown Barker. Portland, Oregon: Binfords and Mort, 1948.
    Letters from Fort Vancouver to the Governor and Committee. Toronto: Champlain Society, 1941-1944.

Mackenzie, Alexander. *Alexander Mackenzie's Voyage to the Pacific Ocean in* 1793. Chicago: R. R. Donnelly and Sons, 1931.
    Voyages From Montreal Through the Continent of North America to the Frozen and Pacific Oceans in 1789 and 1793. New York: New Amsterdam Book Co., 1902.

Meany, Edmond S. *Vancouver's Discovery of Puget Sound*. Portland, Oregon: Binfords and Mort, 1949.

Madariaga, Salvador de. *Hernan Cortes*. New York: Macmillan Co., 1941.

Meares, John. *Memorial of John Meares*. Portland, Oregon: Metropolitan Press, 1933.

Menzies, Archibald. *Menzies' Journal of Vancouver's Voyage April to October, 1792*. Edited by C. F. Newcombe. Victoria, B. C.: W. H. Cullin, 1923.

Mirsky, Jeannette. *The Westward Crossings*. New York: A. Knopf, 1946.

Montgomery, Richard Gill. *White-Headed Eagle*. New York: Macmillan Co., 1934.

Moore, Irene. *Valiant La Verendrye*. Quebec: A. Proulx, 1927.

Morton, Arthur S. *Sir George Simpson*. Portland, Oregon: Binfords and Mort, 1944.

Munford, Kenneth: *John Ledyard: an American Marco Polo*. Portland, Oregon: Binfords and Mort, 1939.

New International Encyclopedia. Second Edition. New York: Dodd, Mead and Co., 1917.

Nute, Grace Lee. *Caesars of the Wilderness*. New York: D. Appleton-Century Co., 1943.

Ober, Frederick Albion. *Hernando Cortes*. New York; Harper and Brothers, 1905.
    Vasco Nunez de Balboa. Same, 1905.

Oregon Historical Quarterly. Portland, Oregon.

Parrington, Vernon Louis. *The Romantic Revolution in America*. New York: Harcourt, Brace and Co., 1927.
    The Colonial Mind. Same, 1927.

Parrish, Philip. *Before the Covered Wagon*. Portland, Oregon: Binfords and Mort, 1931.

Paxson, Frederic Logan. *Last American Frontier*. New York: Macmillan Co., 1928.

Portlock, Nathaniel. *A Voyage Round the World*. Dublin: J. Whitworth, 1789.

Priestley,Herbert Ingram. *The Mexican Nation: a History*. New York: Macmillan Co., 1923.

Quaife, Milo M. *Journals of Captain Meriwether Lewis and Sergeant John Ordway*. Madison, Wisconsin Historical Society, 1916.

Radisson, Pierre Esprit. *Voyages*. Introduction by Gideon D. Skull. New York: Peter Smith, 1943.

Reed, Charles B. *The Masters of Wilderness*. Chicago: Chicago Historical Society, 1909.

Ross, Alexander. *Adventures of the First Settlers on the Oregon or Columbia River*. London: Smith, 1849.
    Same. Edited by M. M. Quaife. Chicago: Donnelly and Sons, 1923.

Schafer, Joseph. *A History of the Pacific Northwest*. New York: Macmillan Co., 1903.

Simons, A. M. *Social Forces in United States History*. New York: Macmillan Co., 1911.

Snowden, Clinton A. *History of Washington*. New York: Century History Co., 1909.

Spencer, Omar C. *Story of Sauvies Island*. Portland, Oregon: Binfords and Mort, 1950.

Strange, James. *James Strange's Journal and Narrative of the Commercial Expedition from Bombay to the Northwest Coast of America*. Madras: Government Press, 1928.

Strawn, Arthur. *Sails and Swords*. New York: Bretano's Publishers, 1928.

Stuart, Robert. *Discovery of the Oregon Trail*. New York: Charles Scribner's Sons, 1935.

Taylor and Maury. *Writings*. Washington: 1853.

Thompson, David. *Journals Relating to Montana and Adjacent Regions*. Edited by M. Catherine White. Missoula, Montana State University Press, 1950.
    Journals. Edited by J. B. Tyrrell. Toronto: Champlain Society, 1911.

Thwaites, Reuben Gold. *Early Western Travels*. Cleveland: Arthur H. Clark Co., 1904.
    A Brief History of Rocky Mountain Exploration. New York: D. Appleton Co., 1904.

Vancouver, George. *A Voyage to the North Pacific Ocean*, London: J. Stockdale, 1801.

Verendrye, la.*Journals and Letters of Pierre Gaultier de Varennes de la Verendrye and His Sons*. Edited by Lawrence J. Burpee. Toronto: Champlain Society, 1927.

Vestal, Stanley. *Jim Bridger, Mountain Man.* New York: Morrow and Co., 1946.

> *King of the Fur Traders.* Boston: Houghton, Mifflin Co., 1940.

Vining, Edward P. *An Inglorious Columbus; or, Evidence That Hwui Shan and a Party of Buddhist Monks from Afghanistan Discovered America in the Fifth Century A. D.* New York: D. Appleton Co., 1885.

Vinton, Stallo. *John Colter, Discoverer of Yellowstone Park.* New York: Edward Eberstadt, 1926.

Wagner, Henry Raup. *The Rise of Fernando Cortes.* Los Angeles: Cortes Society, 1944.

Walker, Sir Edmund. *Introduction to the Journals of Hearne.* Toronto: Champlain Society, 1911.

Wyeth, Nathaniel Jarvis. *The Correspondence and Journals of Captain Nathaniel J. Wyeth.* Edited by F. G. Young. Eugene, Oregon: University Press, 1899.

INDEX

A

Acadia, 51n
Acla, 17, 23-25
Acapulco, 46, 48-49, 91
Adakh island, 72-73
Adams, John, 233n
Adams, John, 78n, 368n
Adams, Point, 161
Addington, Cape, 71
Adventure (Gray), 158-159, 161
Aguilar, Martin de and R., 47, 49-50, 84, 90, 135
Aikens, 283
Aird, 257
Alarcon, Hernando de, 31
Alaska, 8-9, 59-60, 72, 74-76, 77n, 78n, 87, 91, 105, 107, 110, 111n, 116, 123-124, 131, 143, 157, 307, 307n, 370
Albany, 170, 266n
Albany (Knight), 201
Albanel, Father, 177
Albatross (Hunt), 308, 308n, 312
Alberta, 196, 330
Albermarle, 175
Aldan river, 63
Alexander islands, 71
Aleutian islands, 8-9, 91
Algerian pirates, 233n
Alien and Sedition Acts, 233n
Allegheny mountains, 236, 343
Alliance of 1778, 214n
Alneau, Father, 185
Alta California, 80, 86
Alva, Duke, 34
Alvarez, 27n
American Daily Advertiser, 214n
American Fur company, 247n, 263, 270, 276-277, 298n, 344, 358n, 359, 361-363
American Philosophical society, 236
American Revolution, 131, 152, 206, 214n, 37n
Amherst, General, 192
Amsterdam, 53, 170
Amundsen, Roald, 30
Anna, Ivanovna, 61
Ania, Anian, (See also Northwest Passage) 26-33, 38, 40, 50, 52, 56, 73, 79, 94, 110, 132, 135, 138, 167, 174, 179, 181, 193, 201, 211-212, 225n, 261
Anti-Federalists, 237
Anti-Masons, 353n

Appalachian mountains, 79n
Apraxin, Count, 54
Arapahoes, 272n
Argonaut (Meares), 115-116, 119
Arguello, Jose Dario, 91, 155n
Areche, Jose de, 91
Arikara, 246, 259, 266, 270-272, 302, 344-345, 352
Arkansas river, 272
Articles of Confederation, 125n, 214n
Armada, 34, 51
Armstrong, John, 236
Arrow lakes, 341
Ashley creek, 338
Ashley, William Henry, 342-353, 359, 363
Assiniboin Indians, 185-186, 335
Assiniboine river, 185, 193, 343
Astor and Astorians, 263, 269n, 270-271, 275-315, *Tonquin* 279-299, Hunt 300-315, 319, 329, 340, 342, 346, 352, 360-362, 367n
Astrolabe, 110
Athabasca lake, 208, 211, 215-216, 215n, 218, 221, 225, 308, 327, 331, 339-341
Atkinson, General, 349
Atoo, 159
Austin, Moses, 343n
Austrian East India company, 124
Avacha bay, 65, 68-69, 71, 73 (see Kamchatka)
Ayala, Juan de, 86
Ayllon, Lucas Vasquez de, 27
Aymes, 281
Aztecs, 7, 11, 13, 31
Azores, 14

B

Babine mountain, 333
Bacon's rebellion, 51n
Bacri, 233n
Bad Lands, 29
Baffin bay, 100, 105
Baffin land, 175
Bahia de la Ascuncion, 89
Baikal lake, 98n
Baja California, 10
Baker, Mount, 138
Baker's bay, 253
Balboa, Vasco Nunez de, 3, 14, 15-25, 27, 79
Bales, Governor, 266

Baltic, 55
Baltimore, 75, 275
Baltimore, Lord, 201n
Bancroft, Hubert Howe, 30n, 66n, 85n, 103, 103n, 108n, 109, 109n, 112, 112n, 116n, 121n, 122, 122n, 123n, 145n, 157n
Banks, Joseph, 132, 145-147
Baranof, Alexander, 76-78, 78n, 80, 143, 277, 307
Barbary pirates, 162
Barclay, Captain, 121, 124-125, 125n
Barclay sound, 88
Barkley (see Barclay)
Barnett, Mr., 119
Barrell, J., 152-153
"Barren grounds," 200, 205
Barrow, Cape, 120
Barter, Joseph, 244
Basquia, 211
Bastille, 121
Batavia, 240
Batteau, 242
Batts, Elizabeth, 93
Bayly, Governor, 177
"Bay of San Francisco," 42
Bear Lake river, 323, 354
Bear river, 348
Beauharnois, Governor, 182, 184, 188, 189n
Beaver (Sowles), 305-307, 307n, 310
Beaver (Nor'Westers), 318-319
Beaver club, 325
Beaver Head river, 250
Becerra, Diego, 27
Becknell, William, 342
Begg, Alexander, 104n, 176n
Bella Coola river, 229
Bellingham bay, 138
Bengal, 114
Benson, E. F., 34, 35, 38n, 42n
Bentick North Arm, 229
Benton, Thomas, 276
Benyowsky, Count Mauritius, 75, 75n, 211n
Bering island, 69, 70n, 75
Bering sea, 73, 105
Bering strait, 59n, 60
Bering, Vitus Ivanovich, 54, 55-73, 76, 78, 80, 83, 130, 145n, 182, 186n, 203, 222, 235, 245
Berkeley (see Barclay), 125
Berkeley, Governor, 175n
Berthold, 264
Betton, 138
Biddle, Nicholas, 258n
"Big Bellies," 247
Big Hole river, 250, 256
Big Horn mountains, 302, 345

Big Horn river, 266, 269, 346, 349
Big White, Chief, 269
Bitter Root mountains, 251, 357
Black, Arthur, 356, 356n
Black, Captain, 312-313
Blackfeet, 256, 266-269, 302, 336, 244-345, 349, 352, 359
Black hills, 242, 345
Black mountains, 259
Black sea, 55
Blackstone, 235
Blackwater river, 229
Blanco, Cape, 47
Blondeau, Maurice, 318
Bloody Falls massacre, 210
Blue mountains, 304, 357
Bodega y Quadra, Juan Francisco de la, (see Heceta), 86-92, 135, 137-141, 143-144, 161
Bodega bay, 42, 90
Bokhara, fairs, 3
Bolitho, William, 172n
Bolsheretsk, 58, 75
Bombay, 112
Bonaparte (Napoleon), 180, 213
Bonneville, Benjamin, 361
Boston, 78n, 154-159, 161-162, 173, 192-193, 193n, 194, 262, 283, 312n, 320n, 369
Boston massacre, 204
Boston ships, 30, 113
Boullard, 296
Bourbon river, 196
Bourne, E.G., 192n, 195, 195n
Boussole, 110
Bow Indians, 187
Bowman, G., 254n
Bow river, 336
Bradbury, Joseph, 301
Bratton, 244
Brazil, 38, 120
Bretton, Cape, 172
Bridger, Governor, 177
Bridger, James, 342, 345, 348, 357-359, 363
Bridger pass, 347
British Columbia, 297
Brooks, Noah, 259n
Broughton, Lieutenant, 140-141, 161
Brown, T., 152
Brule lake, 339
Bryant, William Cullen, 368n
Bryce, George, 325n
Bucareli y Ursua, Antonio Maria, 84-86, 91, 98n
Buddha, 7, 13
Bull boats, 348, 348n
Burpee, L. J., 191n, 193n, 212n, 338n
Burr, Aaron, 246, 256, 304n

C

Cabeza de Vaca, Alvar Nunez, 31
Cabinet range, 338
Cabot, John and Sebastian, 14
Cabrillo, Juan Rodriguez, 31, 33, 38n, 44, 48-49
Cache valley, 353
Cadboro, 369
Cairo, 98n
Calicut, 14
California, 9, 27, 30, 31, 32, 40, 41, 42n, 44, 46, 48, 60, 78, 80-81, 86, 140-142, 144-145, 155, 353-355, 357
California, Gulf, 27, 47
Callao de Lima, 40, 155
Cameawhait, 251
Camelford, Lord, 150
Campbell, Robert, 358n
Campion, Etienne, 317, 329
Canada, 29, 93-94
Canandaigua, 353n
Canary islands, 133
Cannibalism, 9n, 104, 207, 213n
Canoe river, 341
Canterbury, 191
Canton, 124-125, 153, 156-158, 161, 163, 232, 255n, 277, 293, 307, 320n, 327
Cape Verde islands, 14, 38, 154
Captain Cook (Strange), 112
Careta, 21, 23
Caribbean exploration, 14
Carlos III, 79-80, 91n
Carmelites, 47
Carolina, 172n, 362n
Carolinas settled, 51n
Carson City, 363
Carson, Kit, 360
Cartegena, 37
Carteret, George, 173, 175
Carteret, Philip, 174
Carver, Jonathan, 191-198, 225, 253n
Cascade mountains, 29, 293
Casper, 306
Castille, 18, 31
Catalina island, 32, 48
Catherine I, 57
Catherine II, 74, 76
Cavendish, Thomas, 38n, 45
Cawalho, Juan, 118
Celilo falls, 253
Cerros island, 33
Chagres river, 36
Champlain, Samuel, 51n, 168n, 213
Champlain society, 187n, 202n
Channing, Edward, 237n, 239n, 257, 257n
Chaplin, Lieutenant, 57
Chapman, Charles E., 32n, 46n, 48n,

91n, 98n, 141n, 155n
Champoeg, 369
Charboneau, Toussaint, 247-249, 256, 271n
Charles I (Spain), 27
Charles, King (England), 173, 177-178
Charleston, 142n, 162, 226n
Charlevois, 195
Charlottesville, 238
Charybdis, 307
Chase, Justice, 248n, 257n
Chatham (Vancouver), 132-135, 140-141
Chetka cove, 41
Chequamegon, Point, 171
Chickahominy river, 29
Chili, 39
Chipewyan, 204-205, 213n, 218-219
Chippewa river, 193
Chittenden, Hiram Martin, 266n, 268n, 269n, 270n, 273n, 298n, 302n, 305n, 307n, 311, 346n, 347n, 350, 350n, 352n, 362n, 263, 363n
Chouteau, Auguste Pierre, 268
Chouteau, Pierre, 264, 268
Chukchi, 60
Chukotski, 58
Churchill river and fort, 199-212, 317
Cibola, 31
Cimarron river, 357, 360
Cincinnati, 236, 238, 302
Clapp, Mr., 314
Clappine, Antoine, 303
Claremont, 266n
Clark, George Rogers, 236n, 237, 239
Clark, John, 239
Clark, William, 3, 57, 98n, 145n, 161-162, 181, 185n, 197, 213, 235, 261-262, 265-266, 268-269, 272-273
Clarke, John, 294, 295n, 298, 310
Clark river, 196
Clark's fork, 357
Classet, 136
Clay, Henry, 349n
Clayoquot sound, 88, 121, 126, 156-159, 160n
Clearwater river, 251-252, 255, 336
Clerke, Charles, 97, 104-108, 110, 123n
Clinton-Colden lake, 208
Clinton, DeWitt, 268n
Clive, Robert, 94
Clowy lake, 209
Clyman, James, 347
Coeur d'Alene lake, 357
Coles, John, 283
Colleton, P., 175
Colonel Allen (Hudson's Bay company), 320

Colorado, 347, 353-354, 359
Colorado river, 31, 33, 196-197
Colter, John, 266-269, 302, 346
Columbia (Hudson's Bay company),
116, 119, 320
Columbia Brigade, 323
Columbia Rediviva, 151-162
Columbia river, 78n, 89, 121, 122n,
135, 138, 140, 158, 161, 196, 197,
225n, 231-232, 232n, 250, 252-253,
253n, 256, 270, 276-279, 282, 285,
287-288, 288n, 289, 292, 297-298, 300,
302-305, 307-308, 311-312, 312n, 313-
314, 320, 333, 336-338, 340-341,
366-370
Columbus, Christopher, 4, 6, 8, 14-15,
28, 197, 248, 365
Colnett, James, 116, 119
Coman, Katherine, 170n, 186n, 187n,
233n, 255n, 256n, 321, 321n
Comanches, 360
Concomly, 287
Commander islands, 70n, 71
Commercial company, 237
"Company store" system, 326
Conception (Elisa), 126
Conception, Point, 32, 48
Confederation, Articles of, 75n, 113n
Concord battle, 86n
Connecticut, 115n, 191
Constitution, 279
Constitution, U.S., 115, 121n, 122n,
154n
Constitutional convention, 113n, 215n
Continental army, 87n
Continental Congress, 82n, 84n, 91n
Cook, James, 3, 30, 48, 59n, 91-110,
116, 122-123, 123n, 128-131, 133-134,
141, 145n, 146, 152-153, 202, 203n,
229, 236n, 248
Cook's entry, 282
Cook's inlet, 104
Cook's river, 115, 123, 123n, 126, 143
Copenhagen, 60
Copper, Coppermine, Coppermine
river, 119-212, 317
Copper Indians, 209
Cordillo, Francisco, 27n
Coronado, Francisco Vasquez, 31, 81
Corsica, 180
Cortereal, Anis, 28
Cortereal, Gasper, 14
Cortez, Hernando, 3, 25-28, 31, 79, 150
Cotton gin, 143n
Council of Constance, 4
Council of Indies, 29, 47
"Country of Marked Bodies," 9
Court-martials, 244
Cowlitz river, 288

Cox, Mr. (North West company), 313
Cox, the Owyhee, 297
Craven, 175
Crees, 169, 171, 183
Creoles, 262
"Critical Period," 319n
Croix, Viceroy, 80
Crooks, Ramsay, 271, 301-305, 314n,
362
"Cross of the Order of St. Louis," 188-
189
Crow Indians, 187, 266-267, 301-303,
306, 345, 349, 362
Crusatte, 256
Cruys, Admiral, 55
Cuba, 26
Culfitch, C., 152
Cumberland house, 211, 317, 329,
335n, 336
Cumberland lake, 317
Currey, Thomas (Corry), 317

D

D'Avaugour, Governor, 171
Daedalus, 138, 142
Da Gama, Vasco, 14
Dakota and Dakotas, 185, 186-187, 242,
329, 343
Dalles, 253, 305-306, 340, 369
Darby, J., 152
Darien, 20, 22-23
Dauphin river, 335
Davidson, Gordon Charles, 320, 320n,
325n, 327n, 329n, 330n, 335n
Davila, Pedrarias, 22-25
Day, John, 305-306, 314
Deception bay, 121, 159
Deception pass, 126
Declaration of Independence, 98n, 263
Declaration of Rights, 171n
Dementieff, Abraham, 72
Dent, Mr., 264
De Noyelles, 188
Deschutes river, 253
Destruction island, 87, 125-126
Detering, Henry, 275
Detroit, 214, 238
Devonshire, 37, 97, 131n
Dias, Bartolomeu, 14
Digges island, 175
Diomede island, 59
Disappointment bay, 140
Disappointment cape, 135-136, 161
Discovery (Cook), 97-99, 104-108, 130
Discovery (Knight), 201
Discovery, Port, 126, 138
Discovery (Vancouver), 128-150
Divers Voyages, 28

Dixon entrance, 83, 118
Dixon, George, 91, 123-124, 125n, 157, 163
Dogrib Indians, 217-218
Don river, 263
Donaldson, Mr., 233n
Dorion, Pierre, 245
Dorion, Pierre, Jr., 270, 301-302, 304
Dorsetshire, 202
Drake's bay, 42, 49
Drake, Francis, 3, 29, 34-43, 83, 93, 96-98, 131n, 139, 141, 150, 172, 181, 213
Drake, John, 42n
Drewyer, George, 260-261, 266, 268
Doughty, mutiny of, 38-39
Douglas, James, 366, 368
Douglas, William, 114-118, 121, 156
Dubois river, 241
Duncan, Captain, 157
Duffin, Mr., 121
Duffus, R. L., 272n, 253n, 360n
Duluth, 196
Dupliex, Joseph Francois, 94
Durham, 92
Dutch harbor, 104

E

Eaglet (Stannard), 173-175
East Indies, 40, 55
East India company, 53, 94, 108-109, 112, 119, 231, 320n
Edgecombe, Mount, (Mount Jacinto), 90, 104
Edinburgh, 145
Edmonton, 330
Eisleben, 180
Elgin, 269
Elk river, 193
Elisa, Francisco, 126
Elizabeth I, 3, 34, 38, 41, 42
Elizabethides, 39
Embargo Acts, 268n
Empress of China, 153
Encisco, Martin Fernandez de, 16-18, 22
Enforcement Act, 1809, 268n
English Chief, 215, 217-220, 226
Erie canal, 368n
Erie, Lake, 273n
Eskimos, 104
Eskimo massacre, 210
Essex, 257n
Experiment (Strange), 112
Exploration, motives, 3, 5

F

Fairweather, Mount, 104

Falkland islands, 154, 280
Falmouth, 132-133
Farallones, 42, 84
Farewell address, 233n
Fargo, 196
Farnham, Mr., 314
Federalists, 233n, 235, 239, 241, 257n
Federalism, 162
Federoff, Ivan, 60
Felice (Meares), 114-115, 121-122
Ferdinand of Aragon, 4, 14, 18, 20
Fernandez, Juan, 14
Ferrelo, Bartolome, 31-33, 44, 49
Fidalgo, Salvador, 126-127
Fields, Reuben, 256n
"Fifty-four forty or fight," 85
Finlay, James, 317, 317n, 330
Finlay river, 227, 330
Fiske, John, 4n, 16n, 22, 22n, 25
Fitzpatrick, Thomas, 343, 345-347, 352, 358-362
Flame, 131
Flathead Indians and lake, 298, 348, 353
Flattery, Cape, 9, 103, 125-126, 135
Florez, Viceroy, 116-117, 126
Florida, 14, 27n, 51n, 182n, 235, 305n
Florida Cession, 268n
Flour mills, 370
Floyd, Sergeant, 243n, 246
Fort Atkinson, 244, 347
Fort Augustus, 336, 338
Fort Boise, 363n
Fort Bourbon, 224, 317
Fort Charles, 175, 177, 183
Fort Chipewyan, 215, 217, 222, 225, 233, 327
Fort Churchill, 334
Fort Clark, 247n
Fort Defiance, 158-159
Fort Dusquesne, 213n
Fort Fraser, 331, 333
Fort George (Astoria), 313, 336
Fort George (Saskatchewan), 330
Fort Good Hope, 323
Fort Greenville, 239
Fort Hall, 363n
Fort Henry, 269, 303, 306, 357
Fort Kiowa, 344-345
Fort Kootenay, 337-338
Fort La Riene, 185-186
Fort La Traite, 317
Fort Lisa, 264, 272
Fort Mandan, 242, 247, 247n, 269
Fort Manuel, 272
Fort Maurepass, 185
Fort McLeod, 330
Fort Orange, 170

Fort Osage, 342
Fort Prince of Wales, 199-212
Fort St. James, 331
Fort St. Pierre, 183-184
Fort Sutter, 363
Fort Union, 358n
Fort Vancouver, 356, 356n, 368-369
Fort Wayne, 238
Fort William, 320, 322-324, 336, 341
Fonesca, Bishop, 22
Fonte, Bartholomew de, 29
Forsyth-Richardson and company, 319
Fortuna, 58
Foulweather, Cape, 103
Fox island, 74
Box, Mr., 282-283
Fox river, 192
Fraeb, Henry, 358-360
Franciscans, 46
Franklin, Benjamin, 95n, 99
Franchere, Gabriel, 271, 279-283, 279n, 288-289, 298, 304, 307, 312-313
Fraser, Private, 243n
Fraser lake, 331
Fraser river, 136, 138, 228-229, 232n, 296, 331, 369
Fraser, Simon, 296, 330-333
Frederick the Great, 134
French and Indian war, 152
French revolution, 120-121, 236, 365
Friendly cove, 103-105
Friendly village, 229
Frobisher, Benjamin, 318
Frobisher, James, 317-318
Frobisher, Thomas, 317-318
Fuca, Juan de, 29, 121
Fuca, Juan da, strait, 84, 87-89, 103, 124, 126-127, 136-137, 139, 158-159, 160n
Fuggers, The, 275
Fulton, Robert, 266n, 331
Funter, Captain, 118-119
Fu-Sang, 9-10

G

Gabriel, 58-59
Gage, General, 193n
Gali, Francisco de, 39n, 44
Galileo, 365
Gallatin, Albert, 258n
Gallatin river, 249
Galvaez, 193n
Galvez, Jose de, 80-81
Gama, Jnan de, 65
Gamaland, 65
Garavito, 24
Gass, Patrick, 243n, 246

Genet, "Citizen," 142n, 226n, 233n, 237
George III, 90n, 212n
Georgia, 51n, 199n, 257n
Georgia, Gulf of, 126, 137
Georgia settled, 51n, 60n, 115n
Georgian bay, 170n
Gervais, Jean Baptiste, 358-359
Ghent, W. J., 264n, 269n, 270n, 375n, 306n, 312n, 343n, 346n, 352n
Gibraltar, 3
Gibert, Humphrey, 38n, 44n
Gillam, Captain, 173, 175, 177
Gillam, Junior, 177
Gjoa, 30
Glass, Hugh, 343
Godwin, George, 128, 128n, 131n, 137, 173n, 138n
Golden Hind, 39-42
Golder, F. A., 70n, 72n, 73n
Gollikof, Ivan, 75
Gomez, 14
Gomez de Corban, Toribio, 47-48
Gonner, Father, 181
Gonzales, Don Blas, 155
Good Hope, Cape of, 14, 42, 97, 100-101, 111, 240
Gooseberry, Mr., 174-175
Gore, Lieutenant, 107
Grand Captain of the South, 39
Grand canal, 263
"Grand perch," 322
Grand Rapids, 328
Grande Portage, 183, 317-318, 327, 331, 335-336
Grande Ronde, 304-305, 357
Grant, C., 330
Grasse, Count de, 131
Gravesend, 175, 366
Gray, Robert, 3, 116, 127-128, 136, 140, 143, 151-163, 225n
Gray's Harbor, 159-160
Great Ayton, 92
Great Basin, 357
Great Bear Lake river, 218, 221
Great Falls, 249, 256
"Great Han Country," 9, 10
Great lakes, 11, 170, 174, 181, 182, 214, 223n, 262, 277, 314n, 320n, 328
Great Salt lake, 348 (Grand L.), 351-354
Great Slave lake, 211, 215, 330
Greeley, 347
Green, 347
Green bay, 192
Greenland, 3, 104
Green river, 196, 303, 306, 345-346, 352, 359
Greenhow, Robert, 77n
Greenwich hospital, 95

Gregg, Josiah, 360n
Gregory, John, 214
Gregory-McLeod and company, 214, 318n
Grenville, Point, 87, 136
Grey Coat school, 335n
Grijalva, Hernando de, 27
Groseilliers, Sieur des, 94, 167, 168-179, 365
Grosventres, 247, 258, 266, 361, 361n
Grotius, Hugo, 45
Guatulco, 41, 42n
Guerriere, 306n
Guiana, 14
Guinea, 197
Guion, Captain, 238
Gvosdeff, Michael, 60, 72

H

Hakluyt, Richard, 28
Halsey, Mr., 314
Hamilton, Alexander, 127n, 158n, 237, 246, 256, 257n
Hanna, James, 109-110, 112, 123
Hancock, Cape, 161
Hancock, John, 158
Harmar, General, 236
Harmon, D. W., 333
Haro canal, 126
Haro, Gonzalo, 116
Harper's Ferry, 240
Harrison, William H., 271n, 299n
Harvard college, 51n
Haswell, Robert, 153, 157, 159, 161
Hawaii and Hawaiians, 158, 282, 305, 307-308, 369
Hawkins, John, 35, 97
Haworth, Paul Leland, 171n, 187n, 207n, 331, 331n
Hayes, J., 175
Hearne, Samuel, 50, 198-212, 215, 217, 219n, 221, 223, 225n, 317, 317n, 334, 365
Hebrides islands, 213
Heceta, Bruno (see Bodega), 86-92, 125, 160
Helena, 196
Hell's gulch, 363
Henry IV, 4
Henry, Alexander (elder), 193n
Henry, Alexander (younger), 312, 317, 329, 330n, 339
Henry, Major Andrew, Sr., 269-270, 272, 342-347, 353
Henry fork, 347-348
Henry lake, 269
"Henry Letters," 272n
Henry, Nebraska, 306

Henry, Prince of Portugal, 4, 14
Henry, William, 339
Hennepin, Louis, 5, 195
Hill, Captain, 255n
Hoback river, 303
Hodgenville, 180
Hoh river, 125
Honesdale, 357n
Hood canal, 138
Hood, Mount, 288
Hood, Samuel, 202
Horn, Cape, 40-41, 131, 145, 154, 156
Horse Indians, 187
Horsens, 55
Howse, Joseph, 338n
Howse pass, 337-339
Hudson bay, 51n, 100, 105, 168, 171, 173, 175-178, 181n, 199-212, 231, 262, 277, 319, 325-326
Budson Bay company, 30, 51n, 94, 122, 168, 176, 178-180, 199-212, 233, 242, 263, 313-314, 318, 320, 320n, 321, 323, 327, 330, 333-336, 337n, 338 356-357, 359, 363n, 364-365, 368-370
Hudson, Henry, 51n
Hudson strait, 175-176
Huelva, 45
Huguenots, 51n
Humboldt, Alex von, 6
Hunt, Wilson Price, (see also Astor), 161, 269n, 270-272, 295n, 297, 298n, 300-315, 343
Huss, Jon, 4
Hutchinson, Anne, 4
Hwui Shan, 7-13, 65
"Hyperborean Sea," 219-220

I

Iberville, Pierre le Moyne d', 178
Idaho, 269, 273, 297, 304, 306
Ilimsk, 57
Imperial Eagle, 124-125
Importation act, 257n
Imprisonment for debt, 335n
Incas, 25, 45
India, 114
Indies, 15, 35, 108
Independence rock, 347
Industrial revolution, 100
Iphegenia, 114-118, 121
Inquisition, 79
Inter-colonial wars, 51n, 79n, 201
Inverness-shire, 234
Iowa, 246
Irkutsk, 57
Iroquois, 98n, 169, 170n, 292, 340
Irving, Washington, 268n, 314
Isaac Todd, 320

Isabella, 4, 14
Isla de Dolores, (see Destruction)
Isles of France, 240
Ismyloff, 105
Ivan the Terrible, 53

J

Jacinto, Mount, (see Edgecumbe)
Jackson, Andrew, 356n
Jackson, David E., 343, 350, 359
Jackson hole, 267, 306
Jamestown, 11, 27n, 30n, 51n
Jay's Treaty, 113n, 233n, 319n
Jefferson, Mount, 288
Jefferson river, 249-250
Jeffersonians, 233n
Jefferson, Thomas, 98n, 154n, 162, 193, 233, 235-240, 239n, 243, 244n, 249, 257n, 262
Jersey, 51n
"Jesso," 9
Jesuits, 170n
John Day river, 253
Johnson, William Henry, 169n, 170n, 171n
Joliet, Louis, 5
Jones, John Paul, 110
Juan Fernandez islands, 154-155, 280
Juno, 78n

K

Kalm, Peter, 188n
Kamchatka, 7-8, 53-59, 61, 65-66, 68-69, 71, 73-75, 77, 107, 111, 114
Kaministikwia river, 329
Karakakooa, 158
Kaskaskia, 241, 266
Kayak island (Kayes), 66-67, 71, 73, 104
Keelboat, 242
Keelshies, Captain, 209
Kelly, Hall J., 369
Kendrick, John, 116, 151-162
Kent, 34
Kentucky, 237, 239, 241
Kerr, Robert F., 170n
Kettle falls, 340
Khiva, 3, 263, 348
Kine-pox, 240
King's island, 230
King George, 123
King George men, 369
King George's Sound company, 123
King George's war, 51n
King's Lynn, 128, 131n
King Phillip's war, 51n
King William's war, 51n

Kippis, Andrew, 102, 102n, 103, 103n, 106
Knife river, 247, 269
Knight, James, 201
Knistenaux, 223
Knox, General, 236
Kodiak island, 72, 75-76, 91
Kooskooskee, 252
Kootenae Appee, 336-337
Kootenay falls, 338
Kootenay Indians, 337
Kootenay river and lake, 338
Koumiss, 11
Krenitzin, Captain, 74-75
Krupischef, 60
Kullyspell, 338
Kurds, 54
Kurile islands, 8

L

Labadie, Sylvester, 269
Labrador, 14, 29, 93
La Charette, 245
Lachine, 324, 366
La Corne (Nipawee), 317
Ladrone islands, 75
Lady Washington, 153-162
Lafayette, 346n
La Gabelle, 180
La Galissonierre, Governor, 189n
Lahontan, 195
Laird river, 227
La Jonquiere, Governor, 190
Lake of the Woods, 183, 185, 193, 317
La Liberty, 244
Langle, M. de, 110-111
La Paz bay, 27, 46
Lapensee, Basil, 282
Lapensee, Ignace, 282
La Perouse, de, 110-111,116
La Pierre, Joseph, 281n
Laramie river, 358n, 360
Lark, 307-308, 314
La Rochelle, 170
Larpenteur, Charles, 350n
La Salle, Robert de, 5, 170, 178n
Last Chance, 363
Lauridsen, Peter, 56n, 60n, 64n, 66, 66n, 96n
Laut, Agnes C., 53n, 72n, 135n, 140n, 170n, 171n, 178n, 201n
Leavenworth, Colonel, 344
Le Clerc, 306
Ledyard, John, 98n, 110, 152-153, 236, 236n

Lee, Jason, 4, 369
Lemhi river, 250-251
Lena river, 63-64
Leoncico, 16
Le Roux, M., 215-216, 222, 330
Lesser Slave lake, 335
Levachef, Captain, 74-75
Lewis and Clark, 266-267, 298, 301-302, 314, 329n, 343
Lewis, Mr. (*Tonquin*), 290
Lewis, Meriwether, 3, 57, 98n, 145n, 161-162, 181, 185n, 197, 213, 235-262, 266
Lewis, Reuben, 269
Lewis river, 250
Lexington, battle of, 86n
Lexington, (Missouri,), 352
Li, 10, 12
Liguest, Pierre Laclede, 262
Lincoln, Abraham, 180
Lindbergh, Charles, 4
Lisa, Manuel, 161, 263-274, 276, 301, 301n, 302, 342-343, 346
Literary History of the American Revolution, 192
Little Belt, 282n
Little Big Horn river, 272
"Little Company," 214
"Little Lion," 16, 20
Llama, 7
Lobscheid, Reverend W., 6
Logan, Mount, 29
Lok, Michael, 29
Lolo pass, 251
London, 29, 51n, 143, 172, 174, 178, 195n, 211, 233, 275
London company, 51n
Longeuil, 341n
Long Island, 51n, 98n
Lopez, 155
Louis, King, 110, 177-178, 184, 188
Louisiana, 162, 235, 237, 237n, 239-241, 258, 305n, 319n, 342
Louisville, 236, 239
Lovell, John, 35
Luther, Martin, 180
Luzon, 75
Lydia, 255n
Lyddell, William, 177

M

Macao, 44, 75, 108-109, 115, 118, 122, 158

Mackenzie, Alexander, 9, 57, 176, 181, 197, 213-234, 240, 245, 255, 265, 288n, 296, 318n, 319-320, 324n, 325, 329-331, 333-334, 341, 357
Mackenzie, Geddes, 234
Mackenzie river, 196-197, 215, 217, 323
Macon's bill number two, 269n
Madagascar, 75
Madison, James, 233n, 268n
Madison river, 249, 269
Madrid, 81, 144
Magellan, Fernando, 16, 27n, 28, 83
Magellan, Straits of, 28, 39, 154
Maine, 273n
Majors, Alexander, 351
Malaba, 197
Malay, 3
Maldonado, Lorenzo, 29
Malplaquet, Battle of, 180
"Maltechusets," 30
Mandan, 185, 185n, 186-188, 242-243, 245-247, 256, 266, 269, 271-272, 335
Manhattan, 51n, 170
"Manifest Destiny," 235
Manilla and trade, 40-41, 44-45, 47-48, 50, 81, 83-84
Manito legend, 218
Maquilla, 115
Marble island, 201
Margaret Dollar, 9
Marias river, 249, 256, 257n
Marietta, 113n
Maritime fur trade, 74-75
Marina, 26
Marquette, Jacques, 5, 170
Marshall, John, 233n, 257n
Martin, 131
Martin, John, 262
Martinez, pilot, 84
Martinez, Don Stephen Joseph, 115-121, 157
Marton, 92
Maryland, 51n, 75, 115n, 201n
Maryland Toleration Act, 168n
Massachusetts, 51n, 115n, 153, 158, 171n, 193n
Matchedash bay, 170n
Mather, Cotton, 51n
Matonabbee, 206-212, 217
Maurepas, 183-184, 189
Maxent, Laclede and company, 262
Maya, 63
Mazatlan, 49
MacPherson, John, 114-115
McClellan, Robert, 271, 301-302, 305, 313
McCracken, Hugh, 246

McDonald, Finan, 338
McDougal, Duncan, (McDougall), 279, 282, 292, 298, 298n, 308, 310, 312-313, 313n
McDougal, James, 330
McGill, James, 318
McGillis, Hugh, 335
McGillivray, Duncan, 336n
McGillivray, Simon, 320
McKay, Alexander, 226, 228, 234, 279, 279n, 282, 288, 288n, 289-291
McKenzie, Donald, 297, 298n, 300-301, 305, 310-313
McLean, 366
McLeod lake, 330-331
McLoughlin, David, 367
McLoughlin, John, 3, 97, 320, 356-357, 365-371
McMillan, James, 333
McTavish, J. G., 308, 308n, 312
McTavish, Simon, 318-319, 323
Meat rations, 324
Meares, John, 91, 113-124, 131, 139, 156, 160, 163
Medici, 94, 275
Medicine Bow mountains, 347
Medicine Hat, 196
Medway river, 34-35
Mellon, Andrew, 275
Menard, Pierre, 266, 268
Mendocino, 44, 49, 88, 134-135, 155
Mendoza, Diego Hurtado de, 27, 44
Menendez de Aviles, Pedro, 29
Menzies, Cape, 230
Menzies, Archibald, 132, 136, 145-148
Mercator, 8
Mesaiger, Father, 183
Michaux, Andre, 236-237, 237n
Michigan, Lake, 192
Michilimackinac, 170n, 183, 192-193, 300
Middle Kingdom, 10-11
"Middle pasage," 152
Miller, Joseph, 301, 306
Minnetarees, 249, 256-257
Minnesota, 196
Minnesota river, 193
Misaki, 9
Missionaries in Orient, 4
Mississippi river and country, 27n, 125, 162, 170, 178n, 193-194, 196-197, 233n, 236, 238, 241, 250n, 262, 270, 276, 304n, 335
Missouri river and country, 181, 186, 171, 188, 196-197, 236, 240, 242-243, 246, 248-261, 265-276, 273n, 301-302, 306, 320n, 335, 337, 342-346, 349-350, 352, 358n
Missouri Compromise, 273n

Missouri Fur company, 263, 268, 272-274, 345, 359-364
Mobile, 27n, 180n
Mojave, 354
Mongols, 4
Montana, 196-197, 273, 338, 348, 352, 357, 359
Monterey, 48, 81-82, 84, 86, 88-91, 111, 126, 141, 145, 355
Monterey, Count, 46-47
Monthly Miscellany, 29
Montreal, 168n, 171-172, 182-185, 187, 189-190, 192, 214, 231, 233, 292, 300, 310, 318, 320, 323-326, 328, 341n, 366
Monroe, James, 314n, 368n
Morgan, J. P., 275
"Morgan Killers," 353n
Morgan, William, 353n
Morris, Robert, 275
Morrison, William, 266, 268-269
Moslems, 4
Mountain fur trade, 262-263
Mulberry Hill, 239
"Murderers' Harbor," 155
Muzon, Cape, 83

N

Nadeau, Joseph, 282
"Nampumpeage," 174
Nantucket, 154
Napoleon, 268n, 269n, 367
Napoleonic wars, 367
Narvaez, Panfilo de, 26
Navidad, 31, 34, 49
Navigation Ordinances, 51n
Neah bay, 126-128
Negro slavery, 51n
Nelson river, 196-197
Nepean, Mr., 148-149
Neuman, Karl F., 7
Nevada, 354
New Albion, 97-98
New Amsterdam, 168n
New Archangel, 76
New Caledonia, 130, 331, 333
Newell, Gordon R., 9
New Dungeness, 138
New England, 43n, 98n, 143n
New England Confederation, 51n, 65n
Newfoundland, 14, 51n, 39n, 44n, 93, 174, 327
New Hampshire, 115n
New Hebrides, 130
New International Encyclopedia, 19n, 195n
New Jersey, 175
Newman, John, 244-245

New Mexico, 30
New North West company, 319
New Orleans, 201n, 237, 250, 262, 264, 264n
New South Wales, 141
Newtee (Newity), 289
New Universal Traveler, 192
New Westminster, 333
New York, 122n, 157n, 191, 275, 279, 288, 300, 307n, 311n, 314, 353, 357n, 358n, 362
New Zealand, 95, 97, 101, 111, 130, 134
Nez Perce, 251-252
Nicuesa, Diego de, 19
Niobrara river, 271
Nipawee, 317
Nipigon lake, 181-182
Nizhni-Novgorod, 348
Nodaway, 301, 310
Nombre de Dios, 36-37
Non-Intercourse Act, 268n
Nonsuch (Gillam), 174-175
Nootka, 84, 88, 103-104, 109, 112-113, 115-117, 119-123, 123n, 124, 126-127, 131, 133, 135, 137-140, 142, 144, 153-154, 156-157, 160n, 161, 163, 289
Nootka (Meares), 114, 117
Nordenskjold, 60n
Norfolk, 128
Norfolk sound, 124
Norsemen, 3, 4, 6
"North canoes," 323
North cape, 82
North Dakota, 196, 242
Northern Indians, 204, 207
North Riding, 92
Northwest America, 115-119, 156
North West company, 215, 231, 242, 246, 263, 278, 287-288, 292, 298, 308-309, 311-313, 313n, 314, 316-333; Organization, 317-321; Trade methods, 322-328; Explorers, 329-333, 334-342, 365-367, 367n
Northwest Ordinance, 125n, 215n
Northwest Passage, 30, 52, 100, 138, 167, 201-212, 204n, 209, 211, 215, 220
Norton, Moses, 199-212
Norton, Richard, 199
Nova Scotia, 173, 327
Nullification, 362n
Nuttall, Thomas, 301

O

Oajaca, 41
Oak point, 308n
Ob river, 73
Ochagach, 181

Ogden, Peter Skene, 348, 359, 369
Oglethorpe, James, 51n, 60n, 199n
Ohio company, 113n
Ohio river, 79n, 125n, 241
Ojeda, Alonso de, 14, 16, 18-19
Okanogan legends, 293
Okanogan river and fort, 293-294,
Okanogan river and fort, 293-294, 295n, 296-297, 305, 314
Okhotsk, 57-58, 63-64, 74-75
"Old Establishment," 225
"Old Ironsides," 306n
Old Oregon, 122n, 136, 162
"Old Regime," 236
"Olive Branch Petition," 90n
Olympus, Mount, 84, 121
Omaha, 271-272
Ordinance of 1787, 113n
Ordway, Sergeant, 243n, 243-246, 251, 253-254
Oregon, 34, 42, 49-50, 103, 134, 160, 196-197, 196n, 268, 304, 354n, 355, 364, 370
Oregon Historical Quarterly, 317n
Orient, trade with, 6
Oriental culture, 6-7
Orleans island, 93
Osage Indians, 264
Ostend, 124
Otaheite, 97
Ottawa river, 170n
Our Lady of the Conception, 40
Oviedo y Valdez, Gonzalo Fernandez de, 22
Oxford, 173
Owyhees, 148, 284-285

P

Pacific Fur company, 263, 269n, 276-279, 309, 312, 314
Pack, sizes of, 324
Palliser, Hugh, 93, 96-98
Palouse river, 357
Panama, 21, 28, 36, 50
Panama Congress, 349n
Paris, 99, 111
Park City, 347
Parker, Daniel, 153
Parrington, Vernon Louis, 236n, 275n, 276n
Pasha, 36
Parsnip river, 227, 330
Passy, 99
Paul I, 76
Pawnees, 259, 347
Pawtucket, 143, 233n
Paxson, F. L., 364n
Peace river, 225-228, 230, 232n, 330

Pearls, 18, 21, 26-27, 31, 46-47
Pedlar, 314
Pequot war, 51n
Pelican, 39
Penalosa, Diego de, 30
Pend d'Oreille, 338, 357
Penn, William, 51n, 178n
Perez, Juan, 80-88, 90-92
Perpetua, Cape, 103
Perouse, Comte de, 110-111,116
Perrault, 281
Perry, Mathew C., 51
Perry, Oliver, 273n
Perthshire, 145
Peter the Great, 53-57, 59, 61, 64, 235
Petersham, 128, 150
Petropavlovsk, 65, 107
Philadelphia, 84n, 113n, 154n, 178n, 237, 240, 255n, 258, 275, 275n
Philippines, 40, 44, 44n, 45
Piegans, 336-338
Pierre's hole, 267, 357, 361, 361n
Pierre, S. D., 188
Pigeon river, 193
Pike lake, 208
Pike, Zebulon, 237n, 250n, 257, 272n
Pilcher, John, 273-274, 344-345
Pilgrims, 5, 51n
Pinckney Treaty, 113n
Pin portage, 327
Pinch, Lieutenant, 270
Pinos, Point, 82
Pissarjeff, 64
Pirogue, 242, 289
Pitt, William, 150
Pittsburgh, 238, 241
Pizarro, Francisco, 24-25, 27n
Plains of Abraham, 192
Plata river, 39, 42n
Platte river, 237, 246, 246n, 306, 344, 347
Plymouth, 36-38, 98
Pocahontas, 29
Pocatello, 306
Point George, 285
Polo, Marco, 8, 28, 191
Ponca, 21
Ponce de Leon, Juan, 14
Pond, Peter, 317, 330
Popo Agie, 345-346
Popoff, the Cossack, 56
"Pork-eaters," 322
Portage la Prairie, 329
Port Cox, (see Clayoquot)
Port Conclusion, 143
Port de Francais, 110
Portland canal, 142
Portlock, Nathaniel, 123-124, 125n, 163
Port Nelson, 231

Port Royal, 44n, 173
Port Townsend, 9, 138
Porto Bello, 43
Portola, Gaspar de, 203n
Portmouth, 147
Potts, John, 266-267
Powder river, 359-360
Prairie du Chien, 193
Preble, Commander, 162, 242n
President, 282n
Priestly, Herbert Ingram, 46n
Prince of Wales (Colnett), 116
Prince of Wales, Cape, 105
Prince of Wales island, 83
Prince William sound, 75, 104, 114-115, 124, 126
Princesa Real (Quimper), 126
Princess Royal (Meares), 119
Princessa (Martinez), 157
Printing press, 183n
Protection island, 138
Providence, 168, 168n
Provost, C. J., 21
Provost, Etienne, 342, 347n
Puget, Lieutenant, 136, 159
Puget sound, 91, 103, 136-138
Purchas, His Pilgrims, 29
Puritans, 152
Pryor, Sergeant, 243n

Q

Quadra, (see Bodega y Quadra)
Quaife, Milo M., 244n
Quakers, 51n, 178n
Quebec, 93-94, 177, 180, 189, 201, 327, 341
Queen Charlotte, 123-124
Queen Charlotte islands, 82-84, 110, 123, 157, 159, 161
Quesnel, 331
Quevedo, Juan de, 23
Quimper, Alferez Manuel, 126

R

Racoon, 312
Radisson, Pierre Esprit, 94, 167, 168-180, 190, 365
Rainy lake, 183, 193, 338
Raleigh, Walter, 3, 38n, 44n, 97, 197
Ramboullet decree, 269n
Randolph, John, 349n
Rainier, Mount, 138
Rattlesnake legend, 198
Red Knife, 217
Red lake, 335
Red river, 196, 320, 329, 335
Red River of the North, 333n

Red Deer river, 336
Reduccions, 111, 157
Reed, Charles, B., 367n
Reed, John, 305
Reed, Moses B., 244
Religious liberty, 79n, 168n
Renaissance, 3-4, 14
Representative government, 51n
Resanoff, Nikolai Petrovich, 77n, 78n
Resolution (Cook), 97-99, 107-108, 129-130
Revilla, Gigedo Conde de, 117, 119, 126
Rhode Island, 51n, 78n, 126n, 143n, 152, 168, 168n, 183n
"Rica de Oro," 50-51
"Rica de Plata, 50-51
Rio de la Hacha, 35-36
Rio Grande, 121
"River of the West," 196
Riviere de Loup, 367
Riviere Terre Blanche, 329
Roanoke, 38n, 44n
Robertson, Mr., 327
Robbins, Abigail, 191
Rocky Mountain, 343-344
Rocky mountains, 29, 58, 187, 197, 226-227, 231, 233, 242, 255, 270, 276, 297, 330, 332, 336-337, 339, 342, 352, 356-357, 365
Rocky Mountain Fur company, 342, 358
Rocky Mountain house, 329, 336, 339
Rocky Mountain men, 342-358
Rodney, George B., 131, 134
Rogers, George, 192
Rogue river, 33, 50
Romanzoff, Count, 78n
Rome, 3
Rose, Ed, 301-302, 343, 345
Ross, Alexander, 277, 279, 279n, 280-281, 281n, 283, 285, 288n, 292-298, 300, 304, 311n, 312--314
Royal Society, 95
Rupert's Land, 176
Rupert, Prince, 173, 175
Rupert river, 175
"Rushes pills," 252
Russian American company, 76-78, 91, 163
Russians in North Pacific, 74-78, 80
Russian revolution, 365
Ryo Yei Maru, 9

S

Sacajawea, 248-249, 251, 251n, 254, 256, 271n

Sacramento, 355
Sahara, 3
Saints, Battle of, 131, 145
St. Anthony falls, 193
St. Charles, 242
St. Clair, General, 127n
St. Crois, 51n
St. Croix river, 193
St. Elias, Mount, 29, 66, 104, 110
St. Francis of Assisi, 25
St. Gabriel street, 324
Ste. Genevieve, 342
St. Helena, 145, 147
St, Helens, Mount, 288
St. Julian, 38-39
St. Joseph, 301, 323
St. Lawrence island, 58
St. Lawrence river, 11, 79n, 93, 168, 182n, 196-197, 367
St. Louis, 237, 241-242, 245-248, 255, 257-258, 257n, 262-264, 298n, 301-302, 306, 314, 314n, 342-343, 345-347, 349-350, 352-353, 357n, 359, 362
St. Louis river, 335
St. Malo, 168
St. Patrick bay (St. Joseph), 109
St. Paul, 65, 71-73, 75
St. Peter, 65-68, 70-71, 74-75
St. Petersburg, 53, 56-64, 68, 71, 76, 142
St. Roc, (see Columbia river)
Saleesh house, 338
Salt Lake valley, 347n
Salvatierre, 17
Samarkand, 3, 263
Samwell, Mr., 106
San Blas, 26, 81-82, 84, 86, 90-91, 116, 119, 126-127, 157
San Carlos, 86, 126
San Diego, 47-49
San Diego, 27, 32, 48, 80-82, 203, 353, 355
San Domingo, 16-17
Sand Lake river, 335
Sandwich, Earl of, 95, 97, 102
Sandwich islands, 102-103, 105, 109-110, 113, 115-116, 118, 123, 130, 134, 138, 140, 140n, 141-142, 156-157, 281,
San Gabriel, 355
San Francisco, 32, 42, 50, 80, 82, 89, 115, 139, 141, 155, 155n, 203n, 355
San Jose, 355
San Juan de Ulua, 36
San Lorenzo, (see Nootka)
San Miguel, 21-22, 27
San Miguel islands, 32-33
San Pedro, 32
San Quentin, 31
San Salvador Vitoria, 32

San Sebastian, 14, 16
Santa Ana, 45
Santa Ana, Pedro, 88
Santa Barbara islands, 82
Santa Cruz, 27
Santa Fe, 30, 30n, 262, 272n, 273, 342, 348, 350, 357, 359-360, 360n
Santa Maria, 21
Santa Monica, 32
Santiago, 81-84, 86-87, 89-90
Santo Tomas, 47
Saratoga, 214n
Saskatchewan, 188, 196, 211, 231, 317, 329, 334, 338-339
Sault Ste. Marie, 317, 323
Savelief, Sidor, 72
Sawmill, first, 369
"Sawyer," 242
Schaefer, Joseph, 321, 321n
Schelikof, Gregory, 75-76
Scomalt, 294
Scott, Robert, 96
Scurvy, remedy for, 95
Scylla, 307
Sea cow, 70, 70n
Seal river, 204
Seaton, Mr., 314
Sea Otter (Hanna), 109
Sea Otter harbor, 109
Sea Otter (Tipping), 114
"Search for the Western Sea," 167
Secession, 362n
Selkirk, 320
Selkirk islands, 154
Sequim bay, 126
Seven Cities of Cibola, 31
Seven Years' war, 202
Severn river, 170n
Sevier river, 353
Shannon, George, 243-244
Shaw, Angus, 330
Shays, Daniel, 113n
Shoshone Indians, 249-251, 250n, 303
Shumagin islands, 66-67, 69, 104
Siberia and Siberians, 54, 60-67, 111
Sie-Hao, 12
Sierra mountains, 354-355, 357
Simcoe lake, 170n
Simons, A. M., 152n
Simpson, George, 366-367, 369-370
Sioux, 183, 193n, 237, 245-246, 271, 344, 352
Sioux City, 246
Sir Alexander Mackenzie company, 319
Sitka, 72-73, 76n, 77, 77n, 78n, 90, 142-143, 163
Skeena river, 136, 138, 333
Skottow, Thomas, 92

Skyloo, 294
Slater, Samuel, 142n, 233n
Slave Indians, 217-218
Slave lake and river, 216-217, 222, 224
Slaves, non-importation of, 337n
Smith, Captain, 308, 312
Smith-Jackson-Sublette company, 342, 353-358, 359
Smith, Jedediah S., 343, 345-346, 346n, 348-350, 353-360, 369
Smith, John, 11, 29
Snake river and Indians, 187, 249, 252-253, 269, 297-298, 303-304, 306, 314, 340, 357
Snowden, Clinton A., 60n, 66, 66n, 91n, 107n, 116n, 122n, 124n, 135n, 155n, 158n, 170n, 171n, 176n, 191n, 196n, 197n, 232n, 239n, 255n
Society islands, 130, 134
Somersetshire, 202
Sonora (Felicidad), 86-88, 90
South Carolina, 44n, 162
South pass, 306, 345, 352
South Sea company, 108
Southern Indians, 203-204
Sowles, Captain, 305-308
Spangberg, Martin, 57-58, 63-64, 73
Spanish Main, 15, 36, 38
Spithead, 147
Spokane, 196, 294, 295n, 297, 340-341, 357
Staffordshire, 194
Stalin, Josef, 61n
Stanilaus river, 354
Stamp Act, 192n
Stannard, Captain, 174
Stanovoi mountains, 63
Steller, George William, 66-71, 74. 83
Stillwater river, 191
Stinking lake, 174
Stix, 145
Stoddard, Benjamin, 233n
Stone Indian river, 335
Stornoway, 213
"Stourbridge Lion," 357n
Strange, James, 112, 123, 163
Strawn, Arthur, 15n, 16n, 18n, 19n
Stuart, Alexander, 312
Stuart, David, 279, 292-293, 296, 298-299, 305, 310
Stuart, John, 330-333
Stuart lake, 331, 333
Stuart, Robert, 279-281, 305-306, 314, 314n, 340, 346
Stuart, Wallace W., 317n
Sturgeon lake, 211
Sublette, Milton G., 358-359, 361, 363
Sublette, William L., 343, 345, 353-358, 358n, 359, 362-363

Sung dynasty, 8
Superior, Lake, 170-171, 182, 192-193, 196, 215, 318, 329, 335
Swan, 36
Swan river, 335
Sweetwater river, 345-347, 349
Synd, Lieutenant, 74

T

Table bay, 100
Tacouche Tesse river, 228, 231, 232n, 331, 333
Tahiti, 94
Taos, 262, 348, 248n, 357, 360
Tariff, first protective, 217n
Tartars, 7, 54
Tartar-Mantchoos, 6
Tatoosh, 157, 159
Taylor and Maury, 235n
Tchirikoff, Alexis, 57-58, 60, 63, 65-66, 69, 71-73
Tea tax, 193
Teneriffe, 133-134, 137
Tennessee, 241, 258
Terra Firme, 22
Teton mountains, 303, 348
Teton pass, 267, 306
Teutons, 3
Texas, 343n
Thames river, 132, 175
Three Rivers, 168, 168n, 169-170, 178, 180-181, 188, 321
Thompson, David, 292-293, 299, 329-330, 330n, 334-341
Thompson river, 296-297
Thorn, Captain (see *Tonquin* and Astor)
Three Years Travels through the Interior Parts of North America, 194-195
Three Forks, 249, 269-270, 343
Thwaites, Reuben Gold, 184n, 195, 195n, 212n, 237n, 249n, 254n, 255n, 256n, 282n, 283n, 285, 287n, 288n, 291n, 292n, 294n, 296n, 297n, 301n, 304n, 307n, 310n-314n, 331, 331n
Tibetans, 7
Tierra del Fuego, 40, 120
Tillamook, 155, 258
Tippecanoe, 271n, 299n
Tipping, Captain, 114
Tlama, 7
Tobolsk, 57, 63
Todd and McGill, 318
Tonquin, 279-299, 300, 306, 310, 314
Trinidad, 87
Trinidad, 28

Tongue point, 313n
Townsend Acts, 203n
Treaty of Ghent, 367n
Treaty of Greenville, 233n
Treaty of Joint Occupancy, 354n, 368, 370
Treaty of Paris 1763, 74n, 93, 192, 262
Treaty of Paris 1783, 214n
Treaty of Utrecht, 201n
Treaty of Versailles, 192
Tres Reyes, 47-49
Tripolitan war, 242n, 257n, 279
Tulloch, 362
Turner, John, 356
Turner, Nat, 360n
Turner, Philip, 335n
Twisted Hair's camp, 255

U

Ukamok, 67
Ulloa, Francisco de, 27
Umatilla river and Indians, 253, 304 305, 356
Umpqua river and Indians, 356
Unalaska, 104
Union pass, 303
Uraba, Gulf of, 16, 18
Urak river, 63
Ural mountains, 54, 62-63
United States Bank, First, 127n, 158n
United States Bank, Second, 367n
Utah, 347-348, 359
Utah lake, 348, 353-354
Utrecht, Peace of, 51n

V

Valparaiso, 40, 145, 147
Valley Forge, 102n
Van Couverden, 128
Vancouver, George, and Vancouver island, 76, 91, 103-104, 125, 127, 128-150, 151, 159, 160n, 161, 225n, 232, 289
Van Dieman's Land, 134
Vashon and Vashon island, 131, 138
Velasquez, Diego de, 26
Venice, 29
Vente Cruz, 36
Ventura, 32
Venus, 94
Vera Cruz, 36
Verde, Cape, 14
Verendrye, Pierre Gaultier de Varennes de la and sons, 180-190, 190n, 224, 225n, 228, 237
Vespucci, Amerigo, 14
Vermont, 127n
Victoria, 126

Villafrane, Angel de, 44n
Vining, Edward P., 6n, 7n, 9n, 11n, 12n
Virago H. M. S., 21
Virgin river, 353
Virginia, 29, 51n, 121n, 175n, 182n, 193n, 235, 237-238, 262, 342
Virginia resolutions, 233n
Vizcaino, Sebastian, 3, 45-52, 79
Volga river, 263

W

Wagons, 357n
Waldorf, 275
Wales, William, 202
Walker, Edmund, 212n
Walker, Dame, 92
Walker, John, 92
Walker, Henry, 92
Walla Walla, 255, 257n, 306, 357
War of 1812, 249n, 257n, 272, 272n, 273, 307-308,, 313n, 367n
War of Spanish Succession, 180
Washington, 116
Washington, D.C., 233n, 246-247, 367n
Washington, George, 87n, 102n, 113n, 116n, 131, 153, 153n, 155n, 157n, 158, 162n, 182n, 191n, 199n, 213n, 215n, 226n, 233n, 234n, 237
Washington, Mount, 288
Washington, state, 84, 87, 196, 255, 297
Watape, 323
Wavero, 175
Waxel, 68-69, 71
Wayne, General, 238
Weber river, 347
Weem school, 146
Weeks, Steven, 283, 285
Weippe plain, 252, 255
Weiser river, 304
West Africa, 35
West Indies, 16, 35-36, 42-43, 131
Westminster, 334
Whidbey and Whidbey island, 131, 138
Whiskey rebellion, 113n, 238
Whitby, 92
Whitehall, 145, 335
Whitehouse, Private, 243n
Whitman, Marcus, 4, 369
Whitney, Eli, 143n, 233n, 236n
Whitworth, Richard, 194

Witchcraft trials, 51n
Williams, Roger, 4, 168n
Wilkinson, Benjamin, 269
Wilkinson family, 268
Wilkinson, General, 272n, 304n
Wilkinson-Burr scandal, 276n
Willamette river, 253n, 314, 356, 368-370
Wind river, 267, 303, 345,·357, 357n
Windemere, Lake, 337
Winnipeg, 313
Winnipeg, Lake, 185, 193
Winnipeg river, 317, 335
Winship settlement, 308n
Wisdom river, 256
Wiser, Peter, 266
Wisconsin river, 192-193
Wolfe, General, 192
Women, Country of, 8, 11-12, 65
Women, on Northwest coast, 124
Women, treatment of, 20, 47, 102, 141, 159, 206, 207, 211, 223
Wooton, Richens, 342
World War I, 151
Wyeth, Nathaniel, 361, 363n, 369
Wyoming, 272-273, 306, 347

X

X. Y. Z. affair, 233n
X. Y. company, 319, 329

Y

Yakutsk, 57, 63-64
Yazoo claims, 257n
Yelagin, 73
Yellowstone river, 187, 242, 248, 256, 257n, 266-267, 273, 343-346, 349
Yellowstone Packet, 343-344
York, 242, 243n
York factory, 201, 334
Yorktown, 131
Young's bay, 253
Young, Ewing, 369
Yudoma, 63

Z

Zarate, Don Francisco, 40
Zenger, Peter, 185n
Zunig ay Acereda, Gaspar de, 46